WRITING THROUGH LITERATURE

An Anthology of Literary Texts for Academic Inquiry

Revised Printing

MARY ISBELL

University of Connecticut

Kendall Hunt

publishing company

Cover design by The Sheepdog Group

Kendall Hunt
publishing company

www.kendallhunt.com
Send all inquiries to:
4050 Westmark Drive
Dubuque, IA 52004-1840

Printed in the United States of America
10 9 8 7 6 5 4 3

Contents

ACKNOWLEDGMENTS

Before this edition, this anthology existed in three different editions printed by the University of Connecticut co-op, and I include below the participants in that multi-year collaborative effort. I am most grateful for the texts, assignments, and revisions suggested by these colleagues, all fellow instructors of the "Seminar in Writing Through Literature." Simply put, without these contributions, this anthology would not exist. I am especially thankful for Emily Wojcik's willingness to co-edit the 2010 edition with me and Lori Carriere's work uploading our online resources in 2011. There is no way I could have gathered and revised the example assignments (now available online) without their energy and insight. We were all guided by the pedagogical goals for the course articulated by our then-director of Freshman English, Thomas Recchio. Tom's insistence on writing *through* literature and his presentation of how literature can be used to teach composition provides the inspiration for this entire project, and his feedback on this edition was invaluable. I also thank Sarah Winter, our former co-director of Freshman English, for encouraging us to create our own anthology during those early pilot meetings, and Scott Campbell, Tom Deans, Ellen Carillo, and Steve Mollmann for their feedback as I revised the Introduction.

Writing Through Literature: An Anthology of Literary Texts for Academic Inquiry, 2010
> **Editors:** Emily Wojcik and Mary Isbell
> **Contributors:** Lori Carriere, Ellen Carillo, Tom Deans, Jared Demick, Molly Ferguson, Jonathan Kotchian, Andrew Pfrenger, Mandy Suhr-Sytsma, Patricia R. Taylor
> **Editor of Online Instructor Resources:** Patricia R. Taylor

The Writing Through Literature Anthology 2nd Edition, 2009
> **Managing Editor:** Mary Isbell
> **Editorial Board:** Lori Carriere, Daniela Falco, Toni Fellela, Matthew Harding, Katie Kornacki, Jonathan Kotchian, Michelle Maloney-Mangold, Katie Silbereis, Emily Wojcik

The Writing Through Literature Anthology, 2008
> **Writing Through Literature Pilot Committee:** Katie Costanzo, Katie Silbereis, Matthew Harding, Lynn Menillo, Daniela Falco, Lori Carriere, Emily Wojcik, Jonathan Kotchian, Patricia R. Taylor

INTRODUCTION: WHAT IS WRITING THROUGH LITERATURE?

The primary purpose of this anthology is to present literary texts as the starting point for inquiry instead of material to be mastered. It is designed for a "writing seminar," not an "introduction to literature or a course focused on a narrowly defined period or subject area" (Recchio). You will probably learn something new about literature, but the goal of the course is for you to gain experience in the practice and conventions of academic writing. Because literature is not the object of study in this anthology, readings are not preceded by introductions explaining their importance, nor are they followed by discussion questions. I have excluded these common textbook elements to give you the freedom to determine why a reading is important to you and how you want to use it in your writing. Most students appreciate the freedom of this format (you don't have to agree with your teacher! you are actually encouraged to say if you find something frustrating!), but they also find it challenging. Because no one is telling you what is important, you have to decide on your own. This introduction offers some strategies for navigating these challenges.

The preposition "through" is key to the title of this anthology and the course that inspired it, and I explain the process of "writing through literature" in the coming pages with the metaphor of a lens. Instead of directing you to interpret the meaning of a given text and present that interpretation as an argument with evidence from the text (writing *about* literature), I encourage you to use your interpretation of a text as a lens to consider complex questions that extend beyond the text (writing *through* literature).

Writing through literature is essentially an extension of writing about literature, which you were probably asked to do in high school. The images below illustrate this difference by showing Bob writing two papers: one *about* and one *through* Sherman Alexie's "How to Write the Great American Indian Novel." If you haven't read it before, this short piece begins on page 1 of this anthology.

Writing about Literature

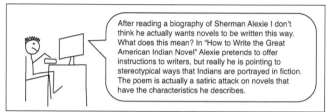

The picture above shows Bob reading "How to Write the Great American Indian Novel" and getting pretty confused. In preparing a short response for class, he decides that he needs more information and reads a short biography of Sherman Alexie. In light of that context, Bob responds that Alexie probably doesn't really want people to write novels that have the features he describes in the poem. When tasked with writing *about* literature, Bob sits down to write his analysis of the poem and argues that Alexie is criticizing novels that have features described in the poem because those novels perpetuate harmful stereotypes. Alexie pretends to offer guidelines for a novel, Bob argues, but he's really offering a satiric attack on novels that have the characteristics he describes. He references the biography of Alexie that informed his analysis and supports his argument with close analysis of several passages in the poem. This is writing about literature because Bob has used writing to interpret the literary text.

The goal of writing *through* literature prompts Bob to use his initial difficulty understanding the text as a lens to consider the value of satire as a social critique. He is guided in this task by a writing assignment that directs him to devise a theory about how satire works in Alexie's poem and then test that theory on two more satiric texts: one that he finds easy to understand and one that initially confuses him.

Writing through Literature

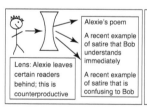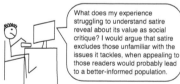

Based on his experience reading Alexie, Bob develops a theory that Alexie confuses some readers, which is counterproductive if the poem is intended as social commentary. He then uses that theory to develop a question to answer through close analysis of all three texts: "What does my experience struggling to understand satire reveal about its value as social critique?" Bob's answer to this question becomes his argument: "satire excludes those unfamiliar with the issues it tackles, when appealing to those readers would probably lead to a better informed population." In other words, Bob works through his experience reading and writing about Alexie's poem to develop a question that extends beyond the poem. Though each scenario above involves a question, the writing about literature question is a variation on "what does this text mean?" while the writing through literature question Bob develops uses his own interpretation to consider the poem in a broader context.

You might think of writing about literature as the starting point for the work of this course. Since the goal of writing about literature is to isolate an interpretation, it allows you to explain what you find significant about a literary text so you can consider your perspective in relation to other interpretations and issues beyond the text. The literary analysis you were asked to do in high school is still very valuable here, in other words, but you will be asked to take your analysis further and ask more complex questions.

In what follows, I recommend several strategies for writing through literature, and I illustrate Bob and three other students using these strategies. The first, "Reading and Responding," encourages you to articulate your own response to a text in writing. The second, "Using a Text as a Lens" involves the work of writing *about* a literary text, since you need to articulate your interpretation of a text to determine how you want to use it in your writing. Placing your own interpretation in dialogue with other texts can reveal differences between your individual perspective and the perspective of others. These differences create a space for inquiry in which you will employ the third strategy of "Questioning"—formulating a complex question to guide your writing project. As you work to answer and refine your question by working closely with a variety of sources, you will be "Arguing and Revising," the fourth strategy. Each of these strategies involves writing, and I have included short assignments for each strategy that can be used with any text. These assignments are meant to prompt informal, exploratory writing; you will likely discover what you think about a text as you write.

The supplementary texts and assignments your instructor assigns will invite you to write *through* literature by bringing other texts into conversation with your interpretation. These other texts might be historical contexts, other literary texts, academic writing, or contemporary texts, and these texts might not be written: assignments might reference songs, films, visual images, and your own experiences as texts. You might also be asked to consider your own initial interpretation in relation to your peers' interpretations or your own changing sense of a text.

Much of what I describe below will make much more sense once you've gone through this process once; in fact, it might be useful to return to this Introduction after your instructor returns your first essay. Keep in mind that you might not be able to fully articulate your question or argument until you revise for your final draft, and you will need to re-interpret parts of the literary text while drafting your argument. It's also very possible that you will jump immediately to an argument you would like to make, and then have to work backwards to determine the question implied by your argument and the interpretation that supports and helps answer that question. All of this is to say that this Introduction does not provide a rigid formula that will automatically churn out academic arguments, but instead offers suggestions on how you might approach the task of writing through literature.

Reading and Responding

The texts included here are known for provoking different reactions from their audiences over the years. Follow your own inclinations in making meaning of these texts. Take notes as you read and underline passages that pique your interest, confuse you, or make you angry. These reactions are invaluable for class discussion, and are especially important as you pursue your own project of writing through that text. You will most likely find that your response to a text only begins to emerge as you write, and that writing also helps you pinpoint the aspect of the text that prompted your response. The "passage-based response," adapted from an assignment by Ellen Carillo[1], is a short assignment that prompts you to articulate in writing what you're thinking after your first reading of a text.

Passage-Based Response

The primary goal of the PBR is for you to articulate your initial observations about a text and begin to consider the implications of your observations. The first step of this assignment is, therefore, a careful reading of the assigned text. As you read, mark passages that you find interesting, confusing, infuriating, brilliant, etc. If you come across words and/or passages you don't understand, look them up and write a definition or paraphrase in the margins. If you don't want to write in your book, use sticky notes.

Ideally, you will work through the assigned text on your own, but of course a simple Google search will turn up summaries paraphrasing the plot, articles explaining the meaning, and student essays offering ideas for essays. Remember that these sources offer someone else's response; your goal is to respond to the original assigned text, so looking to these sources means you veer away from your goal. If you find the text very confusing, referencing a summary can be productive, but you need to return to the task of articulating your response.

After carefully reading the assigned text, select one short passage (about 2-4 sentences) that captured your attention and transcribe it single-spaced onto the top of the page (including the page number from which the passage is taken). Begin by describing why you chose the passage, and then offer your analysis of it. This is a prewriting assignment so your writing can be informal. Your analysis will differ depending on your reason for selecting the passage. If you chose a passage that you didn't understand at first, you should write informally to work through possible ways of understanding the passage. If you understood the text and found one passage interesting, infuriating, brilliant, etc., you should work toward articulating exactly what you think about the passage and begin to think of the larger implications of your response.

Remember, your goal is not to summarize the entire text but to respond to something very specific!

If your response includes something someone else wrote about the text, you must acknowledge where the ideas from that source enter into your response (this means proper in-text citations and a works cited page). Skipping this step is not an option; it is a part of academic writing.

Recommended length: 1-2 double-spaced pages (including single-spaced transcribed passage)

---

1 Carillo's iteration, the passage-based paper, does not include space for students' responses and directs their attention, instead, solely to the textual elements within their chosen passage as a means to honing their abilities to recognize how they construct meaning through reading and writing.

The goal here is not to master the "right" understanding of these literary texts (since there is no "right" answer), but to try to articulate what aspect of the text prompted your reaction. Even if you respond that a text makes no sense, this is okay so long as you cite and puzzle over the section of the text that seems particularly tricky. As you discuss your response in class, you might find that other students have responded very differently—some might like it, or believe that the difficulty works to advance the direction of thought opened up by the text. Pay attention to the passages those students have referenced to explain their own responses, and consider how you would respond to their interpretation based on that evidence. The differences between your interpretation and those of your classmates might provide the first step toward a question that can take you through an extended argument. As you focus on specific passages, you will be working toward isolating an element of the text that interests you.

Because writing through literature does not rely on the general consensus of the meaning of a text, or the "intended" meaning in the rare cases the author reveals it, your genuine reaction to a text and the interpretation that follows will very productively begin the work of using that text in your writing. It is not a problem for you to say that a text bored you, for example, because you can then consider what would intrigue a twenty-first-century college student that isn't present in the text, or why the allusions did not register. The goal of this assignment is to remove the stigma associated with "not getting it," and instead encourage you to consider how and why literary texts may be difficult to understand or interpret. Consider the variations between these four students' responses to Alexie's poem:

As you'll notice, Bob, Angie, Carl, and Dorothy have very different reactions while reading and they select different passages for their responses (you may also notice that they all read standing up and would seem to have the same desk, but we won't concern ourselves with that). Bob is confused and chooses the first two sentences of the poem for his response, explaining that he thinks they reference something he doesn't know about. He looks up a biography of Sherman Alexie and uses that to guess that Alexie might be referencing the way American Indians are portrayed in novels. Angie finds the poem absurd and funny. She picks the most absurd line she can find and tries to determine why it is funny. Carl reasons from the title that Alexie has written instructions and as he reads he notices the abundance of 'must's and 'should's, concluding that this is a pretty demanding "how-to" guide, but also that he would have a hard time writing a novel following these instructions. Dorothy finds a similarity between the description of Indian men in the poem and Jacob in the movie *Twilight*. These differences in interpretation and focus create opportunities for fresh thinking and exchange.

Using a Text as a Lens

We can't know exactly why Sherman Alexie wrote "How to Write the Great American Indian Novel," but we can be fairly certain that he didn't write it as material for college essays. After reading and responding to a literary text—any text really—it becomes your responsibility to decide just how you want to use it in your writing. One way of envisioning that "use" involves thinking of a text as a lens. Referring to a text as a lens is, of course, a figurative construction. It is one thing to literally look through a microscopic lens to see the complexity of an organism at the cellular level and another to "see" the world "through" a text. Unlike an actual lens, literature is not manufactured for this purpose. The texts gathered here for academic inquiry were written in very different contexts by authors motivated by a variety of factors we may never know. It is, therefore, your responsibility to decide how the text will function as a lens.

Using a text as a lens involves interpreting the text, but your interpretation will be geared toward opening inquiry instead of answering the question of a text's meaning completely. Recall the difference between writing about and writing through literature illustrated above. When the goal was writing *about*, Bob developed his initial observation that Alexie probably does not actually want novels to be written the way the poem describes, arguing that the poem is actually a satiric attack on novels that have the characteristics it seems to advocate. When his task was writing *through*, Bob reshaped his response into a lens, "Alexie leaves the uninformed behind; this is counterproductive." You'll notice that this strategy involves interpretation, since Bob had to describe the significance of his frustration reading the poem. This interpretation is important as Bob moves forward to ask questions.

In his excellent guide to academic writing, *Rewriting*, Joseph Harris describes this step as "coming to terms" with a text for your own purposes. Harris defines *coming to terms* as "translat[ing] the language and ideas of a text into words of your own" (15). This is the first of several "moves" Harris describes for academic writing, and he explains it as a process of interpretation:

> In coming to terms, you need both to give a text its due and to show what uses you want to make of it. You are not simply re-presenting a text but incorporating it into your own project as a writer. You thus need not only to explain what you think it means but to say something about the perspective from which you are reading it. In coming to terms with the work of others, then, you also say a good deal about who you are as a writer, about your own interests and values (15).

Harris describes this process as one of "rewriting" a text in your own words, and this has useful parallels to the strategy of using a text as a lens that I have been describing. He clarifies that you will not be "simply re-presenting a text but incorporating it into your own project." As you put a literary text to use as a lens, you will not be summarizing the entire text (a common pitfall when incorporating literature), but instead selecting something very specific that will serve your project. In his essay, Bob does not explain Alexie's entire poem, but uses the moments in the poem that he found frustrating when first reading it to develop his theory of satire. Harris also notes that you will need to "explain what you think it means." Because literary texts (any texts really, as Harris would point out) can be interpreted in such a multitude of ways, you must give your reader some insight into your perspective. That perspective, after all, is guiding your writing project.

You will be making a text into a lens through writing, and that writing will present your interpretation and explain how that interpretation has led to your larger questions. This process of interpretation is often facilitated by class discussion. It was not until Bob came to class and described his confusion upon first reading the poem that he realized that others felt the same way. When the instructor distributed the assignment, Bob decided he wanted to expand on his experience struggling with satire, while Angie, who is also in Bob's class, turned her response into a very different lens. Angie's theory of satire emerges from her sense that Alexie's poem might offend some readers.

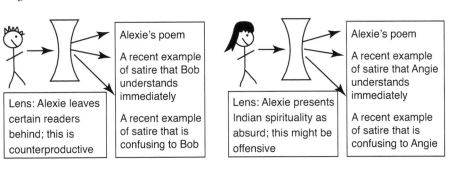

Bob and Angie have the same assignment, but they are not saying the same thing about Alexie. They are also not disagreeing directly; they are simply pursuing different projects.

Carl and Dorothy are in a different class than Bob and Angie. Instead of assigning satirical texts, Carl and Dorothy's instructor assigns two texts from very different periods that depict American Indians: selections from Mary Rowlandson's "A Narrative of the Captivity and Restoration of Mrs. Mary Rowlandson" (1682), included in this anthology, and the popular movie *Twilight* (2008). The assignment asks Carl and Dorothy to use one aspect of Alexie's poem as a lens to view either of these texts and develop a question about the representation of American Indians. Upon first reading Alexie's poem, Dorothy commented on the line, "All white women love Indian men," remarking that it reminded her of the "Team Edward/Team Jacob" craze that followed the release of the second *Twilight* movie in 2009, where Jacob's appeal relies in part on his membership in the Quileute tribe. After deciding to use *Twilight* as her supplementary text, Dorothy turned her initial response into a lens by arguing that Alexie's poem points to the stereotype that all white women love American Indians. Once Carl decided he wanted to work with Rowlandson's narrative, in which she describes being captured and held prisoner by Indians, he decided to shift from his initial response about the repetition of "must" and "should" to develop a lens that would allow him to explore the representation of Indians as violent. He focuses on the difference between the tragic, sad Indian hero in Alexie's poem and the violent savage in Rowlandson's narrative. Like Carl, you may wind up moving beyond your initial response to use a different aspect of a text as a lens; this is very common.

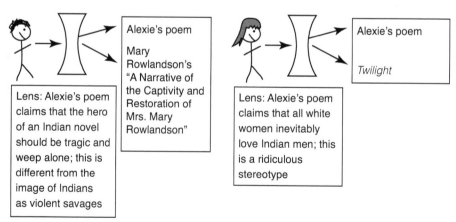

Depending on your assignment, your lens might be a theory you've devised, a term the class has collectively defined, or your interpretation of one aspect of a text. Because each reader brings a different perspective, the possible ways of using a text as a lens are infinite. The important thing is that you find something that intrigues you. The short assignment below prompts you to brainstorm different options for using a text as a lens.

Determining Your Lens

Your initial response to a text should give you some sense of what you might use as a lens for scholarly inquiry, but you may also have encountered other ideas during class discussion or by considering it alongside supplementary texts. In this response, you should consider at least two different aspects of the assigned text that you might use as a lens. Pay attention to the goals of your essay assignment, since they will set parameters within which you should work. Your writing here does not need to be polished; this is an informal pre-writing exercise.

Begin by quoting or paraphrasing from the text to demonstrate the aspect you might use as a lens, and then explain how you interpret that section of the text. Next, brainstorm as many uses of this lens as you can. When you've run out of ideas, move on to another aspect of the text you might use as a lens and start the process again. After you've brainstormed for 1–2 pages, highlight your favorite lens idea.

Questioning

It is important to note that Angie, Bob, Carl, and Dorothy bring very different perspectives to their reading of Alexie, which lead them to develop very different lenses. Differences between your interpretation and those of other students or other assigned texts create a space for critical inquiry. If everyone in the class agreed upon an interpretation and you ran into no contradictions, it would be difficult to formulate an insightful question. Genuine questions are prompted by inconsistency and even disagreement. There is no shortage of contradiction in the literary texts in this anthology, and your writing assignments will also reveal discrepancies and help you formulate provocative questions. The important thing is that you pursue questions emerging from your response to a text—this is the best way to write interesting papers, since your enthusiasm will translate into your writing.

The assignments your instructor gives you will often provide ideas for supplementary texts or questions prompted by class discussion that may complicate your initial interpretation of the lens. Even in these cases where questions abound, you need to decide for yourself what question you want to pursue in your essay. Creating your own question will probably be the most challenging aspect of writing through literature; by doing this often you will be learning a habit of inquiry that will be beneficial beyond this course. As you formulate questions, pay attention to the interrogative words you are using. Questions that can be answered with "yes" or "no" tend to hinder the expansion of your project. Questions that start with "What" can leave you bogged down in summary, though they often lead to other questions. The common question, "What does this mean?" is more of a question for writing *about* literature—a starting point, in other words, rather than something to substantiate an entire academic argument—and this is something you will hopefully have established as you think through your own reaction and interpretation of the text. Questions that begin with "How," "Why," and "To what extent," on the other hand, often lead to exciting insights and analysis that engages academic inquiry on a deeper and more useful level.

The task of writing through literature can be easily misunderstood to mean using a text to get you thinking about a more general issue in the world and leaving the text behind to pursue that issue. In the case of Alexie's poem, this misunderstanding might lead to a question such as, "where do stereotypes of American Indians come from?" This sort of question will establish a project that is bigger than you can tackle in one assignment (or even an entire semester!), so it is best to limit your focus to one text or a set of texts, providing a small test case for your question. The short assignment below prompts you in this task:

Formulating a Question

After reading and responding to the primary text(s) of the assignment and considering your perspective alongside other student responses and supplementary texts, you may begin to notice differences between your response to these texts and the verbal or written responses of others. Your goal here is to articulate your questions about the relationship between all of these texts and work toward one compelling question to pursue in an academic essay. Remember to pay attention to the goals of your essay assignment, since they will set parameters within which you should work. Your writing here does not need to be polished; this is an informal pre-writing exercise. If you get stuck, just start a sentence with interrogative words such as "Why" or "How," since these words cannot be answered with a yes or no.

After brainstorming questions for 1–2 pages, devote your last page to refining the best question that emerged. Make sure your question moves beyond asking a "what" question that will just lead to a summary of a given text or an explanation of a similarity/difference between two texts. Also remember to include the required texts of the assignment in your question since you want your answer (i.e., argument) to deal with them. Conclude by highlighting your best question, and speculating on what you think the answer will be.

Recommended Length: 2–3 double-spaced pages

Though Bob and Angie are working from the same assignment on satire, and Carl and Dorothy are working from the same assignment on the representation of American Indians, you'll see on the next page that they develop very different questions.

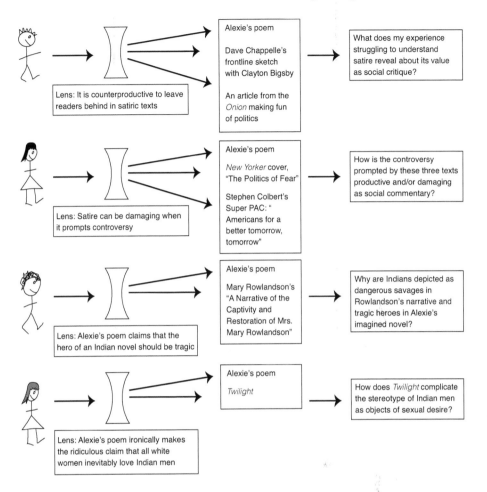

Note in the image above that all of the students view Alexie's poem through their lenses to develop their questions. Angie and Bob were directed by their assignment to create a theory of satire to use as a lens, and even though they developed that theory by reading Alexie, they still test that theory on the poem in its entirety. Though Carl and Dorothy use one aspect of Alexie's poem as a lens, they are using that aspect to look at other features in the poem alongside their other chosen texts.

By creating your own questions, you can begin to read literary texts with the same critical eye necessary for engaging with texts outside of this (or any) classroom. These questions are at the heart of academic inquiry across every discipline—and are essential to becoming a critical thinker in your own right. The student of science, for example, notices a phenomenon in the physical world, formulates and refines a question by looking at existing research on some part of that phenomenon, and then works toward a new way to pursue their specific question (i.e., an experiment). In the study of political science, the source material is often statistical studies or theories of political behavior, but the questions still emerge from phenomena of collective human behavior. Even in the realm of engineering, we see questions such as "Why?" (i.e., "Why can't we create a building 100 stories high?") and "How?" ("How can we increase the speed of this train?"). Indeed, most of our major engineering feats result from questions just like these.

The habit of inquiry and critical analysis learned while writing through literature are applicable to all of these other fields, because the primary skill being honed through this work is the ability to formulate and pursue questions that are generated by what we do not yet know—questions that can be answered in many different ways. In order to pursue these questions, however, you'll need to keep your focus specific and related to your chosen text. As mentioned above, you cannot tackle the root of stereotypes of American Indians in one essay. In the same way, testing the question of why we can't create a building 100 stories high, you would not look at every building, but instead at particular buildings as a manageable sample.

Argument and Revision

Since much of your prewriting will likely involve the formulation of a question for your project, you can think of the final stages as attempting to answer your question through the analysis of primary and secondary texts, and then translating your answer(s) into an argument or thesis. At this point, you have essentially set up an experiment—you now have to actually analyze the text ("results") and answer your question step by step. Academic writing is argument driven, and although the strategies described here place considerable emphasis on establishing a question based on your response to a text, you will likely spend the most time drafting and revising your argument. As mentioned above, this may mean also revising your question, so again it is important to realize this is not an exact formula.

Many students who have undertaken the process of writing through literature have found that they were not sure of their exact question until completing the rough draft. After drafting, students were able to add complexity to a question they began with, or even change the question completely when a particular section of analysis led them to find a new angle on the issue. To return to the experiment example, you may need to change your experiment (the texts you analyze, the questions you ask) to make your project successful. The important thing to remember is that the process of revision begins even as you draft.

While the images so far show the process of writing through literature progressing from response➔lens➔question, you will likely find those arrows reversed as you argue and revise. On the next page, you can see Angie, Bob, Carl, and Dorothy further developing their writing projects:

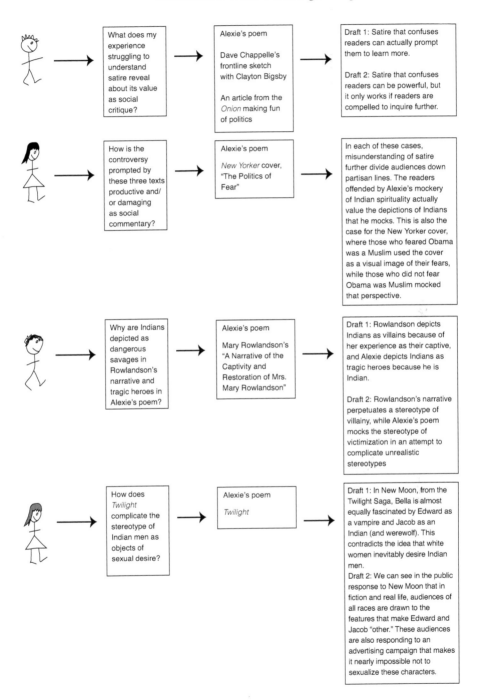

What does my experience struggling to understand satire reveal about its value as social critique?

→ Alexie's poem

Dave Chappelle's frontline sketch with Clayton Bigsby

An article from the *Onion* making fun of politics

→ Draft 1: Satire that confuses readers can actually prompt them to learn more.

Draft 2: Satire that confuses readers can be powerful, but it only works if readers are compelled to inquire further.

How is the controversy prompted by these three texts productive and/or damaging as social commentary?

→ Alexie's poem

New Yorker cover, "The Politics of Fear"

→ In each of these cases, misunderstanding of satire further divide audiences down partisan lines. The readers offended by Alexie's mockery of Indian spirituality actually value the depictions of Indians that he mocks. This is also the case for the New Yorker cover, where those who feared Obama was a Muslim used the cover as a visual image of their fears, while those who did not fear Obama was Muslim mocked that perspective.

Why are Indians depicted as dangerous savages in Rowlandson's narrative and tragic heroes in Alexie's poem?

→ Alexie's poem

Mary Rowlandson's "A Narrative of the Captivity and Restoration of Mrs. Mary Rowlandson"

→ Draft 1: Rowlandson depicts Indians as villains because of her experience as their captive, and Alexie depicts Indians as tragic heroes because he is Indian.

Draft 2: Rowlandson's narrative perpetuates a stereotype of villainy, while Alexie's poem mocks the stereotype of victimization in an attempt to complicate unrealistic stereotypes

How does *Twilight* complicate the stereotype of Indian men as objects of sexual desire?

→ Alexie's poem

Twilight

→ Draft 1: In New Moon, from the Twilight Saga, Bella is almost equally fascinated by Edward as a vampire and Jacob as an Indian (and werewolf). This contradicts the idea that white women inevitably desire Indian men.

Draft 2: We can see in the public response to New Moon that in fiction and real life, audiences of all races are drawn to the features that make Edward and Jacob "other." These audiences are also responding to an advertising campaign that makes it nearly impossible not to sexualize these characters.

As has often been the case with my students, your analysis of a particular text while drafting may contradict the argument you thought you were going to make when you were pre-writing. Often students will ignore limitations or evidence that supports an opposing position for the sake of holding on to their original thesis. I would encourage you to see how those contradictions might complicate your initial argument and, indeed, lead to further inquiry. This leads to more work, but it is valuable work because it has led to new thinking.

To continue with the example above, Carl initially argues in his draft that Rowlandson depicts Indians as villains because of her experience as their captive, and that Alexie depicts Indians as tragic heroes because he is Indian. But as he re-reads the poem, he realizes that Alexie is making fun of that depiction of Indians—though he is an American Indian, he doesn't seem to want them depicted as tragic figures. Carl initially wants to ignore this because it complicates his argument, but instead he revises his argument to accommodate his new discovery. This difference between what he expected to think about the text and his emerging perspective led him to another question: "Why would it be harmful for Indians to be portrayed as tragic figures or savage figures?" The answer to that question led Carl to a far more complex and interesting argument: "Rowlandson's narrative perpetuates a stereotype of villainy, while Alexie's poem mocks the stereotype of victimization in an attempt to complicate unrealistic stereotypes." In a similar way, you may find that your draft concludes with a much different argument than the one you described in the introduction. This is a common occurrence, since it often takes the entire process of drafting to really begin to see an answer emerge. Feedback on your rough draft from your instructor or classmates will help you to clarify points that you might not have even realized you were arguing, and this can guide your revision toward a final polished draft.

It is possible that you will set out to make an argument, never come across any contradictions, and wrap things up tidily in your conclusion. The revision process is still valuable for a draft such as this, since the perspective of other readers can help you think of counterarguments and other avenues that had not occurred to you. This is what happened as Bob drafted and revised his essay. As Bob drafted he realized that he actually learned more about American Indians and their representation in fiction *because* he was confused; his initial theory about the counterproductivity of excluding readers might be wrong. He argued in his first draft that confusing readers actually prompts them to learn more, while readers who "get it" just laugh and move on. At his revision conference, however, another student brought up the point that Bob probably only read more because he had to write a response for class. When Bob admitted that he would probably just ignore things he didn't understand in day-to-day life, he asked a new question: "How does satire work differently when it is assigned and when it is read for pleasure?" He argued in his final draft that satire that confuses readers only works if they are compelled to inquire further. Dorothy was also quite happy with her argument going into her revision conference, which claimed that Bella's almost equal fascination with Edward and Jacob contradicts the idea that white women inevitably desire Indian men. In her revision conference, however, the group was far more interested in discussing the Team Edward/Team Jacob phenomenon and, with a little nudging from her instructor, she decided to focus more in her revisions on why audiences respond the way they do to the *Twilight* series.

Think again of the ambitious engineer, who pursued the question "Why can't we create a building 100 stories high?" This engineer concluded by saying that we could if only we used a new system he had devised. This is an argument, to be sure, but the engineer's colleagues pointed out several flaws in his design that had not occurred to him. Though he didn't recognize these flaws on his own, they nevertheless needed to be confronted. His entire project was not, therefore, useless—it just required revision. The best piece of advice I can give at this introductory stage is that you should become comfortable with your papers changing dramatically from rough to final draft. As one student put it, "Coming from high school, even when I did do all my drafts, [the changes were] really minor ... I never changed my thesis like I did here." This may seem foreign to the way you learned to write in high school, but these are the methods of drafting and revision that will enable you to pursue complex projects and make strong arguments throughout your university career and beyond. This final short assignment I include below can serve as an assignment for reviewing a peer's essay or your own.

Evaluating a Student-Writer's Project

After reading a peer's student essay draft (or your own), describe in a few sentences what you think the author is trying to accomplish with the essay. After explaining this author's project by paraphrasing or quoting from the paper directly, evaluate the success of this project. Taking your sense of the author's goals into account, consider the author's use of source materials and methods of argumentation. You should emphasize what is working well, but also point out what the author has left undone. Since many questions change from rough to final draft, try to quote or paraphrase the question this writer seems to be pursuing and offer feedback on that question. Do you find the question compelling? Do you see ways to make it more complex, or does it need clarification? Is the question answerable with the sources the author has referenced in the essay?

Works Cited

Harris, Joseph. *Rewriting: How to Do Things with Texts*. Logan: Utah State University Press, 2006.

Recchio, Thomas. "1011 Specifics." *Freshman English*. University of Connecticut Freshman English Program, http://freshmanenglish.uconn.edu/instructors/course-descriptions/1011specifics.php (accessed 13 March 2011).

HOW TO WRITE
THE GREAT AMERICAN
INDIAN NOVEL (1996)

Sherman Alexie
b. 1966 Wellpinit, WA

All of the Indians must have tragic features: tragic noses, eyes, and arms. Their hands and fingers must be tragic when they reach for tragic food.

The hero must be a half-breed, half white and half Indian, preferably from a horse culture. He should often weep alone. That is mandatory.

If the hero is an Indian woman, she is beautiful. She must be slender and in love with a white man. But if she loves an Indian man

then he must be a half-breed, preferably from a horse culture. If the Indian woman loves a white man, then he has to be so white

that we can see the blue veins running through his skin like rivers. When the Indian woman steps out of her dress, the white man gasps

at the endless beauty of her brown skin. She should be compared to nature:

brown hills, mountains, fertile valleys, dewy grass, wind, and clear water.

If she is compared to murky water, however, then she must have a secret.

Indians always have secrets, which are carefully and slowly revealed.

Yet Indian secrets can be disclosed suddenly, like a storm.

Indian men, of course, are storms. They should destroy the lives of any white women who choose to love them. All white women love Indian men. That is always the case. White women feign disgust at the savage in blue jeans and T-shirt, but secretly lust after him.

White women dream about half-breed Indian men from horse cultures. Indian men are horses, smelling wild and gamey. When the Indian man unbuttons his pants, the white woman should think of topsoil.

There must be one murder, one suicide, one attempted rape.

"How to Write the Great American Indian Novel" Reprinted from *The Summer of Black Widows*, ©1996 by Sherman Alexie, by permission of Hanging Loose Press.

Alcohol should be consumed. Cars must be driven at high speeds.
Indians must see visions. White people can have the same visions if they are in
love with Indians. If a white person loves an Indian
then the white person is Indian by proximity. White people must
carry
an Indian deep inside themselves. Those interior Indians are half-breed
and obviously from horse cultures. If the interior Indian is male then he must
be a warrior, especially if he is inside a white man.
If the interior Indian is female, then she must be a healer, especially if
she is inside
a white woman. Sometimes there are complications.
An Indian man can be hidden inside a white woman. An Indian
woman
can be hidden inside a white man. In these rare instances,
everybody is a half-breed struggling to learn more about his or her
horse culture.
There must be redemption, of course, and sins must be forgiven.
For this, we need children. A white child and an Indian child, gender not
important, should express deep affection in a childlike way.
In the Great American Indian novel, when it is finally written, all of the white
people will be Indians and all of the Indians will be
ghosts.

BLUEBEARD'S EGG (1983)

Margaret Atwood
b. 1939 Ottawa, Canada

Sally stands at the kitchen window, waiting for the sauce she's reducing to come to a simmer, looking out. Past the garage the lot sweeps downwards, into the ravine, it's a wilderness there, of bushes and branches and what Sally thinks of as vines. It was her idea to have a kind of terrace, built of old railroad ties, with wild flowers growing between them, but Edward says he likes it the way it is. There's a playhouse down at the bottom, near the fence; from here she can just see the roof. It has nothing to do with Edward's kids, in their earlier incarnations, before Sally's time; it's more ancient than that, and falling apart. Sally would like it cleared away. She thinks drunks sleep in it, the men who live under the bridges down there, who occasionally wander over the fence (which is broken down, from where they step on it) and up the hill, to emerge squinting like moles into the light of Sally's well-kept back lawn.

Off to the left is Ed, in his windbreaker; it's officially spring, Sally's blue scylla is in flower, but it's chilly for this time of year. Ed's windbreaker is an old one he won't throw out; it still says WILDCATS, relic of some team he was on in high school, an era so prehistoric Sally can barely imagine it; though picturing Ed at high school is not all that difficult. Girls would have had crushes on him, he would have been unconscious of it; things like that don't change. He's puttering around the rock garden now; some of the rocks stick out too far and are in danger of grazing the side of Sally's Peugeot, on its way to the garage, and he's moving them around. He likes doing things like that, puttering, humming to himself. He won't wear work gloves, though she keeps telling him he could squash his fingers.

Watching his bent back with its frayed, poignant lettering, Sally dissolves; which is not infrequent with her. *My darling Edward*, she thinks. *Edward Bear, of little brain. How I love you.* At times like this she feels very protective of him.

Sally knows for a fact that dumb blondes were loved, not because they were blondes, but because they were dumb. It was their helplessness and confusion that were so sexually attractive, once; not their hair. It wasn't false, the rush of tenderness men must have felt for such women. Sally understands it.

For it must be admitted: Sally is in love with Ed because of his stupidity, his monumental and almost energetic stupidity: energetic, because Ed's stupidity is not passive. He's no mere blockhead; you'd have to be working at it to be that stupid. Does it make Sally feel smug, or smarter than he is, or even smarter than she really is herself? No; on the contrary, it makes her humble. It fills her with wonder that the world can contain such marvels as Ed's colossal and endearing thickness. He is just so *stupid*. Every time he gives her another piece of evidence, another tile that she can glue into place in the vast mosaic of his stupidity she's continually piecing together, she wants to hug him, and often does; and he is so stupid he can never figure out what for.

Because Ed is so stupid he doesn't even know he's stupid. He's a child of luck, a third son who, armed with nothing but a certain feeble-minded amiability, manages to make it through the forest with all its witches and traps and pitfalls and end up with the princess, who is Sally, of course. It helps that he's handsome.

On good days she sees his stupidity as innocence, lamblike, shining with the light of (for instance) green daisied meadows in the sun. (When Sally starts thinking this way about Ed, in terms of the calendar art from the service-station washrooms of her childhood, dredging up images of a boy with curly golden hair, his arm thrown around the neck of an Irish setter—a notorious brainless beast, she reminds herself—she knows she is sliding over the edge, into a ghastly kind of sentimentality, and that she must stop at once, or Ed will vanish, to be replaced by a stuffed fac- simile, useful for little else but an umbrella stand. Ed is a real person, with a lot more to him than these simplistic renditions allow for; which sometimes worries her.) On bad days though, she sees his stupidity as wilfulness, a stubborn determination to shut things out. His obtuseness is a wall, within which he can go about his business, humming to himself, while Sally, locked outside, must hack her way through the brambles with hardly so much as a transparent raincoat between them and her skin.

Why did she choose him (or, to be precise, as she tries to be with herself and sometimes is even out loud, *hunt him down*), when it's clear to everyone she had other options? To Marylynn, who is her best though most recent friend, she's explained it by saying she was spoiled when young by reading too many Agatha Christie murder mysteries, of the kind in which the clever and witty heroine passes over the equally clever and witty first-lead male, who's helped solve the crime, in order to marry the second-lead male, the stupid one, the one who would have been arrested and condemned and executed if it hadn't been for her cleverness. Maybe this is how she sees Ed: if it weren't for her, his blundering too-many-thumbs kind- ness would get him into all sorts of quagmires, all sorts of sink-holes he'd never be able to get himself out of, and then he'd be done for.

"Sink-hole" and "quagmire" are not flattering ways of speaking about other women, but this is what is at the back of Sally's mind; specifically, Ed's two previous wives. Sally didn't exactly extricate him from their clutches. She's never even met the first one, who moved to the west coast fourteen years ago and sends Christmas cards, and the second one was middle-aged and already in the act of severing herself from Ed before Sally came along. (For Sally, "middle-aged" means anyone five years older than she is. It has always meant this. She applies it only to women, however. She doesn't think of Ed as middle-aged, although the gap between them is considerably more than five years.)

Ed doesn't know what happened with these marriages, what went wrong. His protestations of ignorance, his refusal to discuss the finer points, is frustrating to Sally, because she would like to hear the whole story. But it's also cause for anxiety: if he doesn't know what happened with the other two, maybe the same thing could be happening with her and he doesn't know about that, either. Stupidity like Ed's can be a health hazard, for other people. What if he wakes up one day and decides that she isn't the true bride after all, but the false one? Then she will be put into a barrel stuck full of nails and rolled downhill, endlessly, while he is sitting in yet another bridal bed, drinking champagne. She remembers the brand name, because she bought it herself. Champagne isn't the sort of finishing touch that would occur to Ed, though he enjoyed it enough at the time.

But outwardly Sally makes a joke of all this. "He doesn't *know*," she says to Marylynn, laughing a little, and they shake their heads. If it were them, they'd know, all right. Marylynn is in fact divorced, and she can list every single thing that went wrong, item by item. After doing this, she adds that her divorce was one of the best things that ever happened to her. "I was just a nothing before," she says. "It made me pull myself together."

Sally, looking across the kitchen table at Marylynn, has to agree that she is far from being a nothing now. She started out re-doing people's closets, and has worked that up into her own interior-design firm. She does the houses of the newly rich, those who lack ancestral furniture and the confidence to be shabby, and who wish their interiors to reflect a personal taste they do not in reality possess.

"What they want are mausoleums," Marylynn says, "or hotels," and she cheerfully supplies them. "Right down to the ash-trays. Imagine having someone else pick out your ash-trays for you."

By saying this, Marylynn lets Sally know that she's not including her in that category, though Sally did in fact hire her, at the very first, to help with a few details around the house. It was Marylynn who redesigned the wall of closets in the master bedroom and who found Sally's massive Chinese mahogany table, which cost her another seven hundred dollars to have stripped. But it turned out to be perfect, as Marylynn said it would. Now she's dug up a nineteenth-century keyhole desk, which both she and Sally know will be exactly right for the bay-windowed alcove off the living room. "Why do you need it?" Ed said in his puzzled way. "I thought you worked in your study." Sally admitted this, but said they could keep the telephone bills in it, which appeared to satisfy him. She knows exactly what she needs it for: she needs it to sit at, in something flowing, backlit by the morning sunlight, gracefully dashing off notes. She saw a 1940's advertisement for coffee like this once; and the husband was standing behind the chair, leaning over, with a worshipful expression on his face.

Marylynn is the kind of friend Sally does not have to explain any of this to, because it's assumed between them. Her intelligence is the kind Sally respects.

Marylynn is tall and elegant, and makes anything she is wearing seem fashionable. Her hair is prematurely grey and she leaves it that way. She goes in for loose blouses in cream-coloured silk, and eccentric scarves gathered from interesting shops and odd corners of the world, thrown carelessly around her neck and over one shoulder. (Sally has tried this toss in the mirror, but it doesn't work.) Marylynn has a large collection of unusual shoes; she says they're unusual because her feet are so big, but Sally knows better. Sally, who used to think of herself as pretty enough and now thinks of herself as doing quite well for her age, envies Marylynn her bone structure, which will serve her well when the inevitable happens.

Whenever Marylynn is coming to dinner, as she is today—she's bringing the desk, too—Sally takes especial care with her clothes and make-up. Marylynn, she knows, is her real audience for such things, since no changes she effects in herself seem to affect Ed one way or the other, or even to register with him. "You look fine to me" is all he says, no matter how she really looks. (But does she want him to see her more clearly, or not? Most likely not. If he did he would notice the incipient wrinkles, the small pouches of flesh that are not quite there yet, the network forming beneath her eyes. It's better as it is.)

Sally has repeated this remark of Ed's to Marylynn, adding that he said it the day the Jacuzzi overflowed because the smoke alarm went off, because an English muffin she was heating to eat in the bathtub got stuck in the toaster, and she had to spend an hour putting down newspaper and mopping up, and only had half an hour to dress for a dinner they were going to. "Really I looked like the wrath of God," said Sally. These days she finds herself repeating to Marylynn many of the things Ed says: the stupid things. Marylynn is the only one of Sally's friends she has confided in to this extent.

"Ed is cute as a button," Marylynn said. "In fact, he's just like a button: he's so bright and shiny. If he were mine, I'd get him bronzed and keep him on the mantelpiece."

Marylynn is even better than Sally at concocting formulations for Ed's particular brand of stupidity, which can irritate Sally: coming from herself, this sort of comment appears to her indulgent and loving, but from Marylynn it borders on the patronizing. So then she sticks up for Ed, who is by no means stupid about everything. When you narrow it down, there's only one area of life he's hopeless about. The rest of the time he's intelligent enough, some even say brilliant: otherwise, how could he be so successful?

Ed is a heart man, one of the best, and the irony of this is not lost on Sally: who could possibly know less about the workings of hearts, real hearts, the kind symbolized by red satin surrounded by lace and topped by pink bows, than Ed? Hearts with arrows in them. At the same time, the fact that he's a heart man is a large part of his allure. Women corner him on sofas, trap him in bay-windows at cocktail parties, mutter to him in confidential voices at dinner parties. They behave this way right in front of Sally, under her very nose, as if she's invisible, and Ed lets them do it. This would never happen if he were in banking or construction.

As it is, everywhere he goes he is beset by sirens. They want him to fix their hearts. Each of them seems to have a little something wrong—a murmur, a whisper. Or they faint a lot and want him to tell them why. This is always what the conversations are about, according to Ed, and Sally believes it. Once she'd wanted it herself, that mirage. What had she invented for him, in the beginning? A heavy heart, that beat too hard after meals. And he'd been so sweet, looking at her with those stunned brown eyes of his, as if her heart were the genuine topic, listening to her gravely as if he'd never heard any of this twaddle before, advising her to drink less coffee. And she'd felt such triumph, to have carried off her imposture, pried out of him that miniscule token of concern.

Thinking back on this incident makes her uneasy, now that she's seen her own performance repeated so many times, including the hand placed lightly on the heart, to call attention of course to the breasts. Some of these women have been within inches of getting Ed to put his head down on their chests, right there in Sally's living room. Watching all this out of the corners of her eyes while serving the liqueurs, Sally feels the Aztec rise within her. *Trouble with your heart? Get it removed,* she thinks. *Then you'll have no more problems.*

Sometimes Sally worries that she's a nothing, the way Marylynn was before she got a divorce and a job. But Sally isn't a nothing; therefore, she doesn't need a divorce to stop being one. And she's always had a job of some sort; in fact she has one now. Luckily Ed has no objection; he doesn't have much of an objection to anything she does.

Her job is supposed to be full-time, but in effect it's part-time, because Sally can take a lot of the work away and do it at home, and, as she says, with one arm tied behind her back. When Sally is being ornery, when she's playing the dull wife of a fascinating heart man—she does this with people she can't be bothered with—she says she works in a bank, nothing important. Then she watches their eyes dismiss her. When, on the other hand, she's trying to impress, she says she's in P.R. In reality she runs the in-house organ for a trust company, a medium-sized one. This is a thin magazine, nicely printed, which is supposed to make the employees feel that some of the boys are doing worthwhile things out there and are human beings as well. It's still the boys, though the few women in anything resembling key positions are wheeled out regularly, bloused and suited and smiling brightly, with what they hope will come across as confidence rather than aggression.

This is the latest in a string of such jobs Sally has held over the years: comfortable enough jobs that engage only half of her cogs and wheels, and that end up leading nowhere. Technically she's second-in-command: over her is a man who wasn't working out in management, but who couldn't be fired because his wife was related to the chairman of the board. He goes out for long alcoholic lunches and plays a lot of golf, and Sally runs the show. This man gets the official credit for everything Sally does right, but the senior executives in the company take Sally aside when no one is looking and tell her what a great gal she is and what a whiz she is at holding up her end.

The real pay-off for Sally, though, is that her boss provides her with an endless supply of anecdotes. She dines out on stories about his dim-wittedness and pomposity, his lobotomized suggestions about what the two of them should cook up for the magazine; *the organ*, as she says he always calls it. "He says we need some fresh blood to perk up the organ," Sally says, and the heart men grin at her. "He actually said that?" Talking like this about her boss would be reckless—you never know what might get back to him, with the world as small as it is—if Sally were afraid of losing her job, but she isn't. There's an unspoken agreement between her and this man: they both know that if she goes, he goes, because who else would put up with him? Sally might angle for his job, if she were stupid enough to disregard his family connections, if she coveted the trappings of power. But she's just fine where she is. Jokingly, she says she's reached her level of incompetence. She says she suffers from fear of success.

Her boss is white-haired, slender, and tanned, and looks like an English gin ad. Despite his vapidity he's outwardly distinguished, she allows him that. In truth she pampers him outrageously, indulges him, covers up for him at every turn, though she stops short of behaving like a secretary: she doesn't bring him coffee. They both have a secretary who does that anyway. The one time he made a pass at her, when he came in from lunch visibly reeling, Sally was kind about it.

Occasionally, though not often, Sally has to travel in connection with her job. She's sent off to places like Edmonton, where they have a branch. She interviews the boys at the middle and senior levels; they have lunch, and the boys talk about ups and downs in oil or the slump in the real-estate market. Then she gets taken on tours of shopping plazas under construction. It's always windy, and grit blows into her face. She comes back to home base and writes a piece on the youthfulness and vitality of the West.

She teases Ed, while she packs, saying she's going off for a rendezvous with a dashing financier or two. Ed isn't threatened; he tells her to enjoy herself, and she hugs him and tells him how much she will miss him. He's so dumb it doesn't occur to him she might not be joking. In point of fact, it would have been quite possible for Sally to have had an affair, or at least a one- or two-night stand, on several of these occasions: she knows when those chalk lines are being drawn, when she's being dared to step over them. But she isn't interested in having an affair with anyone but Ed.

She doesn't eat much on the planes; she doesn't like the food. But on the return trip, she invariably saves the pre-packaged parts of the meal, the cheese in its plastic wrap, the miniature chocolate bar, the bag of pretzels. She ferrets them away in her purse. She thinks of them as supplies, that she may need if she gets stuck in a strange airport, if they have to change course because of snow or fog, for instance. All kinds of things could happen, although they never have. When she gets home she takes the things from her purse and throws them out.

Outside the window Ed straightens up and wipes his earthsmeared hands down the sides of his pants. He begins to turn, and Sally moves back from the window so he won't see that she's watching. She doesn't like it to be too obvious. She shifts her attention to the sauce: it's in the second stage of a *sauce suprême*, which will make all the difference to the chicken. When Sally was learning this sauce, her cooking instructor quoted one of the great chefs, to the effect that the chicken was merely a canvas. He meant as in painting, but Sally, in an undertone to the woman next to her, turned it around. "Mine's canvas anyway, sauce or no sauce," or words to that effect.

Gourmet cooking was the third night course Sally has taken. At the moment she's on her fifth, which is called *Forms of Narrative Fiction*. It's half reading and half writing assignments—the instructor doesn't believe you can understand an art form without at least trying it yourself—and Sally purports to be enjoying it. She tells her friends she takes night courses to keep her brain from atrophying, and her friends find this amusing: whatever else may become of Sally's brain, they say, they don't see atrophying as an option. Sally knows better, but in any case there's always room for improvement. She may have begun taking the courses in the belief that this would make her more interesting to Ed, but she soon gave up on that idea: she appears to be neither more nor less interesting to Ed now than she was before.

Most of the food for tonight is already made. Sally tries to be well organized: the overflowing Jacuzzi was an aberration. The cold watercress soup with walnuts is chilling in the refrigerator, the chocolate mousse ditto. Ed, being Ed, prefers meatloaf to sweetbreads with pine nuts, butterscotch pudding made from a package to chestnut purée topped with whipped cream. (Sally burnt her fingers peeling the chestnuts. She couldn't do it the easy way and buy it tinned.) Sally says Ed's preference for this type of food comes from being pre-programmed by hospital cafeterias when he was younger: show him a burned sausage and a scoop of instant mashed potatoes and he salivates. So it's only for company that she can unfurl her *boeuf en daube* and her salmon *en papillote*, spread them forth to be savoured and praised.

What she likes best about these dinners though is setting the table, deciding who will sit where and, when she's feeling mischievous, even what they are likely to say. Then she can sit and listen to them say it. Occasionally she prompts a little.

Tonight will not be very challenging, since it's only the heart men and their wives, and Marylynn, whom Sally hopes will dilute them. The heart men are forbidden to talk shop at Sally's dinner table, but they do it anyway. "Not what you really want to listen to while you're eating," says Sally. "All those tubes and valves." Privately she thinks they're a conceited lot, all except Ed. She can't resist needling them from time to time.

"I mean," she said to one of the leading surgeons, "basically it's just an exalted form of dress-making, don't you think?"

"Come again?" said the surgeon, smiling. The heart men think Sally is one hell of a tease.

"It's really just cutting and sewing, isn't it?" Sally murmured. The surgeon laughed.

"There's more to it than that," Ed said, unexpectedly, solemnly.

"What more, Ed?" said the surgeon. "You could say there's a lot of embroidery, but that's in the billing." He chuckled at himself.

Sally held her breath. She could hear Ed's verbal thought processes lurching into gear. He was delectable.

"Good judgement," Ed said. His earnestness hit the table like a wet fish. The surgeon hastily downed his wine.

Sally smiled. This was supposed to be a reprimand to her, she knew, for not taking things seriously enough. *Oh, come on, Ed*, she could say. But she knows also, most of the time, when to keep her trap shut. She should have a light-up JOKE sign on her forehead, so Ed would be able to tell the difference.

The heart men do well. Most of them appear to be doing better than Ed, but that's only because they have, on the whole, more expensive tastes and fewer wives. Sally can calculate these things and she figures Ed is about par.

These days there's much talk about advanced technologies, which Sally tries to keep up on, since they interest Ed. A few years ago the heart men got themselves a new facility. Ed was so revved up that he told Sally about it, which was unusual for him. A week later Sally said she would drop by the hospital at the end of the day and pick Ed up and take him out for dinner; she didn't feel like cooking, she said. Really she wanted to check out the facility; she likes to check out anything that causes the line on Ed's excitement chart to move above level.

At first Ed said he was tired, that when the day came to an end he didn't want to prolong it. But Sally wheedled and was respectful, and finally Ed took her to see his new gizmo. It was in a cramped, darkened room with an examining table in it. The thing itself looked like a television screen hooked up to some complicated hardware. Ed said that they could wire a patient up and bounce sound waves off the heart and pick up the echoes, and they would get a picture on the screen, an actual picture, of the heart in motion. It was a thousand times better than an electrocardiogram, he said: they could see the faults, the thickenings and cloggings, much more clearly.

"Colour?" said Sally.

"Black and white," said Ed.

Then Sally was possessed by a desire to see her own heart, in motion, in black and white, on the screen. At the dentist's she always wants to see the X-rays of her teeth, too, solid and glittering in her cloudy head. "Do it," she said, "I want to see how it works," and though this was the kind of thing Ed would ordinarily evade or tell her she was being silly about, he didn't need much persuading. He was fascinated by the thing himself, and he wanted to show it off.

He checked to make sure there was nobody real booked for the room. Then he told Sally to slip out of her clothes, the top half, brassière and all. He gave her a paper gown and turned his back modestly while she slipped it on, as if he didn't see her body every night of the week. He attached electrodes to her, the ankles and one wrist, and turned a switch and fiddled with the dials. Really a technician was supposed to do this, he told her, but he knew how to run the machine himself. He was good with small appliances.

Sally lay prone on the table, feeling strangely naked. "What do I do?" she said.

"Just lie there," said Ed. He came over to her and tore a hole in the paper gown, above her left breast. Then he started running a probe over her skin. It was wet and slippery and cold, and felt like the roller on a roll-on deodorant.

"There," he said, and Sally turned her head. On the screen was a large grey object, like a giant fig, paler in the middle, a dark line running down the centre. The sides moved in and out; two wings fluttered in it, like an uncertain moth's.

"That's it?" said Sally dubiously. Her heart looked so insubstantial, like a bag of gelatin, something that would melt, fade, disintegrate, if you squeezed it even a little.

Ed moved the probe, and they looked at the heart from the bottom, then the top. Then he stopped the frame, then changed it from a positive to a negative image. Sally began to shiver.

"That's wonderful," she said. He seemed so distant, absorbed in his machine, taking the measure of her heart, which was beating over there all by itself, detached from her exposed and under his control.

Ed unwired her and she put on her clothes again, neutrally, as if he were actually a doctor. Nevertheless this transaction, this whole room, was sexual in a way she didn't quite understand; it was clearly a dangerous place. It was like a massage parlour, only for women. Put a batch of women in there with Ed and they would never want to come out. They'd want to stay in there while he ran his probe over their wet skins and pointed out to them the defects of their beating hearts.

"Thank you," said Sally.

Sally hears the back door open and close. She feels Ed approaching, coming through the passages of the house towards her, like a small wind or a ball of static electricity. The hair stands up on her arms. Sometimes he makes her so happy she thinks she's about to burst; other times she thinks she's about to burst anyway.

He comes into the kitchen, and she pretends not to notice. He puts his arms around her from behind, kisses her on the neck. She leans back, pressing herself into him. What they should do now is go into the bedroom (or even the living room, even the den) and make love, but it wouldn't occur to Ed to make love in the middle of the day. Sally often comes across articles in magazines about how to improve your sex life, which leave her feeling disappointed, or reminiscent: Ed is not Sally's first and only man. But she knows she shouldn't expect too much of Ed. If Ed were more experimental, more interested in variety, he would be a different kind of man altogether: slyer, more devious, more observant, harder to deal with.

As it is, Ed makes love in the same way, time after time, each movement following the others in an exact order. But it seems to satisfy him. Of course it satisfies him: you can always tell when men are satisfied. It's Sally who lies awake, afterwards, watching the pictures unroll across her closed eyes.

Sally steps away from Ed, smiles at him. "How did you make out with the women today?" she says.

"What women?" says Ed absently, going towards the sink. He knows what women.

"The ones out there, hiding in the forsythia," says Sally. "I counted at least ten. They were just waiting for a chance."

She teases him frequently about these troops of women, which follow him around everywhere, which are invisible to Ed but which she can see as plain as day.

"I bet they hang around outside the front door of the hospital," she will say, "just waiting till you come out. I bet they hide in the linen closets and jump out at you from behind, and then pretend to be lost so you'll take them by the short cut. It's the white coat that does it. None of those women can resist the white coats. They've been conditioned by Young Doctor Kildare."

"Don't be silly," says Ed today, with equanimity. Is he blushing, is he embarrassed? Sally examines his face closely, like a geologist with an aerial photograph, looking for telltale signs of mineral treasure: markings, bumps, hollows. Everything about Ed means something, though it's difficult at times to say what.

Now he's washing his hands at the sink, to get the earth off. In a minute he'll wipe them on the dish towel instead of using the hand towel the way he's supposed to. Is that complacency, in the back turned to her? Maybe there really are these hordes of women, even though she's made them up. Maybe they really do behave that way. His shoulders are slightly drawn up: is he shutting her out?

"I know what they want," she goes on. "They want to get into that little dark room of yours and climb up onto your table. They think you're delicious. They'll gobble you up. They'll chew you into tiny pieces. There won't be anything left of you at all, only a stethoscope and a couple of shoelaces."

Once Ed would have laughed at this, but today he doesn't. Maybe she's said it, or something like it, a few times too often. He smiles though, wipes his hands on the dish towel, peers into the fridge. He likes to snack.

"There's some cold roast beef," Sally says, baffled.

Sally takes the sauce off the stove and sets it aside for later: she'll do the last steps just before serving. It's only two-thirty. Ed has disappeared into the cellar, where Sally knows he will be safe for a while. She goes into her study, which used to be one of the kids' bedrooms, and sits down at her desk. The room has never been completely redecorated: there's still a bed in it, and a dressing table with a blue flowered flounce Sally helped pick out, long before the kids went off to university: "flew the coop," as Ed puts it.

Sally doesn't comment on the expression, though she would like to say that it wasn't the first coop they flew. Her house isn't even the real coop, since neither of the kids is hers. She'd hoped for a baby of her own when she married Ed, but she didn't want to force the issue. Ed didn't object to the idea, exactly, but he was neutral about it, and Sally got the feeling he'd had enough babies already. Anyway, the other two wives had babies, and look what happened to them. Since their actual fates have always been vague to Sally, she's free to imagine all kinds of things, from drug addiction to madness. Whatever it was resulted in Sally having to bring up their kids, at least from puberty onwards. The way it was presented by the first wife was that it was Ed's turn now. The second wife was more oblique: she said that the child wanted to spend some time with her father. Sally was left out of both these equations, as if the house wasn't a place she lived in, not really, so she couldn't be expected to have any opinion.

Considering everything, she hasn't done badly. She likes the kids and tries to be a friend to them, since she can hardly pretend to be a mother. She describes the three of them as having an easy relationship. Ed wasn't around much for the kids, but it's him they want approval from, not Sally; it's him they respect. Sally is more like a confederate, helping them get what they want from Ed.

When the kids were younger, Sally used to play Monopoly with them, up at the summer place in Muskoka Ed owned then but has since sold. Ed would play too, on his vacations and on the weekends when he could make it up. These games would all proceed along the same lines. Sally would have an initial run of luck and would buy up everything she had a chance at. She didn't care whether it was classy real estate, like Boardwalk or Park Place, or those dingy little houses on the other side of the tracks; she would even buy train stations, which the kids would pass over, preferring to save their cash reserves for better investments. Ed, on the other hand, would plod along, getting a little here, a little there. Then, when Sally was feeling flush, she would blow her money on next-to-useless luxuries such as the electric light company; and when the kids started to lose, as they invariably did, Sally would lend them money at cheap rates or trade them things of her own, at a loss. Why not? She could afford it.

Ed meanwhile would be hedging his bets, building up blocks of property, sticking houses and hotels on them. He preferred the middle range, respectable streets but not flashy. Sally would land on his spaces and have to shell out hard cash. Ed never offered deals, and never accepted them. He played a lone game, and won more often than not. Then Sally would feel thwarted. She would say she guessed she lacked the killer instinct; or she would say that for herself she didn't care, because after all it was only a game, but he ought to allow the kids to win, once in a while. Ed couldn't grasp the concept of allowing other people to win. He said it would be condescending towards the children, and anyway you couldn't arrange to have a dice game turn out the way you wanted it to, since it was partly a matter of chance. If it was chance, Sally would think, why were the games so similar to one another? At the end, there would be Ed, counting up his paper cash, sorting it out into piles of bills of varying denominations, and Sally, her vast holdings dwindled to a few shoddy blocks on Baltic Avenue, doomed to foreclosure: extravagant, generous, bankrupt.

On these nights, after the kids were asleep, Sally would have two or three more rye-and-gingers than were good for her. Ed would go to bed early—winning made him satisfied and drowsy—and Sally would ramble about the house or read the endings of murder mysteries she had already read once before, and finally she would slip into bed and wake Ed up and stroke him into arousal, seeking comfort.

Sally has almost forgotten these games. Right now the kids are receding, fading like old ink, Ed on the contrary looms larger and larger, the outlines around him darkening. He's constantly developing, like a Polaroid print, new colours emerging, but the result remains the same: Ed is a surface, one she has trouble getting beneath.

"Explore your inner world," said Sally's instructor in *Forms of Narrative Fiction*, a middle-aged woman of scant fame who goes in for astrology and the Tarot pack and writes short stories, which are not published in any of the magazines Sally reads. "Then there's your outer one," Sally said afterwards, to her friends. "For instance, she should really get something done about her hair." She made this trivial and mean remark because she's fed up with her inner world; she doesn't need to explore it. In her inner world is Ed, like a doll within a Russian wooden doll, and in Ed is Ed's inner world; which she can't get at.

She takes a crack at it anyway: Ed's inner world is a forest, which looks something like the bottom part of their ravine lot, but without the fence. He wanders around in there, among the trees, not heading in any special direction. Every once in a while he comes upon a strange-looking plant, a sickly plant choked with weeds and briars. Ed kneels, clears a space around it, does some pruning, a little skilful snipping and cutting, props it up. The plant revives, flushes with health, sends out a grateful red blossom. Ed continues on his way. Or it may be a conked-out squirrel, which he restores with a drop from his flask of magic elixir. At set intervals an angel appears, bringing him food. It's always meatloaf. That's fine with Ed, who hardly notices what he eats, but the angel is getting tired of being an angel. Now Sally begins thinking about the angel: why are its wings frayed and dingy grey around the edges, why is it looking so withered and frantic? This is where all Sally's attempts to explore Ed's inner world end up.

She knows she thinks about Ed too much. She knows she should stop. She knows she shouldn't ask, "Do you still love me?" in the plaintive tone that sets even her own teeth on edge. All it achieves is that Ed shakes his head, as if not understanding why she would ask this, and pats her hand. "Sally, Sally," he says, and everything proceeds as usual; except for the dread that seeps into things, the most ordinary things, such as rearranging the chairs and changing the burnt-out lightbulbs. But what is it she's afraid of? She has what they call everything: Ed, their wonderful house on a ravine lot, something she's always wanted. (But the hill is jungly, and the house is made of ice. It's held together only by Sally, who sits in the middle of it, working on a puzzle. The puzzle is Ed. If she should ever solve it, if she should ever fit the last cold splinter into place, the house will melt and flow away down the hill, and then . . .) It's a bad habit, fooling around with her head this way. It does no good. She knows that if she could quit she'd be happier. She ought to be able to: she's given up smoking.

She needs to concentrate her attention on other things. This is the real reason for the night courses, which she picks almost at random, to coincide with the evenings Ed isn't in. He has meetings, he's on the boards of charities, he has trouble saying no. She runs the courses past herself, mediaeval history, cooking, anthropology, hoping her mind will snag on something; she's even taken a course in geology, which was fascinating, she told her friends, all that magma. That's just it: everything is fascinating, but nothing enters her. She's always a star pupil, she does well on the exams and impresses the teachers, for which she despises them. She is familiar with her brightness, her techniques; she's surprised other people are still taken in by them.

Forms of Narrative Fiction started out the same way. Sally was full of good ideas, brimming with helpful suggestions. The workshop part of it was anyway just like a committee meeting, and Sally knew how to run those, from behind, without seeming to run them: she'd done it lots of times at work. Bertha, the instructor, told Sally she had a vivid imagination and a lot of untapped creative energy. "No wonder she never gets anywhere, with a name like Bertha," Sally said, while having coffee afterwards with two of the other night-coursers. "It goes with her outfits, though." (Bertha sports the macramé look, with health-food sandals and bulky-knit sweaters and handweave skirts that don't do a thing for her square figure, and too many Mexican rings on her hands, which she doesn't wash often enough.) Bertha goes in for assignments, which she calls learning by doing. Sally likes assignments: she likes things that can be completed and then discarded, and for which she gets marks.

The first thing Bertha assigned was The Epic. They read *The Odyssey* (selected passages, in translation, with a plot summary of the rest); then they poked around in James Joyce's *Ulysses*, to see how Joyce had adapted the epic form to the modern-day novel. Bertha had them keep a Toronto notebook, in which they had to pick out various spots around town as the ports of call in *The Odyssey*, and say why they had chosen them. The notebooks were read out loud in class, and it was a scream to see who had chosen what for Hades. (The Mount Pleasant Cemetery, McDonald's, where, if you eat the forbidden food, you never get back to the land of the living, the University Club with its dead ancestral souls, and so forth.) Sally's was the hospital, of course; she had no difficulty with the trench filled with blood, and she put the ghosts in wheelchairs.

After that they did The Ballad, and read gruesome accounts of murders and betrayed love. Bertha played them tapes of wheezy old men singing traditionally, in the Doric mode, and assigned a newspaper scrapbook, in which you had to clip and paste up-to-the-minute equivalents. The *Sun* was the best newspaper for these. The fiction that turned out to go with this kind of plot was the kind Sally liked anyway, and she had no difficulty concocting a five-page murder mystery, complete with revenge.

But now they are on Folk Tales and the Oral Tradition, and Sally is having trouble. This time, Bertha wouldn't let them read anything. Instead she read to them, in a voice, Sally said, that was like a gravel truck and was not conducive to reverie. Since it was the Oral Tradition, they weren't even allowed to take notes; Bertha said the original hearers of these stories couldn't read, so the stories were memorized. "To re-create the atmosphere," said Bertha, "I should turn out the lights. These stories were always told at night." "To make them creepier?" someone offered. "No," said Bertha. "In the days, they worked." She didn't do that, though she did make them sit in a circle.

"You should have seen us," Sally said afterwards to Ed, "sitting in a circle, listening to fairy stories. It was just like kindergarten. Some of them even had their mouths open. I kept expecting her to say, 'If you need to go, put up your hand.'" She was meaning to be funny, to amuse Ed with this account of Bertha's eccentricity and the foolish appearance of the students, most of them middle-aged, sitting in a circle as if they had never grown up at all. She was also intending to belittle the course, just slightly. She always did this with her night courses, so Ed wouldn't get the idea there was anything in her life that was even remotely as important as he was. But Ed didn't seem to need this amusement or this belittlement. He took her information earnestly, gravely, as if Bertha's behaviour was, after all, only the procedure of a specialist. No one knew better than he did that the procedures of specialists often looked bizarre or incomprehensible to onlookers. "She probably has her reasons," was all he would say.

The first stories Bertha read them, for warm-ups ("No memorizing for *her*," said Sally), were about princes who got amnesia and forgot about their true loves and married girls their mothers had picked out for them. Then they had to be rescued, with the aid of magic. The stories didn't say what happened to the women the princes had already married, though Sally wondered about it. Then Bertha read them another story, and this time they were supposed to remember the features that stood out for them and write a five-page transposition, set in the present and cast in the realistic mode. ("In other words," said Bertha, "no real magic.") They couldn't use the Universal Narrator, however: they had done that in their Ballad assignment. This time they had to choose a point of view. It could be the point of view of anyone or anything in the story, but they were limited to one only. The story she was about to read, she said, was a variant of the Bluebeard motif, much earlier than Perrault's sentimental rewriting of it. In Perrault, said Bertha, the girl has to be rescued by her brothers; but in the earlier version things were quite otherwise.

This is what Bertha read, as far as Sally can remember:

There were once three young sisters. One day a beggar with a large basket on his back came to the door and asked for some bread. The eldest sister brought him some, but no sooner had she touched him than she was compelled to jump into his basket, for the beggar was really a wizard in disguise. ("So much for United Appeal," Sally murmured. "She should have said, 'I gave at the office.'") The wizard carried her away to his house in the forest, which was large and richly furnished. "Here you will be happy with me, my darling," said the wizard, "for you will have everything your heart could desire."

This lasted for a few days. Then the wizard gave the girl an egg and a bunch of keys. "I must go away on a journey," he said, "and I am leaving the house in your charge. Preserve this egg for me, and carry it about with you everywhere; for a great misfortune will follow from its loss. The keys open every room in the house. You may go into each of them and enjoy what you find there, but do not go into the small room at the top of the house, on pain of death." The girl promised, and the wizard disappeared.

At first the girl contented herself with exploring the rooms, which contained many treasures. But finally her curiosity would not let her alone. She sought out the smallest key, and, with beating heart, opened the little door at the top of the house. Inside it was a large basin full of blood, within which were the bodies of many women, which had been cut to pieces; nearby were a chopping block and an axe. In her horror, she let go of the egg, which fell into the basin of blood. In vain did she try to wipe away the stain: every time she succeeded in removing it; back it would come.

The wizard returned, and in a stern voice asked for the egg and the keys. When he saw the egg, he knew at once she had disobeyed him and gone into the forbidden room. "Since you have gone into the room against my will," he said, "you shall go back into it against your own." Despite her pleas he threw her down, dragged her by the hair into the little room, hacked her into pieces and threw her body into the basin with the others.

Then he went for the second girl, who fared no better than her sister. But the third was clever and wily. As soon as the wizard had gone, she set the egg on a shelf, out of harm's way, and then went immediately and opened the forbidden door. Imagine her distress when she saw the cut-up bodies of her two beloved sisters; but she set the parts in order, and they joined together and her sisters stood up and moved, and were living and well. They embraced each other, and the third sister hid the other two in a cupboard.

When the wizard returned he at once asked for the egg. This time it was spotless. "You have passed the test," he said to the third sister. "You shall be my bride." ("And second prize," said Sally, to herself this time, "is *two* weeks in Niagara Falls.") The wizard no longer had any power over her, and had to do whatever she asked. There was more, about how the wizard met his come-uppance and was burned to death, but Sally already knew which features stood out for her.

At first she thought the most important thing in the story was the forbidden room. What would she put in the forbidden room, in her present-day realistic version? Certainly not chopped-up women. It wasn't that they were too unrealistic, but they were certainly too sick, as well as being too obvious. She wanted to do something more clever. She thought it might be a good idea to have the curious woman open the door and find nothing there at all, but after mulling it over she set this notion aside. It would leave her with the problem of why the wizard would have a forbidden room in which he kept nothing.

That was the way she was thinking right after she got the assignment, which was a full two weeks ago. So far she's written nothing. The great temptation is to cast herself in the role of the cunning heroine, but again it's too predictable. And Ed certainly isn't the wizard; he's nowhere near sinister enough. If Ed were the wizard, the room would contain a forest, some ailing plants and feeble squirrels, and Ed himself, fixing them up; but then, if it were Ed the room wouldn't even be locked, and there would be no story.

Now, as she sits at her desk, fiddling with her felt-tip pen, it comes to Sally that the intriguing thing about the story, the thing she should fasten on, is the egg. Why an egg? From the night course in Comparative Folklore she took four years ago, she remembers that the egg can be a fertility symbol, or a necessary object in African spells, or something the world hatched out of. Maybe in this story it's a symbol of virginity, and that is why the wizard requires it unbloodied. Women with dirty eggs get murdered, those with clean ones get married.

But this isn't useful either. The concept is so outmoded. Sally doesn't see how she can transpose it into real life without making it ridiculous, unless she sets the story in, for instance, an immigrant Portuguese family, and what would she know about that?

Sally opens the drawer of her desk and hunts around in it for her nail file. As she's doing this, she gets the brilliant idea of writing the story from the point of view of the egg. Other people will do the other things: the clever girl, the wizard, the two blundering sisters, who weren't smart enough to lie, and who will have problems afterwards, because of the thin red lines running all over their bodies, from where their parts joined together. But no one will think of the egg. How does it feel, to be the innocent and passive cause of so much misfortune?

(Ed isn't the Bluebeard: Ed is the egg. Ed Egg, blank and pristine and lovely. Stupid, too. Boiled, probably. Sally smiles fondly.)

But how can there be a story from the egg's point of view, if the egg is so closed and unaware? Sally ponders this, doodling on her pad of lined paper. Then she resumes the search for her nail file. Already it's time to begin getting ready for her dinner party. She can sleep on the problem of the egg and finish the assignment tomorrow, which is Sunday. It's due on Monday, but Sally's mother used to say she was a whiz at getting things done at the last minute.

After painting her nails with *Nuit Magique*, Sally takes a bath, eating her habitual toasted English muffin while she lies in the tub. She begins to dress, dawdling; she has plenty of time. She hears Ed coming up out of the cellar; then she hears him in the bathroom, which he has entered from the hall door. Sally goes in through the other door, still in her slip. Ed is standing at the sink with his shirt off, shaving. On the weekends he leaves it until necessary, or until Sally tells him he's too scratchy.

Sally slides her hands around his waist, nuzzling against his naked back. He has very smooth skin, for a man. Sally smiles to herself: she can't stop thinking of him as an egg.

"Mmm," says Ed. It could be appreciation, or the answer to a question Sally hasn't asked and he hasn't heard, or just an acknowledgement that she's there.

"Don't you ever wonder what I think about?" Sally says. She's said this more than once, in bed or at the dinner table, after dessert. She stands behind him, watching the swaths the razor cuts in the white of his face, looking at her own face reflected in the mirror, just the eyes visible above his naked shoulder. Ed, lathered, is Assyrian, sterner than usual; or a frost-covered Arctic explorer; or demi-human, a white-bearded forest mutant. He scrapes away at himself, methodically destroying the illusion.

"But I already know what you think about," says Ed.

"How?" Sally says, taken aback.

"You're always telling me," Ed says, with what might be resignation or sadness; or maybe this is only a simple statement of fact.

Sally is relieved. If that's all he's going on, she's safe.

Marylynn arrives half an hour early, her pearl-coloured Porsche leading two men in a delivery truck up the driveway. The men install the keyhole desk, while Marylynn supervises: it looks, in the alcove, exactly as Marylynn has said it would, and Sally is delighted. She sits at it to write the cheque. Then she and Marylynn go into the kitchen, where Sally is finishing up her sauce, and Sally pours them each a Kir. She's glad Marylynn is here: it will keep her from dithering, as she tends to do just before people arrive. Though it's only the heart men, she's still a bit nervous. Ed is more likely to notice when things are wrong than when they're exactly right.

Marylynn sits at the kitchen table, one arm draped over the chairback, her chin on the other hand; she's in soft grey, which makes her hair look silver, and Sally feels once again how banal it is to have ordinary dark hair like her own, however well-cut, however shiny. It's the confidence she envies, the negligence. Marylynn doesn't seem to be trying at all, ever.

"Guess what Ed said today?" Sally says.

Marylynn leans further forward. "What?" she says, with the eagerness of one joining in a familiar game.

"He said, 'Some of these femininists go too far,'" Sally reports. "'Femininists.' Isn't that sweet?"

Marylynn holds the pause too long, and Sally has a sudden awful thought: maybe Marylynn thinks she's showing off, about Ed. Marylynn has always said she's not ready for another marriage yet; still, Sally should watch herself, not rub her nose in it. But then Marylynn laughs indulgently, and Sally, relieved, joins in.

"Ed is unbelievable," says Marylynn. "You should pin his mittens to his sleeves when he goes out in the morning."

"He shouldn't be let out alone," says Sally.

"You should get him a seeing-eye dog," says Marylynn, "to bark at women."

"Why?" says Sally, still laughing but alert now, the cold beginning at the ends of her fingers. Maybe Marylynn knows something she doesn't; maybe the house is beginning to crumble, after all.

"Because he can't see them coming," says Marylynn. "That's what you're always telling me."

She sips her Kir; Sally stirs the sauce. "I bet he thinks I'm a femininist," says Marylynn.

"You?" says Sally. "Never." She would like to add that Ed has given no indication of thinking anything at all about Marylynn, but she doesn't. She doesn't want to take the risk of hurting her feelings.

The wives of the heart men admire Sally's sauce; the heart men talk shop, all except Walter Morly, who is good at by-passes. He's sitting beside Marylynn, and paying far too much attention to her for Sally's comfort. Mrs. Morly is at the other end of the table, not saying much of anything, which Marylynn appears not to notice. She keeps on talking to Walter about St. Lucia, where they've both been.

So after dinner, when Sally has herded them all into the living room for coffee and liqueurs, she takes Marylynn by the elbow. "Ed hasn't seen our desk yet," she says, "not up close. Take him away and give him your lecture on nineteenth-century antiques. Show him all the pigeon-holes. Ed loves pigeon-holes." Ed appears not to get this.

Marylynn knows exactly what Sally is up to. "Don't worry," she says, "I won't rape Dr. Morly; the poor creature would never survive the shock," but she allows herself to be shunted off to the side with Ed.

Sally moves from guest to guest, smiling, making sure everything is in order. Although she never looks directly, she's always conscious of Ed's presence in the room, any room; she perceives him as a shadow, a shape seen dimly at the edge of her field of vision, recognizable by the outline. She likes to know where he is, that's all. Some people are on their second cup of coffee. She walks towards the alcove: they must have finished with the desk by now.

But they haven't, they're still in there. Marylynn is bending forward, one hand on the veneer. Ed is standing too close to her, and as Sally comes up behind them she sees his left arm, held close to his side, the back of it pressed against Marylynn, her shimmering upper thigh, her ass to be exact. Marylynn does not move away.

It's a split second, and then Ed sees Sally and the hand is gone; there it is, on top of the desk, reaching for a liqueur glass.

"Marylynn needs more Tia Maria," he says. "I just told her that people who drink a little now and again live longer." His voice is even, his face is as level as ever, a flat plain with no signposts.

Marylynn laughs. "I once had a dentist who I swear drilled tiny holes in my teeth, so he could fix them later," she says.

Sally sees Ed's hand outstretched towards her, holding the empty glass. She takes it, smiling, and turns away. There's a roaring sound at the back of her head; blackness appears around the edges of the picture she is seeing, like a television screen going dead. She walks into the kitchen and puts her cheek against the refrigerator and her arms around it, as far as they will go. She remains that way, hugging it; it hums steadily, with a sound like comfort. After a while she lets go of it and touches her hair, and walks back into the living room with the filled glass.

Marylynn is over by the french doors, talking with Walter Morly. Ed is standing by himself, in front of the fireplace, one arm on the mantelpiece, his left hand out of sight in his pocket.

Sally goes to Marylynn, hands her the glass. "Is that enough?" she says.

Marylynn is unchanged. "Thanks, Sally," she says, and goes on listening to Walter, who has dragged out his usual piece of mischief: some day, when they've perfected it, he says, all hearts will be plastic, and this will be a vast improvement on the current model. It's an obscure form of flirtation. Marylynn winks at Sally, to show that she knows he's tedious. Sally, after a pause, winks back.

She looks over at Ed, who is staring off into space, like a robot which has been parked and switched off. Now she isn't sure whether she really saw what she thought she saw. Even if she did, what does it mean? Maybe it's just that Ed, in a wayward intoxicated moment, put his hand on the nearest buttock, and Marylynn refrained from a shriek or a flinch out of good breeding or the desire not to offend him. Things like this have happened to Sally.

Or it could mean something more sinister: a familiarity between them, an understanding. If this is it, Sally has been wrong about Ed, for years, forever. Her version of Ed is not something she's perceived but something that's been perpetrated on her, by Ed himself, for reasons of his own. Possibly Ed is not stupid. Possibly he's enormously clever. She thinks of moment after moment when this cleverness, this cunning, would have shown itself if it were there, but didn't. She has watched him so carefully. She remembers playing Pick Up Sticks, with the kids, Ed's kids, years ago: how if you moved one stick in the tangle, even slightly, everything else moved also.

She won't say anything to him. She can't say anything: she can't afford to be wrong, or to be right either. She goes back into the kitchen and begins to scrape the plates. This is unlike her—usually she sticks right with the party until it's over—and after a while Ed wanders out. He stands silently, watching her. Sally concentrates on the scraping: dollops of *sauce suprême* slide into the plastic bag, shreds of lettuce, rice, congealed and lumpy. What is left of her afternoon.

"What are you doing out here?" Ed asks at last.

"Scraping the plates," Sally says, cheerful, neutral. "I just thought I'd get a head start on tidying up."

"Leave it," says Ed. "The woman can do that in the morning." That's how he refers to Mrs. Rudge, although she's been with them for three years now: *the woman*. And Mrs. Bird before her, as though they are interchangeable. This has never bothered Sally before. "Go on out there and have a good time."

Sally puts down the spatula, wipes her hands on the hand towel, puts her arms around him, holds on tighter than she should. Ed pats her shoulder. "What's up?" he says; then, "Sally, Sally." If she looks up, she will see him shaking his head a little, as if he doesn't know what to do about her. She doesn't look up.

Ed has gone to bed. Sally roams the house, fidgeting with the debris left by the party. She collects empty glasses, picks up peanuts from the rug. After a while she realizes that she's down on her knees, looking under a chair, and she's forgotten what for. She goes upstairs, creams off her make-up, does her teeth, undresses in the darkened bedroom and slides into bed beside Ed, who is breathing deeply as if asleep. *As if.*

Sally lies in bed with her eyes closed. What she sees is her own heart, in black and white, beating with that insubstantial moth-like flutter, a ghostly heart, torn out of her and floating in space, an animated valentine with no colour. It will go on and on forever; she has no control over it. But now she's seeing the egg, which is not small and cold and white and inert but larger than a real egg and golden pink, resting in a nest of brambles, glowing softly as though there's something red and hot inside it. It's almost pulsing; Sally is afraid of it. As she looks it darkens: rose-red, crimson. This is something the story left out, Sally thinks: the egg is alive, and one day it will hatch. But what will come out of it?

THE LESSON (1972)

Toni Cade Bambara
b. 1939 New York
d. 1995 Philadephia

Back in the days when everyone was old and stupid or young and foolish and me and Sugar were the only ones just right, this lady moved on our block with nappy hair and proper speech and no makeup. And quite naturally we laughed at her, laughed the way we did at the junk man who went about his business like he was some big-time president and his sorry-ass horse his secretary. And we kinda hated her too, hated the way we did the winos who cluttered up our parks and pissed on our handball walls and stank up our hallways and stairs so you couldn't halfway play hide-and-seek without a goddamn gas mask. Miss Moore was her name. The only woman on the block with no first name. And she was black as hell, cept for her feet, which were fish-white and spooky. And she was always planning these boring-ass things for us to do, us being my cousin, mostly, who lived on the block cause we all moved North the same time and to the same apartment then spread out gradual to breathe. And our parents would yank our heads into some kinda shape and crisp up our clothes so we'd be presentable for travel with Miss Moore, who always looked like she was going to church, though she never did. Which is just one of things the grown-ups talked about when they talked behind her back like a dog. But when she came calling with some sachet she'd sewed up or some gingerbread she'd made or some book, why then they'd all be too embarrassed to turn her down and we'd get handed over all spruced up. She'd been to college and said it was only right that she should take responsibility for the young ones' education, and she not even related by marriage or blood. So they'd go for it. Specially Aunt Gretchen. She was the main gofer in the family. You got some ole dumb shit foolishness you want somebody to go for, you send for Aunt Gretchen. She been screwed into the go-along for so long, it's a blood-deep natural thing with her. Which is how she got saddled with me and Sugar and Junior in the first place while our mothers were in a la-de-da apartment up the block having a good ole time.

So this one day Miss Moore rounds us all up at the mailbox and it's puredee hot and she's knockin herself out about arithmetic. And school suppose to let up in summer I heard, but she don't never let up. And the starch in my pinafore scratching the shit outta me and I'm really hating this nappy-head bitch and her goddamn college degree. I'd much rather go to the pool or to the show where it's cool. So me and Sugar leaning on the mailbox being surly, which is a Miss Moore word. And Flyboy checking out what everybody brought for lunch. And Fat Butt already wasting his peanut-butter-and-jelly sandwich like the pig he is. And Junebug punchin on Q.T.'s arm for potato chips. And Rosie Giraffe shifting from one hip to the other waiting for somebody to step on her foot or ask her if she from Georgia so she can kick ass, preferably Mercedes'. And Miss Moore asking us do we know what money is, like we a bunch of retards. I mean real money, she say, like it's only poker chips or monopoly papers we lay on the grocer. So right away I'm tired of this and say so. And would much rather snatch Sugar and go to the Sunset and terrorize the West Indian kids and take their hair ribbons and their money too. And Miss Moore files that remark away for next week's lesson on brotherhood, I can tell. And finally I say we oughta get to the subway cause it's cooler and besides we might meet some cute boys. Sugar done swiped her mama's lipstick, so we ready.

So we heading down the street and she's boring us silly about what things cost and what our parents make and how much goes for rent and how money ain't divided up right in this country. And then she gets to the part about we all poor and live in the slums, which I don't feature. And I'm ready to speak on that, but she steps out in the street and hails two cabs just like that. Then she hustles half the crew in with her and hands me a five-dollar bill and tells me to calculate 10 percent tip for the driver. And we're off. Me and Sugar and Junebug and Flyboy hangin out the window and hollering to everybody, putting lipstick on each other cause Flyboy a faggot anyway, and making farts with our sweaty armpits. But I'm mostly trying to figure how to spend this money. But they all fascinated with the meter ticking and Junebug starts laying bets as to how much it'll read when Flyboy can't hold his breath no more. Then Sugar lays bets as to how much it'll be when we get there. So I'm stuck. Don't nobody want to go for my plan, which is to jump out at the next light and run off to the first bar-b-que we can find. Then the driver tells us to get the hell out cause we there already. And the meter reads eighty-five cents. And I'm stalling to figure out the tip and Sugar say give him a dime. And I decide he don't need it bad as I do, so later for him. But then he tries to take off with Junebug foot still in the door so we talk about his mama something ferocious. Then we check out that we on Fifth Avenue and everybody dressed up in stockings. One lady in fur coat, hot as it is. White folks crazy.

"This is the place," Miss Moore say, presenting it to us in the voice she uses at the museum. "Let's look in the windows before we go in."

"Can we steal?" Sugar asks very serious like she's getting the ground rules squared away before she plays. "I beg your pardon," say Miss Moore, and we fall out. So she leads us around the windows of the toy store and me and Sugar screamin, "This is mine, that's mine, I gotta have that, that was made for me, I was born for that," till Big Butt drowns us out.

"Hey, I'm goin to buy that there."

"That there? You don't even know what it is, stupid."

"I do so," he say punchin on Rosie Giraffe. "It's a microscope."

"Whatcha gonna do with a microscope, fool?"

"Look at things."

"Like what, Ronald?" ask Miss Moore. And Big Butt ain't got the first notion. So here go Miss Moore gabbing about the thousands of bacteria in a drop of water and the somethinorother in a speck of blood and the million and one living things in the air around us is invisible to the naked eye. And what she say that for? Junebug go to town on that "naked" and we rolling. Then Miss Moore ask what it cost. So we all jam into the window smudgin it up and the price tag say $300. So then she ask how long'd take for Big Butt and Junebug to save up their allowances. "Too long," I say. "Yeh," adds Sugar, "outgrown it by that time." And Miss Moore say no, you never outgrow learning instruments. "Why, even medical students and interns and," blah, blah, blah. And we ready to choke Big Butt for bringing it up in the first damn place.

"This here costs four hundred eighty dollars," say Rosie Giraffe. So we pile up all over her to see what she pointin out. My eyes tell me it's a chunk of glass cracked with something heavy, and different-color inks dripped into the splits, then the whole thing put into a oven or something. But for $480 it don't make sense.

"That's a paperweight made of semi-precious stones fused together under tremendous pressure," she explains slowly, with her hands doing the mining and all the factory work.

"So what's a paperweight?" asks Rosie Giraffe.

"To weigh paper with, dumbbell," say Flyboy, the wise man from the East.

"Not exactly," say Miss Moore, which is what she say when you warm or way off too. "It's to weigh paper down so it won't scatter and make your desk untidy." So right away me and Sugar curtsy to each other and then to Mercedes who is more the tidy type.

"We don't keep paper on top of the desk in my class," say Junebug, figuring Miss Moore crazy or lyin one.

"At home, then," she say. "Don't you have a calendar and a pencil case and a blotter and a letter-opener on your desk at home where you do your homework?" And she know damn well what our homes look like cause she nosys around in them every chance she gets.

"I don't even have a desk," say Junebug. "Do we?"

"No. And I don't get no homework neither," say Big Butt.

"And I don't even have a home," say Flyboy like he do at school to keep the white folks off his back and sorry for him. Send this poor kid to camp posters, is his specialty.

"I do," says Mercedes. "I have a box of stationery on my desk and a picture of my cat. My godmother bought the stationery and the desk. There's a big rose on each sheet and the envelopes smell like roses."

"Who wants to know about your smelly-ass stationery," say Rosie Giraffe fore I can get my two cents in.

"It's important to have a work area all your own so that . . . "

"Will you look at this sailboat, please," say Flyboy, cuttin her off and pointin to the thing like it was his. So once again we tumble all over each other to gaze at this magnificent thing in the toy store which is just big enough to maybe sail two kittens across the pond if you strap them to the posts tight. We all start reciting the price tag like we in assembly. "Handcrafted sailboat of fiberglass at one thousand one hundred ninety-five dollars."

"Unbelievable," I hear myself say and am really stunned. I read it again for myself just in case the group recitation put me in a trance. Same thing. For some reason this pisses me off. We look at Miss Moore and she lookin at us, waiting for I dunno what.

"Who'd pay all that when you can buy a sailboat set for a quarter at Pop's, a tube of glue for a dime, and a ball of string for eight cents? It must have a motor and a whole lot else besides," I say. "My sailboat cost me about fifty cents."

"But will it take water?" say Mercedes with her smart ass.

"Took mine to Alley Pond Park once," say Flyboy. "String broke, Lost it. Pity."

"Sailed mine in Central Park and it keeled over and sank. Had to ask my father for another dollar."

"And you got the strap," laugh Big Butt. "The jerk didn't even have a string on it. My old man wailed on his behind."

Little Q. T. was staring hard at the sailboat and you could see he wanted it bad. But he too little and somebody'd just take it from him. So what the hell. "This boat for kids, Miss Moore?"

"Parents silly to buy something like that just to get all broke up," say Rosie Giraffe.

"That much money it should last forever," I figure.

"My father'd buy it for me if I wanted it."

"Your father, my ass," say Rosie Giraffe getting a chance to finally push Mercedes.

"Must be rich people shop here," say Q. T.

"You are a very bright boy," say Flyboy. "What was your first clue?" And he rap him on the head with the back of his knuckles, since Q. T. the only one he could get away with. Though Q. T. liable to come up behind you years later and get his licks in when you half expect it.

"What I want to know is," I says to Miss Moore though I never talk to her, I wouldn't give the bitch that satisfaction, "is how much a real boat costs? I figure a thousand'd get you a yacht any day."

"Why don't you check that out," she says, "and report back to the group?" Which really pains my ass. If you gonna mess up a perfectly good swim day least you could do is have some answers. "Let's go in," she say like she got something up her sleeve. Only she don't lead the way. So me and Sugar turn the corner to where the entrance is, but when we get there I kinda hang back. Not that I'm scared, what's there to be afraid of, just a toy store. But I feel funny, shame. But what I got to be shamed about? Got as much right to go in as anybody. But somehow I can't seem to get hold of the door, so I step away for Sugar to lead. But she hangs back too. And I look at her and she looks at me and this is ridiculous. I mean, damn, I have never ever been shy about doing nothing or going nowhere. But then Mercedes steps up and then Rosie Giraffe and Big Butt crowd in behind and shove, and next thing we all stuffed into the doorway with only Mercedes squeezing past us, smoothing out her jumper and walking right down the aisle. Then the rest of us tumble in like a glued-together jigsaw done all wrong. And people lookin at us. And it's like the time me and Sugar crashed into the Catholic church on a dare. But once we got in there and everything so hushed and holy and the candles and the bowin and the handkerchiefs on all the drooping heads, I just couldn't go through with the plan. Which was for me to run up to the altar and do a tap dance while Sugar played the nose flute and messed around in the holy water. And Sugar kept givin me the elbow. Then later teased me so bad I tied her up in the shower and turned it on and locked her in. And she'd be there till this day if Aunt Gretchen hadn't finally figured I was lyin about the boarder takin a shower.

Same thing in the store. We all walkin on tiptoe and hardly touchin the games and puzzles and things. And I watched Miss Moore who is steady watchin us like she waitin for a sign. Like Mama Drewery watches the sky and sniffs the air and takes note of just how much slant is in the bird formation. Then me and Sugar bump smack into each other, so busy gazing at the toys, specially the sailboat. But we don't laugh and go into our fat-lady bump-stomach routine. We just stare at that price tag. Then Sugar run a finger over the whole boat. And I'm jealous and want to hit her. Maybe not her, but I sure want to punch somebody in the mouth.

"Watcha bring us here for, Miss Moore?"

"You sound angry, Sylvia. Are you mad about something?" Givin me one of them grins like she tellin a grown-up joke that never turns out to be funny. And she's lookin very closely at me like maybe she plannin to do my portrait from memory. I'm mad, but I won't give her that satisfaction. So I slouch around the store bein very bored and say, "Let's go."

Me and Sugar at the back of the train watchin the tracks whizzin by large then small then gettin gobbled up in the dark. I'm thinkin about this tricky toy I saw in the store. A clown that somersaults on a bar then does chin-ups just cause you yank lightly at his leg. Cost $35. I could see me askin my mother for a $35 birthday clown. "You wanna who that costs what?" she'd say, cocking her head to the side to get a better view of the hole in my head. Thirty-five dollars could buy new bunk beds for Junior and Gretchen's boy. Thirty-five dollars and the whole household could go visit Granddaddy Nelson in the country. Thirty-five dollars would pay for the rent and the piano bill too. Who are these people that spend that much for performing clowns and $1,000 for toy sailboats? What kinda work they do and how they live and how come we ain't in on it? Where we are is who we are, Miss Moore always pointin out. But it don't necessarily have to be that way, she always adds then waits for somebody to say that poor people have to wake up and demand their share of the pie and don't none of us know what kind of pie she talkin about in the first damn place. But she ain't so smart cause I still got her four dollars from the taxi and she sure ain't gettin it. Messin up my day with this shit. Sugar nudges me in my pocket and winks.

Miss Moore lines us up in front of the mailbox where we started from, seem like years ago, and I got a headache for thinkin so hard. And we lean all over each other so we can hold up under the draggy-ass lecture she always finishes us off with at the end before we thank her for borin us to tears. But she just looks at us like she readin tea leaves. Finally she say, "Well, what did you think of F. A. O. Schwartz?"

Rosie Giraffe mumbles, "White folks crazy."

"I'd like to go there again when I get my birthday money," says Mercedes, and we shove her out the pack so she has to lean on the mailbox by herself.

"I'd like a shower. Tiring day," say Flyboy.

Then Sugar surprises me by sayin, "You know, Miss Moore, I don't think all of us here put together eat in a year what that sailboat costs." And Miss Moore lights up like somebody goosed her. "And?" she say, urging Sugar on. Only I'm standin on her foot so she don't continue.

"Imagine for a minute what kind of society it is in which some people can spend on a toy what it would cost to feed a family of six or seven. What do you think?"

"I think," say Sugar pushing me off her feet like she never done before, cause I whip her ass in a minute, "that this is not much of a democracy if you ask me. Equal chance to pursue happiness means an equal crack at the dough, don't it?" Miss Moore is besides herself and I am disgusted with Sugar's treachery. So I stand on her foot one more time to see if she'll shove me. She shuts up, and Miss Moore looks at me, sorrowfully I'm thinkin. And somethin weird is goin on, I can feel it in my chest.

"Anybody else learn anything today?" lookin dead at me.

I walk away and Sugar has to run to catch up and don't even seem to notice when I shrug her arm off my shoulder.

"Well, we got four dollars anyway," she says.

"Uh hunh."

"We could go to Hascombs and get half a chocolate layer and then go to the Sunset and still have plenty money for potato chips and ice-cream sodas."

"Uh hunh."

"Race you to Hascombs," she say.

We start down the block and she gets ahead which is O.K. by me cause I'm goin to the West End and then over to the Drive to think this day through. She can run if she want to and even run faster. But ain't nobody gonna beat me at nuthin.

BEAUTY AND THE BEAST (1756)

Jeanne-Marie LePrince de Beaumont
1711 Rouen, France
1780 Savoy, France

There was once a very rich merchant, who had six children, three sons, and three daughters; being a man of sense, he spared no cost for their education, but gave them all kinds of masters. His daughters were extremely handsome, especially the youngest. When she was little everybody admired her, and called her "The little Beauty;" so that, as she grew up, she still went by the name of Beauty, which made her sisters very jealous.

The youngest, as she was handsomer, was also better than her sisters. The two eldest had a great deal of pride, because they were rich. They gave themselves ridiculous airs, and would not visit other merchants' daughters, nor keep company with any but persons of quality. They went out every day to parties of pleasure, balls, plays, concerts, and so forth, and they laughed at their youngest sister, because she spent the greatest part of her time in reading good books.

As it was known that they were great fortunes, several eminent merchants made their addresses to them; but the two eldest said, they would never marry, unless they could meet with a duke, or an earl at least. Beauty very civilly thanked them that courted her, and told them she was too young yet to marry, but chose to stay with her father a few years longer.

All at once the merchant lost his whole fortune, excepting a small country house at a great distance from town, and told his children with tears in his eyes, they must go there and work for their living. The two eldest answered, that they would not leave the town, for they had several lovers, who they were sure would be glad to have them, though they had no fortune; but the good ladies were mistaken, for their lovers slighted and forsook them in their poverty. As they were not beloved on account of their pride, everybody said; they do not deserve to be pitied, we are very glad to see their pride humbled, let them go and give themselves quality airs in milking the cows and minding their dairy. But, added they, we are extremely concerned for Beauty, she was such a charming, sweet-tempered creature, spoke so kindly to poor people, and was of such an affable, obliging behavior. Nay, several gentlemen would have married her, though they knew she had not a penny; but she told them she could not think of leaving her poor father in his misfortunes, but was determined to go along with him into the country to comfort and attend him. Poor Beauty at first was sadly grieved at the loss of her fortune; "but," said she to herself, "were I to cry ever so much, that would not make things better, I must try to make myself happy without a fortune."

When they came to their country house, the merchant and his three sons applied themselves to husbandry and tillage; and Beauty rose at four in the morning, and made haste to have the house clean, and dinner ready for the family. In the beginning she found it very difficult, for she had not been used to work as a servant, but in less than two months she grew stronger and healthier than ever. After she had done her work, she read, played on the harpsichord, or else sung whilst she spun.

On the contrary, her two sisters did not know how to spend their time; they got up at ten, and did nothing but saunter about the whole day, lamenting the loss of their fine clothes and acquaintance. "Do but see our youngest sister," said they, one to the other, "what a poor, stupid, mean-spirited creature she is, to be contented with such an unhappy dismal situation."

The good merchant was of quite a different opinion; he knew very well that Beauty outshone her sisters, in her person as well as her mind, and admired her humility and industry, but above all her humility and patience; for her sisters not only left her all the work of the house to do, but insulted her every moment.

The family had lived about a year in this retirement, when the merchant received a letter with an account that a vessel, on board of which he had effects, was safely arrived. This news had liked to have turned the heads of the two eldest daughters, who immediately flattered themselves with the hopes of returning to town, for they were quite weary of a country life; and when they saw their father ready to set out, they begged of him to buy them new gowns, headdresses, ribbons, and all manner of trifles; but Beauty asked for nothing for she thought to herself, that all the money her father was going to receive, would scarce be sufficient to purchase everything her sisters wanted.

"What will you have, Beauty?" said her father.

"Since you have the goodness to think of me," answered she, "be so kind to bring me a rose, for as none grows hereabouts, they are a kind of rarity." Not that Beauty cared for a rose, but she asked for something, lest she should seem by her example to condemn her sisters' conduct, who would have said she did it only to look particular.

The good man went on his journey, but when he came there, they went to law with him about the merchandise, and after a great deal of trouble and pains to no purpose, he came back as poor as before.

He was within thirty miles of his own house, thinking on the pleasure he should have in seeing his children again, when going through a large forest he lost himself. It rained and snowed terribly; besides, the wind was so high, that it threw him twice off his horse, and night coming on, he began to apprehend being either starved to death with cold and hunger, or else devoured by the wolves, whom he heard howling all round him, when, on a sudden, looking through a long walk of trees, he saw a light at some distance, and going on a little farther perceived it came from a place illuminated from top to bottom. The merchant returned God thanks for this happy discovery, and hastened to the place, but was greatly surprised at not meeting with any one in the outer courts. His horse followed him, and seeing a large stable open, went in, and finding both hay and oats, the poor beast, who was almost famished, fell to eating very heartily; the merchant tied him up to the manger, and walking towards the house, where he saw no one, but entering into a large hall, he found a good fire, and a table plentifully set out with but one cover laid. As he was wet quite through with the rain and snow, he drew near the fire to dry himself. "I hope," said he, "the master of the house, or his servants will excuse the liberty I take; I suppose it will not be long before some of them appear."

He waited a considerable time, until it struck eleven, and still nobody came. At last he was so hungry that he could stay no longer, but took a chicken, and ate it in two mouthfuls, trembling all the while. After this he drank a few glasses of wine, and growing more courageous he went out of the hall, and crossed through several grand apartments with magnificent furniture, until he came into a chamber, which had an exceeding good bed in it, and as he was very much fatigued, and it was past midnight, he concluded it was best to shut the door, and go to bed.

It was ten the next morning before the merchant waked, and as he was going to rise he was astonished to see a good suit of clothes in the room of his own, which were quite spoiled; certainly, said he, this palace belongs to some kind fairy, who has seen and pitied my distress. He looked through a window, but instead of snow saw the most delightful arbors, interwoven with the beautifullest flowers that were ever beheld. He then returned to the great hall, where he had supped the night before, and found some chocolate ready made on a little table. "Thank you, good Madam Fairy," said he aloud, "for being so careful, as to provide me a breakfast; I am extremely obliged to you for all your favors."

The good man drank his chocolate, and then went to look for his horse, but passing through an arbor of roses he remembered Beauty's request to him, and gathered a branch on which were several; immediately he heard a great noise, and saw such a frightful Beast coming towards him, that he was ready to faint away.

"You are very ungrateful," said the Beast to him, in a terrible voice; "I have saved your life by receiving you into my castle, and, in return, you steal my roses, which I value beyond any thing in the universe, but you shall die for it; I give you but a quarter of an hour to prepare yourself, and say your prayers."

The merchant fell on his knees, and lifted up both his hands, "My lord," said he, "I beseech you to forgive me, indeed I had no intention to offend in gathering a rose for one of my daughters, who desired me to bring her one."

"My name is not My Lord," replied the monster, "but Beast; I don't love compliments, not I. I like people to speak as they think; and so do not imagine, I am to be moved by any of your flattering speeches. But you say you have got daughters. I will forgive you, on condition that one of them come willingly, and suffer for you. Let me have no words, but go about your business, and swear that if your daughter refuse to die in your stead, you will return within three months."

The merchant had no mind to sacrifice his daughters to the ugly monster, but he thought, in obtaining this respite, he should have the satisfaction of seeing them once more, so he promised, upon oath, he would return, and the Beast told him he might set out when he pleased, "but," added he, "you shall not depart empty handed; go back to the room where you lay, and you will see a great empty chest; fill it with whatever you like best, and I will send it to your home," and at the same time Beast withdrew.

"Well," said the good man to himself, "if I must die, I shall have the comfort, at least, of leaving something to my poor children." He returned to the bedchamber, and finding a great quantity of broad pieces of gold, he filled the great chest the Beast had mentioned, locked it, and afterwards took his horse out of the stable, leaving the palace with as much grief as he had entered it with joy. The horse, of his own accord, took one of the roads of the forest, and in a few hours the good man was at home.

His children came round him, but instead of receiving their embraces with pleasure, he looked on them, and holding up the branch he had in his hands, he burst into tears. "Here, Beauty," said he, "take these roses, but little do you think how dear they are like to cost your unhappy father," and then related his fatal adventure. Immediately the two eldest set up lamentable outcries, and said all manner of ill-natured things to Beauty, who did not cry at all.

"Do but see the pride of that little wretch," said they; "she would not ask for fine clothes, as we did; but no truly, Miss wanted to distinguish herself, so now she will be the death of our poor father, and yet she does not so much as shed a tear."

"Why should I," answered Beauty, "it would be very needless, for my father shall not suffer upon my account, since the monster will accept of one of his daughters, I will deliver myself up to all his fury, and I am very happy in thinking that my death will save my father's life, and be a proof of my tender love for him."

"No, sister," said her three brothers, "that shall not be, we will go find the monster, and either kill him, or perish in the attempt."

"Do not imagine any such thing, my sons," said the merchant, "Beast's power is so great, that I have no hopes of your overcoming him. I am charmed with Beauty's kind and generous offer, but I cannot yield to it. I am old, and have not long to live, so can only loose a few years, which I regret for your sakes alone, my dear children."

"Indeed father," said Beauty, "you shall not go to the palace without me, you cannot hinder me from following you." It was to no purpose all they could say. Beauty still insisted on setting out for the fine palace, and her sisters were delighted at it, for her virtue and amiable qualities made them envious and jealous.

The merchant was so afflicted at the thoughts of losing his daughter, that he had quite forgot the chest full of gold, but at night when he retired to rest, no sooner had he shut his chamber door, than, to his great astonishment, he found it by his bedside; he was determined, however, not to tell his children, that he was grown rich, because they would have wanted to return to town, and he was resolved not to leave the country but he trusted Beauty with the secret, who informed him, that two gentlemen came in his absence, and courted her sisters, she begged her father to consent to their marriage and give them fortunes for she was so good, that she loved them and forgave heartily all their ill usage. These wicked creatures rubbed their eyes with an onion to force some tears when they parted with their sister, but her brothers were really concerned. Beauty was the only one who did not shed tears at parting, because she would not increase their uneasiness.

The horse took the direct road to the palace, and towards evening they perceived it illuminated as at first. The horse went of himself into the stable, and the good man and his daughter came into the great hall, where they found a table splendidly served up, and two covers. The merchant had no heart to eat, but Beauty, endeavoring to appear cheerful, sat down to table, and helped him. "Afterwards," thought she to herself, "Beast surely has a mind to fatten me before he eats me, since he provides such plentiful entertainment." When they had supped they heard a great noise, and the merchant, all in tears, bid his poor child, farewell, for he thought Beast was coming. Beauty was sadly terrified at his horrid form, but she took courage as well as she could, and the monster having asked her if she came willingly; "ye—e— es," said she, trembling.

The beast responded, "You are very good, and I am greatly obliged to you; honest man, go your ways tomorrow morning, but never think of coming here again."

"Farewell Beauty, farewell Beast," answered he, and immediately the monster withdrew. "Oh, daughter," said the merchant, embracing Beauty, "I am almost frightened to death, believe me, you had better go back, and let me stay here."

"No, father," said Beauty, in a resolute tone, "you shall set out tomorrow morning, and leave me to the care and protection of providence." They went to bed, and thought they should not close their eyes all night; but scarce were they laid down, than they fell fast asleep, and Beauty dreamed, a fine lady came, and said to her, "I am content, Beauty, with your good will, this good action of yours in giving up your own life to save your father's shall not go unrewarded." Beauty waked, and told her father her dream, and though it helped to comfort him a little, yet he could not help crying bitterly, when he took leave of his dear child.

As soon as he was gone, Beauty sat down in the great hall, and fell a crying likewise; but as she was mistress of a great deal of resolution, she recommended herself to God, and resolved not to be uneasy the little time she had to live; for she firmly believed Beast would eat her up that night.

However, she thought she might as well walk about until then, and view this fine castle, which she could not help admiring; it was a delightful pleasant place, and she was extremely surprised at seeing a door, over which was written, "Beauty's Apartment." She opened it hastily, and was quite dazzled with the magnificence that reigned throughout; but what chiefly took up her attention, was a large library, a harpsichord, and several music books. "Well," said she to herself, "I see they will not let my time hang heavy upon my hands for want of amusement." Then she reflected, "Were I but to stay here a day, there would not have been all these preparations." This consideration inspired her with fresh courage, and opening the library she took a book, and read these words, in letters of gold:

Welcome Beauty, banish fear, You are queen and mistress here. Speak your wishes, speak your will, Swift obedience meets them still.

"Alas," said she, with a sigh, "there is nothing I desire so much as to see my poor father, and know what he is doing." She had no sooner said this, when casting her eyes on a great looking glass, to her great amazement, she saw her own home, where her father arrived with a very dejected countenance. Her sisters went to meet him, and notwithstanding their endeavors to appear sorrowful, their joy, felt for having got rid of their sister, was visible in every feature. A moment after, everything disappeared, and Beauty's apprehensions at this proof of Beast's complaisance.

At noon she found dinner ready, and while at table, was entertained with an excellent concert of music, though without seeing anybody. But at night, as she was going to sit down to supper, she heard the noise Beast made, and could not help being sadly terrified. "Beauty," said the monster, "will you give me leave to see you sup?"

"That is as you please," answered Beauty trembling.

"No," replied the Beast, "you alone are mistress here; you need only bid me gone, if my presence is troublesome, and I will immediately withdraw. But, tell me, do not you think me very ugly?"

"That is true," said Beauty, "for I cannot tell a lie, but I believe you are very good natured."

"So I am," said the monster, "but then, besides my ugliness, I have no sense; I know very well, that I am a poor, silly, stupid creature."

"Tis no sign of folly to think so," replied Beauty, "for never did fool know this, or had so humble a conceit of his own understanding."

"Eat then, Beauty," said the monster, "and endeavor to amuse yourself in your palace, for everything here is yours, and I should be very uneasy, if you were not happy."

"You are very obliging," answered Beauty, "I own I am pleased with your kindness, and when I consider that, your deformity scarce appears."

"Yes, yes," said the Beast, "my heart is good, but still I am a monster."

"Among mankind," says Beauty, "there are many that deserve that name more than you, and I prefer you, just as you are, to those, who, under a human form, hide a treacherous, corrupt, and ungrateful heart."

"If I had sense enough," replied the Beast, "I would make a fine compliment to thank you, but I am so dull, that I can only say, I am greatly obliged to you."

Beauty ate a hearty supper, and had almost conquered her dread of the monster; but she had like to have fainted away, when he said to her, "Beauty will you be my wife?"

She was some time before she dared answer, for she was afraid of making him angry, if she refused. At last, however, she said trembling; "no Beast." Immediately the poor monster went to sigh, and hissed so frightfully, that the whole palace echoed. But Beauty soon recovered her fright, for Beast having said, in a mournful voice, "then farewell, Beauty," left the room; and only turned back, now and then, to look at her as he went out.

When Beauty was alone, she felt a great deal of compassion for poor Beast. "Alas," said she, "'tis thousand pities, anything so good natured should be so ugly."

Beauty spent three months very contentedly in the palace. Every evening Beast paid her a visit, and talked to her, during supper, very rationally; with plain good common sense, but never with what the world calls wit; and Beauty daily discovered some valuable qualifications in the monster, and seeing him often had so accustomed her to his deformity, that, far from dreading the time of his visit, she would often look on her watch to see when it would be nine, for the Beast never missed coming at that hour. There was but one thing that gave Beauty any concern, which was, that every night, before she went to bed, the monster always asked her, if she would be his wife. One day she said to him, "Beast, you make me very uneasy, I wish I could consent to marry you, but I am too sincere to make you believe that will ever happen; I shall always esteem you as a friend, endeavor to be satisfied with this."

"I must," said the Beast, "for, alas! I know too well my own misfortune, but then I love you with the tenderest affection. However, I ought to think myself happy, that you will stay here; promise me never to leave me."

Beauty blushed at these words; she had seen in her glass, that her father had pined himself sick for the loss of her, and she longed to see him again. "I could," answered she, "indeed, promise never to leave you entirely, but I have so great a desire to see my father, that I shall fret to death, if you refuse me that satisfaction."

"I had rather die myself," said the monster, "than give you the least uneasiness. I will send you to your father, you shall remain with him, and poor Beast will die with grief."

"No," said Beauty, weeping, "I love you too well to be the cause of your death. I give you my promise to return in a week. You have shown me that my sisters are married, and my brothers gone to the army; only let me stay a week with my father, as he is alone."

"You shall be there tomorrow morning," said the Beast, "but remember your promise. You need only lay your ring on a table before you go to bed, when you have a mind to come back. Farewell Beauty." Beast sighed, as usual, bidding her good night, and Beauty went to bed very sad at seeing him so afflicted. When she waked the next morning, she found herself at her father's, and having rung a little bell, that was by her bedside, she saw the maid come, who, the moment she saw her, gave a loud shriek, at which the good man ran up stairs, and thought he should have died with joy to see his dear daughter again. He held her fast locked in his arms above a quarter of an hour. As soon as the first transports were over, Beauty began to think of rising, and was afraid she had no clothes to put on; but the maid told her, that she had just found, in the next room, a large trunk full of gowns, covered with gold and diamonds. Beauty thanked good Beast for his kind care, and taking one of the plainest of them, she intended to make a present of the others to her sisters. She scarce had said so when the trunk disappeared. Her father told her, that Beast insisted on her keeping them herself, and immediately both gowns and trunk came back again.

Beauty dressed herself, and in the meantime they sent to her sisters who hastened thither with their husbands. They were both of them very unhappy. The eldest had married a gentleman, extremely handsome indeed, but so fond of his own person, that he was full of nothing but his own dear self, and neglected his wife. The second had married a man of wit, but he only made use of it to plague and torment everybody, and his wife most of all. Beauty's sisters sickened with envy, when they saw her dressed like a princess, and more beautiful than ever, nor could all her obliging affectionate behavior stifle their jealousy, which was ready to burst when she told them how happy she was. They went down into the garden to vent it in tears; and said one to the other, in what way is this little creature better than us, that she should be so much happier? "Sister," said the oldest, "a thought just strikes my mind; let us endeavor to detain her above a week, and perhaps the silly monster will be so enraged at her for breaking her word, that he will devour her."

"Right, sister," answered the other, "therefore we must show her as much kindness as possible." After they had taken this resolution, they went up, and behaved so affectionately to their sister, that poor Beauty wept for joy. When the week was expired, they cried and tore their hair, and seemed so sorry to part with her, that she promised to stay a week longer.

In the meantime, Beauty could not help reflecting on herself, for the uneasiness she was likely to cause poor Beast, whom she sincerely loved, and really longed to see again. The tenth night she spent at her father's, she dreamed she was in the palace garden, and that she saw Beast extended on the grass plat, who seemed just expiring, and, in a dying voice, reproached her with her ingratitude. Beauty started out of her sleep, and bursting into tears. "Am I not very wicked," said she, "to act so unkindly to Beast; that has studied so much, to please me in everything? Is it his fault if he is so ugly, and has so little sense? He is kind and good, and that is sufficient. Why did I refuse to marry him? I should be happier with the monster than my sisters are with their husbands; it is neither wit, nor a fine person, in a husband, that makes a woman happy, but virtue, sweetness of temper, and complaisance, and Beast has all these valuable qualifications. It is true, I do not feel the tenderness of affection for him, but I find I have the highest gratitude, esteem, and friendship; I will not make him miserable, were I to be so ungrateful I should never forgive myself." Beauty having said this, rose, put her ring on the table, and then laid down again; scarce was she in bed before she fell asleep, and when she waked the next morning, she was overjoyed to find herself in the Beast's palace.

She put on one of her richest suits to please him, and waited for evening with the utmost impatience, at last the wished-for hour came, the clock struck nine, yet no Beast appeared. Beauty then feared she had been the cause of his death; she ran crying and wringing her hands all about the palace, like one in despair, after having sought for him everywhere, she recollected her dream, and flew to the panal in the garden, where she dreamed she saw him. There she found poor Beast stretched out quite senseless, and, as she imagined, dead. She threw herself upon him without any dread, and finding his heart beat still, she fetched some water from the canal, and poured it on his head. Beast opened his eyes, and said to Beauty, "You forgot your promise, and I was so afflicted for having lost you, that I resolved to starve myself, but since I have the happiness of seeing you once more, I die satisfied."

"No, dear Beast," said Beauty, "you must not die. Live to be my husband; from this moment I give you my hand, and swear to be none but yours. Alas! I thought I had only a friendship for you, but the grief I now feel convinces me, that I cannot live without you." Beauty scarce had pronounced these words, when she saw the palace sparkle with light; and fireworks, instruments of music, everything seemed to give notice of some great event. But nothing could fix her attention; she turned to her dear Beast, for whom she trembled with fear; but how great was her surprise! Beast was disappeared, and she saw, at her feet, one of the loveliest princes that eye ever beheld; who returned her thanks for having put an end to the charm, under which he had so long resembled a Beast. Though this prince was worthy of all her attention, she could not forbear asking where Beast was.

"You see him at your feet, said the prince. A wicked fairy had condemned me to remain under that shape until a beautiful virgin should consent to marry me. The fairy likewise enjoined me to conceal my understanding. There was only you in the world generous enough to be won by the goodness of my temper, and in offering you my crown I can't discharge the obligations I have to you."

Beauty, agreeably surprised, gave the charming prince her hand to rise; they went together into the castle, and Beauty was overjoyed to find, in the great hall, her father and his whole family, whom the beautiful lady, that appeared to her in her dream, had conveyed thither.

"Beauty," said this lady, "come and receive the reward of your judicious choice; you have preferred virtue before either wit or beauty, and deserve to find a person in whom all these qualifications are united. You are going to be a great queen. I hope the throne will not lessen your virtue, or make you forget yourself. As to you, ladies," said the fairy to Beauty's two sisters, "I know your hearts, and all the malice they contain. Become two statues, but, under this transformation, still retain your reason. You shall stand before your sister's palace gate, and be it your punishment to behold her happiness; and it will not be in your power to return to your former state, until you own your faults, but I am very much afraid that you will always remain statues. Pride, anger, gluttony, and idleness are sometimes conquered, but the conversion of a malicious and envious mind is a kind of miracle."

Immediately the fairy gave a stroke with her wand, and in a moment all that were in the hall were transported into the prince's dominions. His subjects received him with joy. He married Beauty, and lived with her many years, and their happiness—as it was founded on virtue—was complete.

Source: *The Young Misses Magazine, Containing Dialogues between a Governess and Several Young Ladies of Quality Her Scholars*, by Madam Prince de Beaumont, 4th ed., —v. 1 (London: C. Nourse, 1783), pp. 45–67. First published in 1756 in France under the title *Magasin des enfans, ou dialogues entre une sage gouvernante et plusieure de ses élèves*. The first English translation appeared in 1757.

- Spelling and punctuation revised by D. L. Ashliman.
- The French title of "Beauty and the Beast" is "La Belle et la Bête."

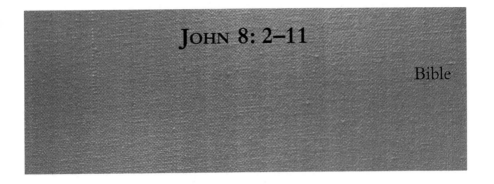

JOHN 8: 2–11

Bible

KING JAMES VERSION

²And early in the morning he came again into the temple, and all the people came unto him; and he sat down, and taught them. ³And the scribes and Pharisees brought unto him a woman taken in adultery; and when they had set her in the midst, ⁴they say unto him, Master, this woman was taken in adultery, in the very act. ⁵Now Moses in the law commanded us, that such should be stoned: but what sayest thou? ⁶This they said, tempting him, that they might have to accuse him. But Jesus stooped down, and with his finger wrote on the ground, as though he heard them not. ⁷So when they continued asking him, he lifted up himself, and said unto them, he that is without sin among you, let him first cast a stone at her. ⁸And again he stooped down, and wrote on the ground. ⁹And they which heard it, being convicted by their own conscience, went out one by one, beginning at the eldest, even unto the last: and Jesus was left alone, and the woman standing in the midst. ¹⁰When Jesus had lifted up himself, and saw none but the woman, he said unto her, Woman, where are those thine accusers? Hath no man condemned thee? ¹¹She said, No man, Lord. And Jesus said unto her, Neither do I condemn thee: go, and sin no more.

NEW REVISED STANDARD VERSION

²Early in the morning he came again to the temple. All the people came to him and he sat down and began to teach them. ³The scribes and the Pharisees brought a woman who had been caught in adultery; and making her stand before all of them, ⁴they said to him, 'Teacher, this woman was caught in the very act of committing adultery. ⁵Now in the law Moses commanded us to stone such women. Now what do you say?' ⁶They said this to test him, so that they might have some charge to bring against him. Jesus bent down and wrote with his finger on the

ground. [7]When they kept on questioning him, he straightened up and said to them, 'Let anyone among you who is without sin be the first to throw a stone at her.' [8]And once again he bent down and wrote on the ground. [9]When they heard it, they went away, one by one, beginning with the elders; and Jesus was left alone with the woman standing before him. [10]Jesus straightened up and said to her, 'Woman, where are they? Has no one condemned you?' [11]She said, 'No one, sir.' And Jesus said, 'Neither do I condemn you. Go your way, and from now on do not sin again.'

PIERRE MENARD, AUTHOR
OF THE *QUIXOTE* (1939)

Jorge Luis Borges
b. 1899 Buenos Aires, Argentina
d. 1986, Geneva, Switzerland

The visible *œuvre* left by this novelist can be easily and briefly enumerated, unpardonable, therefore, are the omissions and additions perpetrated by Mme. Henri Bachelier in a deceitful catalog that a certain newspaper, whose Protestant leanings are surely no secret, has been so inconsiderate as to inflict upon that newspaper's deplorable readers—few and Calvinist (if not Masonic and circumcised) though they be. Menard's true friends have greeted that catalog with alarm, and even with a degree of sadness. One might note that only yesterday were we gathered before his marmoreal place of rest, among the dreary cypresses, and already Error is attempting to tarnish his bright Memory.... Most decidedly, a brief rectification is imperative.

I am aware that it is easy enough to call my own scant authority into question. I hope, nonetheless, that I shall not be prohibited from mentioning two high testimonials. The baroness de Bacourt (at whose unforgettable *vendredis* I had the honor to meet the mourned-for poet) has been so kind as to approve the lines that follow. Likewise, the countess de Bagnoregio, one of the rarest and most cultured spirits of the principality of Monaco (now of Pittsburgh, Pennsylvania, following her recent marriage to the international philanthropist Simon Kautzsch—a man, it grieves me to say, vilified and slandered by the victims of his disinterested operations), has sacrificed "to truth and to death" (as she herself has phrased it) the noble reserve that is the mark of her distinction, and in an open letter, published in the magazine *Luxe*, bestows upon me her blessing. Those commendations are sufficient, I should think.

I have said that the *visible* product of Menard's pen is easily enumerated. Having examined his personal files with the greatest care, I have established that his body of work consists of the following pieces:

   a)   a symbolist sonnet that appeared twice (with variants) in the review *La Conque* (in the numbers for March and October, 1899);

b)   a monograph on the possibility of constructing a poetic vocabulary from concepts that are neither synonyms nor periphrastic locutions for the concepts that inform common speech, "but are, rather, ideal objects created by convention essentially for the needs of poetry" (Nîmes, 1901);

c)   a monograph on "certain connections or affinities" between the philosophies of Descartes, Leibniz, and John Wilkins (Nîmes, 1903);

d)   a monograph on Leibniz' *Characteristica universalis* (Nîmes, 1904);

e)   a technical article on the possibility of enriching the game of chess by eliminating one of the rook's pawns (Menard proposes, recommends, debates, and finally rejects this innovation);

f)   a monograph on Ramon Lull's *Ars magna generalis* (Nîmes, 1906);

g)   a translation, with introduction and notes, of Ruy López de Segura's *Libro de la invención liberal y arte del juego del axedrez* (Paris, 1907);

h)   drafts of a monograph on George Boole's symbolic logic;

i)   a study of the essential metrical rules of French prose, illustrated with examples taken from Saint-Simon (*Revue des langues romanes*, Montpellier, October 1909);

j)   a reply to Luc Durtain (who had countered that no such rules existed), illustrated with examples taken from Luc Durtain (*Revue des langues romanes*, Montpellier, December 1909);

k)   a manuscript translation of Quevedo's *Aguja de navegar cultos*, titled *Laboussole des précieux*;

l)   a foreword to the catalog of an exhibit of lithographs by Carolus Hourcade (Nîmes, 1914);

m)   a work entitled *Les problèmes d'un problème* (Paris, 1917), which discusses in chronological order the solutions to the famous problem of Achilles and the tortoise (two editions of this work have so far appeared; the second bears an epigraph consisting of Leibniz' advice "*Ne craignez point, monsieur, la tortue*," and brings up to date the chapters devoted to Russell and Descartes);

n)   a dogged analysis of the "syntactical habits" of Toulet (*N.R.F.*, March 1921) (Menard, I recall, affirmed that censure and praise were sentimental operations that bore not the slightest resemblance to criticism);

o)   a transposition into alexandrines of Paul Valéry's *Cimetière marin* (*N.R.F.*, January 1928);

p)   a diatribe against Paul Valéry, in Jacques Reboul's *Feuilles pour la suppression de la realité* (which diatribe, I might add parenthetically, states the exact reverse of Menard's true opinion of Valéry; Valéry understood this, and the two men's friendship was never imperiled);

q)   a "definition" of the countess de Bagnoregio, in the "triumphant volume" (the phrase is that of another contributor, Gabriele d'Annunzio) published each year by that lady to rectify the inevitable biases of the popular press and to present "to the world and all of Italy" a true picture of her person, which was so exposed (by reason of her beauty and her bearing) to erroneous and/or hasty interpretations;

r)   a cycle of admirable sonnets dedicated to the baroness de Bacourt (1934);

s) a handwritten list of lines of poetry that owe their excellence to punctuation.[1]

This is the full extent (save for a few vague sonnets of occasion destined for Mme. Henri Bachelier's hospitable, or greedy, *album des souvenirs*) of the *visible* life-work of Pierre Menard, in proper chronological order. I shall turn now to the other, the subterranean, the interminably heroic production—the *œuvre nonpareil*, the *œuvre* that must remain—for such are our human limitations!—unfinished. This work, perhaps the most significant writing of our time, consists of the ninth and thirty-eighth chapters of Part I of *Don Quixote* and a fragment of Chapter XXII. I know that such a claim is on the face of it absurd; justifying that "absurdity" shall be the primary object of this note.[2]

Two texts, of distinctly unequal value, inspired the undertaking. One was that philological fragment by Novalis—number 2005 in the Dresden edition, to be precise—which outlines the notion of *total identification* with a given author. The other was one of those parasitic books that set Christ on a boulevard, Hamlet on La Cannabière, or don Quixote on Wall Street. Like every man of taste, Menard abominated those pointless travesties, which, Menard would say, were good for nothing but occasioning a plebeian delight in anachronism or (worse yet) captivating us with the elementary notion that all times and places are the same, or are different. It might be more interesting, he thought, though of contradictory and superficial execution, to attempt what Daudet had so famously suggested: conjoin in a single figure (Tartarin, say) both the Ingenious Gentleman don Quixote and his squire. . . .

Those who have insinuated that Menard devoted his life to writing a contemporary *Quixote* besmirch his illustrious memory. Pierre Menard did not want to compose *another* Quixote, which surely is easy enough—he wanted to compose *the* Quixote. Nor, surely, need one be obliged to note that his goal was never a mechanical transcription of the original; he had no intention of *copying* it. His admirable ambition was to produce a number of pages which coincided—word for word and line for line—with those of Miguel de Cervantes.

"My purpose is merely astonishing," he wrote me on September 30, 1934, from Bayonne. "The final term of a theological or metaphysical proof—the world around us, or God, or chance, or universal Forms—is no more final, no more uncommon, than my revealed novel. The sole difference is that philosophers publish pleasant volumes containing the intermediate stages of their work, while I am resolved to suppress those stages of my own." And indeed there is not a single draft to bear witness to that years-long labor.

---

[1] Mme. Henri Bachelier also lists a literal translation of Quevedo's literal translation of St. Francis de Sales's *Introduction à la vie dévote*. In Pierre Menard's library there is no trace of such a work. This must be an instance of one of our friend's droll jokes, misheard or misunderstood.

[2] I did, I might say, have the secondary purpose of drawing a small sketch of the figure of Pierre Menard—but how dare I compete with the gilded pages I am told the baroness de Bacourt is even now preparing, or with the delicate sharp *crayon* of Carolus Hourcade?

Initially, Menard's method was to be relatively simple: Learn Spanish, return to Catholicism; fight against the Moor or Turk, forget the history of Europe from 1602 to 1918—*be* Miguel de Cervantes. Pierre Menard weighed that course (I know he pretty thoroughly mastered seventeenth-century Castilian) but he discarded it as too easy. Too impossible, rather!, the reader will say. Quite so, but the undertaking was impossible from the outset, and of all the impossible ways of bringing it about, this was the least interesting. To be a popular novelist of the seventeenth century in the twentieth seemed to Menard to be a diminution. Being, somehow, Cervantes, and arriving thereby at the Quixote—that looked to Menard less challenging (and therefore less interesting) than continuing to be Pierre Menard and coming to the Quixote *through the experiences of Pierre Menard.* (It was that conviction, by the way, that obliged him to leave out the autobiographical foreword to Part II of the novel. Including the prologue would have meant creating another character—"Cervantes"—and also presenting Quixote through that character's eyes, not Pierre Menard's. Menard, of course, spurned that easy solution.) "The task I have undertaken is not *in essence* difficult," I read at another place in that letter. "If I could just be immortal, I could do it." Shall I confess that I often imagine that he did complete it, and that I read the Quixote—the *entire* Quixote—as if Menard had conceived it? A few nights ago, as I was leafing through Chapter XXVI (never attempted by Menard), I recognized our friend's style, could almost hear his voice in this marvelous phrase: "the nymphs of the rivers, the moist and grieving Echo." That wonderfully effective linking of one adjective of emotion with another of physical description brought to my mind a line from Shakespeare, which I recall we discussed one afternoon:

Where a malignant and a turban'd Turk . . .

Why the Quixote? my reader may ask. That choice, made by a Spaniard, would not have been incomprehensible, but it no doubt is so when made by a *Symboliste* from Nîmes, a devotee essentially of Poe—who begat Baudelaire, who begat Mallarmé, who begat Valéry, who begat M. Edmond Teste. The letter mentioned above throws some light on this point. "The *Quixote,*" explains Menard,

> deeply interests me, but does not seem to me—*comment dirai-je?*— inevitable. I cannot imagine the universe without Poe's ejaculation "Ah, bear in mind this garden was enchanted!" or the *Bateau ivre* or the *Ancient Mariner,* but I know myself able to imagine it without the Quixote. (I am speaking, of course, of my personal ability, not of the historical resonance of those works.) The *Quixote* is a contingent work; the *Quixote* is not necessary. I can premeditate committing it to writing, as it were—I can write it—without falling into a tautology. At the age of twelve or thirteen I read it—perhaps read it cover to cover, I cannot recall. Since then, I have carefully reread certain chapters, those which, at least for the moment, I shall not attempt. I have also glanced at the interludes, the comedies, the *Galatea,* the Exemplary Novels, the undoubtedly laborious *Travails of Persiles and Sigismunda,* and the poetic

Voyage to Parnassus . . . . My general recollection of the *Quixote*, simplified by forgetfulness and indifference, might well be the equivalent of the vague foreshadowing of a yet unwritten book. Given that image (which no one can in good conscience deny me), my problem is, without the shadow of a doubt, much more difficult than Cervantes'. My obliging predecessor did not spurn the collaboration of chance; his method of composition for the immortal book was a bit *à la diable*, and he was often swept along by the inertiæ of the language and the imagination. I have assumed the mysterious obligation to reconstruct, word for word, the novel that for him was spontaneous. This game of solitaire I play is governed by two polar rules: the first allows me to try out formal or psychological variants; the second forces me to sacrifice them to the "original" text and to come, by irrefutable arguments, to those eradications. . . . In addition to these first two artificial constraints there is another, inherent to the project. Composing the *Quixote* in the early seventeenth century was a reasonable, necessary, perhaps even inevitable undertaking; in the early twentieth, it is virtually impossible. Not for nothing have three hundred years elapsed, freighted with the most complex events. Among those events, to mention but one, is the *Quixote* itself.

In spite of those three obstacles, Menard's fragmentary Quixote is more subtle than Cervantes'. Cervantes crudely juxtaposes the humble provincial reality of his country against the fantasies of the romance, while Menard chooses as his "reality" the land of Carmen during the century that saw the Battle of Lepanto and the plays of Lope-de Vega. What burlesque brushstrokes of local color that choice would have inspired in a Maurice Barrès or a Rodríguez Larreta*! Yet Menard, with perfect naturalness, avoids them. In his work, there are no gypsy goings-on or conquistadors or mystics or Philip IIs or *autos da fé*. He ignores, overlooks—or banishes—local color. That disdain posits a new meaning for the "historical novel." That disdain condemns *Salammbô*, with no possibility of appeal.

No less amazement visits one when the chapters are considered in isolation. As an example, let us look at Part I, Chapter XXXVIII, "which treats of the curious discourse that Don Quixote made on the subject of arms and letters." It is a matter of common knowledge that in that chapter, don Quixote (like Quevedo in the analogous, and later, passage in *La hora de todos*) comes down against letters and in favor of arms. Cervantes was an old soldier; from him, the verdict is understandable. But that *Pierre Menard's* don Quixote—a contemporary of *La trahison des clercs* and Bertrand Russell—should repeat those cloudy sophistries! Mme. Bachelier sees in them an admirable (typical) subordination of the author to the psychology of the hero; others (lacking all perspicacity) see them as a *transcription* of the Quixote; the baroness de Bacourt, as influenced by Nietzsche. To that third interpretation (which I consider irrefutable), I am not certain I dare to add a fourth, though it agrees very well with the almost divine modesty of Pierre Menard: his resigned or ironic habit of putting forth ideas that were the exact opposite of those he actually held. (We should recall that diatribe against

Paul Valéry in the ephemeral Surrealist journal edited by Jacques Reboul.) The Cervantes text and the Menard text are verbally identical, but the second is almost infinitely richer. (More *ambiguous*, his detractors will say—but ambiguity is richness.)

It is a revelation to compare the *Don Quixote* of Pierre Menard with that of Miguel de Cervantes. Cervantes, for example, wrote the following (Part I, Chapter IX):

> . . . truth, whose mother is history, rival of time, depository of deeds, witness of the past, exemplar and adviser to the present, and the future's counselor.

This catalog of attributes, written in the seventeenth century, and written by the "ingenious layman" Miguel de Cervantes, is mere rhetorical praise of history. Menard, on the other hand, writes:

> . . . truth, whose mother is history, rival of time, depository of deeds, witness of the past, exemplar and adviser to the present, and the future's counselor.

History, the *mother* of truth!—the idea is staggering. Menard, a contemporary of William James, defines history not as a *delving into* reality but as the very *fount* of reality. Historical truth, for Menard, is not "what happened"; it is what we *believe* happened. The final phrases—*exemplar and adviser to the present, and the future's counselor*—are brazenly pragmatic.

The contrast in styles is equally striking. The archaic style of Menard who is, in addition, not a native speaker of the language in which he writes—is somewhat affected. Not so the style of his precursor, who employs the Spanish of his time with complete naturalness.

There is no intellectual exercise that is not ultimately pointless. A philosophical doctrine is, at first, a plausible description of the universe; the years go by, and it is a mere chapter—if not a paragraph or proper noun—in the history of philosophy. In literature, that "falling by the wayside," that loss of "relevance," is even better known. The Quixote, Menard remarked, was first and foremost a pleasant book; it is now an occasion for patriotic toasts grammatical arrogance, obscene *de luxe* editions. Fame is a form—perhaps the worst form—of incomprehension.

Those nihilistic observations were not new; what was remarkable was the decision that Pierre Menard derived from them. He resolved to anticipate the vanity that awaits all the labors of mankind; he undertook a task of infinite complexity, a task futile from the outset. He dedicated his scruples and his nights "lit by midnight oil" to repeating in a foreign tongue a book that already existed. His drafts were endless; he stubbornly corrected, and he ripped up thousands of handwritten pages. He would allow no one to see them, and took care that they not survive him.[3] In vain have I attempted to reconstruct them.

I have reflected that it is legitimate to see the "final" Quixote as a kind of palimpsest, in which the traces—faint but not undecipherable—of our friend's "previous" text must shine through. Unfortunately, only a second Pierre Menard, reversing the labors of the first, would be able to exhume and revive those Troys. . . .

"Thinking, meditating, imagining," he also wrote me, "are not anomalous acts—they are the normal respiration of the intelligence. To glorify the occasional exercise of that function, to treasure beyond price ancient and foreign thoughts, to recall with incredulous awe what some *doctor universalis* thought, is to confess our own languor, or our own *barbarie*. Every man should be capable of all ideas, and I believe that in the future he shall be."

Menard has (perhaps unwittingly) enriched the slow and rudimentary art of reading by means of a new technique—the technique of deliberate anachronism and fallacious attribution. That technique, requiring infinite patience and concentration, encourages us to read the *Odyssey* as though it came after the *Æneid*, to read Mme. Henri Bachelier's *Le jardin du Centaure* as though it were written by Mme. Henri Bachelier. This technique fills the calmest books with adventure. Attributing the *Imitatio Christi* to Louis Ferdinand Céline or James Joyce—is that not sufficient renovation of those faint spiritual admonitions?

Nîmes, 1939

---

[3]I recall his square-ruled notebooks, his black crossings-out, his peculiar typographical symbols, and his insect-like handwriting. In the evening, he liked to go out for walks on the outskirts of Nîmes; he would often carry along a notebook and make a cheery bonfire.

Anna O (1895)

Josef Breuer
b. 1842 Vienna
d. 1925 Vienna

II

CASE HISTORIES

(Breuer and Freud)

CASE 1

Fräulein Anna O. (Breuer)

At the time of her falling ill (in 1880) Fräulein Anna O. was twenty-one years old. She may be regarded as having had a moderately severe neuropathic heredity, since some psychoses had occurred among her more distant relatives. Her parents were normal in this respect. She herself had hitherto been consistently healthy and had shown no signs of neurosis during her period of growth. She was markedly intelligent, with an astonishingly quick grasp of things and penetrating intuition. She possessed a powerful intellect which would have been capable of digesting solid mental pabulum and which stood in need of it—though without receiving it after she had left school. She had great poetic and imaginative gifts, which were under the control of a sharp and critical common sense. Owing to this latter quality she was *completely unsuggestible*; she was only influenced by arguments, never by mere assertions. Her will-power was energetic, tenacious and persistent; sometimes it reached the pitch of an obstinacy which only gave way out of kindness and regard for other people.

One of her essential character traits was sympathetic kindness. Even during her illness she herself was greatly assisted by being able to look after a number of poor, sick people, for she was thus able to satisfy a powerful instinct. Her states of feeling always tended to a slight exaggeration, alike of cheerfulness and gloom; hence she was sometimes subject to moods. The element of sexuality was astonishingly undeveloped in her. The patient, whose life became known to me to an extent to which one person's life is seldom known to another, had never been in love; and in all the enormous number of hallucinations which occurred during her illness that element of mental life never emerged.

This girl, who was bubbling over with intellectual vitality, led an extremely monotonous existence in her puritanically-minded family. She embellished her life in a manner which probably influenced her decisively in the direction of her illness, by indulging in systematic day-dreaming, which she described as her 'private theatre'. While everyone thought she was attending, she was living through fairy tales in her imagination; but she was always on the spot when she was spoken to, so that no one was aware of it. She pursued this activity almost continuously while she was engaged on her household duties, which she discharged unexceptionably. I shall presently have to describe the way in which this habitual day-dreaming while she was well passed over into illness without a break.

The course of the illness fell into several clearly separable phases:

(A) Latent incubation. From the middle of July, 1880, till about December 10. This phase of an illness is usually hidden from us; but in this case, owing to its peculiar character, it was completely accessible; and this in itself lends no small pathological interest to the history. I shall describe this phase presently.

(B) The manifest illness. A psychosis of a peculiar kind, paraphasia, a convergent squint, severe disturbances of vision, paralyses (in the form of contractures), complete in the right upper and both lower extremities, partial in the left upper extremity, paresis of the neck muscles. A gradual reduction of the contracture to the right-hand extremities. Some improvement, interrupted by a severe psychical trauma (the death of the patient's father) in April, after which there followed

(C) A period of persisting somnambulism, subsequently alternating with more normal states. A number of chronic symptoms persisted till December, 1881.

(D) Gradual cessation of the pathological states and symptoms up to June, 1882.

In July, 1880, the patient's father, of whom she was passionately fond, fell ill of a peripleuritic abscess which failed to clear up and to which he succumbed in April, 1881. During the first months of the illness Anna devoted her whole energy to nursing her father, and no one was much surprised when by degrees her own health greatly deteriorated. No one, perhaps not even the patient herself, knew what was happening to her; but eventually the state of weakness, anaemia and distaste for food became so bad that to her great sorrow she was no longer allowed to continue nursing the patient. The immediate cause of this was a very severe cough, on account of which I examined her for the first time. It was a typical *tussis nervosa*. She soon began to display a marked craving for rest during the afternoon, followed in the evening by a sleep-like state and afterwards a highly excited condition.

At the beginning of December a convergent squint appeared. An ophthalmic surgeon explained this (mistakenly) as being due to paresis of one abducens. On December 11 the patient took to her bed and remained there until April 1.

There developed in rapid succession a series of severe disturbances which were *apparently* quite new: left-sided occipital headache; convergent squint (diplopia), markedly increased by excitement; complaints that the walls of the room seemed to be falling over (affection of the obliquus); disturbances of vision which it was hard to analyse; paresis of the muscles of the front of the neck, so that finally the patient could only move her head by pressing it backwards between her raised shoulders and moving her whole back; contracture and anaesthesia of the right upper, and, after a time, of the right lower extremity. The latter was fully extended, adducted and rotated inwards. Later the same symptom appeared in the left lower extremity and finally in the left arm, of which, however, the fingers to some extent retained the power of movement. So, too, there was no complete rigidity in the shoulder-joints. The contracture reached its maximum in the muscles of the upper arms. In the same way, the region of the elbows turned out to be the most affected by anaesthesia when, at a later stage, it became possible to make a more careful test of this. At the beginning of the illness the anaesthesia could not be efficiently tested, owing to the patient's resistance arising from feelings of anxiety.

It was while the patient was in this condition that I undertook her treatment, and I at once recognized the seriousness of the psychical disturbance with which I had to deal. Two entirely distinct states of consciousness were present which alternated very frequently and without warning and which became more and more differentiated in the course of the illness. In one of these states she recognized her surroundings; she was melancholy and anxious, but relatively normal. In the other state she hallucinated and was 'naughty'—that is to say, she was abusive, used to throw the cushions at people, so far as the contractures at various times allowed, tore buttons off her bedclothes and linen with those of her fingers which she could move, and so on. At this stage of her illness if something had been moved in the room or someone had entered or left it [during her other state of consciousness] she would complain of having 'lost' some time and would remark upon the gap in her train of conscious thoughts. Since those about her tried to deny this and to soothe her when she complained that she was going mad, she would, after throwing the pillows about, accuse people of doing things to her and leaving her in a muddle, etc.

These '*absences*' had already been observed before she took to her bed; she used then to stop in the middle of a sentence, repeat her last words and after a short pause go on talking. These interruptions gradually increased till they reached the dimensions that have just been described; and during the climax of the illness, when the contractures had extended to the left side of her body, it was only for a short time during the day that she was to any degree normal. But the disturbances invaded even her moments of relatively clear consciousness. There were extremely rapid changes of mood leading to excessive but quite temporary high spirits, and at other times severe anxiety, stubborn opposition to every therapeutic effort and frightening hallucinations of black snakes, which was how she saw her hair, ribbons and similar things. At the same time she kept on telling herself not to be so silly: what she was seeing was really only her hair, etc. At moments when her mind was quite clear she would complain of the profound darkness in her head, of not being able to think, of becoming blind and deaf, of having two selves, a real one and an evil one which forced her to behave badly, and so on.

In the afternoons she would fall into a somnolent state which lasted till about an hour after sunset. She would then wake up and complain that something was tormenting her—or rather, she would keep repeating in the impersonal form 'tormenting, tormenting'. For alongside of the development of the contractures there appeared a deep-going functional disorganization of her speech. It first became noticeable that she was at a loss to find words, and this difficulty gradually increased. Later she lost her command of grammar and syntax; she no longer conjugated verbs, and eventually she used only infinitives, for the most part incorrectly formed from weak past participles; and she omitted both the definite and indefinite article. In the process of time she became almost completely deprived of words. She put them together laboriously out of four or five languages and became almost unintelligible. When she tried to write (until her contractures entirely prevented her doing so) she employed the same jargon. For two weeks she became completely dumb and in spite of making great and continuous efforts to speak she was unable to say a syllable. And now for the first time the psychical mechanism of the disorder became clear. As I knew, she had felt very much offended over something and had determined not to speak about it. When I guessed this and obliged her to talk about it, the inhibition, which had made any other kind of utterance impossible as well, disappeared.

This change coincided with a return of the power of movement to the extremities of the left side of her body, in March, 1881. Her paraphasia receded; but thenceforward she spoke only in English—apparently, however, without knowing that she was doing so. She had disputes with her nurse who was, of course, unable to understand her. It was only some months later that I was able to convince her that she was talking English. Nevertheless, she herself could still understand the people about her who talked German. Only in moments of extreme anxiety did her power of speech desert her entirely, or else she would use a mixture of all sorts of languages. At times when she was at her very best and most free, she talked French and Italian. There was complete amnesia between these times and those at which she talked English. At this point, too, her squint began to diminish and made its appearance only at moments of great excitement. She was once again able to support her head. On the first of April she got up for the first time.

On the fifth of April her adored father died. During her illness she had seen him very rarely and for short periods. This was the most severe psychical trauma that she could possibly have experienced. A violent outburst of excitement was succeeded by profound stupor which lasted about two days and from which she emerged in a greatly changed state. At first she was far quieter and her feelings of anxiety were much diminished. The contracture of her right arm and leg persisted as well as their anaesthesia, though this was not deep. There was a high degree of restriction of the field of vision: in a bunch of flowers which gave her much pleasure she could only see one flower at a time. She complained of not being able to recognize people. Normally, she said, she had been able to recognize faces without having to make any deliberate effort; now she was obliged to do laborious 'recognizing work'[1] and had to say to herself 'this person's nose is such-and-such, his hair is such-and-such, so he must be so-and-so'. All the people she saw seemed like wax figures without

---

1. [In English in the original.]

any connection with her. She found the presence of some of her close relatives very distressing and this negative attitude grew continually stronger. If someone whom she was ordinarily pleased to see came into the room, she would recognize him and would be aware of things for a short time, but would soon sink back into her own broodings and her visitor was blotted out. I was the only person whom she always recognized when I came in; so long as I was talking to her she was always in contact with things and lively, except for the sudden interruptions caused by one of her hallucinatory '*absences*'.

She now spoke only English and could not understand what was said to her in German. Those about her were obliged to talk to her in English; even the nurse learned to make herself to some extent understood in this way. She was, however, able to read French and Italian. If she had to read one of these aloud, what she produced, with extraordinary fluency, was an admirable extempore English translation.

She began writing again, but in a peculiar fashion. She wrote with her left hand, the less stiff one, and she used Roman printed letters, copying the alphabet from her edition of Shakespeare.

She had eaten extremely little previously, but now she refused nourishment altogether. However, she allowed me to feed her, so that she very soon began to take more food. But she never consented to eat bread. After her meal she invariably rinsed out her mouth and even did so if, for any reason, she had not eaten anything—which shows how absentminded she was about such things.

Her somnolent states in the afternoon and her deep sleep after sunset persisted. If, after this, she had talked herself out (I shall have to explain what is meant by this later) she was clear in mind, calm and cheerful.

This comparatively tolerable state did not last long. Some ten days after her father's death a consultant was brought in, whom, like all strangers, she completely ignored while I demonstrated all her peculiarities to him. 'That's like an examination,'[2] she said, laughing, when I got her to read a French text aloud in English. The other physician intervened in the conversation and tried to attract her attention, but in vain. It was a genuine 'negative hallucination' of the kind which has since so often been produced experimentally. In the end he succeeded in breaking through it by blowing smoke in her face. She suddenly saw a stranger before her, rushed to the door to take away the key and fell unconscious to the ground. There followed a short fit of anger and then a severe attack of anxiety which I had great difficulty in calming down. Unluckily I had to leave Vienna that evening, and when I came back several days later I found the patient much worse. She had gone entirely without food the whole time, was full of anxiety and her hallucinatory *absences* were filled with terrifying figures, death's heads and skeletons. Since she acted these things through as though she was experiencing them and in part put them into words, the people around her became aware to a great extent of the content of these hallucinations.

The regular order of things was; the somnolent state in the afternoon, followed after sunset by the deep hypnosis for which she invented the technical name of 'clouds'.[3] If during this she was able to narrate the hallucinations she had had in the

2. [In English in the original.]   3. [In English in the original.]

course of the day, she would wake up clear in mind, calm and cheerful. She would sit down to work and write or draw far into the night quite rationally. At about four she would go to bed. Next day the whole series of events would be repeated. It was a truly remarkable contrast: in the day-time the irresponsible patient pursued by hallucinations, and at night the girl with her mind completely clear.

In spite of her euphoria at night, her psychical condition deteriorated steadily. Strong suicidal impulses appeared which made it seem inadvisable for her to continue living on the third floor. Against her will, therefore, she was transferred to a country house in the neighbourhood of Vienna (on June 7, 1881). I had never threatened her with this removal from her home, which she regarded with horror, but she herself had, without saying so, expected and dreaded it. This event made it clear once more how much the affect of anxiety dominated her psychical disorder. Just as after her father's death a calmer condition had set in, so now, when what she feared had actually taken place, she once more became calmer. Nevertheless, the move was immediately followed by three days and nights completely without sleep or nourishment, by numerous attempts at suicide (though, so long as she was in a garden, these were not dangerous), by smashing windows and so on, and by hallucinations unaccompanied by *absences*—which she was able to distinguish easily from her other hallucinations. After this she grew quieter, let the nurse feed her and even took chloral at night.

Before continuing my account of the case, I must go back once more and describe one of its peculiarities which I have hitherto mentioned only in passing. I have already said that throughout the illness up to this point the patient fell into a somnolent state every afternoon and that after sunset this period passed into a deeper sleep—'clouds'. (It seems plausible to attribute this regular sequence of events merely to her experience while she was nursing her father, which she had had to do for several months. During the nights she had watched by the patient's bedside or had been awake anxiously listening till the morning; in the afternoons she had lain down for a short rest, as is the usual habit of nurses. This pattern of waking at night and sleeping in the afternoons seems to have been carried over into her own illness and to have persisted long after the sleep had been replaced by a hypnotic state.) After the deep sleep had lasted about an hour she grew restless, tossed to and fro and kept repeating 'tormenting, tormenting', with her eyes shut all the time. It was also noticed how, during her *absences* in day-time she was obviously creating some situation or episode to which she gave a clue with a few muttered words. It happened then—to begin with accidentally but later intentionally—that someone near her repeated one of these phrases of hers while she was complaining about the 'tormenting'. She at once joined in and began to paint some situation or tell some story, hesitatingly at first and in her paraphasic jargon; but the longer she went on the more fluent she became, till at last she was speaking quite correct German. (This applies to the early period before she began talking English only.) The stories were always sad and some of them very charming, in the style of Hans Andersen's *Picture-book without Pictures*, and, indeed, they were probably constructed on that model. As a rule their starting-point or central situation was of a girl anxiously sitting by a sick-bed. But she also built up her stories on quite other topics.—A few moments after she had finished her narrative she would wake up, obviously, calmed down, or, as she called it, 'gehäglich'.[4] During the night she would again become restless, and in the morning, after a couple of hours' sleep, she was visibly involved in some other set of ideas.—If for any reason she was unable to tell me the story during her evening hypnosis she failed to calm down afterwards, and on the following day she had to tell me *two* stories in order for this to happen.

The essential features of this phenomenon—the mounting up and intensification of her *absences* into her auto-hypnosis in the evening, the effect of the products of her imagination as psychical stimuli and the easing and removal of her state of stimulation when she gave utterance to them in her hypnosis—remained constant throughout the whole eighteen months during which she was under observation.

The stories naturally became still more tragic after her father's death. It was not, however, until the deterioration of her mental condition, which followed when her state of somnambulism was forcibly broken into in the way already described, that her evening narratives ceased to have the character of more or less freely-created poetical compositions and changed into a string of frightful and terrifying hallucinations. (It was already possible to arrive at these from the patient's behaviour during the day.) I have already described how completely her mind was relieved when, shaking with fear and horror, she had reproduced these frightful images and given verbal utterance to them.

While she was in the country, when I was unable to pay her daily visits, the situation developed as follows. I used to visit her in the evening, when I knew I should find her in her hypnosis, and I then relieved her of the whole stock of imaginative products which she had accumulated since my last visit. It was essential that this should be effected completely if good results were to follow. When this was done she became perfectly calm, and next day she would be agreeable, easy to manage, industrious and even cheerful; but on the second day she would be increasingly moody, contrary and unpleasant, and this would become still more marked on the third day. When she was like this it was not always easy to get her to talk, even in her hypnosis. She aptly described this procedure, speaking seriously, as a 'talking cure', while she referred to it jokingly as 'chimney-sweeping'.[5] She knew that after she had given utterance to her hallucinations she would lose all her obstinacy and what she described as her 'energy'; and when, after some comparatively long interval, she was in a bad temper, she would refuse to talk, and I was obliged to overcome her unwillingness by urging and pleading and using devices such as repeating a formula with which she was in the habit of introducing her stories. But she would never begin to talk until she had satisfied herself of my identity by carefully feeling my hands. On those nights on which she had not been calmed by verbal utterance it was necessary to fall back upon chloral. I had tried it on a few earlier occasions, but I was obliged to give her 5 grammes, and sleep was preceded by a state of intoxication which lasted for some hours. When I was present this state was euphoric, but in my absence it was highly disagreeable and characterized by

---

4. [She used this made-up word instead of the regular German 'behaglich,' meaning 'comfortable.']

5. [These two phrases are in English in the original.]

anxiety as well as excitement. (It may be remarked incidentally that this severe state of intoxication made no difference to her constractures.) I had been able to avoid the use of narcotics, since the verbal utterance of her hallucinations calmed her even though it might not induce sleep; but when she was in the country the nights on which she had not obtained hypnotic relief were so unbearable that in spite of everything it was necessary to have recourse to chloral. But it became possible gradually to reduce the dose.

The persisting somnambulism did not return. But on the other hand the alternation between two states of consciousness persisted. She used to hallucinate in the middle of a conversation, run off, start climbing up a tree, etc. If one caught hold of her, she would very quickly take up her interrupted sentence without knowing anything about what had happened in the interval. All these hallucinations, however, came up and were reported on in her hypnosis.

Her condition improved on the whole. She took nourishment without difficulty and allowed the nurse to feed her; except that she asked for bread but rejected it the moment it touched her lips. The paralytic contracture of the leg diminished greatly. There was also an improvement in her power of judgement and she became much attached to my friend Dr. B., the physician who visited her. She derived much benefit from a Newfoundland dog which was given to her and of which she was passionately fond. On one occasion, though, her pet made an attack on a cat, and it was splendid to see the way in which the frail girl seized a whip in her left hand and beat off the huge beast with it to rescue his victim. Later, she looked after some poor, sick people, and this helped her greatly.

It was after I returned from a holiday trip which lasted several weeks that I received the most convincing evidence of the pathogenic and exciting effect brought about by the ideational complexes which were produced during her *absences*, or *condition seconde*, and of the fact that these complexes were disposed of by being given verbal expression during hypnosis. During this interval no 'talking cure' had been carried out, for it was impossible to persuade her to confide what she had to say to anyone but me—not even to Dr. B. to whom she had in other respects become devoted. I found her in a wretched moral state, inert, unamenable, ill-tempered, even malicious. It became plain from her evening stories that her imaginative and poetic vein was drying up. What she reported was more and more concerned with her hallucinations and, for instance, the things that had annoyed her during the past days. These were clothed in imaginative shape, but were merely formulated in stereotyped images rather than elaborated into poetic productions. But the situation only became tolerable after I had arranged for the patient to be brought back to Vienna for a week and evening after evening made her tell me three to five stories. When I had accomplished this, everything that had accumulated during the weeks of my absence had been worked off. It was only now that the former rhythm was re-established: on the day after her giving verbal utterance to her phantasies she was amiable and cheerful, on the second day she was more irritable and less agreeable and on the third positively 'nasty'. Her moral state was a function of the time that had elapsed since her last utterance. This was because every one of the spontaneous products of her imagination and every event which had been assimilated by the pathological part of her mind persisted as a psychical stimulus until it had been narrated in her hypnosis, after which it completely ceased to operate.

When, in the autumn, the patient returned to Vienna (though to a different house from the one in which she had fallen ill), her condition was bearable, both physically and mentally; for very few of her experiences—in fact only her more striking ones—were made into psychical stimuli in a pathological manner. I was hoping for a continuous and increasing improvement, provided that the permanent burdening of her mind with fresh stimuli could be prevented by her giving regular verbal expression to them. But to begin with I was disappointed. In December there was a marked deterioration of her psychical condition. She once more became excited, gloomy and irritable. She had no more 'really good days' even when it was impossible to detect anything that was remaining 'stuck' inside her. Towards the end of December, at Christmas time, she was particularly restless, and for a whole week in the evenings she told me nothing new but only the imaginative products which she had elaborated under the stress of great anxiety and emotion during the Christmas of 1880 [a year earlier]. When the scenes had been completed she was greatly relieved.

A year had now passed since she had been separated from her father, and had taken to her bed, and from this time on her condition became clearer and was systematized in a very peculiar manner. Her alternating states of consciousness, which were characterized by the fact that, from morning onwards, her *absences* (that is to say, the emergence of her *condition seconde*) always became more frequent as the day advanced and took entire possession by the evening—these alternating states had differed from each other previously in that one (the first) was normal and the second alienated; now, however, they differed further in that in the first she lived, like the rest of us, in the winter of 1881–2, whereas in the second she lived in the winter of 1880–1, and had completely forgotten all the subsequent events. The one thing that nevertheless seemed to remain conscious most of the time was the fact that her father had died. She was carried back to the previous year with such intensity that in the new house she hallucinated her old room, so that when she wanted to go to the door she knocked up against the stove which stood in the same relation to the window as the door did in the old room. The change-over from one state to another occurred spontaneously but could also be very easily brought about by any sense-impression which vividly recalled the previous year. One had only to hold up an orange before her eyes (oranges were what she had chiefly lived on during the first part of her illness) in order to carry her over from the year 1882 to the year 1881. But this transfer into the past did not take place in a general or indefinite manner; she lived through the previous winter day by day. I should only have been able to *suspect* that this was happening, had it not been that every evening during the hypnosis she talked through whatever it was that had excited her on the same day in 1881, and had it not been that a private diary kept by her mother in 1881 confirmed beyond a doubt the occurrence of the underlying events. This re-living of the previous year continued till the illness came to its final close in June, 1882.

It was interesting here, too, to observe the way in which these revived psychical stimuli belonging to her secondary state made their way over into her first, more normal one. It happened, for instance, that one morning the patient said to me laughingly that she had no idea what was the matter but she was angry with me. Thanks to the diary I knew what was happening; and, sure enough, this was gone through again in the evening hypnosis: I had annoyed the patient very much on the same evening in 1881. Or another time she told me there was something the matter with her eyes; she was seeing colours wrong. She knew she was wearing a brown dress but she saw it as a blue one. We soon found that she could distinguish all the colours of the visual test-sheets correctly and clearly, and that the disturbance only related to the dress-material. The reason was that during the same period in 1881 she had been very busy with a dressing-gown for her father, which was made with the same material as her present dress, but was blue instead of brown. Incidentally, it was often to be seen that these emergent memories showed their effect in advance; the disturbance of her normal state would occur earlier on, and the memory would only gradually be awakened in her *condition seconde*.

Her evening hypnosis was thus heavily burdened, for we had to talk off not only her contemporary imaginative products but also the events and 'vexations'[6] of 1881. (Fortunately I had already relieved her at the time of the imaginative products of that year.) But in addition to all this the work that had to be done by the patient and her physician was immensely increased by a third group of separate disturbances which had to be disposed of in the same manner. These were the psychical events involved in the period of incubation of the illness between July and December, 1880; it was they that had produced the whole of the hysterical phenomena, and when they were brought to verbal utterance the symptoms disappeared.

When this happened for the first time—when, as a result of an accidental and spontaneous utterance of this kind, during the evening hypnosis, a disturbance which had persisted for a considerable time vanished—I was greatly surprised. It was in the summer during a period of extreme heat, and the patient was suffering very badly from thirst; for, without being able to account for it in any way, she suddenly found it impossible to drink. She would take up the glass of water she longed for, but as soon as it touched her lips she would push it away like someone suffering from hydrophobia. As she did this, she was obviously in an *absence* for a couple of seconds. She lived only on fruit, such as melons, etc., so as to lessen her tormenting thirst. This had lasted for some six weeks, when one day during hypnosis she grumbled about her English lady-companion whom she did not care for, and went on to describe, with every sign of disgust, how she had once gone into that lady's room and how her little dog—horrid creature!—had drunk out of a glass there. The patient had said nothing, as she had wanted to be polite. After giving further energetic expression to the anger she had held back, she asked for something to drink, drank a large quantity of water without any difficulty and woke from her hypnosis with the glass at her lips; and thereupon the disturbance vanished, never to return. A number of extremely obstinate whims were similarly removed after she had described the experiences which had given rise to them. She took a great step forward when the first of her chronic symptoms disappeared in the same way—the contracture of her right leg, which, it is true, had already diminished a great deal. These findings—that in the case of this patient the hysterical phenomena disappeared as soon as the event which had given rise to them was reproduced in her hypnosis—made it possible to arrive at a therapeutic technical procedure which left nothing to be desired in its logical consistency and systematic application. Each individual symptom in this complicated case was taken separately in hand; all the occasions on which it had appeared were described in reverse order, starting before the time when the patient became bed-ridden and going back to the event which had led to its first appearance. When this had been described the symptom was permanently removed.

In this way her paralytic contractures and anaesthesias, disorders of vision and hearing of every sort, neuralgias, coughing, tremors, etc., and finally her disturbances of speech were 'talked away'. Amongst the disorders of vision, the following, for instance, were disposed of separately: the convergent squint with diplopia; deviation of both eyes to the right, so that when her hand reached out for something it always went to the left of the object; restriction of the visual field; central amblyopia; macropsia; seeing a death's head instead of her father; inability to read. Only a few scattered phenomena (such, for instance, as the extension of the paralytic contractures to the left side of her body) which had developed while she was confined to bed, were untouched by this process of analysis, and it is probable, indeed, that they had in fact no immediate psychical cause.

It turned out to be quite impracticable to shorten the work by trying to elicit in her memory straight away the first provoking cause of her symptoms. She was unable to find it, grew confused, and things proceeded even more slowly than if she was allowed quietly and steadily to follow back the thread of memories on which she had embarked. Since the latter method, however, took too long in the evening hypnosis, owing to her being over-strained and distraught by 'talking out' the two other sets of experiences—and owing, too, to the reminiscences needing time before they could attain sufficient vividness—we evolved the following procedure. I used to visit her in the morning and hypnotize her. (Very simple methods of doing this were arrived at empirically.) I would next ask her to concentrate her thoughts on the symptom we were treating at the moment and to tell me the occasions on which it had appeared. The patient would proceed to describe in rapid succession and under brief headings the external events concerned and these I would jot down. During her subsequent evening hypnosis she would then, with the help of my notes, give me a fairly detailed account of these circumstances.

An example will show the exhaustive manner in which she accomplished this. It was our regular experience that the patient did not hear when she was spoken to. It was possible to differentiate this passing habit of not hearing as follows:

(*a*) Not hearing when someone came in, while her thoughts were abstracted. 108 separate detailed instances of this, mentioning the persons and circumstances, often with dates. First instance: not hearing her father come in.

(*b*) Not understanding when several people were talking. 27 instances. First instance: her father, once more, and an acquaintance.

6. [In English in the original.]

(c)   Not hearing when she was alone and directly addressed. 50 instances. Origin: her father having vainly asked her for some wine.

(d)   Deafness brought on by being shaken (in a carriage, etc.). 15 instances. Origin: having been shaken angrily by her young brother when he caught her one night listening at the sickroom door.

(e)   Deafness brought on by fright at a noise. 37 instances. Origin: a choking fit of her father's, caused by swallowing the wrong way.

(f)   Deafness during deep *absence*. 12 instances.

(g)   Deafness brought on by listening hard for a long time, so that when she was spoken to she failed to hear. 54 instances.

Of course all these episodes were to a great extent identical in so far as they could be traced back to states of abstraction or *absences* or to fright. But in the patient's memory they were so clearly differentiated, that if she happened to make a mistake in their sequence she would be obliged to correct herself and put them in the right order; if this was not done her report came to a standstill. The events she described were so lacking in interest and significance and were told in such detail that there could be no suspicion of their having been invented. Many of these incidents consisted of purely internal experiences and so could not be verified; others of them (or circumstances attending them) were within the recollection of people in her environment.

This example, too, exhibited a feature that was always observable when a symptom was being 'talked away': the particular symptom emerged with greater force while she was discussing it. Thus during the analysis of her not being able to hear she was so deaf that for part of the time I was obliged to communicate with her in writing. The first provoking cause was habitually a fright of some kind, experienced while she was nursing her father—some oversight on her part, for instance.

The work of remembering was not always an easy matter and sometimes the patient had to make great efforts. On one occasion our whole progress was obstructed for some time because a recollection refused to emerge. It was a question of a particularly terrifying hallucination. While she was nursing her father she had seen him with a death's head. She and the people with her remembered that once, while she still appeared to be in good health, she had paid a visit to one of her relatives. She had opened the door and all at once fallen down unconscious. In order to get over the obstruction to our progress she visited the same place again and, on entering the room, again fell to the ground unconscious. During her subsequent evening hypnosis the obstacle was surmounted. As she came into the room, she had seen her pale face reflected in a mirror hanging opposite the door; but it was not herself that she saw but her father with a death's head.—We often noticed that her dread of a memory, as in the present instance, inhibited its emergence, and this had to be brought about forcibly by the patient or physician.

The following incident, among others, illustrates the high degree of logical consistency of her states. During this period, as has already been explained, the patient was always in her *condition seconde*—that is, in the year 1881—at night. On one occasion she woke up during the night, declaring that she had been taken away from home once again, and became so seriously excited that the whole household was alarmed. The reason was simple. During the previous evening the talking cure had cleared up her disorder of vision, and this applied also to her *condition seconde*. Thus when she woke up in the night she found herself in a strange room, for her family had moved house in the spring of 1881. Disagreeable events of this kind were avoided by my always (at her request) shutting her eyes in the evening and giving her a suggestion that she would not be able to open them till I did so myself on the following morning. The disturbance was only repeated once, when the patient cried in a dream and opened her eyes on waking up from it.

Since this laborious analysis for her symptoms dealt with the summer months of 1880, which was the preparatory period of her illness, I obtained complete insight into the incubation and pathogenesis of this case of hysteria, and I will now describe them briefly.

In July, 1880, while he was in the country, her father fell seriously ill of a sub-pleural abscess. Anna shared the duties of nursing him with her mother. She once woke up during the night in great anxiety about the patient, who was in a high fever; and she was under the strain of expecting the arrival of a surgeon from Vienna who was to operate. Her mother had gone away for a short time and Anna was sitting at the bedside with her right arm over the back of her chair. She fell into a waking dream and saw a black snake coming towards the sick man from the wall to bite him. (It is most likely that there were in fact snakes in the field behind the house and that these had previously given the girl a fright; they would thus have provided the material for her hallucination.) She tried to keep the snake off, but it was as though she was paralysed. Her right arm, over the back of the chair, had gone to sleep and had become anaesthetic and paretic; and when she looked at it the fingers turned into little snakes with death's heads (the nails). (It seems probable that she had tried to use her paralysed right arm to drive off the snake and that its anaesthesia and paralysis had consequently become associated with the hallucination of the snake.) When the snake vanished, in her terror she tried to pray. But language failed her: she could find no tongue in which to speak, till at last she thought of some children's verses in English and then found herself able to think and pray in that language. The whistle of the train that was bringing the doctor whom she expected broke the spell.

Next day, in the course of a game, she threw a quoit into some bushes; and when she went to pick it out, a bent branch revived her hallucination of the snake, and simultaneously her right arm became rigidly extended. Thenceforward the same thing invariably occurred whenever the hallucination was recalled by some object with a more or less snake-like appearance. This hallucination, however, as well as the contracture only appeared during the short *absences* which became more and more frequent from that night onwards. (The contracture did not become stabilized until December, when the patient broke down completely and took to her bed permanently.) As a result of some particular event which I cannot find recorded in my notes and which I no longer recall, the contracture of the right leg was added to that of the right arm.

Her tendency to auto-hypnotic *absences* was from now on established. On the morning after the night I have described, while she was waiting for the surgeon's arrival, she fell into such a fit of abstraction that he finally arrived in the room without her having heard his approach. Her persistent anxiety interfered with her eating and gradually led to intense feelings of nausea. Apart from this, indeed, each of her hysterical symptoms arose during an affect. It is not quite certain whether in every case a momentary state of *absence* was involved, but this seems probable in view of the fact that in her waking state the patient was totally unaware of what had been going on.

I cannot feel much regret that the incompleteness of my notes makes it impossible for me to enumerate all the occasions on which her various hysterical symptoms appeared. She herself told me them in every single case, with the one exception I have mentioned; and, as I have already said, each symptom disappeared after she had described its first occurrence.

In this way, too, the whole illness was brought to a close. The patient herself had formed a strong determination that the whole treatment should be finished by the anniversary of the day on which she was moved into the country [June 7]. At the beginning of June, accordingly, she entered into the 'talking cure' with the greatest energy. On the last day—by the help of re-arranging the room so as to resemble her father's sickroom—she reproduced the terrifying hallucination which I have described above and which constituted the root of her whole illness. During the original scene she had only been able to think and pray in English; but immediately after its reproduction she was able to speak German. She was moreover free from the innumerable disturbances which she had previously exhibited.[7] After this she left Vienna and travelled for a while; but it was a considerable time before she regained her mental balance entirely. Since then she has enjoyed complete health.

There were two psychical characteristics present in the girl while she was still completely healthy which acted as predisposing causes for her subsequent hysterical illness:

(1)   Her monotonous family life and the absence of adequate intellectual occupation left her with an unemployed surplus of mental liveliness and energy, and this found an outlet in the constant activity of her imagination.

(2)   This led to a habit of day-dreaming (her 'private theatre'), which laid the foundations for a dissociation of her mental personality. Nevertheless a dissociation of this degree is still within the bounds of normality. Reveries and reflections during a more or less mechanical occupation do not in themselves imply a pathological splitting of consciousness, since if they are interrupted—if, for instance, the subject is spoken to—the normal

---

7. [At this point (so Freud once told the present editor (James Strachey), with his finger on an open copy of the book) there is a hiatus in the text. What he had in mind and went on to describe was the occurrence which marked the end of Anna O.'s treatment. . . . [I]t is enough to say here that, when the treatment had apparently reached a successful end, the patient suddenly made manifest to Breuer the presence of a strong unanalyzed positive transference of an unmistakably sexual nature. (Behind these technical terms lies a dramatic story: after Breuer had said good-bye to his patient, about to go off on a trip with his wife who had become jealous of her husband's interesting patient, he was suddenly called back that very evening to discover that she was in the throes of a hysterical pregnancy, claiming to be carrying Breuer's child. It was this occurrence, Freud believed, that caused Breuer to hold back the publication of the case history for so many years and that led ultimately to his abandonment of all further collaboration in Freud's researches.

unity of consciousness is restored; nor, presumably, is any amnesia present. In the case of Anna O., however, this habit prepared the ground upon which the affect of anxiety and dread was able to establish itself in the way I have described, when once that affect had transformed the patient's habitual day-dreaming into a hallucinatory *absence*. It is remarkable how completely the earliest manifestation of her illness in its beginnings already exhibited its main characteristics, which afterwards remained unchanged for almost two years.

The question now arises how far the patient's statements are to be trusted and whether the occasions and mode of origin of the phenomena were really as she represented them. So far as the more important and fundamental events are concerned, the trustworthiness of her account seems to me to be beyond question. As regards the symptoms disappearing after being 'talked away', I cannot use this as evidence; it may very well be explained by suggestion. But I always found the patient entirely truthful and trustworthy. The things she told me were intimately bound up with what was most sacred to her. Whatever could be checked by other people was fully confirmed. Even the most highly gifted girl would be incapable of concocting a tissue of data with such a degree of internal consistency as was exhibited in the history of this case. It cannot be disputed, however, that precisely her consistency may have led her (in perfectly good faith) to assign to some of her symptoms a precipitating cause which they did not in fact possess. But this suspicion, too, I consider unjustified. The very insignificance of so many of those causes, the irrational character of so many of the connections involved, argue in favour of their reality. The patient could not understand how it was that dance music made her cough; such a construction is too meaningless to have been deliberate. (It seemed very likely to me, incidentally, that each of her twinges of conscience brought on one of her regular spasms of the glottis and that the motor impulses which she felt—for she was very fond of dancing— transformed the spasm into a *tussis nervosa*.) Accordingly, in my view the patient's statements were entirely trustworthy and corresponded to the facts.

Every one of her hypnoses in the evening afforded evidence that the patient was entirely clear and well-ordered in her mind and normal as regards her feeling and volition so long as none of the products of her secondary state was acting as a stimulus 'in the unconscious'. The extremely marked psychosis which appeared whenever there was any considerable interval in this unburdening process showed the degree to which those products influenced the psychical events of her 'normal' state. It is hard to avoid expressing the situation by saying that the patient was split into two personalities of which one was mentally normal and the other insane. The sharp division between the two states in the present patient only exhibits more clearly, in my opinion, what has given rise to a number of unexplained problems in many other hysterical patients. It was especially noticeable in Anna O. how much the products of her bad self, as she herself called it, affected her moral habit of mind. If these products had not been continually disposed of, we should have been faced by a hysteric of the malicious type—refractory, lazy, disagreeable and ill-natured; but, as it was, after the removal of those stimuli her true character, which was the opposite of all these, always reappeared at once.

The final cure of the hysteria deserves a few more words. It was accompanied, as I have already said, by considerable disturbances and a deterioration in the patient's mental condition. I had a very strong impression that the numerous products of her secondary state which had been quiescent were now forcing their way into consciousness; and though in the first instance they were being remembered only in her secondary state, they were nevertheless burdening and disturbing her normal one. It remains to be seen whether it may not be that the same origin is to be traced in other cases in which a chronic hysteria terminates in a psychosis.

GWENDOLYN BROOKS

b. 1917 Topeka, KS
d. 2000 Chicago, IL

Sadie and Maud (1945)

Maud went to college.
Sadie stayed home.
Sadie scraped life
With a fine toothed comb.

She didn't leave a tangle in
Her comb found every strand.
Sadie was one of the livingest chicks
In all the land.

Sadie bore two babies
Under her maiden name.
Maud and Ma and Papa
Nearly died of shame.

When Sadie said her last so-long
Her girls struck out from home.
(Sadie left as heritage
Her fine-toothed comb.)

Maud, who went to college,
Is a thin brown mouse.
She is living all alone
In this old house.

We Real Cool (1963)

THE POOL PLAYERS. SEVEN AT THE GOLDEN SHOVEL.

We real cool. We
Left School. We

Lurk late. We
Strike straight. We

Sing sin. We
Thin gin. We

Jazz June. We
Die soon.

My Last Duchess (1842)

Robert Browning
b. 1812, Camberwell, England
d. 1889, Venice, Italy

Ferrara

That's my last Duchess painted on the wall,
Looking as if she were alive; I call
That piece a wonder, now; Frà Pandolf's hands
Worked busily a day, and there she stands.
Will't please you sit and look at her? I said
"Frà Pandolf" by design, for never read
Strangers like you that pictured countenance,
The depth and passion of its earnest glance,
But to myself they turned (since none puts by
The curtain I have drawn for you, but I)
And seemed as they would ask me, if they durst,
How such a glance came there; so, not the first
Are you to turn and ask thus. Sir, 'twas not
Her husband's presence only, called that spot
Of joy into the Duchess' cheek: perhaps
Frà Pandolf chanced to say "Her mantle laps
Over my Lady's wrist too much," or "Paint
Must never hope to reproduce the faint
Half-flush that dies along her throat": such stuff
Was courtesy, she thought, and cause enough
For calling up that spot of joy. She had
A heart—how shall I say?—too soon made glad,
Too easily impressed; she liked whate'er
She looked on, and her looks went everywhere.
Sir, 'twas all one! My favor at her breast,
The dropping of the daylight in the West,

The bough of cherries some officious fool
Broke in the orchard for her, the white mule
She rode with round the terrace—all and each
Would draw from her alike the approving speech,
Or blush, at least. She thanked men,—good; but thanked
Somehow—I know not how—as if she ranked
My gift of a nine-hundred-years-old name
With anybody's gift. Who'd stoop to blame
This sort of trifling? Even had you skill
In speech—(which I have not)—to make your will
Quite clear to such an one, and say, "Just this
Or that in you disgusts me; here you miss,
Or there exceed the mark"—and if she let
Herself be lessoned so, nor plainly set
Her wits to yours, forsooth, and made excuse,
—E'en then would be some stooping, and I choose
Never to stoop. Oh, Sir, she smiled, no doubt,
Whene'er I passed her; but who passed without
Much the same smile? This grew; I gave commands;
Then all smiles stopped together. There she stands
As if alive. Will't please you rise? We'll meet
The company below, then. I repeat,
The Count your Master's known munificence
Is ample warrant that no just pretence
Of mine for dowry will be disallowed;
Though his fair daughter's self, as I avowed
At starting, is my object. Nay, we'll go
Together down, Sir! Notice Neptune, though,
Taming a sea-horse, thought a rarity,
Which Claus of Innsbruck cast in bronze for me.

HOLY SONNETS (1633)

John Donne
b. 1572 London, England
d. 1631 London, England

I

Thou hast made me, and shall thy work decay?
Repair me now, for now mine end doth haste,
I run to death, and death meets me as fast,
And all my pleasures are like yesterday;
I dare not move my dim eyes any way,
Despair behind, and death before doth cast
Such terror, and my feeble flesh doth waste
By sin in it, which it t'wards hell doth weigh;
Only thou art above, and when towards thee
By thy leave I can look, I rise again;
But our old subtle foe so tempteth me,
That not one hour my self I can sustain;
Thy Grace may wing me to prevent his art,
And thou like Adamant draw mine iron heart.

II

As due by many titles I resign
My self to Thee, O God; first I was made
By Thee, and for Thee, and when I was decayed
Thy blood bought that, the which before was Thine;
I am Thy son, made with Thy Self to shine,
Thy servant, whose pains Thou hast still repaid,
Thy sheep, thine image, and, till I betrayed
My self, a temple of Thy Spirit divine;
Why doth the devil then usurp on me?
Why doth he steal, nay ravish that's thy right?

Except thou rise and for thine own work fight,
Oh I shall soon despair, when I do see
That thou lov'st mankind well, yet wilt not choose me,
And Satan hates me, yet is loth to lose me.

III

O might those sighs and tears return again
Into my breast and eyes, which I have spent,
That I might in this holy discontent
Mourn with some fruit, as I have mourned in vain;
In mine Idolatry what showers of rain
Mine eyes did waste! what griefs my heart did rent!
That sufferance was my sin; now I repent;
'Cause I did suffer I must suffer pain.
Th' hydropic drunkard, and night-scouting thief,
The itchy lecher, and self-tickling proud
Have the remembrance of past joys for relief
Of comming ills. To (poor) me is allowed
No ease; for long, yet vehement grief hath been
Th' effect and cause, the punishment and sin.

IV

Oh my black soul! now art thou summoned
By sickness, death's herald, and champion;
Thou art like a pilgrim, which abroad hath done
Treason, and durst not turn to whence he is fled;
Or like a thief, which till death's doom be read,
Wisheth himself delivered from prison,
But damned and haled to execution,
Wisheth that still he might be imprisoned.
Yet grace, if thou repent, thou canst not lack;
But who shall give thee that grace to begin?
Oh make thy self with holy mourning black,
And red with blushing, as thou art with sin;
Or wash thee in Christ's blood, which hath this might
That being red, it dyes red souls to white.

V

I am little world made cunningly
Of Elements, and an Angelike spright,
But black sinne hath betraid to endlesse night
My worlds both parts, and (oh) both parts must die.
You which beyond that heaven which was most high
Have found new sphears, and of new lands can write,

Powre new seas in mine eyes, that so I might
Drowne my world with my weeping earnestly,
Or wash it if it must be drown'd no more;
But oh it must be burnt! alas the fire
Of lust and envie have burnt it heretofore,
And made it fouler; Let their flames retire,
And burne me o Lord, with a fiery zeale
Of thee and thy house, which doth in eating heale.

VI

This is my play's last scene, here heavens appoint
My pilgrimage's last mile; and my race
Idly, yet quickly run, hath this last pace,
My span's last inch, my minute's latest point,
And gluttonous death, will instantly unjoint
My body and soul, and I shall sleep a space;
But my ever-waking part shall see that face,
Whose fear already shakes my every joint:
Then, as my soul, t' heaven her first seat, takes flight,
And earth-born body in the earth shall dwell,
So fall my sins that all may have their right
(To where they're bred, and would press me) to hell.
Impute me righteous, thus purged of evil,
For thus I leave the world, the flesh, the devil.

VII

At the round earth's imagined corners, blow
Your trumpets, Angels, and arise, arise
From death, you numberless infinities
Of souls, and to your scattered bodies go,
All whom the flood did, and fire shall o'erthrow,
All whom war, dearth, age, agues, tyrannies,
Despair, law, chance, hath slain, and you whose eyes,
Shall behold God, and never taste death's woe.
But let them sleep, Lord, and me mourn a space,
For, if above all these, my sins abound,
'Tis late to ask abundance of thy grace,
When we are there; here on this lowly ground,
Teach me how to repent; for that's as good
As if thou hadst seal'd my pardon, with thy blood.

VIII

If faithful souls be alike glorified
As angels, then my father's soul doth see,

And adds this even to full felicity,
That valiantly I hell's wide mouth o'erstride:
But if our minds to these souls be descried
By circumstances, and by signs that be
Apparent in us, not immediately,
How shall my mind's white truth by them be tried?
They see idolatrous lovers weep and mourn,
And vile blasphemous conjurers to call
On Jesus name, and Pharisaical
Dissemblers feigne devotion. Then turn,
O pensive soul, to God, for he knows best
Thy true grief, for he put it in my breast.

IX

If poisonous minerals, and if that tree
Whose fruit threw death on else immortal us,
If lecherous goats, if serpents envious
Cannot be damn'd, alas, why should I be?
Why should intent or reason, born in me,
Make sins, else equal, in me more heinous?
And mercy being easy, and glorious
To God, in his stern wrath why threatens he?
But who am I, that dare dispute with thee,
O God? Oh, of thine only worthy blood
And my tears, make a heavenly Lethean flood,
And drown in it my sins' black memory.
That thou remember them, some claim as debt;
I think it mercy, if thou wilt forget.

X

Death be not proud, though some have called thee
Mighty and dreadful, for thou art not so,
For those whom thou think'st thou dost overthrow,
Die not, poor death, nor yet canst thou kill me.
From rest and sleep, which but thy pictures be,
Much pleasure, then from thee, much more must flow,
And soonest our best men with thee do go,
Rest of their bones, and soul's delivery.
Thou art slave to Fate, Chance, kings, and desperate men,
And dost with poison, war, and sickness dwell,
And poppy, or charms can make us sleep as well,
And better than thy stroke; why swell'st thou then?
One short sleep past, we wake eternally,
And death shall be no more; death, thou shalt die.

XI

Spit in my face you Jews, and pierce my side,
Buffet, and scoff, scourge, and crucify me,
For I have sinned, and sinned, and only he
Who could do no iniquity hath died:
But by my death can not be satisfied
My sins, which pass the Jews' impiety:
They killed once an inglorious man, but I
Crucify him daily, being now glorified.
Oh let me, then, his strange love still admire:
Kings pardon, but he bore our punishment.
And Jacob came clothed in vile harsh attire
But to supplant, and with gainful intent:
God clothed himself in vile man's flesh, that so
He might be weak enough to suffer woe.

XII

Why are we by all creatures waited on?
Why do the prodigal elements supply
Life and food to me, being more pure than I,
Simple, and further from corruption?
Why brook'st thou, ignorant horse, subjection?
Why dost thou, bull, and bore so seelily,
Dissemble weakness, and by one man's stroke die,
Whose whole kind you might swallow and feed upon?
Weaker I am, woe is me, and worse than you,
You have not sinned, nor need be timorous.
But wonder at a greater wonder, for to us
Created nature doth these things subdue,
But their Creator, whom sin nor nature tied,
For us, His creatures, and His foes, hath died.

XIII

What if this present were the world's last night?
Mark in my heart, O soul, where thou dost dwell,
The picture of Christ crucified, and tell
Whether that countenance can thee affright,
Tears in his eyes quench the amazing light,
Blood fills his frowns, which from his pierced head fell.
And can that tongue adjudge thee unto hell,
Which prayed forgiveness for his foes' fierce spite?
No, no; but as in my idolatry
I said to all my profane mistresses,

Beauty, of pity, foulness only is
A sign of rigour: so I say to thee,
To wicked spirits are horrid shapes assigned,
This beauteous form assures a piteous mind.

XIV

Batter my heart, three-person'd God; for you
As yet but knock, breathe, shine, and seek to mend;
That I may rise, and stand, o'erthrow me and bend
Your force, to break, blow, burn and make me new.
I, like an usurpt town, to another due,
Labour to admit you, but Oh, to no end,
Reason your viceroy in me, me should defend,
But is captiv'd, and proves weak or untrue.
Yet dearly I love you, and would be loved fain,
But am betroth'd unto your enemy:
Divorce me, untie, or break that knot again,
Take me to you, imprison me, for I
Except you enthrall me, never shall be free,
Nor ever chaste, except you ravish me.

XV

Wilt thou love God, as he thee? Then digest,
My soul, this wholesome meditation,
How God the Spirit, by angels waited on
In heaven, doth make his Temple in thy breast.
The Father having begot a Son most blest,
And still begetting, (for he ne'er be gone)
Hath deigned to choose thee by adoption,
Co-heir t' his glory, and Sabbath' endless rest.
And as a robbed man, which by search doth find
His stol'n stuff sold, must lose or buy 't again:
The Son of glory came down, and was slain,
Us whom he'd made, and Satan stol'n, to unbind.
'Twas much that man was made like God before,
But, that God should be made like man, much more.

XVI

Father, part of his double interest
Unto thy kingdom, thy Son gives to me,
His jointure in the knotty Trinity
He keeps, and gives to me his death's conquest.
This Lamb, whose death with life the world hath blest,
Was from the world's beginning slain, and he

Hath made two Wills which with the Legacy
Of his and thy kingdom do thy Sons invest.
Yet such are thy laws that men argue yet
Whether a man those statutes can fulfil;
None doth; but all-healing grace and spirit
Revive again what law and letter kill.
Thy law's abridgement, and thy last command
Is all but love; Oh let this last Will stand!

XVII

Since she whom I lov'd hath payd her last debt
To Nature, and to hers, and my good is dead,
And her Scule early into heaven ravished,
Wholly on heavenly things my mind is sett.
Here the admyring her my mind did whett
To seeke thee God; so streames do shew their head;
But though I have found thee, and thou my thirst hast fed,
A holy thirsty dropsy melts mee yet.
But why should I begg more Love, when as thou
Dost wooe my soule for hers; offring all thine:
And dost not only feare least I allow
My Love to Saints and Angels things divine,
But in thy tender jealousy dost doubt
Least in the World. Fleshe, yea Devill put thee out.

XVIII

Show me dear Christ, thy spouse so bright and clear.
What! is it she which on the other shore
Goes richly painted? or which, robb'd and tore,
Laments and mourns in Germany and here?
Sleeps she a thousand, then peeps up one year?
Is she self-truth, and errs? now new, now outwore?
Doth she, and did she, and shall she evermore
On one, on seven, or on no hill appear?
Dwells she with us, or like adventuring knights
First travel we to seek, and then make love?
Betray, kind husband, thy spouse to our sights,
And let mine amorous soul court thy mild Dove,
Who is most true and pleasing to thee then
When she'is embrac'd and open to most men.

XIX

Oh, to vex me, contraries meet in one:
Inconstancy unnaturally hath begot

A constant habit; that when I would not
I change in vows, and in devotion.
As humorous is my contrition
As my profane love, and as soon forgot:
As riddlingly distempered, cold and hot,
As praying, as mute; as infinite, as none.
I durst not view heaven yesterday; and today
In prayers and flattering speeches I court God:
Tomorrow I quake with true fear of his rod.
So my devout fits come and go away
Like a fantastic ague; save that here
Those are my best days, when I shake with fear.

The Love Song
of J. Alfred Prufrock (1915)

T.S. Eliot
b. 1888 St. Louis, MO
d. 1965 London, England

S'io credesse che mia risposta fosse
A persona che mai tornasse al mondo,
Questa fiamma staria senza piu scosse.
Ma percioche giammai di questo fondo
Non torno vivo alcun, s'i'odo il vero,
Senza tema d'infamia ti rispondo.

Let us go then, you and I,
When the evening is spread out against the sky
Like a patient etherized upon a table;
Let us go, through certain half-deserted streets,
The muttering retreats
Of restless nights in one-night cheap hotels
And sawdust restaurants with oyster-shells:
Streets that follow like a tedious argument
Of insidious intent
To lead you to an overwhelming question. . .
Oh, do not ask, "What is it?"

Let us go and make our visit.
In the room the women come and go
Talking of Michelangelo.

The yellow fog that rubs its back upon the window-panes,
The yellow smoke that rubs its muzzle on the window-panes,
Licked its tongue into the corners of the evening,
Lingered upon the pools that stand in drains,
Let fall upon its back the soot that falls from chimneys,

Slipped by the terrace, made a sudden leap,
And seeing that it was a soft October night,
Curled once about the house, and fell asleep.

And indeed there will be time
For the yellow smoke that slides along the street,
Rubbing its back upon the window-panes;
There will be time, there will be time
To prepare a face to meet the faces that you meet;
There will be time to murder and create,
And time for all the works and days of hands
That lift and drop a question on your plate;
Time for you and time for me,
And time yet for a hundred indecisions,
And for a hundred visions and revisions,
Before the taking of a toast and tea.

In the room the women come and go
Talking of Michelangelo.

And indeed there will be time
To wonder, "Do I dare?" and, "Do I dare?"
Time to turn back and descend the stair,
With a bald spot in the middle of my hair—
(They will say: "How his hair is growing thin!")
My morning coat, my collar mounting firmly to the chin,
My necktie rich and modest, but asserted by a simple pin—
(They will say: "But how his arms and legs are thin!")
Do I dare
Disturb the universe?
In a minute there is time
For decisions and revisions which a minute will reverse.
For I have known them all already, known them all:
Have known the evenings, mornings, afternoons,
I have measured out my life with coffee spoons;
I know the voices dying with a dying fall
Beneath the music from a farther room.
      So how should I presume?

And I have known the eyes already, known them all—
The eyes that fix you in a formulated phrase,
And when I am formulated, sprawling on a pin,
When I am pinned and wriggling on the wall,
Then how should I begin
To spit out all the butt-ends of my days and ways?
      And how should I presume?

And I have known the arms already, known them all—
Arms that are braceleted and white and bare
(But in the lamplight, downed with light brown hair!)
Is it perfume from a dress
That makes me so digress?
Arms that lie along a table, or wrap about a shawl.
    And should I then presume?
    And how should I begin?

Shall I say, I have gone at dusk through narrow streets
And watched the smoke that rises from the pipes
Of lonely men in shirt-sleeves, leaning out of windows? . . .

I should have been a pair of ragged claws
Scuttling across the floors of silent seas.

And the afternoon, the evening, sleeps so peacefully!
Smoothed by long fingers,
Asleep . . . tired . . . or it malingers,
Stretched on the floor, here beside you and me.
Should I, after tea and cakes and ices,
Have the strength to force the moment to its crisis?
But though I have wept and fasted, wept and prayed,
Though I have seen my head (grown slightly bald) brought in upon a platter,
I am no prophet — and here's no great matter;
I have seen the moment of my greatness flicker,
And I have seen the eternal Footman hold my coat, and snicker,
And in short, I was afraid.

And would it have been worth it, after all,
After the cups, the marmalade, the tea,
Among the porcelain, among some talk of you and me,
Would it have been worth while,
To have bitten off the matter with a smile,
To have squeezed the universe into a ball
To roll it towards some overwhelming question,
To say: "I am Lazarus, come from the dead,
Come back to tell you all, I shall tell you all"—
If one, settling a pillow by her head
    Should say: "That is not what I meant at all;
    That is not it, at all."

And would it have been worth it, after all,
Would it have been worth while,
After the sunsets and the dooryards and the sprinkled streets,
After the novels, after the teacups, after the skirts that trail along the floor—

And this, and so much more?—
It is impossible to say just what I mean!
But as if a magic lantern threw the nerves in patterns on a screen:
Would it have been worth while
If one, settling a pillow or throwing off a shawl,
And turning toward the window, should say:
    "That is not it at all,
    That is not what I meant, at all."

No! I am not Prince Hamlet, nor was meant to be;
Am an attendant lord, one that will do
To swell a progress, start a scene or two,
Advise the prince; no doubt, an easy tool,
Deferential, glad to be of use,
Politic, cautious, and meticulous;
Full of high sentence, but a bit obtuse;
At times, indeed, almost ridiculous—
Almost, at times, the Fool.

I grow old . . . I grow old . . .
I shall wear the bottoms of my trousers rolled.

Shall I part my hair behind? Do I dare to eat a peach?
I shall wear white flannel trousers, and walk upon the beach.
I have heard the mermaids singing, each to each.

I do not think that they will sing to me.

I have seen them riding seaward on the waves
Combing the white hair of the waves blown back
When the wind blows the water white and black.
We have lingered in the chambers of the sea
By sea-girls wreathed with seaweed red and brown
Till human voices wake us, and we drown.

JEFFTY IS FIVE (1977)

Harlan Ellison®
b. 1934 Cleveland, Ohio

When I was five years old, there was a little kid I played with: Jeffty. His real name was Jeff Kirizer, and everyone who played with him called him Jeffty. We were five years old together, and we had good times playing together.

When I was five, a Clark Bar was as fat around as the gripping end of a Louisville Slugger, and pretty nearly six inches long, and they used real chocolate to coat it, and it crunched very nicely when you bit into the center, and the paper it came wrapped in smelled fresh and good when you peeled off one end to hold the bar so it wouldn't melt onto your fingers. Today, a Clark Bar is as thin as a credit card, they use something artificial and awful-tasting instead of pure chocolate, the thing is soft and soggy, it costs fifteen or twenty cents instead of a decent, correct nickel, and they wrap it so you think it's the same size it was twenty years ago, only it isn't; it's slim and ugly and nasty tasting and not worth a penny, much less fifteen or twenty cents.

When I was that age, five years old, I was sent away to my Aunt Patricia's home in Buffalo, New York, for two years. My father was going through "bad times" and Aunt Patricia was very beautiful, and had married a stock-broker. They took care of me for two years. When I was seven, I came back home and went to find Jeffty, so we could play together.

I was seven. Jeffty was still five. I didn't notice any difference. I didn't know:

I was only seven.

When I was seven years old, I used to lie on my stomach in front of our Atwater-Kent radio and listen to swell stuff. I had tied the ground wire to the radiator, and I would lie there with my coloring books and my Crayolas (when there were only sixteen colors in the big box), and listen to the NBC Red network: Jack Benny on the *Jell-O Program, Amos. 'n' Andy*, Edgar Bergen and Charlie McCarthy on the *Chase and Sanborn Program, One Man's Family, First Nighter;* the NBC Blue network: *Easy Aces*, the *Jergens Program* with Walter Winchell, *Information Please, Death Valley Days*; and best of all, the Mutual Network with *The Green Hornet, The Lone Ranger, The Shadow*, and *Quiet, Please*. Today, I turn on my car radio and go from one end of the dial to the other and all I get is 100 strings orchestras, banal housewives and insipid truckers discussing their kinky sex lives with arrogant talk show hosts, country and western drivel and rock music so loud it hurts my ears.

When I was ten, my grandfather died of old age and I was "a troublesome kid," and they sent me off to military school, so I could be "taken in hand."

I came back when I was fourteen. Jeffty was still five.

When I was fourteen years old, I used to go to the movies on Saturday afternoons and a matinee was ten cents and they used real butter on the popcorn and I could always be sure of seeing a western like Lash LaRue, or Wild Bill Elliott as Red Ryder with Bobby Blake as Little Beaver, or Roy Rogers, or Johnny Mack Brown; a scary picture like *House of Horrors* with Rondo Hatton as the Strangler, or *The Cat People*, or *The Mummy*, or *I Married a Witch* with Fredric March and Veronica Lake; plus an episode of a great serial like *The Shadow* with Victor Jory, or *Dick Tracy* or *Flash Gordon;* and three cartoons; a James Fitzpatrick TravelTalk; Movietone News; and a sing-along and, if I stayed on till evening, Bingo or Keeno; and free dishes. Today, I go to movies and see Clint Eastwood blowing people's heads apart like ripe cantaloupes.

At eighteen, I went to college Jeffty was still five. I came back during the summers, to work at my Uncle Joe's jewelry store. Jeffty hadn't changed. Now I knew there was something different about him, something wrong, something weird. Jeffty was still five years old, not a day older.

At twenty-two, I came home for keeps. To open a Sony television franchise in town, the first one. I saw Jeffty from time to time. He was five.

Things are better in a lot of ways. People don't die from some of the old diseases any more. Cars go faster and get you there more quickly on better roads. Shirts are softer and silkier. We have paperback books, even though they cost as much as a good hardcover used to. When I'm running short in the bank, I can live off credit cards till things even out. But I still think we've lost a lot of good stuff. Did you know you can't buy linoleum any more, only vinyl floor covering? There's no such thing as oilcloth any more; you'll never again smell that special, sweet smell from your grandmother's kitchen. Furniture isn't made to last thirty years or longer because they took a survey and found that young homemakers like to throw their furniture out and bring in all new, color-coded borax every seven years. Records don't feel right; they're not thick and solid like the old ones, they're thin and you can bend them . . . that doesn't seem right to me. Restaurants don't serve cream in pitchers any more, just that artificial glop in little plastic tubs, and one is never enough to get coffee the right color. You can make a dent in a car fender with only a sneaker. Everywhere you go, all the towns look the same with Burger Kings and McDonald's and 7-Elevens and Taco Bells and motels and shopping centers. Things may be better, but why do I keep thinking about the past?

What I mean by five years old is not that Jeffty was retarded. I don't think that's what it was. Smart as a whip for five years old; very bright, quick, cute, a funny kid.

But he was three feet tall, small for his age, and perfectly formed: no big head, no strange jaw, none of that. A nice, normal-looking five-year-old kid. Except that he was the same age as I was: twenty-two.

When he spoke, it was with the squeaking, soprano voice of a five-year-old; when he walked, it was with the little hops and shuffles of a five-year-old; when he talked to you, it was about the concerns of a five-year-old ... comic books, playing soldier, using a clothes pin to attach a stiff piece of cardboard to the front fork of his bike so the sound it made when the spokes hit was like a motorboat, asking questions like *why does that thing do that like that,* how high is up, how old is old, why is grass green, what's an elephant look like? At twenty-two, he was five.

Jeffty's parents were a sad pair. Because I was still a friend of Jeffty's, still let him hang around with me in the store, sometimes took him to the county fair or to the miniature golf or the movies, I wound up spending time with *them.* Not that I much cared for them, because they were so awfully depressing. But then, I suppose one couldn't expect much more from the poor devils. They had an alien thing in their home, a child who had grown no older than five in twenty-two years, who provided the treasure of that special childlike state indefinitely, but who also denied them the joys of watching the child grow into a normal adult.

Five is a wonderful time of life for a little kid ... or it *can* be, if the child is relatively free of the monstrous beastliness other children indulge in. It is a time when the eyes are wide open and the patterns are not yet set; a time when one has not yet been hammered into accepting everything as immutable and hopeless; a time when the hands cannot do enough, the mind cannot learn enough, the world is infinite and colorful and filled with mysteries. Five is a special time before they take the questing, unquenchable, quixotic soul of the young dreamer and thrust it into dreary schoolroom boxes. A time before they take the trembling hands that want to hold everything, touch everything, figure everything out, and make them lie still on desktops. A time before people begin saying "act your age" and "grow up" or "you're behaving like a baby." It is a time when a child who acts adolescent is still cute and responsive and everyone's pet. A time of delight, of wonder, of innocence.

Jeffty had been stuck in that time, just five, just so.

But for his parents it was an ongoing nightmare from which no one—not social workers, not priests, not child psychologists, not teachers, not friends, not medical wizards, not psychiatrists, no one—could slap or shake them awake. For seventeen years their sorrow had grown through stages of parental dotage to concern, from concern to worry, from worry to fear, from fear to confusion, from confusion to anger, from anger to dislike, from dislike to naked hatred, and finally, from deepest loathing and revulsion to a stolid, depressive acceptance.

John Kinzer was a shift foreman at the Balder Tool & Die plant. He was a thirty-year man. To everyone but the man living it, his was a spectacularly uneventful life. In no way was he remarkable ... save that he had fathered a twenty-two-year-old five-year-old.

John Kinzer was a small man; soft, with no sharp angles; with pale eyes that never seemed to hold mine for longer than a few seconds. He continually shifted in his chair during conversations, and seemed to see things in the upper corners of the room, things no one else could see ... or wanted to see. I suppose the word that best suited him was *haunted.* What his life had become ... well, *haunted* suited him.

Leona Kinzer tried valiantly to compensate. No matter what hour of the day I visited, she always tried to foist food on me. And when Jeffty was in the house she was always at *him* about eating: "Honey, would you like an orange? A nice orange? Or a tangerine? I have tangerines. I could peel a tangerine for you." But there was clearly such fear in her, fear of her own child, that the offers of sustenance always had a faintly ominous tone.

Leona Kinzer had been a tall woman, but the years had bent her. She seemed always to be seeking some area of wallpapered wall or storage niche into which she could fade, adopt some chintz or rose-patterned protective coloration and hide forever in plain sight of the child's big brown eyes, pass her a hundred times a day and never realize she was there, holding her breath, invisible. She always had an apron tied around her waist, and her hands were red from cleaning. As if by maintaining the environment immaculately she could pay off her imagined sin: having given birth to this strange creature.

Neither of them watched television very much. The house was usually dead silent, not even the sibilant whispering of water in the pipes, the creaking of timbers settling, the humming of the refrigerator. Awfully silent, as if time itself had taken a detour around that house.

As for Jeffty, he was inoffensive. He lived in that atmosphere of gentle dread and dulled loathing and if he understood it, he never remarked in any way. He played, as a child plays, and seemed happy. But he must have sensed, in the way of a five-year-old, just how alien he was in their presence.

Alien. No, that wasn't right. He was *too* human, if anything. But out of phase, out of synch with the world around him, and resonating to a different vibration than his parents, God knows. Nor would other children play with him. As they grew past him, they found him at first childish, then uninteresting, then simply frightening as their perceptions of aging became clear and they could see he was not affected by time as they were. Even the little ones, his own age, who might wander into the neighborhood, quickly came to shy away from him like a dog in the street when a car backfires.

Thus, I remained his only friend. A friend of many years. Five years. Twenty-two years. I liked him; more than I can say. And never knew exactly why. But I did, without reserve.

But because we spent time together, I found I was also—polite society—spending time with John and Leona Kinzer. Dinner, Saturday afternoons sometimes, an hour or so when I'd bring Jeffty back from a movie. They were grateful: slavishly so. It relieved them of the embarrassing chore of going out with him, or having to pretend before the world that they were loving parents with a perfectly normal, happy, attractive child. And their gratitude extended to hosting me. Hideous, every moment of their depression, hideous.

I felt sorry for the poor devils, but I despised them for their inability to love Jeffty, who was eminently lovable.

I never let on, of course, even during the evenings in their company that were awkward beyond belief.

We would sit there in the darkening living room—*always* dark or darkening, as if kept in shadow to hold back what the light might reveal to the world outside through the bright eyes of the house—we would sit and silently stare at one another. They never knew what to say to me.

"So how are things down at the plant?" I'd say to John Kinzer.

He would shrug. Neither conversation nor life suited him with any ease or grace. "Fine, just fine," he would say, finally.

And we would sit in silence again.

"Would you like a nice piece of coffee cake?" Leona would say. "I made it fresh just this morning." Or deep dish green apple pie. Or milk and toll-house cookies. Or a brown betty pudding.

"No, no, thank you, Mrs. Kinzer; Jeffty and I grabbed a couple of cheeseburgers on the way home." And again, silence.

Then, when the stillness and the awkwardness became too much even for them (and who knew how long that total silence reigned when they were alone, with that thing they never talked about any more, hanging between them), Leona Kinzer would say, "I think he's asleep."

John Kinzer would say, "I don't hear the radio playing."

Just so, it would go on like that, until I could politely find excuse to bolt away on some flimsy pretext. Yes, that was the way it would go on, every time, just the same . . . except once.

"I don't know what to do any more," Leona said. She began crying. "There's no change, not one day of peace."

Her husband managed to drag himself out of the old easy chair, and he went to her. He bent and tried to soothe her, but it was clear from the graceless way in which he touched her graying hair that the ability to be compassionate had been stunned in him. "Shhh, Leona, it's all right. Shhh." But she continued crying. Her hands scraped gently at the antimacassars on the arms of the chair.

Then she said, "Sometimes I wish he had been stillborn."

John looked up into the corners of the room. For the nameless shadows that were always watching him? Was it God he was seeking in those spaces? "You don't mean that," he said to her, softly, pathetically, urging her with body tension and trembling in his voice to recant before God took notice of the terrible thought. But she meant it; she meant it very much.

I managed to get away quickly that evening. They didn't want witnesses to their shame. I was glad to go.

And for a week I stayed away. From them, from Jeffty, from their street, even from that end of town.

I had my own life. The store, accounts, suppliers' conferences, poker with friends, pretty women I took to well-lit restaurants, my own parents, putting anti-freeze in the car, complaining to the laundry about too much starch in the collars and cuffs, working out at the gym, taxes, catching Jan or David (whichever one it was) stealing from the cash register. I had my own life.

But not even *that* evening could keep me from Jeffty. He called me at the store and asked me to take him to the rodeo. We chummed it up as best a twenty-two-year-old with other interests *could* . . . with a five-year-old. I never dwelled on what bound us together; I always thought it was simply the years. That, and affection for a kid who could have been the little brother I never had. (Except I *remembered* when we had played together, when we had both been the same age; I *remembered* that period, and Jeffty was still the same.)

And then, one Saturday afternoon, I came to take him to a double feature, and things I should have noticed so many times before, I first began to notice only that afternoon.

I came walking up to the Kinzer house, expecting Jeffty to be sitting on the front porch steps, or in the porch glider, waiting for me. But he was nowhere in sight.

Going inside, into that darkness and silence, in the midst of May sunshine, was unthinkable. I stood on the front walk for a few moments, then cupped my hands around my mouth and yelled, "Jeffty? Hey, Jeffty, come on out, let's go. We'll be late."

His voice came faintly, as if from under the ground.

"Here I am, Donny."

I could hear him, but I couldn't see him. It was Jeffty, no question about it: as Donald H. Horton, President and Sole Owner of The Horton TV & Sound Center, no one but Jeffty called me Donny. He had never called me anything else.

(Actually, it isn't a lie. I *am*, as far as the public is concerned, Sole Owner of the Center. The partnership with my Aunt Patricia is only to repay the loan she made me, to supplement the money I came into when I was twenty-one, left to me when I was ten by my grandfather. It wasn't a very big loan, only eighteen thousand, but I asked her to be a silent partner, because of when she had taken care of me as a child.)

"Where are you, Jeffty?"

"Under the porch in my secret place."

I walked around the side of the porch, and stooped down and pulled away the wicker grating. Back in there, on the pressed dirt, Jeffty had built himself a secret place. He had comics in orange crates, he had a little table and some pillows, it was lit by big fat candles, and we used to hide there when we were both . . . five.

"What'cha up to?" I asked, crawling in and pulling the grate closed behind me. It was cool under the porch, and the dirt smelled comfortable, the candles smelled clubby and familiar. Any kid would feel at home in such a secret place: there's never been a kid who didn't spend the happiest, most productive, most deliciously mysterious times of his life in such a secret place.

"Playin'," he said. He was holding something golden and round. It filled the palm of his little hand.

"You forget we were going to the movies?"

"Nope. I was just waitin' for you here."

"Your mom and dad home?"

"Momma."

I understood why he was waiting under the porch. I didn't push it any further. "What've you got there?"

"Captain Midnight Secret Decoder Badge," he said, showing it to me on his flattened palm.

I realized I was looking at it without comprehending what it was for a long time. Then it dawned on me what a miracle Jeffty had in his hand. A miracle that simply could *not* exist.

"Jeffty," I said softly, with wonder in my voice, "where'd you get that?"

"Came in the mail today. I sent away for it."

"It must have cost a lot of money."

"Not so much. Ten cents an' two inner wax seals from two jars of Ovaltine."

"May I see it?" My voice was trembling, and so was the hand I extended. He gave it to me and I held the miracle in the palm of my hand. It was *wonderful*.

You remember. *Captain Midnight* went on the radio nationwide in 1940. It was sponsored by Ovaltine. And every year they issued a Secret Squadron Decoder Badge. And every day at the end of the program, they would give you a clue to the next days installment in a code that only kids with the official badge could decipher. They stopped making those wonderful Decoder Badges in 1949. I remember the one I had in 1945: it was beautiful. It had a magnifying glass in the center of the code dial. *Captain Midnight* went off the air in 1950, and though I understand it was a short-lived television series in the mid-Fifties, and though they issued Decoder Badges in 1955 and 1956, as far as the *real* badges were concerned, they never made one after 1949.

The Captain Midnight Code-O-Graph I held in my hand, the one Jeffty said he had gotten in the mail for ten cents (*ten cents!!!*) and two Ovaltine labels, was brand new, shiny gold metal, not a dent or a spot of rust on it like the old ones you can find at exorbitant prices in collectible shoppes from time to time . . . it was a *new* Decoder. And the date on it was *this* year.

But *Captain Midnight* no longer existed. Nothing like it existed on the radio. I'd listened to the one or two weak imitations of old-time radio the networks were currently airing, and the stories were dull, the sound effects bland, the whole feel of it wrong, out of date, cornball. Yet I held a *new* Code-O-Graph.

"Jeffty, tell me about this," I said.

"Tell you what, Donny? It's my new Capt'n Midnight Secret Decoder Badge. I use it to figger out what's gonna happen tomorrow."

"Tomorrow how?"

"On the program."

"*What* program?

He stared at me as if I was being purposely stupid. "On Capt'n *Midnight! Boy!*" I was being dumb.

I still couldn't get it straight. It was right there, right out in the open, and I still didn't know what was happening. "You mean one of those records they made of the old-time radio programs? Is that what you mean, Jeffty?"

"What records?" he asked. He didn't know what *I* meant.

We stared at each other there under the porch. And then I said, very slowly, almost afraid of the answer, "Jeffty, how do you hear *Captain Midnight?*"

"Every day. On the radio. On my radio. Every day at five-thirty."

News. Music, dumb music, and news. That's what was on the radio every day at 5:30. Not *Captain Midnight*. The Secret Squadron hadn't been on the air in twenty years.

"Can we hear it tonight?" I asked.

"Boy!" he said. I was being dumb. I knew it from the way he said it; but I didn't know *why*. Then it dawned on me: this was Saturday. *Captain Midnight* was on Monday through Friday. Not on Saturday or Sunday.

"We goin' to the movies?"

He had to repeat himself twice. My mind was somewhere else. Nothing definite. No conclusions. No wild assumptions leapt to. Just off somewhere trying to figure it out, and concluding—as *you* would have concluded, as *any*one would have concluded rather than accepting the truth, the impossible and wonderful truth—just finally concluding there was a simple explanation I didn't yet perceive. Something mundane and dull, like the passage of time that steals all good, old things from us, packratting trinkets and plastic in exchange. And all in the name of Progress.

"We goin' to the movies, Donny?"

"You bet your boots we are, kiddo," I said. And I smiled. And I handed him the Code-O-Graph. And he put it in his side pants pocket. And we crawled out from under the porch. And we went to the movies. And neither of us said anything about *Captain Midnight* all the rest of that day. And there wasn't a ten-minute stretch, all the rest of that day, that I didn't think about it.

It was Inventory all that next week. I didn't see Jeffty till late Thursday. I confess I left the store in the hands of Jan and David, told them I had some errands to run, and left early. At 4:00. I got to the Kinzers' right around 4:45. Leona answered the door, looking exhausted and distant. "Is Jeffty around?" She said he was upstairs in his room . . .

. . . listening to the radio.

I climbed the stairs two at a time.

All right, I had finally made that impossible, illogical leap. Had the stretch of belief involved anyone but Jeffty, adult or child. I would have reasoned out more explicable answers. But it *was* Jeffty, clearly another kind of vessel of life, and what he might experience should not be expected to fit into the ordered scheme.

I admit it: I *wanted* to hear what I heard.

Even with the door closed. I recognized the program:

"*There he goes, Tennessee, Get him!*"

There was the heavy report of a rifle shot and the keening whine of the slug ricochering, and then the same voice yelled triumphantly, "*Got him! D-e-a-a-a-d center!*"

He was listening to the American Broadcasting Company, 790 kilocycles, and he was hearing *Tennessee Jed*, one of my most favorite programs from the Forties, a western adventure I had not heard in twenty years, because it had not existed for twenty years.

I sat down on the top step of the stairs, there in the upstairs hall of the Kinzer home, and I listened to the show. It wasn't a rerun of an old program, because there were occasional references in the body of the drama to current cultural and technological developments, and phrases that had not existed in common usage in the Forties aerosol spray cans, laserasing of tattoos, Tanzania, the word "uptight."

I could not ignore the fact. Jeffty was listening to a *new* segment of *Tennessee Jed*.

I ran downstairs and out the front door to my car. Leona must have been in the kitchen. I turned the key and punched on the radio and spun the dial to 790 kilocycles. The ABC station. Rock music.

I sat there for a few moments, then ran the dial slowly from one end to the other. Music, news, talk shows. No *Tennessee Jed*. And it was a Blaupunkt, the best radio I could get. I wasn't missing some perimeter station. It simply was not there!

After a few moments I turned off the radio and the ignition and went back upstairs quietly. I sat down on the top step and listened to the entire program. It was *wonderful*.

Exciting, imaginative, filled with everything I remembered as being most innovative about radio drama. But it was modern. It wasn't an antique, re-broadcast to assuage the need of that dwindling listenership who longed for the old days. It was a new show, with all the old voices, but still young and bright. Even the commercials were for currently available products, but they weren't as loud or as insulting as the screamer ads one heard on radio these days.

And when *Tennessee Jed* went off at 5:00, I heard Jeffty spin the dial on his radio till I heard the familiar voice of the announcer Glenn Riggs proclaim, "*Presenting Hop Harrigan! America's ace of the airwaves!*" There was the sound of an airplane in flight. It was a prop plane, *not* a jet! Not the sound kids today have grown up with, but the sound *I* grew up with, the *real* sound of an airplane, the growling, revving, throaty sound of the kind of airplanes G-8 and His Battle Aces flew, the kind Captain Midnight flew, the kind Hop Harrigan flew. And then I heard Hop say, "*CX-4 calling control tower. CX-4 calling control tower. Standing by!*" A pause, then, "*Okay, this is Hop Harrigan . . . coming in!*"

And Jeffty, who had the same problem all of us kids had had in the Forties with programming that pitted equal favorites against one another on different stations, having paid his respects to Hop Harrigan and Tank Tinker, spun the dial and went back to ABC, where I heard the stroke of a gong, the wild cacophony of nonsense Chinese chatter, and the announcer yelled, "*T-e-e-e-rry and the Pirates!*"

I sat there on the top step and listened to Terry and Connie and Flip Corkin and, so help me God, Agnes Moorehead as The Dragon Lady, all of them in a new adventure that took place in a Red China that had not existed in the days of Milton Caniff's 1937 version of the Orient, with river pirates and Chiang Kai-shek and warlords and the naive Imperialism of American gunboat diplomacy.

Sat, and listened to the whole show, and sat even longer to hear *Superman* and part of *Jack Armstrong, The All American Boy* and part of *Captain Midnight*, and John Kinzer came home and neither he nor Leona came upstairs to find out what had happened to me, or where Jeffty was, and sat longer, and found I had started crying, and could not stop, just sat there with tears running down my face, into the corners of my mouth, sitting and crying until Jeffty heard me and opened his door and saw me and came out and looked at me in childish confusion as I heard the station break for the Mutual Network and they began the theme music of *Tom Mix*, "When It's Round-up Time in Texas and the Bloom Is on the Sage," and Jeffty touched my shoulder and smiled at me, with his mouth and his big brown eyes, and said, "Hi, Donny. Wanna come in an listen to the radio with me?"

Hume denied the existence of an absolute space, in which each thing has its place; Borges denies the existence of one single time, in which all events are linked.

Jeffty received radio programs from a place that could not, in logic, in the natural scheme of the space-time universe as conceived by Einstein, exist. But that wasn't all he received. He got mail order premiums that no one was manufacturing. He read comic books that had been defunct for three decades. He saw movies with actors who had been dead for twenty years. He was the receiving terminal for endless joys and pleasures of the past that the world had dropped along the way. On its headlong suicidal flight toward New Tomorrows, the world had razed its treasurehouse of simple happinesses, had poured concrete over its playgrounds, had abandoned its elfin stragglers, and all of it was being impossibly, miraculously shunted back into the present through Jeffty. Revivified, updated, the traditions maintained but contemporaneous. Jeffty was the unbidding Aladdin whose very nature formed the magic lampness of his reality.

And he took me into his world with him.

Because he trusted me.

We had breakfast of Quaker Puffed Wheat Sparkies and warm Ovaltine we drank out of *this* year's Little Orphan Annie Shake-Up Mugs. We went to the movies and while everyone else was seeing a comedy starring Goldie Hawn and Ryan O'Neal, Jeffty and I were enjoying Humphrey Bogart as the professional thief Parker in John Huston's brilliant adaptation of the Donald Westlake novel *Slayground*. The second feature was Spencer Tracy, Carole Lombard and Laird Cregar in the Val Lewton–produced film of *Leiningen Versus the Ants*.

Twice a month we went down to the newsstand and bought the current pulp issues of *The Shadow, Doc Savage* and *Startling Stories*. Jeffty and I sat together and I read to him from the magazines. He particularly liked the new short novel by Henry Kuttner. "The Dreams of Achilles," and the new Stanley G. Weinbaum series of short stories set in the subatomic particle universe of Redurna. In September we enjoyed the first installment of the new Robert E. Howard Conan novel, *Isle of the Black Ones*, in *Weird Tales*; and in August we were only mildly disappointed by Edgar Rice Burroughs's fourth novella in the Jupiter series featuring John Carter of Batsoom—"Corsairs of Jupiter." But the editor of *Argosy All-Story Weekly* promised there would be two more stories in the series, and it was such an unexpected revelation for Jeffty and me that it dimmed our disappointment at the lessened quality of the current story.

We read comics together, and Jeffty and I both decided—separately, before we came together to discuss it—that our favorite characters were Doll Man, Airboy and The Heap. We also adored the George Carlson strips in *Jingle Jangle Comics*, particularly the Pie-Face Prince of Old Pretzleburg stories, which we read together and laughed over, even though I had to explain some of the esoteric puns to Jeffty who was too young to have that kind of subtle wit.

How to explain it? I can't. I had enough physics in college to make some offhand guesses, but I'm more likely wrong than right. The laws of the conservation of energy occasionally break. These are laws that physicists call "weakly violated." Perhaps Jeffty was a catalyst for the weak violation of conservation laws we're only now beginning to realize exist. I tried doing some reading in the area—muon decay of the "forbidden" kind: gamma decay that doesn't include the muon neutrino among its products—but nothing I encountered, not even the latest readings from the Swiss Institute for Nuclear Research near Zurich, gave me an insight. I was thrown back on a vague acceptance of the philosophy that the real name for "science" is *magic*.

No explanations, but enormous good times.

The happiest time of my life.

I had the "real" world, the world of my store and my friends and my family, the world of profit&loss, of taxes and evenings with young women who talked about going shopping or the United Nations, or the rising cost of coffee and microwave ovens. And I had Jeffty's world, in which I existed only when I was with him. The things of the past he knew as fresh and new, I could experience only when in his company. And the membrane between the two worlds grew ever thinner, more luminous and transparent. I had the best of both worlds. And knew, somehow, that I could carry nothing from one to the other.

Forgetting that, for just a moment, betraying Jeffty by forgetting, brought an end to it all.

Enjoying myself so much, I grew careless and failed to consider how fragile the relationship between Jeffty's world and my world really was. There is a reason why the present begrudges the existence of the past. I never really understood. Nowhere in the beast books, where survival is shown in battles between claw and fang, tentacle and poison sac, is there recognition of the ferocity the present always brings to bear on the past. Nowhere is there a detailed statement of how the present lies in wait for What-Was, waiting for it to become Now-This-Moment so it can shred it with its merciless jaws.

Who could know such a thing . . . at any age . . . and certainly not at my age . . . who could understand such a thing?

I'm trying to exculpate myself. I can't. It was my fault.

It was another Saturday afternoon.

"What's playing today?" I asked him, in the car, on the way downtown.

He looked up at me from the other side of the front seat and smiled one of his best smiles. 'Ken Maynard in *Bullwhip Justice* an' *The Demolished Man*." He kept smiling, as if he'd really put one over on me. I looked at him with disbelief.

"You're *kidding*!" I said, delighted. "Bester's *The Demolished Man*?" He nodded his head, delighted at my being delighted. He knew it was one of my favorite books. "Oh, that's super!"

"Super *duper*," he said.

"Who's in it?"

"Franchot Tone, Evelyn Keyes, Lionel Barrymore and Elisha Cook, Jr." He was much more knowledgeable about movie actors than I'd ever been. He could name the character actors in any movie he'd ever seen. Even the crowd scenes.

"And cartoons?" I asked.

"Three of 'em: a *Little Lulu*, a *Donald Duck* and a *Bugs Bunny*. An' a *Pete Smith Specialty* an', a Lew Lehr *Monkeys is da C-r-r-r-aziest Peoples*."

"Oh boy!" I said. I was grinning from ear to ear. And then I looked down and saw the pad of purchase order forms on the seat. I'd forgotten to drop it off at the store.

"Gotta stop by the Center," I said. "Gotta drop off something. It'll only take a minute."

"Okay," Jeffty said. "But we won't be late, will we?"

"Not on your tintype, kiddo," I said.

When I pulled into the parking lot behind the Center, he decided to come in with me and we'd walk over to the theater. It's not a large town. There are only two movie houses, the Utopia and the Lyric. We were going to the Utopia and it was only three blocks from the Center.

I walked into the store with the pad of forms, and it was bedlam. David and Jan were handling two customers each, and there were people standing around waiting to be helped. Jan turned a look on me and her face was a horror-mask of pleading. David was running from the stockroom to the showroom and all he could murmur as he whipped past was "Help!" and then he was gone.

"Jeffty," I said, crouching down, "listen, give me a few minutes. Jan and David are in trouble with all these people. We won't be late, I promise. Just let me get rid of a couple of these customers." He looked nervous, but nodded okay.

I motioned to a chair and said, "Just sit down for a while and I'll be right with you."

He went to the chair, good as you please, though he knew what was happening, and he sat down.

I started taking care of people who wanted color television sets. This was the first really substantial batch of units we'd gotten in—color television was only now becoming reasonably priced and this was Sony's first promotion—and it was bonanza time for me. I could see paying off the loan and being out in front for the first time with the Center. It was business.

In my world, good business comes first.

Jeffty sat there and stared at the wall. Let me tell you about the wall.

Stanchion and bracket designs had been rigged from floor to within two feet of the ceiling. Television sets had been stacked artfully on the wall. Thirty-three television sets. All playing at the same time. Black and white, color, little ones, big ones, all going at the same time.

Jeffty sat and watched thirty-three television sets, on a Saturday afternoon. We can pick up a total of thirteen channels including the UHF educational stations. Golf was on one channel; baseball was on a second; celebrity bowling was on a third; the fourth channel was a religious seminar; a teenage dance show was on the fifth; the sixth was a rerun of a situation comedy; the seventh was a rerun of a police show; eighth was a nature program showing a man fly-casting endlessly; ninth was news and conversation; tenth was a stock car race; eleventh was a man doing logarithms on a blackboard; twelfth was a woman in a leotard doing setting-up exercises; and on the thirteenth channel was a badly animated cartoon show in Spanish. All but six of the shows were repeated on three sets. Jeffty sat and watched that wall of television on a Saturday afternoon while I sold as fast and as hard as I could, to pay back my Aunt Patricia and stay in touch with my world. It was business.

I should have known better. I should have understood about the present and the way it kills the past. But I was selling with both hands. And when I finally glanced over at Jeffty, half an hour later, he looked like another child.

He was sweating. That terrible fever sweat when you have stomach flu. He was pale, as pasty and pale as a worm, and his little hands were gripping the arms of the chair so tightly I could see his knuckles in bold relief. I dashed over to him, excusing myself from the middle-aged couple looking at the new 21″ Mediterranean model.

"Jeffty!"

He looked at me, but his eyes didn't track. He was in absolute terror. I pulled him out of the chair and started toward the front door with him, but the customers I'd deserted yelled at me, "Hey!" The middle-aged man said, "You wanna sell me this thing or don't you?"

I looked from him to Jeffty and back again. Jeffty was like a zombie. He had come where I'd pulled him. His legs were rubbery and his feet dragged. The past, being eaten by the present, the sound of something in pain.

I clawed some money out of my pants pocket and jammed it into Jeffty's hand. "Kiddo . . . listen to me . . . get out of here right now!" He still couldn't focus properly. "*Jeffty*," I said as tightly as I could, "*listen* to me!" The middle-aged customer and his wife were walking toward us. "Listen, kiddo, get out of here right this minute. Walk over to the Utopia and buy the tickets. I'll be right behind you." The middle-aged man and his wife were almost on us. I shoved Jeffty through the door and watched him stumble away in the wrong direction, then stop as if gathering his wits, turn and go back past the front of the Center and in the direction of the Utopia. "Yes sir," I said, straightening up and facing them, "yes, ma'am, that is one terrific set with some sensational features! If you'll just step back here with me . . ."

There was a terrible sound of something hurting, but I couldn't tell from which channel; or from which set, it was coming.

Most of it I learned later, from the girl in the ticket booth, and from some people I knew who came to me to tell me what had happened. By the time I got to the Utopia, nearly twenty minutes later, Jeffty was already beaten to a pulp and had been taken to the Manager's office.

"Did you see a very little boy, about five years old, with big brown eyes and straight brown hair . . . he was waiting for me?"

"Oh, I think that's the little boy those kids beat up?"

"What!?! *Where is he?*"

"They took him to the Manager's office. No one knew who he was or where to find his parents—"

A young girl wearing an usher's uniform was kneeling down beside the couch, placing a wet paper towel on his face.

I took the towel away from her and ordered her out of the office.

She looked insulted and snorted something rude, but she left. I sat on the edge of the couch and tried to swab away the blood from the lacerations without opening the wounds where the blood had caked. Both his eyes were swollen shut. His mouth was ripped badly. His hair was matted with dried blood.

He had been standing in line behind two kids in their teens. They started selling tickets at 12:30 and the show started at 1:00. The doors weren't opened till 12:45. He had been waiting, and the kids in front of him had had a portable radio. They were listening to the ball game. Jeffty had wanted to hear some program, God knows what it might have been, *Grand Central Station, Let's Pretend, Land of the Lost,* God only knows which one it might have been.

He had asked if he could borrow their radio to hear the program for a minute, and it had been a commercial break or something, and the kids had given him the radio, probably out of some malicious kind of courtesy that would permit them to take offense and rag the little boy. He had changed the station . . . and they'd been unable to get it to go back to the ball game. It was locked into the past, on a station that was broadcasting a program that didn't exist for anyone but Jeffty.

They had beaten him badly . . . as everyone watched.

And then they had run away.

I had left him alone, left him to fight off the present without sufficient weaponry. I had betrayed him for the sale of a 21" Mediterranean console television, and now his face was pulped meat. He moaned something inaudible and sobbed softly.

"Shhh, it's okay, kiddo, it's Donny. I'm here, I'll get you home, it'll be okay."

I should have taken him straight to the hospital. I don't know why I didn't. I should have. I should have done that.

When I carried him through the door, John and Leona Kinzer just stared at me. They didn't move to take him from my arms. One of his hands was hanging down. He was conscious, but just barely. They stared, there in the semi-darkness of a Saturday afternoon in the present. I looked at them. "A couple of kids beat him up at the theater." I raised him a few inches in my arms and extended him. They stared at me, at both of us, with nothing in their eyes, without movement. "Jesus Christ," I shouted, "he's been beaten! He's your son! Don't you even want to touch him? What the hell kind of people are you?!"

Then Leona moved toward me very slowly. She stood in front of us for a few seconds, and there was a leaden stoicism in her face that was terrible to see. It said, *I have been in this place before, many times, and I cannot bear to be in it again; but I am here now.*

So I gave him to her. God help me. I gave him over to her.

And she took him upstairs to bathe away his blood and his pain.

John Kinzer and I stood in our separate places in the dim living room of their home, and we stared at each other. He had nothing to say to me.

I shoved past him and fell into a chair. I was shaking.

I heard the bath water running upstairs.

After what seemed a very long time Leona came downstairs, wiping her hands on her apron. She sat down on the sofa and after a moment John sat down beside her. I heard the sound of rock music from upstairs.

"Would you like a piece of nice pound cake?" Leona said.

I didn't answer. I was listening to the sound of the music. Rock music. On the radio. There was a table lamp on the end table beside the sofa. It cast a dim and futile light in the shadowed living room. *Rock music from the present, on a radio upstairs?* I started to say something, and then I *knew* . . . Oh, God . . . *no!*

I jumped up just as the sound of hideous crackling blotted out the music, and the table lamp dimmed and dimmed and flickered. I screamed something. I don't know what it was, and ran for the stairs.

Jeffty's parents did not move. They sat there with their hands folded, in that place they had been for so many years.

I fell twice rushing up the stairs.

There isn't much on television that can hold my interest. I bought an old cathedral-shaped Philco radio in a second-hand store, and I replaced all the burnt-out parts with the original tubes from old radios I could cannibalize that still worked. I don't use transistors or printed circuits. They wouldn't work. I've sat in front of that set for hours sometimes, running the dial back and forth as slowly as you can imagine, so slowly it doesn't look as if it's moving at all sometimes.

But I can't find *Captain Midnight* or *The Land of the Lost* or *The Shadow* or *Quiet, Please.*

So she did love him, still, a little bit, even after all those years. I can't hate them: they only wanted to live in the present world again. That isn't such a terrible thing.

It's a good world, all things considered. It's much better than it used to be, in a lot of ways. People don't die from the old diseases any more. They die from new ones, but that's Progress, isn't it?

Isn't it?

Tell me.

Somebody please tell me.

THE YELLOW WALLPAPER (1892)

Charlotte Perkins Gilman
b. 1860 Hartford, CT
d. 1935 Pasadena, CA

It is very seldom that mere ordinary people like John and myself secure ancestral halls for the summer.

A colonial mansion, a hereditary estate, I would say a haunted house and reach the height of romantic felicity—but that would be asking too much of fate!

Still I will proudly declare that there is something queer about it.

Else, why should it be let so cheaply? And why have stood so long untenanted?

John laughs at me, of course, but one expects that.

John is practical in the extreme. He has no patience with faith, an intense horror of superstition, and he scoffs openly at any talk of things not to be felt and seen and put down in figures.

John is a physician, and *perhaps*—(I would not say it to a living soul, of course, but this is dead paper and a great relief to my mind)—*perhaps* that is one reason I do not get well faster.

You see, he does not believe I am sick! And what can one do?

If a physician of high standing, and one's own husband, assures friends and relatives that there is really nothing the matter with one but temporary nervous depression—a slight hysterical tendency—what is one to do?

My brother is also a physician, and also of high standing, and he says the same thing.

So I take phosphates or phosphites—whichever it is—and tonics, and air and exercise, and journeys, and am absolutely forbidden to "work" until I am well again.

Personally, I disagree with their ideas.

Personally, I believe that congenial work, with excitement and change, would do me good.

But what is one to do?

I did write for a while in spite of them; but it *does* exhaust me a good deal—having to be so sly about it, or else meet with heavy opposition.

I sometimes fancy that in my condition, if I had less opposition and more society and stimulus—but John says the very worst thing I can do is to think about my condition, and I confess it always makes me feel bad.

So I will let it alone and talk about the house.

The most beautiful place! It is quite alone, standing well back from the road, quite three miles from the village. It makes me think of English places that you read about, for there are hedges and walls and gates that lock, and lots of separate little houses for the gardeners and people.

There is a *delicious* garden! I never saw such a garden—large and shady, full of box-bordered paths, and lined with long grape-covered arbors with seats under them.

There were greenhouses, but they are all broken now.

There was some legal trouble, I believe, something about the heirs and co-heirs; anyhow, the place has been empty for years.

That spoils my ghostliness, I am afraid, but I don't care—there is something strange about the house—I can feel it.

I even said so to John one moonlight evening, but he said what I felt was a draught, and shut the window.

I get unreasonably angry with John sometimes. I'm sure I never used to be so sensitive. I think it is due to this nervous condition.

But John says if I feel so I shall neglect proper self-control; so I take pains to control myself—before him, at least, and that makes me very tired.

I don't like our room a bit. I wanted one downstairs that opened onto the piazza and had roses all over the window, and such pretty old-fashioned chintz hangings! But John would not hear of it.

He said there was only one window and not room for two beds, and no near room for him if he took another.

He is very careful and loving, and hardly lets me stir without special direction.

I have a schedule prescription for each hour in the day; he takes all care from me, and so I feel basely ungrateful not to value it more.

He said he came here solely on my account, that I was to have perfect rest and all the air I could get. "Your exercise depends on your strength, my dear," said he, "and your food somewhat on your appetite; but air you can absorb all the time." So we took the nursery at the top of the house.

It is a big, airy room, the whole floor nearly, with windows that look all ways, and air and sunshine galore. It was nursery first, and then playroom and gymnasium, I should judge, for the windows are barred for little children, and there are rings and things in the walls.

The paint and paper look as if a boys' school had used it. It is stripped off—the paper—in great patches all around the head of my bed, about as far as I can reach, and in a great place on the other side of the room low down. I never saw a worse paper in my life. One of those sprawling, flamboyant patterns committing every artistic sin.

It is dull enough to confuse the eye in following, pronounced enough constantly to irritate and provoke study, and when you follow the lame uncertain curves for a little distance they suddenly commit suicide—plunge off at outrageous angles, destroy themselves in unheard-of contradictions.

The color is repellent, almost revolting: a smouldering unclean yellow, strangely faded by the slow-turning sunlight. It is a dull yet lurid orange in some places, a sickly sulphur tint in others.

No wonder the children hated it! I should hate it myself if I had to live in this room long.

There comes John, and I must put this away—he hates to have me write a word.

We have been here two weeks, and I haven't felt like writing before, since that first day.

I am sitting by the window now, up in this atrocious nursery, and there is nothing to hinder my writing as much as I please, save lack of strength.

John is away all day, and even some nights when his cases are serious.

I am glad my case is not serious!

But these nervous troubles are dreadfully depressing.

John does not know how much I really suffer. He knows there is no reason to suffer, and that satisfies him.

Of course it is only nervousness. It does weigh on me so not to do my duty in any way!

I meant to be such a help to John, such a real rest and comfort, and here I am a comparative burden already!

Nobody would believe what an effort it is to do what little I am able—to dress and entertain, and order things.

It is fortunate Mary is so good with the baby. Such a dear baby!

And yet I *cannot* be with him, it makes me so nervous.

I suppose John never was nervous in his life. He laughs at me so about this wallpaper!

At first he meant to repaper the room, but afterward he said that I was letting it get the better of me, and that nothing was worse for a nervous patient than to give way to such fancies.

He said that after the wallpaper was changed it would be the heavy bed-stead, and then the barred windows, and then that gate at the head of the stairs, and so on.

"You know the place is doing you good," he said, "and really, dear, I don't care to renovate the house just for a three months' rental."

"Then do let us go downstairs," I said. "There are such pretty rooms there."

Then he took me in his arms and called me a blessed little goose, and said he would go down cellar, if I wished, and have it whitewashed into the bargain.

But he is right enough about the beds and windows and things.

It is as airy and comfortable a room as anyone need wish, and, of course, I would not be so silly as to make him uncomfortable just for a whim.

I'm really getting quite fond of the big room, all but that horrid paper.

Out of one window I can see the garden—those mysterious deep-shaded arbors, the riotous old-fashioned flowers, and bushes and gnarly trees.

Out of another I get a lovely view of the bay and a little private wharf belonging to the estate. There is a beautiful shaded lane that runs down there from the house. I always fancy I see people walking in these numerous paths and arbors, but John has cautioned me not to give way to fancy in the least. He says that with my imaginative power and habit of story-making, a nervous weakness like mine is sure to lead to all manner of excited fancies, and that I ought to use my will and good sense to check the tendency. So I try.

I think sometimes that if I were only well enough to write a little it would relieve the press of ideas and rest me.

But I find I get pretty tired when I try.

It is so discouraging not to have any advice and companionship about my work. When I get really well, John says we will ask Cousin Henry and Julia down for a long visit; but he says he would as soon put fireworks in my pillow-case as to let me have those stimulating people about now.

I wish I could get well faster.

But I must not think about that. This paper looks to me as if it *knew* what a vicious influence it had!

There is a recurrent spot where the pattern lolls like a broken neck and two bulbous eyes stare at you upside down.

I get positively angry with the impertinence of it and the everlastingness. Up and down and sideways they crawl, and those absurd unblinking eyes are everywhere. There is one place where two breadths didn't match, and the eyes go all up and down the line, one a little higher than the other.

I never saw so much expression in an inanimate thing before, and we all know how much expression they have! I used to lie awake as a child and get more entertainment and terror out of blank walls and plain furniture than most children could find in a toy-store.

I remember what a kindly wink the knobs of our big old bureau used to have, and there was one chair that always seemed like a strong friend.

I used to feel that if any of the other things looked too fierce I could always hop into that chair and be safe.

The furniture in this room is no worse than inharmonious, however, for we had to bring it all from downstairs. I suppose when this was used as a playroom they had to take the nursery things out, and no wonder! I never saw such ravages as the children have made here.

The wallpaper, as I said before, is torn off in spots, and it sticketh closer than a brother[3]—they must have had perseverance as well as hatred.

Then the floor is scratched and gouged and splintered, the plaster itself is dug out here and there, and this great heavy bed, which is all we found in the room, looks as if it had been through the wars.

But I don't mind it a bit—only the paper.

There comes John's sister. Such a dear girl as she is, and so careful of me! I must not let her find me writing.

She is a perfect and enthusiastic housekeeper, and hopes for no better profession. I verily believe she thinks it is the writing which made me sick!

But I can write when she is out, and see her a long way off from these windows.

There is one that commands the road, a lovely shaded winding road, and one that just looks off over the country. A lovely country, too, full of great elms and velvet meadows.

---

3. Proverbs 18.24.

This wallpaper has a kind of sub-pattern in a different shade, a particularly irritating one, for you can only see it in certain lights, and not clearly then.

But in the places where it isn't faded and where the sun is just so—I can see a strange, provoking, formless sort of figure that seems to skulk about behind that silly and conspicuous front design.

There's sister on the stairs!

Well, the Fourth of July is over! The people are all gone, and I am tired out. John thought it might do me good to see a little company, so we just had Mother and Nellie and the children down for a week.

Of course I didn't do a thing. Jennie sees to everything now.

But it tired me all the same.

John says if I don't pick up faster he shall send me to Weir Mitchell[4] in the fall.

But I don't want to go there at all. I had a friend who was in his hands once, and she says he is just like John and my brother, only more so!

Besides, it is such an undertaking to go so far.

I don't feel as if it was worthwhile to turn my hand over for anything, and I'm getting dreadfully fretful and querulous.

I cry at nothing, and cry most of the time.

Of course I don't when John is here, or anybody else, but when I am alone.

And I am alone a good deal just now. John is kept in town very often by serious cases, and Jennie is good and lets me alone when I want her to.

So I walk a little in the garden or down that lovely lane, sit on the porch under the roses, and lie down up here a good deal.

I'm getting really fond of the room in spite of the wallpaper. Perhaps *because* of the wallpaper.

It dwells in my mind so!

I lie here on this great immovable bed—it is nailed down, I believe—and follow that pattern about by the hour. It is as good as gymnastics, I assure you. I start, we'll say, at the bottom, down in the corner over there where it has not been touched, and I determine for the thousandth time that I *will* follow that pointless pattern to some sort of a conclusion.

I know a little of the principle of design, and I know this thing was not arranged on any laws of radiation, or alternation, or repetition, or symmetry, or anything else that I ever heard of.

It is repeated, of course, by the breadths, but not otherwise.

Looked at in one way, each breadth stands alone; the bloated curves and flourishes—a kind of "debased Romanesque" with delirium tremens[5]—go waddling up and down in isolated columns of fatuity.

But, on the other hand, they connect diagonally, and the sprawling outlines run off in great slanting waves of optic horror, like a lot of wallowing sea-weeds in full chase.

---

4. Silas Weir Mitchell (1829–1914), American nerve specialist, who popularized the "rest cure" and who treated Gilman herself.

5. Trembling delirium associated with alcoholism. "Romanesque": a highly decorative style of architecture.

The whole thing goes horizontally, too, at least it seems so, and I exhaust myself trying to distinguish the order of its going in that direction.

They have used a horizontal breadth for a frieze, and that adds wonderfully to the confusion.

There is one end of the room where it is almost intact, and there, when the crosslights fade and the low sun shines directly upon it, I can almost fancy radiation after all—the interminable grotesque seems to form around a common center and rush off in headlong plunges of equal distraction.

It makes me tired to follow it. I will take a nap, I guess.

I don't know why I should write this.

I don't want to.

I don't feel able.

And I know John would think it absurd. But I *must* say what I feel and think in some way—it is such a relief!

But the effort is getting to be greater than the relief.

Half the time now I am awfully lazy, and lie down ever so much. John says I mustn't lose my strength, and has me take cod liver oil and lots of tonics and things, to say nothing of ale and wine and rare meat.

Dear John! He loves me very dearly, and hates to have me sick. I tried to have a real earnest reasonable talk with him the other day, and tell him how I wish he would let me go and make a visit to Cousin Henry and Julia.

But he said I wasn't able to go, nor able to stand it after I got there; and I did not make out a very good case for myself, for I was crying before I had finished.

It is getting to be a great effort for me to think straight. Just this nervous weakness, I suppose.

And dear John gathered me up in his arms, and just carried me upstairs and laid me on the bed, and sat by me and read to me till it tired my head.

He said I was his darling and his comfort and all he had, and that I must take care of myself for his sake, and keep well.

He says no one but myself can help me out of it, that I must use my will and self-control and not let any silly fancies run away with me.

There's one comfort—the baby is well and happy, and does not have to occupy this nursery with the horrid wallpaper.

If we had not used it, that blessed child would have! What a fortunate escape! Why, I wouldn't have a child of mine, an impressionable little thing, live in such a room for worlds.

I never thought of it before, but it is lucky that John kept me here after all; I can stand it so much easier than a baby, you see.

Of course I never mention it to them any more—I am too wise—but I keep watch for it all the same.

There are things in that wallpaper that nobody knows about but me, or ever will.

Behind that outside pattern the dim shapes get clearer every day.

It is always the same shape, only very numerous.

And it is like a woman stooping down and creeping about behind that pattern. I don't like it a bit. I wonder—I begin to think—I wish John would take me away from here!

It is so hard to talk with John about my case, because he is so wise, and because he loves me so.

But I tried it last night.

It was moonlight. The moon shines in all around just as the sun does.

I hate to see it sometimes, it creeps so slowly, and always comes in by one window or another.

John was asleep and I hated to waken him, so I kept still and watched the moonlight on that undulating wallpaper till I felt creepy.

The faint figure behind seemed to shake the pattern, just as if she wanted to get out.

I got up softly and went to feel and see if the paper *did* move, and when I came back John was awake.

"What is it, little girl?" he said. "Don't go walking about like that—you'll get cold."

I thought it was a good time to talk, so I told him that I really was not gaining here, and that I wished he would take me away.

"Why, darling!" said he. "Our lease will be up in three weeks, and I can't see how to leave before.

"The repairs are not done at home, and I cannot possibly leave town just now. Of course, if you were in any danger, I could and would, but you really are better, dear, whether you can see it or not. I am a doctor, dear, and I know. You are gaining flesh and color, your appetite is better, I feel really much easier about you."

"I don't weigh a bit more," said I, "nor as much; and my appetite may be better in the evening when you are here but it is worse in the morning when you are away!"

"Bless her little heart!" said he with a big hug. "She shall be as sick as she pleases! But now let's improve the shining hours[6] by going to sleep, and talk about it in the morning!"

"And you won't go away?" I asked gloomily.

"Why, how can I, dear? It is only three weeks more and then we will take a nice little trip of a few days while Jennie is getting the house ready. Really, dear, you are better!"

"Better in body perhaps—" I began, and stopped short, for he sat up straight and looked at me with such a stern, reproachful look that I could not say another word.

"My darling," said he, "I beg of you, for my sake and for our child's sake, as well as for your own, that you will never for one instant let that idea enter your mind! There is nothing so dangerous, so fascinating, to a temperament like yours. It is a false and foolish fancy. Can you not trust me as a physician when I tell you so?"

So of course I said no more on that score, and we went to sleep before long. He thought I was asleep first, but I wasn't and lay there for hours trying to decide whether that front pattern and the back pattern really did move together or separately.

---

6. From the popular moral poem by Isaac Watts "Against Idleness and Mischief" (1715). "How doth the little busy bee / Improve each shining hour, / And gather honey all the day / From every opening flower!"

On a pattern like this, by daylight, there is a lack of sequence, a defiance of law, that is a constant irritant to a normal mind.

The color is hideous enough, and unreliable enough, and infuriating enough, but the pattern is torturing.

You think you have mastered it, but just as you get well under way in following, it turns a back-somersault and there you are. It slaps you in the face, knocks you down, and tramples upon you. It is like a bad dream.

The outside pattern is a florid arabesque,[7] reminding one of a fungus. If you can imagine a toadstool in joints, an interminable string of toadstools, budding and sprouting in endless convolutions—why, that is something like it.

That is, sometimes!

There is one marked peculiarity about this paper, a thing nobody seems to notice but myself, and that is that it changes as the light changes.

When the sun shoots in through the east window—I always watch for that first long, straight ray—it changes so quickly that I never can quite believe it.

That is why I watch it always.

By moonlight—the moon shines in all night when there is a moon—I wouldn't know it was the same paper.

At night in any kind of light, in twilight, candlelight, lamplight, and worst of all by moonlight, it becomes bars! The outside pattern, I mean, and the woman behind it is as plain as can be.

I didn't realize for a long time what the thing was that showed behind, that dim sub-pattern, but now I am quite sure it is a woman.

By daylight she is subdued, quiet. I fancy it is the pattern that keeps her so still. It is so puzzling. It keeps me quiet by the hour.

I lie down ever so much now. John says it is good for me, and to sleep all I can.

Indeed he started the habit by making me lie down for an hour after each meal.

It is a very bad habit, I am convinced, for you see, I don't sleep.

And that cultivates deceit, for I don't tell them I'm awake—oh, no!

The fact is I am getting a little afraid of John.

He seems very queer sometimes, and even Jennie has an inexplicable look.

It strikes me occasionally, just as a scientific hypothesis, that perhaps it is the paper!

I have watched John when he did not know I was looking, and come into the room suddenly on the most innocent excuses, and I've caught him several times *looking at the paper!* And Jennie too. I caught Jennie with her hand on it once.

She didn't know I was in the room, and when I asked her in a quiet, a very quiet voice, with the most restrained manner possible, what she was doing with the paper, she turned around as if she had been caught stealing, and looked quite angry—asked me why I should frighten her so!

Then she said that the paper stained everything it touched, that she had found yellow smooches on all my clothes and John's and she wished we would be more careful!

Did not that sound innocent? But I know she was studying that pattern, and I am determined that nobody shall find it out but myself!

---

7. An intricate pattern of interlaced lines.

Life is very much more exciting now than it used to be. You see, I have something more to expect, to look forward to, to watch. I really do eat better, and am more quiet than I was.

John is so pleased to see me improve! He laughed a little the other day, and said I seemed to be flourishing in spite of my wallpaper.

I turned it off with a laugh. I had no intention of telling him it was *because* of the wallpaper—he would make fun of me. He might even want to take me away.

I don't want to leave now until I have found it out. There is a week more, and I think that will be enough.

I'm feeling so much better!

I don't sleep much at night, for it is so interesting to watch developments; but I sleep a good deal during the daytime.

In the daytime it is tiresome and perplexing.

There are always new shoots on the fungus, and new shades of yellow all over it. I cannot keep count of them, though I have tried conscientiously.

It is the strangest yellow, that wallpaper! It makes me think of all the yellow things I ever saw—not beautiful ones like buttercups, but old, foul, bad yellow things.

But there is something else about that paper—the smell! I noticed it the moment we came into the room, but with so much air and sun it was not bad. Now we have had a week of fog and rain, and whether the windows are open or not, the smell is here.

It creeps all over the house.

I find it hovering in the dining-room, skulking in the parlor, hiding in the hall, lying in wait for me on the stairs.

It gets into my hair.

Even when I go to ride, if I turn my head suddenly and surprise it—there is that smell!

Such a peculiar odor, too! I have spent hours in trying to analyze it, to find what it smelled like.

It is not bad—at first—and very gentle, but quite the subtlest, most enduring odor I ever met.

In this damp weather it is awful. I wake up in the night and find it hanging over me.

It used to disturb me at first. I thought seriously of burning the house—to reach the smell.

But now I am used to it. The only thing I can think of that it is like is the *color* of the paper! A yellow smell.

There is a very funny mark on this wall, low down, near the mopboard. A streak that runs round the room. It goes behind every piece of furniture, except the bed, a long, straight, even *smooch*, as if it had been rubbed over and over.

I wonder how it was done and who did it, and what they did it for. Round and round and round—round and round and round—it makes me dizzy!

I really have discovered something at last.

Through watching so much at night, when it changes so, I have finally found out.

The front pattern *does* move—and no wonder! The woman behind shakes it!

Sometimes I think there are a great many women behind, and sometimes only one, and she crawls around fast, and her crawling shakes it all over.

Then in the very bright spots she keeps still, and in the very shady spots she just takes hold of the bars and shakes them hard.

And she is all the time trying to climb through. But nobody could climb through that pattern—it strangles so; I think that is why it has so many heads.

They get through, and then the pattern strangles them off and turns them upside down, and makes their eyes white!

If those heads were covered or taken off it would not be half so bad.

I think that woman gets out in the daytime!

And I'll tell you why—privately—I've seen her!

I can see her out of every one of my windows!

It is the same woman, I know, for she is always creeping, and most women do not creep by daylight.

I see her in that long shaded lane, creeping up and down. I see her in those dark grape arbors, creeping all around the garden.

I see her on that long road under the trees, creeping along, and when a carriage comes she hides under the blackberry vines.

I don't blame her a bit. It must be very humiliating to be caught creeping by daylight!

I always lock the door when I creep by daylight. I can't do it at night, for I know John would suspect something at once.

And John is so queer now that I don't want to irritate him. I wish he would take another room! Besides, I don't want anybody to get that woman out at night but myself.

I often wonder if I could see her out of all the windows at once.

But, turn as fast as I can, I can only see out of one at one time.

And though I always see her, she *may* be able to creep faster than I can turn! I have watched her sometimes away off in the open country, creeping as fast as a cloud shadow in a wind.

If only that top pattern could be gotten off from the under one! I mean to try it, little by little.

I have found out another funny thing, but I shan't tell it this time! It does not do to trust people too much.

There are only two more days to get this paper off, and I believe John is beginning to notice. I don't like the look in his eyes.

And I heard him ask Jennie a lot of professional questions about me. She had a very good report to give.

She said I slept a good deal in the daytime.

John knows I don't sleep very well at night, for all I'm so quiet!

He asked me all sorts of questions, too, and pretended to be very loving and kind.

As if I couldn't see through him!

Still, I don't wonder he acts so, sleeping under this paper for three months.

It only interests me, but I feel sure John and Jennie are affected by it.

Hurrah! This is the last day, but it is enough. John is to stay in town over night, and won't be out until this evening.

Jennie wanted to sleep with me—the sly thing; but I told her I should undoubtedly rest better for a night all alone.

That was clever, for really I wasn't alone a bit! As soon as it was moonlight and that poor thing began to crawl and shake the pattern, I got up and ran to help her.

I pulled and she shook. I shook and she pulled, and before morning we had peeled off yards of that paper.

A strip about as high as my head and half around the room.

And then when the sun came and that awful pattern began to laugh at me, I declared I would finish it today!

We go away tomorrow, and they are moving all my furniture down again to leave things as they were before.

Jennie looked at the wall in amazement, but I told her merrily that I did it out of pure spite at the vicious thing.

She laughed and said she wouldn't mind doing it herself, but I must not get tired.

How she betrayed herself that time!

But I am here, and no person touches this paper but Me—not *alive!*

She tried to get me out of the room—it was too patent! But I said it was so quiet and empty and clean now that I believed I would lie down again and sleep all I could, and not to wake me even for dinner—I would call when I woke.

So now she is gone, and the servants are gone, and the things are gone, and there is nothing left but that great bedstead nailed down, with the canvas mattress we found on it.

We shall sleep downstairs tonight, and take the boat home tomorrow.

I quite enjoy the room, now it is bare again.

How those children did tear about here!

This bedstead is fairly gnawed!

But I must get to work.

I have locked the door and thrown the key down into the front path.

I don't want to go out, and I don't want to have anybody come in, till John comes.

I want to astonish him.

I've got a rope up here that even Jennie did not find. If that woman does get out, and tries to get away, I can tie her!

But I forgot I could not reach far without anything to stand on!

This bed will *not* move!

I tried to lift and push it until I was lame, and then I got so angry I bit off a little piece at one corner—but it hurt my teeth.

Then I peeled off all the paper I could reach standing on the floor. It sticks horribly and the pattern just enjoys it! All those strangled heads and bulbous eyes and waddling fungus growths just shriek with derision!

I am getting angry enough to do something desperate. To jump out of the window would be admirable exercise, but the bars are too strong even to try.

Besides I wouldn't do it. Of course not. I know well enough that a step like that is improper and might be misconstrued.

I don't like to *look* out of the windows even—there are so many of those creeping women, and they creep so fast.

I wonder if they all come out of that wallpaper as I did?

But I am securely fastened now by my well-hidden rope—you don't get *me* out in the road there!

I suppose I shall have to get back behind the pattern when it comes night, and that is hard!

It is so pleasant to be out in this great room and creep around as I please!

I don't want to go outside. I won't, even if Jennie asks me to.

For outside you have to creep on the ground, and everything is green instead of yellow.

But here I can creep smoothly on the floor, and my shoulder just fits in that long smooch around the wall, so I cannot lose my way.

Why, there's John at the door!

It is no use, young man, you can't open it!

How he does call and pound!

Now he's crying to Jennie for an axe.

It would be a shame to break down that beautiful door!

"John, dear!" said I in the gentlest voice. "The key is down by the front steps, under a plantain[8] leaf!"

That silenced him for a few moments.

Then he said, very quietly indeed, "Open the door, my darling!"

"I can't," said I. "The key is down by the front door under a plantain leaf!" And then I said it again, several times, very gently and slowly, and said it so often that he had to go and see, and he got it of course, and came in. He stopped short by the door.

"What is the matter?" he cried. "For God's sake, what are you doing!"

I kept on creeping just the same, but I looked at him over my shoulder.

"I've got out at last," said I, "in spite of you and Jane. And I've pulled off most of the paper, so you can't put me back!"

Now why should that man have fainted? But he did, and right across my path by the wall, so that I had to creep over him every time!

1892

WHY I WROTE THE YELLOW WALLPAPER?

Many and many a reader has asked that. When the story first came out, in the *New England Magazine* about 1891, a Boston physician made protest in *The Transcript*. Such a story ought not to be written, he said; it was enough to drive anyone mad to read it.

Another physician, in Kansas I think, wrote to say that it was the best description of incipient insanity he had ever seen, and—begging my pardon—had I been there?

Now the story of the story is this:

For many years I suffered from a severe and continuous nervous breakdown tending to melancholia—and beyond. During about the third year of this trouble I went, in devout faith and some faint stir of hope, to a noted specialist in nervous diseases, the best known in the country. This wise man put me to bed and applied the rest cure, to which a still good physique responded so promptly that he concluded there was nothing much the matter with me, and sent me home with solemn advice to "live as domestic a life as far as possible;" to "have but two hours' intellectual life a day," and "never to touch pen, brush or pencil again as long as I lived." This was in 1887.

I went home and obeyed those directions for some three months, and came so near the border line of utter mental ruin that I could see over.

Then, using the remnants of intelligence that remained, and helped by a wise friend, I cast the noted specialist's advice to the winds and went to work again— work, the normal life of every human being; work, in which is joy and growth and service, without which one is a pauper and a parasite; ultimately recovering some measure of power.

Being naturally moved to rejoicing by this narrow escape. I wrote *The Yellow Wallpaper*, with its embellishments and additions to carry out the ideal (I never had hallucinations or objections to my mural decorations) and sent a copy to the physician who so nearly drove me mad. He never acknowledged it.

The little book is valued by alienists and as a good specimen of one kind of literature. It has to my knowledge saved one woman from a similar fate—so terrifying her family that they let her out into normal activity and she recovered.

But the best result is this. Many years later I was told that the great specialist had admitted to friends of his that he had altered his treatment of neurasthenia since reading *The Yellow Wallpaper*.

It was not intended to drive people crazy, but to save people from being driven crazy, and it worked.

TRIFLES (1916)

Susan Glaspell
b. 1876 Davenport, IA
d. 1948 Provincetown, MA

CHARACTERS

GEORGE HENDERSON, *County Attorney*   MRS. PETERS
HENRY PETERS, *Sheriff*   MRS. HALE
LEWIS HALE, *A Neighboring Farmer*

SCENE. *The kitchen in the now abandoned farmhouse of John Wright, a gloomy kitchen, and left without having been put in order—unwashed pans under the sink, a loaf of bread outside the breadbox, a dish towel on the table—other signs of incompleted work. At the rear the outer door opens and the* SHERIFF *comes in followed by the* COUNTY ATTORNEY *and* HALE. *The* SHERIFF *and* HALE *are men in middle life, the* COUNTY ATTORNEY *is a young man; all are much bundled up and go at once to the stove. They are followed by two women—the* SHERIFF'S WIFE *first; she is a slight wiry woman, a thin nervous face.* MRS. HALE *is larger and would ordinarily be called more comfortable looking, but she is disturbed now and looks fearfully about as she enters. The women have come in slowly, and stand close together near the door.*

COUNTY ATTORNEY,   [*Rubbing his hands.*] This feels good. Come up to the fire, ladies.
MRS. PETERS   [*After taking a step forward.*] I'm not—cold.
SHERIFF   [*Unbuttoning his overcoat and stepping away from the stove as if to mark the beginning of official business.*] Now, Mr. Hale, before we move things about, you explain to Mr. Henderson just what you saw when you came here yesterday morning.
COUNTY ATTORNEY   By the way, has anything been moved? Are things just as you left them yesterday?
SHERIFF   [*Looking about.*] It's just the same. When it dropped below zero last night I thought I'd better send Frank out this morning to make a fire for us—no use

getting pneumonia with a big case on, but I told him not to touch anything except the stove—and you know Frank.

COUNTY ATTORNEY   Somebody should have been left here yesterday.

SHERIFF   Oh—yesterday. When I had to send Frank to Morris Center for that man who went crazy—I want you to know I had my hands full yesterday, I knew you could get back from Omaha by today and as long as I went over everything here myself—

COUNTY ATTORNEY   Well, Mr. Hale, tell just what happened when you came here yesterday morning.

HALE   Harry and I had started to town with a load of potatoes. We came along the road from my place and as I got here I said, "I'm going to see if I can't get John Wright to go in with me on a party telephone."[1] I spoke to Wright about it once before and he put me off, saying folks talked too much anyway, and all he asked was peace and quiet—I guess you know about how much he talked himself; but I thought maybe if I went to the house and talked about it before his wife, though I said to Harry that I didn't know as what his wife wanted made much difference to John.

COUNTY ATTORNEY Let's talk about that later, Mr. Hale. I do want to talk about that, but tell now just what happened when you got to the house.

HALE   I didn't hear or see anything; I knocked at the door, and still it was all quiet inside. I knew they must be up, it was past eight o'clock. So I knocked again, and I thought I heard somebody say, "Come in." I wasn't sure, I'm not sure yet, but I opened the door—this door [*Indicating the door by which the two women are still standing*] and there in that rocker— [*Pointing to it.*] sat Mrs. Wright.

[*They all look at the rocker.*]

COUNTY ATTORNEY   What—was she doing?

HALE   She was rockin' back and forth. She had her apron in her hand and was kind of—pleating it.

COUNTY ATTORNEY   And how did she—look?

HALE   Well, she looked queer.

COUNTY ATTORNEY   How do you mean—queer?

HALE   Well, as if she didn't know what she was going to do next. And kind of done up.

COUNTY ATTORNEY   How did she seem to feel about your coming?

HALE   Why, I don't think she minded—one way or other. She didn't pay much attention. I said, "How do, Mrs. Wright, it's cold, ain't it?" And she said, "Is it?"— and went on kind of pleating at her apron. Well, I was surprised; she didn't ask me to come up to the stove, or to set down, but just sat there, not even looking at me, so I said, "I want to see John." And then she—laughed. I guess you would call it a laugh. I thought of Harry and the team outside, so I said a little sharp: "Can't I see John?" "No," she says, kind o' dull like. "Ain't he home?" says I. "Yes," says she, "he's home." "Then why can't I see him?" I asked her, out of

---

1. I.e., a single telephone line shared by two or four households.

patience. "'Cause he's dead," says she. "*Dead?*" says I. She just nodded her head, not getting a bit excited, but rockin' back and forth. "Why—where is he?" says I; not knowing what to say. She just pointed upstairs—like that [*Himself pointing to the room above*]. I got up, with the idea of going up there. I walked from there to here—then I says, "Why, what did he die of?" "He died of a rope round his neck," says she, and just went on pleatin' at her apron. Well, I went out and called Harry. I thought I might—need help. We went upstairs and there he was lyin'—

COUNTY ATTORNEY   I think I'd rather have you go into that upstairs, where you can point it all out. Just go on now with the rest of the story.

HALE   Well, my first thought was to get that rope off. It looked . . . [*Stops, his face twitches.*] . . . but Harry, he went up to him, and he said, "No, he's dead all right, and we'd better not touch anything." So we went back down stairs. She was still sitting that same way. "Has anybody been notified?" I asked. "No," says she, unconcerned. "Who did this, Mrs. Wright?" said Harry. He said it businesslike—and she stopped pleatin' of her apron. "I don't know," she says. "You don't *know?*" says Harry. "No," says she. "Weren't you sleepin' in the bed with him?" says Harry. "Yes," says she, "but I was on the inside." "Somebody slipped a rope round his neck and strangled him and you didn't wake up?" says Harry. "I didn't wake up," she said after him. We must 'a looked as if we didn't see how that could be, for after a minute she said, "I sleep sound." Harry was going to ask her more questions but I said maybe we ought to let her tell her story first to the coroner, or the sheriff, so Harry went fast as he could to Rivers' place, where there's a telephone.

COUNTY ATTORNEY   And what did Mrs. Wright do when she knew that you had gone for the coroner?

HALE   She moved from that chair to this one over here [*Pointing to a small chair in the corner.*] and just sat there with her hands held together and looking down. I got a feeling that I ought to make some conversation, so I said I had come in to see if John wanted to put in a telephone, and at that she started to laugh, and then she stopped and looked at me—scared. [*The* COUNTY ATTORNEY, *who has had his notebook out, makes a note.*] I dunno, maybe it wasn't scared. I wouldn't like to say it was. Soon Harry got back, and then Dr. Lloyd came, and you, Mr. Peters, and so I guess that's all I know that you don't.

COUNTY ATTORNEY   [*Looking around.*] I guess we'll go upstairs first—and then out to the barn and around there. [*To the* SHERIFF.] You're convinced that there was nothing important here—nothing that would point to any motive.

SHERIFF   Nothing here but kitchen things.

[*The* COUNTY ATTORNEY, *after again looking around the kitchen, opens the door of a cupboard closet. He gets up on a chair and looks on a shelf. Pulls his hand away, sticky.*]

COUNTY ATTORNEY   Here's a nice mess.

[*The women draw nearer.*]

MRS. PETERS   [*To the other woman.*] Oh, her fruit; it did freeze. [*To the* COUNTY ATTORNEY.] She worried about that when it turned so cold. She said the fire'd go out and her jars would break.

SHERIFF   Well, can you beat the women! Held for murder and worryin' about her preserves.

COUNTY ATTORNEY   I guess before we're through she may have something more serious than preserves to worry about.

HALE   Well, women are used to worrying over trifles.

[*The two women move a little closer together.*]

COUNTY ATTORNEY   [*With the gallantry of a young politician.*] And yet, for all their worries, what would we do without the ladies? [*The women do not unbend. He goes to the sink, takes a dipperful of water from the pail and pouring it into a basin, washes his hands. Starts to wipe them on the roller towel, turns it for a cleaner place.*] Dirty towels! [*Kicks his foot against the pans under the sink.*] Not much of a housekeeper, would you say, ladies?

MRS. HALE   [*Stiffly.*] There's a great deal of work to be done on a farm.

COUNTY ATTORNEY   To be sure. And yet [*With a little bow to her.*] I know there are some Dickson county farmhouses which do not have such roller towels.

[*He gives it a pull to expose its full length again.*]

MRS. HALE   Those towels get dirty awful quick. Men's hands aren't always as clean as they might be.

COUNTY ATTORNEY.   Ah, loyal to your sex, I see. But you and Mrs. Wright were neighbors. I suppose you were friends, too.

MRS. HALE   [*Shaking her head.*] I've not seen much of her of late years I've not been in this house—it's more than a year.

COUNTY ATTORNEY   And why was that? You didn't like her?

MRS. HALE I liked her all well enough. Farmers' wives have their hands full, Mr. Henderson. And then—

COUNTY ATTORNEY   Yes—?

MRS. HALE   [*Looking about.*] It never seemed a very cheerful place.

COUNTY ATTORNEY   No—it's not cheerful. I shouldn't say she had the home-making instinct.

MRS. HALE   Well, I don't know as Wright had, either.

COUNTY ATTORNEY   You mean that they didn't get on very well?

MRS. HALE No, I don't mean anything. But I don't think a place'd be any cheer-fuller for John Wright's being in it.

COUNTY ATTORNEY   I'd like to talk more of that a little later. I want to get the lay of things upstairs now.

[*He goes to the left, where three steps lead to a stair door.*]

SHERIFF   I suppose anything Mrs. Peter does'll be all right. She was to take in some clothes for her, you know, and a few little things. We left in such a hurry yesterday.

COUNTY ATTORNEY   Yes, but I would like to see what you take, Mrs. Peters, and keep an eye out for anything that might be of use to us.

MRS. PETERS   Yes, Mr. Henderson.

[*The women listen to the men's steps on the stairs, then look about the kitchen.*]

MRS. HALE   I'd hate to have men coming into my kitchen, snooping around and criticizing.

[*She arranges the pans under sink which the* COUNTY ATTORNEY *had shoved out of place.*]

MRS. PETERS   Of course it's no more than their duty.

MRS. HALE   Duty's all right, but I guess that deputy sheriff that came out to make the fire might have got a little of this on. [*Gives the roller towel a pull.*] Wish I'd thought of that sooner. Seems mean to talk about her for not having things slicked up when she had to come away in such a hurry.

MRS. PETERS   [*Who has gone to a small table in the left rear corner of the room, and lifted one end of a towel that covers a pan.*] She had bread set.
  [*Stands still.*]

MRS. HALE   [*Eyes fixed on a loaf of bread beside the breadbox, which is on a low shelf at the other side of the room. Moves slowly toward it.*] She was going to put this in there. [*Picks up loaf, then abruptly drops it. In a manner of returning to familiar things.*] It's a shame about her fruit. I wonder if it's all gone. [*Gets up on the chair and looks.*] I think there's some here that's all right, Mrs. Peters. Yes—here; [*Holding it toward the window.*] this is cherries, too. [*Looking again.*] I declare I believe that's the only one. [*Gets down, bottle in her hand. Goes to the sink and wipes it off on the outside.*] She'll feel awful bad after all her hard work in the hot weather. I remember the afternoon I put up my cherries last summer.
  [*She puts the bottle on the big kitchen table, center of the room. With a sigh, is about to sit down in the rocking-chair. Before she is seated realizes what chair it is; with a slow look at it, steps back. The chair which she has touched rocks back and forth.*]

MRS. PETERS   Well, I must get those things from the front room closet. [*She goes to the door at the right, but after looking into the other room, steps back.*] You coming with me, Mrs. Hale? You could help me carry them.
  [*They go in the other room; reappear,* MRS. PETERS *carrying a dress and skirt,* MRS. HALE *following with a pair of shoes.*]

MRS. PETERS   My, it's cold in there.
  [*She puts the clothes on the big table, and hurries to the stove.*]

MRS. HALE   [*Examining her skirt.*] Wright was close. I think maybe that's why she kept so much to herself. She didn't even belong to the Ladies Aid. I suppose she felt she couldn't do her part, and then you don't enjoy things when you feel shabby. She used to wear pretty clothes and be lively, when she was Minnie Foster, one of the town girls singing in the choir. But that—oh, that was thirty years ago. This all you was to take in?

MRS. PETERS   She said she wanted an apron. Funny thing to want, for there isn't much to get you dirty in jail, goodness knows. But I suppose just to make her feel more natural. She said they was in the top drawer in this cupboard. Yes, here. And then her little shawl that always hung behind the door. [*Opens stair door and looks.*] Yes, here it is.
  [*Quickly shuts door leading upstairs.*]

MRS. HALE   [*Abruptly moving toward her.*] Mrs. Peters?

MRS. PETERS   Yes, Mrs. Hale?

MRS. HALE   Do you think she did it?

MRS. PETERS   [*In a frightened voice.*] Oh, I don't know.

MRS. HALE   Well, I don't think she did. Asking for an apron and her little shawl. Worrying about her fruit.

MRS. PETERS [*Starts to speak, glances up, where footsteps are heard in the room above. In a low voice.*] Mr. Peters says it looks bad for her. Mr. Henderson is awful sarcastic in a speech and he'll make fun of her sayin' she didn't wake up.

MRS. HALE Well, I guess John Wright didn't wake when they was slipping that rope under his neck.

MRS. PETERS No, it's strange. It must have been done awful crafty and still. They say it was such a—funny way to kill a man, rigging it all up like that.

MRS. HALE That's just what Mr. Hale said. There was a gun in the house He says that's what he can't understand.

MRS. PETERS Mr. Henderson said coming out that what was needed for the case was a motive; something to show anger, or—sudden feeling.

MRS. HALE [*Who is standing by the table.*] Well, I don't see any signs of anger around here. [*She puts her hand on the dish towel which lies on the table, stands looking down at table, one half of which is clean, the other half messy.*] It's wiped to here. [*Makes a move as if to finish work, then turns and looks at loaf of bread outside the breadbox. Drops towel. In that voice of coming back to familiar things.*] Wonder how they are finding things upstairs. I hope she had it a little more red-up² up there. You know, it seems kind of sneaking. Locking her up in town and then coming out here and trying to get her own house to turn against her!

MRS. PETERS But Mrs. Hale, the law is the law.

MRS. HALE I s'pose 'tis. [*Unbuttoning her coat.*] Better loosen up your things, Mrs. Peters. You won't feel them when you go out.

[MRS. PETERS *takes off her fur tippet, goes to hang it on hook at back of room, stands looking at the under part of the small corner table.*]

MRS. PETERS She was piecing a quilt.

[*She brings the large sewing basket and they look at the bright pieces.*]

MRS. HALE It's log cabin pattern. Pretty, isn't it? I wonder if she was goin' to quilt it or just knot it?

[*Footsteps have been heard coming down the stairs. The* SHERIFF *enters followed by* HALE *and the* COUNTY ATTORNEY.]

SHERIFF They wonder if she was going to quilt it or just knot it!

[*The men laugh; the women look abashed.*]

COUNTY ATTORNEY [*Rubbing his hands over the stove.*] Frank's fire didn't do much up there, did it? Well, let's go out to the barn and get that cleared up.

[*The men go outside.*]

MRS. HALE [*Resentfully.*] I don't know as there's anything so strange, our takin' up our time with little things while we're waiting for them to get the evidence. [*She sits down at the big table smoothing out a block with decision.*] I don't see as it's anything to laugh about.

MRS. PETERS [*Apologetically.*] Of course they've got awful important things on their minds.

[*Pulls up a chair and joins* MRS. HALE *at the table.*]

MRS. HALE [*Examining another block.*] Mrs. Peters, look at this one. Here, this is the one she was working on, and look at the sewing! All the rest of it has been

2. Tidied up.

so nice and even. And look at this! It's all over the place! Why, it looks as if she didn't know what she was about!

[*After she has said this they look at each other, then start to glance back at the door. After an instant* MRS. HALE *has pulled at a knot and ripped the sewing.*]

MRS. PETERS Oh, what are you doing, Mrs. Hale?

MRS. HALE [*Mildly.*] Just pulling out a stitch or two that's not sewed very good. [*Threading a needle.*] Bad sewing always made me fidgety.

MRS. PETERS [*Nervously.*] I don't think we ought to touch things.

MRS. HALE I'll just finish up this end. [*Suddenly stopping and leaning forward.*] Mrs. Peters?

MRS. PETERS Yes, Mrs. Hale?

MRS. HALE What do you suppose she was so nervous about?

MRS. PETERS Oh—I don't know. I don't know as she was nervous. I sometimes sew awful queer when I'm just tired. [MRS. HALE *starts to say something, looks at* MRS. PETERS, *then goes on sewing.*] Well, I must get these things wrapped up. They may be through sooner than we think. [*Putting apron and other things together.*] I wonder where I can find a piece of paper, and string.

MRS. HALE In that cupboard, maybe.

MRS. PETERS [*Looking in cupboard.*] Why, here's a birdcage. [*Holds it up.*] Did she have a bird, Mrs. Hale?

MRS. HALE Why, I don't know whether she did or not—I've not been here for so long. There was a man around last year selling canaries cheap, but I don't know as she took one; maybe she did. She used to sing real pretty herself.

MRS. PETERS [*Glancing around.*] Seems funny to think of a bird here. But she must have had one, or why would she have a cage? I wonder what happened to it.

MRS. HALE I s'pose maybe the cat got it.

MRS. PETERS No, she didn't have a cat. She's got that feeling some people have about cats—being afraid of them. My cat got in her room and she was real upset and asked me to take it out.

MRS. HALE My sister Bessie was like that. Queer, ain't it?

MRS. PETERS [*Examining the cage.*] Why, look at this door. It's broke. One hinge is pulled apart.

MRS. HALE [*Looking too.*] Looks as if someone must have been rough with it.

MRS. PETERS Why, yes.

[*She brings the cage forward and puts it on the table.*]

MRS. HALE I wish if they're going to find any evidence they'd be about it. I don't like this place.

MRS. PETERS But I'm awful glad you came with me, Mrs. Hale. It would be lonesome for me sitting here alone.

MRS. HALE It would, wouldn't it? [*Dropping her sewing.*] But I tell you what I do wish, Mrs. Peters. I wish I had come over sometimes when she was here. I—[*Looking around the room.*]—wish I had.

MRS. PETERS But of course you were awful busy, Mrs. Hale—your house and your children.

MRS. HALE I could've come. I stayed away because it weren't cheerful—and that's why I ought to have come. I—I've never liked this place. Maybe because it's down in a hollow and you don't see the road. I dunno what it is but it's a lonesome place and always was. I wish I had come over to see Minnie Foster sometimes. I can see now—

[*Shakes her head.*]

MRS. PETERS   Well, you mustn't reproach yourself, Mrs. Hale. Some how we just don't see how it is with other folks until—something comes up.

MRS. HALE   Not having children makes less work—but it makes a quiet house, and Wright out to work all day, and no company when he did come in. Did you know John Wright, Mrs. Peters?

MRS. PETERS   Not to know him: I've seen him in town. They say he was a good man.

MRS. HALE   Yes—good; he didn't drink, and kept his word as well as most I guess, and paid his debts. But he was a hard man, Mrs. Peters. Just to pass the time of day with him—[*Shivers.*] Like a raw wind that gets to the bone. [*Pauses, her eye falling on the cage.*] I should think she would 'a wanted a bird. But what do you suppose went with it?

MRS. PETERS   I don't know, unless it got sick and died.

[*She reaches over and swings the broken door, swings it again. Both women watch it.*]

MRS. HALE   You weren't raised round here, were you? [MRS. PETERS *shakes her head.*] You didn't know—her?

MRS. PETERS   Not till they brought her yesterday.

MRS. HALE   She—come to think of it, she was kind of like a bird herself—real sweet and pretty, but kind of timid and—fluttery. How—she—did—change. [*Silence; then as if struck by a happy thought and relieved to get back to every day things.*] Tell you what, Mrs. Peters, why don't you take the quilt in with you? It might take up her mind.

MRS. PETERS   Why, I think that's a real nice idea, Mrs. Hale. There couldn't possibly be any objection to it, could there? Now, just what would I take? I wonder if her patches are in here—and her things.

[*They look in the sewing basket.*]

MRS. HALE   Here's some red. I expect this has got sewing things in it. [*Brings out a fancy box.*] What a pretty box. Looks like something somebody would give you. Maybe her scissors are in here. [*Opens box. Suddenly puts her hand to her nose.*] Why—[MRS. PETERS *bends nearer, then turns her face away.*] There's something wrapped up in this piece of silk.

MRS. PETERS   Why, this isn't her scissors.

MRS. HALE   [*Lifting the silk.*] Oh, Mrs. Peters—it's—

[MRS. PETERS *bends closer.*]

MRS. PETERS   It's the bird.

MRS. HALE   [*Jumping up.*] But, Mrs. Peters—look at it! Its neck! Look at its neck! It's all—other side to.

MRS. PETERS   Somebody—wrung—its—neck.

[*Their eyes meet. A look of growing comprehension, of horror. Steps are heard outside.* MRS. HALE *slips box under quilt pieces, and sinks into her chair. Enter* SHERIFF *and* COUNTY ATTORNEY. MRS. PETERS *rises.*]

COUNTY ATTORNEY   [*As one turning from serious things to little pleasantries.*] Well, ladies, have you decided whether she was going to quilt it or knot it?

MRS. PETERS   We think she was going to—knot it.

COUNTY ATTORNEY   Well, that's interesting, I'm sure. [*Seeing the birdcage.*] Has the bird flown?

MRS. HALE   [*Putting more quilt pieces over the box.*] We think the—cat got it.

COUNTY ATTORNEY   [*Preoccupied.*] Is there a cat?

[MRS. HALE *glances in a quick covert way at* MRS. PETERS.]

MRS. PETERS   Well, not now. They're superstitious, you know. They leave.

COUNTY ATTORNEY [*To* SHERIFF PETERS, *continuing an interrupted conversation.*] No sign at all of anyone having come from the outside. Their own rope. Now let's go up again and go over it piece by piece. [*They start upstairs.*] It would have to have been someone who knew just the—

[MRS. PETERS *sits down. The two women sit there not looking at one another, but as if peering into something and at the same time holding back. When they talk now it is in the manner of feeling their way over strange ground, as if afraid of what they are saying, but as if they can not help saying it.*]

MRS. HALE   She liked the bird. She was going to bury it in that pretty box.

MRS. PETERS   [*In a whisper.*] When I was a girl—my kitten—there was a boy took a hatchet, and before my eyes—and before I could get there—[*Covers her face an instant.*] If they hadn't held me back I would have—[*Catches herself, looks upstairs where steps are heard, falters weakly.*] hurt him.

MRS. HALE   [*With a slow look around her.*] I wonder how it would seem never to have had any children around. [*Pause.*] No, Wright wouldn't like the bird—a thing that sang. She used to sing. He killed that, too.

MRS. PETERS   [*Moving uneasily.*] We don't know who killed the bird.

MRS. HALE   I knew John Wright.

MRS. PETERS   It was an awful thing was done in this house that night, Mrs. Hale. Killing a man while he slept, slipping a rope around his neck that choked the life out of him.

MRS. HALE   His neck. Choked, the life out of him.

[*Her hand goes out and rests on the birdcage.*]

MRS. PETERS   [*With rising voice.*] We don't know who killed him. We don't know.

MRS. HALE   [*Her own feeling not interrupted.*] If there'd been years and years of nothing, then a bird to sing to you, it would be awful—still, after the bird was still.

MRS. PETERS   [*Something within her speaking.*] I know what stillness is. When we homesteaded in Dakota, and my first baby died—after he was two years old, and me with no other then—

MRS. HALE   [*Moving.*] How soon do you suppose they'll be through, looking for the evidence?

MRS. PETERS   I know what stillness is. [*Pulling herself back.*] The law has got to punish crime, Mrs. Hale.

MRS. HALE   [*Not as if answering that.*] I wish you'd seen Minnie Foster when she wore a white dress with blue ribbons and stood up there in the choir and sang. [*A look around the room.*] Oh, I wish I'd come over here once in a while! That was a crime! That was a crime! Who's going to punish that?

MRS. PETERS [*Looking upstairs.*] We mustn't—take on.

MRS. HALE I might have known she needed help! I know how things can be—for women. I tell you, it's queer, Mrs. Peters. We live close together and we live far apart. We all go through the same things—it's all just different kind of the same thing. [*Brushes her eyes; noticing the bottle of fruit, reaches out for it.*] If I was you I wouldn't tell her her fruit was gone. Tell her it ain't. Tell her it's all right. Take this in to prove it to her. She—she may never know whether it was broke or not.

MRS. PETERS [*Takes the bottle, looks about for something to wrap it in; takes petticoat from the clothes brought from the other room, very nervously begins winding this around the bottle. In a false voice.*] My, it's a good thing the men couldn't hear us. Wouldn't they just laugh! Getting all stirred up over a little thing like a—dead canary. As if that could have anything to do with—with—wouldn't they laugh!

   [*The men are heard coming down stairs.*]

MRS. HALE [*Under her breath.*] Maybe they would—maybe they wouldn't

COUNTY ATTORNEY No, Peters, it's all perfectly clear except a reason for doing it. But you know juries when it comes to women. If there was some definite thing. Something to show—something to make a story about—a thing that would connect up with this strange way of doing it—you.

   [*The women's eyes meet for an instant. Enter HALE from outer door*]

HALE Well, I've got the team around. Pretty cold out there.

COUNTY ATTORNEY I'm going to stay here a while by myself. [*To the SHERIFF.*] You can send Frank out for me, can't you? I want to go over everything. I'm not satisfied that we can't do better.

SHERIFF Do you want to see what Mrs. Peters is going to take in?

   [*The COUNTY ATTORNEY goes to the table, picks up the apron, laughs.*]

COUNTY ATTORNEY Oh, I guess they're not very dangerous things the ladies have picked out. [*Moves a few things about, disturbing the quilt pieces which cover the box. Steps back.*] No, Mrs. Peters doesn't need supervising. For that matter, a sheriff's wife is married to the law. Ever think of it that way, Mrs. Peters?

MRS. PETERS Not—just that way.

SHERIFF [*Chuckling.*] Married to the law. [*Moves toward the other room.*] I just want you to come in here a minute, George. We ought to take a look at these windows.

COUNTY ATTORNEY [*Scoffingly.*] Oh, windows!

SHERIFF We'll be right out, Mr. Hale.

   [*HALE goes outside. The SHERIFF follows the COUNTY ATTORNEY into the other room. Then MRS. HALE rises, hands tight together, looking intensely at MRS. PETERS, whose eyes make a slow turn, finally meeting MRS. HALE's. A moment MRS. HALE holds her, then her own eyes point the way to where the box is concealed. Suddenly MRS. PETERS throws back quilt pieces and tries to put the box in the bag she is wearing. It is too big. She opens box, starts to take bird out, cannot touch it, goes to pieces, stands there helpless. Sound of a knob turning in the other room. MRS. HALE snatches the box and puts it in the pocket of her big coat. Enter COUNTY ATTORNEY and SHERIFF.*]

COUNTY ATTORNEY   [*Facetiously.*] Well, Henry, at least we found out that
she was not going to quilt it. She was going to—what is it you call it, ladies?
MRS. HALE   [*Her hand against her pocket.*] We call it—knot it, Mr. Henderson.

CURTAIN

1916

Fitcher's Bird (1812)

Jacob Grimm
b. 1785 Hessen, Germany
d. 1863 Berlin
Wilhelm Grimm
b. 1786 Hessen
d. 1859 Berlin

Once upon a time there was a sorcerer who disguised himself as a poor man, went begging from house to house, and captured beautiful girls. No one knew where he took them, for none of them ever returned.

One day he came to the door of a man who had three beautiful daughters. He appeared to be a poor, weak beggar, and he carried a pack basket on his back, as though he wanted to collect some benevolent offerings in it. He asked for a bit to eat, and when the oldest daughter came out to give him a piece of bread, he simply touched her, and she was forced to jump into his pack basket. Then he hurried away with powerful strides and carried her to his house, which stood in the middle of a dark forest.

Everything was splendid in the house, and he gave her everything that she wanted. He said, "My dear, you will like it here with me. You will have everything that your heart desires."

So it went for a few days, and then he said to her, "I have to go away and leave you alone for a short time. Here are the house keys. You may go everywhere and look at everything except for the one room that this little key here unlocks. I forbid you to go there on the penalty of death."

He also gave her an egg, saying, "Take good care of this egg. You should carry it with you at all times, for if you should loose it great misfortune would follow."

She took the keys and the egg, and promised to take good care of everything.

As soon as he had gone she walked about in the house from top to bottom examining everything. The rooms glistened with silver and gold, and she thought that she had never seen such splendor.

Finally she came to the forbidden door. She wanted to pass it by, but curiosity gave her no rest. She examined the key. It looked like any other one. She put it into the lock and twisted it a little, and then the door sprang open.

What did she see when she stepped inside? A large bloody basin stood in the middle, inside which there lay the cut up parts of dead girls. Nearby there was a wooden block with a glistening ax lying on it.

She was so terrified that the egg, which she was holding in her hand, fell into the basin. She got it out again and wiped off the blood, but it was to no avail, for it always came back. She wiped and scrubbed, but she could not get rid of the stain.

Not long afterward the man returned from his journey, and he immediately asked for the key and the egg. She handed them to him, shaking all the while, for he saw from the red stain that she had been in the blood chamber.

"You went into that chamber against my will," he said, "and now against your will you shall go into it once again. Your life is finished."

He threw her down, dragged her by her hair into the chamber, cut off her head on the block, then cut her up into pieces, and her blood flowed out onto the floor. Then he threw her into the basin with the others.

"Now I will go get the second one," said the sorcerer, and, again disguised as a poor man, he went to their house begging.

The second sister brought him a piece of bread, and, as he had done to the first one, he captured her by merely touching her, and he carried her away. It went with her no better than it had gone with her sister. She let herself be led astray by her curiosity, opened the blood chamber and looked inside. When he returned she paid with her life.

Then he went and captured the third sister, but she was clever and sly. After he had given her the keys and the egg, and had gone away, she carefully put the egg aside, and then examined the house, entering finally the forbidden chamber.

Oh, what she saw! He two dear sisters were lying there in the basin, miserably murdered and chopped to pieces. In spite of this she proceeded to gather their parts together, placing them back in order: head, body, arms, and legs. Then, when nothing else was missing, the parts began to move. They joined together, and the two girls opened their eyes and came back to life. Rejoicing, they kissed and hugged one another.

When the man returned home he immediately demanded the keys and the egg, and when he was unable to detect any trace of blood on them, he said, "You have passed the test. You shall be my bride."

He now had no more power over her and had to do whatever she demanded.

"Good," she answered, "but first you must take a basketful of gold to my father and mother. You yourself must carry it there on your back. In the meanwhile I shall make preparations for the wedding."

Then she ran to her sisters, whom she had hidden in a closet, and said, "The moment is here when I can rescue you. The evildoer himself shall carry you home. As soon as you have arrived at home send help to me."

She put them both into a basket, then covered them entirely with gold, so that nothing could be seen of them.

Then she called the sorcerer in and said, "Now carry this basket away, but you are not to stop and rest underway. Take care, for I shall be watching you through my little window."

The sorcerer lifted the basket onto his back and walked away with it. However, it pressed down so heavily on him that the sweat ran from his face. He sat down, wanting to rest, but immediately one of the girls in the basket called out, "I am looking through my little window, and I can see that you are resting. Walk on!"

He thought that his bride was calling to him, so he got up again. Then he again wanted to sit down, but someone immediately called out, "I am looking through my little window, and I can see that you are resting. Walk on!"

Every time that he stopped walking, someone called out, and he had to walk on until, groaning and out of breath, he brought the basket with the gold and the two girls to their parents' house.

At home the bride was making preparations for the wedding feast, to which she had had the sorcerer's friends invited. Then she took a skull with grinning teeth, adorned it with jewelry and with a wreath of flowers, carried it to the attic window, and let it look out.

When everything was ready she dipped herself into a barrel of honey, then cut open the bed and rolled around in it until she looked like a strange bird, and no one would have been able to recognize her. Then she walked out of the house.

Underway some of the wedding guests met her, and they asked, "You, Fitcher's bird, where are you coming from?"

"I am coming from Fitcher's house."

"What is his young bride doing there?"

"She has swept the house from bottom to top, and now she is looking out of the attic window."

Finally her bridegroom met her. He was slowly walking back home, and, like the others, he asked, "You, Fitcher's bird, where are you coming from?"

"I am coming from Fitcher's house."

"What is my young bride doing there?"

"She has swept the house from bottom to top, and now she is looking out of the attic window."

The bridegroom looked up. Seeing the decorated skull, he thought it was his bride, and he waved a friendly greeting to her.

After he and all his guests had gone into the house, the bride's brothers and relatives arrived. They had been sent to rescue her. After closing up all the doors of the house so that no one could escape, they set it afire, and the sorcerer, together with his gang, all burned to death.

SWEAT (1926)

Zora Neale Hurston
b. 1891 Alabama
d. 1960 Florida

It was eleven o'clock of a Spring night in Florida. It was Sunday. Any other night, Delia Jones would have been in bed for two hours by this time. But she was a washwoman, and Monday morning meant a great deal to her. So she collected the soiled clothes on Saturday when she returned the clean things. Sunday night after church, she sorted them and put the white things to soak. It saved her almost a half day's start. A great hamper in the bedroom held the clothes that she brought home. It was so much neater than a number of bundles lying around.

She squatted in the kitchen floor beside the great pile of clothes, sorting them into small heaps according to color, and humming a song in a mournful key, but wondering through it all where Sykes, her husband, had gone with her horse and buckboard[1].

Just then something long, round, limp and black fell upon her shoulders and slithered to the floor beside her. A great terror took hold of her. It softened her knees and dried her mouth so that it was a full minute before she could cry out or move. Then she saw that it was the big bull whip her husband liked to carry when he drove.

She lifted her eyes to the door and saw him standing there bent over with laughter at her fright. She screamed at him.

"Sykes, what you throw dat whip on me like dat? You know it would skeer me—looks just like a snake, an' you knows how skeered Ah is of snakes.

"Course Ah knowed it! That's how come Ah done it." He slapped his leg with his hand and almost rolled on the ground in his mirth. "If you such a big fool dat you got to have a fit over a earth worm or a string, Ah don't keer how bad Ah skeer you."

"You aint got no business doing it. Gawd knows it's a sin. Some day Ah'm gointuh drop dead from some of yo' foolishness. 'Nother thing, where you been wid mah rig? Ah feeds dat pony. He aint fuh you to be drivin' wid no bull whip."

[1]buckboard an open wagon.

"Yo sho is one aggravatin' nigger woman!" he declared and stepped into the room. She resumed her work and did not answer him at once. "Ah done tole you time and again to keep them white folks clothes outa dis house."

He picked up the whip and glared down at her. Delia went on with her work She went out into the yard and returned with a galvanized tub and set it on the washbench. She saw that Sykes had kicked all of the clothes together again, and now stood in her way truculently, his whole manner hoping, *praying*, for an argument. But she walked calmly around him and commenced to re-sort the things.

"Next time, Ah'm gointer to kick 'em outdoors," he threatened as he struck a match along the leg of his corduroy breeches.

Delia never looked up from her work, and her thin, stooped shoulders sagged further.

"Ah aint for no fuss t'night Sykes. Ah just come from taking sacrament at the church house."

He snorted scornfully. "Yeah, you just come from de church house on a Sunday night, but heah you is gone to work on them clothes. You aint nothing but a hypocrite. One of them amen-corner Christians—sing, whoop, shout, then come home and wash white folks clothes on the Sabbath."

He stepped roughly upon the whitest pile of things, kicking them helter-skelter as he crossed the room. His wife gave a little scream of dismay, and quickly gathered them together again.

"Sykes, you quit grindin' dirt into these clothes! How can Ah git through by Sat'day if Ah don't start on Sunday?"

"Ah don't keer if you never git through. Anyhow, Ah done promised Gawd and a couple of other men, Ah aint gointer have it in mah house. Don't gimme no lip neither, else Ah'll throw 'em out and put mah fist up side yo' head to boot."

Delia's habitual meekness seemed to slip from her shoulders like a blown scarf. She was on her feet; her poor little body, her bare knuckly hands bravely defying the strapping hulk before her.

"Looka heah, Sykes, you done gone too fur. Ah been married to you fur fifteen years, and Ah been takin' in washin' for fifteen years. Sweat, sweat, sweat! Work and sweat, cry and sweat, pray and sweat!"

"What's that got to do with me?" he asked brutally.

"What's it got to do with you, Sykes? Mah tub of suds is filled yo' belly with vittles more times than yo' hands is filled it. Mah sweat is done paid for this house and Ah reckon Ah kin keep on sweatin in it."

She seized the iron skillet from the stove and struck a defensive pose, which act surprised him greatly, coming from her. It cowed him and he did not strike her as he usually did.

"Naw you won't," she panted, "that ole snaggle-toothed black woman you runrin' with aint comin' heah to pile up on *mah* sweat and blood. You aint paid for nothin' on this place, and Ah'm gointer stay right heah till Ah'm toted out foot foremost."

"Well, you better quit gittin' me riled up, else they'll be totin' you out sooner than you expect. Ah'm so tired of you Ah don't know whut to do. Gawd! how Ah hates skinny wimmen!"

A little awed by this new Delia, he sidled out of the door and slammed the back gate after him. He did not say where he had gone; but she knew too well. She knew very well that he would not return until nearly daybreak also. Her work over, she went on to bed but not to sleep at once. Things had come to a pretty pass!

She lay awake, gazing upon the debris that cluttered their matrimonial trail. Not an image left standing along the way. Anything like flowers had long ago been drowned in the salty stream that had been pressed from her heart. Her tears, her sweat, her blood. She had brought love to the union and he had brought a longing for the flesh. Two months after the wedding, he had given her the first brutal beating. She had the memory of numerous trips to Orlando with all of his wages when he had returned to her penniless, even before the first year had passed. She was young and soft then, but now she thought of her knotty muscled limbs, her harsh knuckly hands, and drew herself up into an unhappy little ball in the middle of the big feather bed. Too late now to hope for love, even if it were not Bertha it would be someone else. This case differed from the others only in that she was bolder than the others. Too late for everything except her little home. She had built it for her old days, and planted one by one the trees and flowers there. It was lovely to her, lovely.

Somehow before sleep came, she found herself saying aloud: "Oh well, whatever goes over the Devil's back, is got to come under his belly. Sometime or ruther, Sykes, like everybody else, is gointer reap his sowing." After that she was able to build a spiritual earthworks against her husband. His shells could no longer reach her. *Amen.* She went to sleep and slept until he announced his presence in bed by kicking her feet and rudely snatching the cover away.

"Gimme some kivah heah, an' git yo' damn foots over on yo' own side! Ah oughter mash you in yo' mouf fuh drawing dat skillet on me."

Delia went clear to the rail without answering him. A triumphant indifference to all that he was or did.

The week was as full of work for Delia as all other weeks, and Saturday found her behind her little pony; collecting and delivering clothes.

It was a hot, hot day near the end of July. The village men on Joe Clarke's porch even chewed cane listlessly. They did not hurl the cane-knots as usual. They let them dribble over the edge of the porch. Even conversation had collapsed under the heat.

"Heah comes Delia Jones," Jim Merchant said, as the shaggy pony came round the bend of the road toward them. The rusty buckboard was heaped with baskets of crisp, clean laundry.

"Yep," Joe Lindsay agreed, "Hot or col', rain or shine, jes ez reg lar ez de weeks roll roun' Delia carries 'em an' fetches 'em on Sat'day."

"She better if she wanter eat," said Moss. "Syke Jones aint wuth de shot an' powder hit would tek tuh kill 'em. Not to *bub* he aint."

"He sho' aint," Walter Thomas chimed in. "It's too bad, too, cause she wuz a right pritty lil trick when he got huh. Ah'd uh mah'ied huh mahseft it' he hadnter beat me to it."

Delia nodded briefly at the men as she drove past.

"Too much knockin will ruin *any* 'oman. He done beat huh nough tuh kill three women let lone change they looks," said Elijah Mosely. How Syke kin stommuck dat big black greasy Mogu he's layin' roun' wid, gits me. Ah swear dat eight rock couldn't kiss a sardine can "Ah done thowed out de back do way las' yeah."

"Aw, she's fat, thass how come. He's allus been crazy bout fat women," put in Merchant. "He'd a' been tied up wid one long time ago if he could a found one tuh have him. Did Ah tell yuh bout him come sidlin' roun' *mah* wife—bringin' her a basket uh pee-cans outa his yard fuh a present? Yes-sir, mah wife! She to! him tuh take 'em right straight back home, cause Delia works so hard ovah dat washtub she reckon everything en de place taste lak sweat an' soap-suds. Ah jus' wisht Ah'd a' caught 'im 'roun' dere! Ah'd a' made his hips ketch on fiah down dat shell road."

"Ah know he done it, too. Ah sees 'im grinnin' at every oman dat passes," Walter Thomas said. "But even so, he useter eat some mighty big hunks uh humble pie tuh git dat lil' 'oman he got. She wuz ez pritty ez a speckled pup! Dat wuz fifteen yeahs ago. He useter be so skeered uh losin' huh, she could make him do some parts of a husband's duty. Dey never wuz de same in de mind."

"There oughter be a law about him," said Lindsay. "He aint fit tuh carry guts tuh a bear!"

Clarke spoke for the first time. "Taint no law on earth dat kin make a man be decent if it aint in 'im. There's plenty men dat takes a wife lak dey do a joint uh sugar-cane. It's round, juicy an' sweet when dey gits it. But dey squeeze an' grind squeeze an' grind an' wring tell dey wring every drop uh pleasure dat's in 'em out. When dey's satisfied dat dey is wring dry, dey treats 'em jes lak dey do a cane-chew. Dey thows 'em away. Dey knows whut dey is doin' while dey is at it, an' hates theirselves fuh it but they keeps on hangin' after huh tell she's empty. Den dey hates huh fuh bein' a cane-chew an' in de way."

"We oughter take Syke an' dat stray oman uh his'n down in Lake Howell swamp an' lay on de rawhide till they cain't say 'Lawd a' mussy.' He allus wuz uh ovahbearin' niggah, but since dat white 'oman from up north done teached 'im how to run a automobile, he done got too biggety to live—an' we oughter kill 'im," Old Man Anderson advised.

A grunt of approval went around the porch. But the heat was melting their civic virtue and Elijah Moseley began to bait Joe Clarke.

"Come on, Joe, git a melon outa dere an' slice it up for yo' customers. We'se all sufferin' wid de heat. De bear's done got *me!*"

"Thass right. Joe, a watermelon is jes' whut Ah needs tuh cure de eppizudicks." Walter Thomas joined forces with Moseley. "Come on dere, Joe. We all is steady customers an you aint set us up in a long time. Ah chooses dat long, bowlegged Floridy favorite."

"A god, an' be dough. You all gimme twenty cents and slice away," Clarke retorted. "Ah needs a col' slice m'self. Heah, everybody chip in. Ah'll lend y'll mah meat knife."

The money was quickly subscribed and the huge melon brought forth. At that moment, Sykes and Bertha arrived. A determined silence fell on the porch and the melon was put away again.

Merchant snapped down the blade of his jackknife and moved toward the store door.

"Come on in, Joe, an' gimme a slab uh sow belly an' uh pound uh coffee—almost fuhgot 'twas Sat'day. Got to git on home." Most of the men left also.

Just then Delia drove past on her way home, as Sykes was ordering magnificently for Bertha. It pleased him for Delia to see.

"Git whutsoever yo' heart desires, Honey. Wait a minute, Joe. Give huh two bottles uh strawberry soda-water, uh quart uh parched groundpeas, an' a block uh chewin' gum."

With all this they left the store, with Sykes reminding Bertha that this was his town and she could have it if she wanted it.

The men returned soon after they left, and held their watermelon feast. "Where did Syke Jones git dat 'oman from nohow?" Lindsay asked.

"Ovah Apopka. Guess dey musta been cleanin' out de town when she lef. She don't look lak a thing but a hunk uh liver wid hair on it."

"Well, she sho' kin squall," Dave Carter contributed. "When she gits ready tuh laff, she jes' opens huh mouf an' latches it back tuh de las' notch. No ole grandpa alligator down in Lake Bell aint got nothin' on huh."

Bertha had been in town three months now. Sykes was still paying her room rent at Della Lewis'—the only house in town that would have taken her in. Sykes took her frequently to Winter Park to "stomps."[4] He still assured her that he was the swellest man in the state.

"Sho' you kin have dat lil' ole house soon's Ah kin git dat 'oman outa dere. Everything b'longs tuh me an' you sho' kin have it. Ah sho' 'bominates uh skinny 'oman. Lawdy, you sho' is got one portly shape on you! You kin git *anything* you wants. Dis is *mah* town an' you sho' kin have it.

Delia's work-worn knees crawled over the earth in Gethsemane and on the rocks of Calvary many, many times during these months. She avoided the villagers and meeting places in her effort to be blind and deaf. But Bertha nullified this to a degree, by coming to Delia's house to call Sykes out to her at the gate.

Delia and Sykes fought all the time now with no peaceful interludes. They slept and ate in silence. Two or three times Delia had attempted a timid friendliness, but she was repulsed each time. It was plain that the breaches must remain agape.

The sun had burned July to August. The heat streamed down like a million hot arrows, smiting all things living upon the earth. Grass withered, leaves browned, snakes went blind in shedding and men and dogs went mad. Dog days!

Delia came home one day and found Sykes there before her. She wondered, but started to go on into the house without speaking, even though he was standing in the kitchen door and she must either stoop under his arm or ask him to move. He made no room for her. She noticed a soap box beside the steps, but paid no particular attention to it, knowing that he must have brought it there. As she was stooping to pass under his outstretched arm, he suddenly pushed her backward, laughingly.

"Look in de box dere Delia. Ah done brung yuh somethin'!!"

She nearly fell upon the box in her stumbling, and when she saw what it held, she all but fainted outright.

"Syke! Syke, mah Gawd! You take dat rattlesnake 'way from heah! You *gottuh*. Oh, Jesus, have mussy!"

"Ah aint gut tuh do nuthin' uh de kin'—fact is Ah aint got tuh do nothin' but die. Taint no use uh you puttin' on airs makin' out lak you sceered uh dat snake—he's gointer stay right heah tell he die. He wouldn't bite me cause Ah knows how tuh handle 'im. Nohow he wouldn't risk breakin' out his fangs 'gin *yo'* skinny laigs."

"Naw, now Syke, don't keep dat thing 'roun' heah tuh skeer me tuh death. You knows Ah'm even feared uh earth worms. Thass de biggest snake Ah evah did see. Kill 'im Syke, please."

"Doan ast me tuh do nothin 'fuh yuh. Goin 'roun' tryin' to be so damn asterperious. Naw, Ah aint gonna kill it. Ah think uh damn sight mo' uh him dan you! Dat's a nice snake an' anybody doan lak 'im kin jes' hit de grit."

The village soon heard that Sykes had the snake, and came to see and ask questions.

"How de hen-fire did you ketch dat six-foot rattler, Syke?" Thomas asked.

"He's full uh frogs so he caint hardly move, thass how Ah eased up on 'm But Ah'm a snake charmer an' knows how tuh handle 'em. Shux, dat aint nothin'. Ah could ketch one eve'y day if Ah so wanted tuh."

"Whut he needs is a heavy hick'ry club leaned real heavy on his head. Dat's de bes 'way tuh charm a rattlesnake."

"Naw, Walt, y'll jes' don't understand dese diamon' backs lak Ah do," said Sykes in a superior tone of voice.

The village agreed with Walter, but the snake stayed on. His box remained by the kitchen door with its screen wire covering. Two or three days later it had digested its meal of frogs and literally came to life. It rattled at every movement in the kitchen or the yard. One day as Delia came down the kitchen steps she saw his chalky white fangs curved like scimitars hung in the wire meshes. This time she did not run away with averted eyes as usual. She stood for a long time in the doorway in a red fury that grew bloodier for every second that she regarded the creature that was her torment.

That night she broached the subject as soon as Sykes sat down to the table.

"Syke, Ah wants you tuh take dat snake way fum heah. You done starved me an' Ah put up widcher, you done beat me an Ah took dat, but you done kilt all mah insides bringin' dat varmint heah."

Sykes poured out a saucer full of coffee and drank it deliberately before he answered her.

"A whole lot Ah keer bout how you feels inside uh out. Dat snake aint goin' no damn wheah till Ah gits ready fuh 'im tuh go. So fur as beatin' is concerned, yuh aint took near all dat you gointer take ef yuh stay 'roun' *me.*"

Delia pushed back her plate and got up from the table. "Ah hates you. Sykes," she said calmly. "Ah hates you tuh de same degree dat Ah useter love yuh. Ah done took an' took till mah belly is full up tuh mah neck. Dat's de reason Ah got mah letter fum de church an' moved mah membership tuh Woodbridge—so Ah don't haftuh take no sacrament wid yuh. Ah don't wantuh see yuh, 'roun' me atall. Lay 'roun' wid dat 'oman all yuh wants tuh, but gwan 'way fum me an' mah house. Ah hates yuh lak uh suck-egg dog."

Sykes almost let the huge wad of corn bread and collard greens he was chewing fall out of his mouth in amazement. He had a hard time whipping himself to the proper fury to try to answer Delia.

"Well, Ah'm glad you does hate me. Ah'm sho tiahed uh you hangin' ontuh me. Ah don't want yuh. Look at yuh stringey ole neck! Yo' raw-bony laigs an' arms is enough tuh cut uh man tuh death. You looks jes lak de devvul's doll-baby tuh *me*. You cain't hate me no worse dan Ah hates you. Ah been hatin' *you* fuh years."

"Yo' ole black hide don't look lak nothin' tuh me, but uh passle uh wrinkled up rubber, wid yo' big ole yeahs flappin' on each side lak uh paih uh buzzard wings. Don't think Ah'm gointuh be run 'way fum mah house neither. Ah'm goin' tuh de white folks about *you*, mah young man, de very nex' time you lay yo' han's on me. Mah cup is done run ovah." Delia said this with no signs of fear and Sykes departed from the house, threatening her, but made not the slightest move to carry out any of them.

That night he did not return at all, and the next day being Sunday, Delia was glad that she did not have to quarrel before she hitched up her pony and drove the four miles to Woodbridge.

She stayed to the night service—"love feast"—which was very warm and full of spirit. In the emotional winds her domestic trials were borne far and wide so that she sang as she drove homeward.

"Jurden water, black an' col'
Chills de body, not de soul
An' Ah wantah cross Jurden in uh calm time."

She came from the barn to the kitchen door and stopped.

"Whut's de mattah, ol' satan, you aint kickin' up yo' racket?" She addressed the snake's box. Complete silence. She went on into the house with a new hope in its birth struggles. Perhaps her threat to go to the white folks had frightened Sykes! Perhaps he was sorry! Fifteen years of misery and suppression had brought Delia to the place where she would hope *anything* that looked towards a way over or through her wall of inhibitions.

She felt in the match safe behind the stove at once for a match. There was only one there.

"Dat niggah wouldn't fetch nothin heah tuh save his rotten neck, but he kin run thew whut Ah brings quick enough. Now he done toted off nigh on tuh haff uh box uh matches. He done had dat 'oman heah in mah house, too."

Nobody but a woman could tell how she knew this even before she struck the match. But she did and it put her into a new fury.

Presently she brought in the tubs to put the white things to soak. This time she decided she need not bring the hamper out of the bedroom; she would go in there and do the sorting. She picked up the pot-bellied lamp and went in. The room was small and the hamper stood hard by the foot of the white iron bed. She could sit and reach through the bedposts—resting as she worked.

"Ah wantah cross Jurden in uh calm time." She was singing again. The mood of the "love feast" had returned. She threw back the lid of the basket almost gaily. Then, moved by both horror and terror, she sprang back toward the door. *There lay the snake in the basket!* He moved sluggishly at first, but even as she turned round and round, jumped up and down in an insanity of fear, he began to stir vigorously. She saw him pouring his awful beauty from the basket upon the bed, then she seized the lamp and ran as fast as she could to the kitchen. The wind from the open door blew out the light and the darkness added to her terror. She sped to the darkness of the yard, slamming the door after her before she thought to set down the lamp. She did not feel safe even on the ground, so she climbed up in the hay barn.

There for an hour or more she lay sprawled upon the hay a gibbering wreck.

Finally she grew quiet, and after that, coherent thought. With this, stalked through her a cold, bloody rage. Hours of this. A period of introspection, a space of retrospection, then a mixture of both. Out of this an awful calm.

"Well, Ah done de bes' Ah could. If things aint right, Gawd knows taint mah fault."

She went to sleep—a twitchy sleep—and woke up to a faint gray sky. There was a loud hollow sound below. She peered out. Sykes was at the wood-pile, demolishing a wire-covered box.

He hurried to the kitchen door, but hung outside there some minutes before he entered, and stood some minutes more inside before he closed it after him.

The gray in the sky was spreading. Delia descended without fear now, and crouched beneath the low bedroom window. The drawn shade shut out the dawn, shut in the night. But the thin walls held back no sound.

"Dat ol' scratch is woke up now!" She mused at the tremendous whirr inside, which every woodsman knows, is one of the sound illusions. The rattler is a ventriloquist. His whirr sounds to the right, to the left, straight ahead, behind, close under foot—everywhere but where it is. Woe to him who guesses wrong unless he is prepared to hold up his end of the argument! Sometimes he strikes without rattling at all.

Inside, Sykes heard nothing until he knocked a pot lid off the stove while trying to reach the match safe in the dark. He had emptied his pockets at Bertha's.

The snake seemed to wake up under the stove and Sykes made a quick leap into the bedroom. In spite of the gin he had had his head was clearing now.

"Mah Gawd!" he chattered. "Ef Ah could only strack uh light!"

The rattling ceased for a moment as he stood paralyzed. He waited. It seemed that the snake waited also.

"Oh, fuh de light! Ah thought he'd be too sick"—Sykes was muttering to himself when the whirr began again, closer, right underfoot this time. Long before this, Sykes' ability to think had been flattened down to primitive instinct and he leaped—onto the bed.

Outside Delia heard a cry that might have come from a maddened chimpanzee, a stricken gorilla. All the terror, all the horror, all the rage that man possibly could express, without a recognizable human sound.

A tremendous stir inside there, another series of animal screams, the intermittent whirr of the reptile. The shade torn violently down from the window letting in the red dawn, a huge brown hand seizing the window stick, great dull blows upon the wooden floor punctuating the gibberish of sound long after the rattle of the snake had abruptly subsided. All this Delia could see and hear from her place beneath the window, and it made her ill. She crept over to the four-o'clocks[7] and stretched herself on the cool earth to recover.

She lay there. "Delia, Delia" She could hear Sykes calling in a most despairing tone as one who expected no answer. The sun crept on up, and he called. Delia

---

7. four-o'clocks flowers that open in the late afternoon.

could not move—her legs were gone flabby. She never moved, he called, and the sun kept rising.

"Mah Gawd!" She heard him moan. "Mah Gawd fum Heben!" She heard him stumbling about and got up from her flower-bed. The sun was growing warm. As she approached the door she heard him call out hopefully. "Delia, is dat you Ah heah?"

She saw him on his hands and knees as soon as she reached the door. He crept an inch or two toward her—all that he was able, and she saw his horribly swollen neck and his one open eye shining with hope. A surge of pity too strong to support bore her away from that eye that must, could not, fail to see the tubs. He would see the lamp. Orlando with its doctors was too far. She could scarcely reach the Chinaberry tree, where she waited in the growing heat while inside she knew the cold river was creeping up and up to extinguish that eye which must know by now that she knew.

[1926]

Araby (1914)

James Joyce
b. 1882 Rathgar (Dublin Suburb), Ireland
d. 1941 Zurich, Switzerland

North Richmond Street, being blind, was a quiet street except at the hour when the Christian Brothers' School set the boys free. An uninhabited house of two storeys stood at the blind end, detached from its neighbours in a square ground. The other houses of the street, conscious of decent lives within them, gazed at one another with brown imperturbable faces.

The former tenant of our house, a priest, had died in the back drawing-room. Air, musty from having been long enclosed, hung in all the rooms, and the waste room behind the kitchen was littered with old useless papers. Among these I found a few paper-covered books, the pages of which were curled and damp: *The Abbot*, by Walter Scott, *The Devout Communicant*, and *The Memoirs of Vidocq*. I liked the last best because its leaves were yellow. The wild garden behind the house contained a central apple-tree and a few straggling bushes, under one of which I found the late tenant's rusty bicycle-pump. He had been a very charitable priest; in his will he had left all his money to institutions and the furniture of his house to his sister.

When the short days of winter came, dusk fell before we had well eaten our dinners. When we met in the street the houses had grown sombre. The space of sky above us was the colour of ever-changing violet and towards it the lamps of the street lifted their feeble lanterns. The cold air stung us and we played till our bodies glowed. Our shouts echoed in the silent street. The career of our play brought us through the dark muddy lanes behind the houses, where we ran the gauntlet of the rough tribes from the cottages, to the back doors of the dark dripping gardens where odours arose from the ashpits, to the dark odorous stables where a coachman smoothed and combed the horse or shook music from the buckled harness. When we returned to the street, light from the kitchen windows had filled the areas. If my uncle was seen turning the corner, we hid in the shadow until we had seen him safely housed. Or if Mangan's sister came out on the doorstep to call her brother in to his tea, we watched her from our shadow peer up and down the street. We waited to see whether she would remain or go in and, if she remained, we left our shadow and walked up to Mangan's steps resignedly. She was waiting for us, her figure defined by the light from the half-opened door. Her brother always teased her before he obeyed, and I stood by the railings looking at her. Her dress swung as she moved her body, and the soft rope of her hair tossed from side to side.

Every morning I lay on the floor in the front parlour watching her door. The blind was pulled down to within an inch of the sash so that I could not be seen. When she came out on the doorstep my heart leaped. I ran to the hall, seized my books and followed her. I kept her brown figure always in my eye and, when we came near the point at which our ways diverged, I quickened my pace and passed her. This happened morning after morning. I had never spoken to her, except for a few casual words, and yet her name was like a summons to all my foolish blood.

Her image accompanied me even in places the most hostile to romance. On Saturday evenings when my aunt went marketing I had to go to carry some of the parcels. We walked through the flaring streets, jostled by drunken men and bargaining women, amid the curses of labourers, the shrill litanies of shop-boys who stood on guard by the barrels of pigs' cheeks, the nasal chanting of street-singers, who sang a *come-all-you* about O'Donovan Rossa, or a ballad about the troubles in our native land. These noises converged in a single sensation of life for me: I imagined that I bore my chalice safely through a throng of foes. Her name sprang to my lips at moments in strange prayers and praises which I myself did not understand. My eyes were often full of tears (I could not tell why) and at times a flood from my heart seemed to pour itself out into my bosom. I thought little of the future. I did not know whether I would ever speak to her or not or, if I spoke to her, how I could tell her of my confused adoration. But my body was like a harp and her words and gestures were like fingers running upon the wires.

One evening I went into the back drawing-room in which the priest had died. It was a dark rainy evening and there was no sound in the house. Through one of the broken panes I heard the rain impinge upon the earth, the fine incessant needles of water playing in the sodden beds. Some distant lamp or lighted window gleamed below me. I was thankful that I could see so little. All my senses seemed to desire to veil themselves and, feeling that I was about to slip from them, I pressed the palms of my hands together until they trembled, murmuring: 'O love! O love!' many times.

At last she spoke to me. When she addressed the first words to me I was so confused that I did not know what to answer. She asked me was I going to *Araby*. I forgot whether I answered yes or no. It would be a splendid bazaar; she said she would love to go.

'And why can't you?' I asked.

While she spoke she turned a silver bracelet round and round her wrist. She could not go, she said, because there would be a retreat that week in her convent. Her brother and two other boys were fighting for their caps, and I was alone at the railings. She held one of the spikes, bowing her head towards me. The light from the lamp opposite our door caught the white curve of her neck, lit up her hair that rested there and, falling, lit up the hand upon the railing. It fell over one side of her dress and caught the white border of a petticoat, just visible as she stood at ease.

'It's well for you,' she said.

'If I go,' I said, 'I will bring you something.'

What innumerable follies laid waste my waking and sleeping thoughts after that evening! I wished to annihilate the tedious intervening days. I chafed against the work of school. At night in my bedroom and by day in the classroom her image came between me and the page I strove to read. The syllables of the word *Araby* were called to me through the silence in which my soul luxuriated and cast an Eastern enchantment over me. I asked for leave to go to the bazaar on Saturday night. My aunt was surprised, and hoped it was not some Freemason affair. I answered few questions in class. I watched my master's face pass from amiability to sternness; he hoped I was not beginning to idle. I could not call my wandering thoughts together. I had hardly any patience with the serious work of life which, now that it stood between me and my desire, seemed to me child's play, ugly monotonous child's play.

On Saturday morning I reminded my uncle that I wished to go to the bazaar in the evening. He was fussing at the hallstand, looking for the hat-brush, and answered me curtly:

'Yes, boy, I know.'

As he was in the hall I could not go into the front parlour and lie at the window. I felt the house in bad humour and walked slowly towards the school. The air was pitilessly raw and already my heart misgave me.

When I came home to dinner my uncle had not yet been home. Still it was early. I sat staring at the clock for some time and, when its ticking began to irritate me, I left the room. I mounted the staircase and gained the upper part of the house. The high, cold, empty, gloomy rooms liberated me and I went from room to room singing. From the front window I saw my companions playing below in the street. Their cries reached me weakened and indistinct and, leaning my forehead against the cool glass, I looked over at the dark house where she lived. I may have stood there for an hour, seeing nothing but the brown-clad figure cast by my imagination, touched discreetly by the lamplight at the curved neck, at the hand upon the railings and at the border below the dress.

When I came downstairs again I found Mrs Mercer sitting at the fire. She was an old, garrulous woman, a pawnbroker's widow, who collected used stamps for some pious purpose. I had to endure the gossip of the tea-table. The meal was prolonged beyond an hour and still my uncle did not come. Mrs Mercer stood up to go: she was sorry she couldn't wait any longer, but it was after eight o'clock and she did not like to be out late, as the night air was bad for her. When she had gone I began to walk up and down the room, clenching my fists. My aunt said:

'I'm afraid you may put off your bazaar for this night of Our Lord.'

At nine o'clock I heard my uncle's latchkey in the hall door. I heard him talking to himself and heard the hallstand rocking when it had received the weight of his overcoat. I could interpret these signs. When he was midway through his dinner I asked him to give me the money to go to the bazaar. He had forgotten.

'The people are in bed and after their first sleep now,' he said.

I did not smile. My aunt said to him energetically:

'Can't you give him the money and let him go? You've kept him late enough as it is.'

My uncle said he was very sorry he had forgotten. He said he believed in the old saying: 'All work and no play makes Jack a dull boy.' He asked me where I was going and, when I told him a second time, he asked me did I know *The Arab's Farewell to his Steed*. When I left the kitchen he was about to recite the opening lines of the piece to my aunt.

I held a florin tightly in my hand as I strode down Buckingham Street towards the station. The sight of the streets thronged with buyers and glaring with gas recalled to me the purpose of my journey. I took my seat in a third-class carriage of a deserted train. After an intolerable delay the train moved out of the station slowly. It crept onward among ruinous houses and over the twinkling river. At Westland Row Station a crowd of people pressed to the carriage doors; but the porters moved them back, saying that it was a special train for the bazaar. I remained alone in the bare carriage. In a few minutes the train drew up beside an improvised wooden platform. I passed out on to the road and saw by the lighted dial of a clock that it was ten minutes to ten. In front of me was a large building which displayed the magical name.

I could not find any sixpenny entrance and, fearing that the bazaar would be closed, I passed in quickly through a turnstile, handing a shilling to a weary-looking man. I found myself in a big hall girded at half its height by a gallery. Nearly all the stalls were closed and the greater part of the hall was in darkness. I recognized a silence like that which pervades a church after a service. I walked into the centre of the bazaar timidly. A few people were gathered about the stalls which were still open. Before a curtain, over which the words *Café Chantant* were written in coloured lamps, two men were counting money on a salver. I listened to the fall of the coins.

Remembering with difficulty why I had come, I went over to one of the stalls and examined porcelain vases and flowered tea-sets. At the door of the stall a young lady was talking and laughing with two young gentlemen. I remarked their English accents and listened vaguely to their conversation.

'O, I never said such a thing!'

'O, but you did!'

'O, but I didn't!'

'Didn't she say that?'

'Yes. I heard her.'

'O, there's a . . . fib!'

Observing me, the young lady came over and asked me did I wish to buy anything. The tone of her voice was not encouraging; she seemed to have spoken to me out of a sense of duty. I looked humbly at the great jars that stood like eastern guards at either side of the dark entrance to the stall and murmured:

'No, thank you.'

The young lady changed the position of one of the vases and went back to the two young men. They began to talk of the same subject. Once or twice the young lady glanced at me over her shoulder.

I lingered before her stall, though I knew my stay was useless, to make my interest in her wares seem the more real. Then I turned away slowly and walked down the middle of the bazaar. I allowed the two pennies to fall against the sixpence in my pocket. I heard a voice call from one end of the gallery that the light was out. The upper part of the hall was now completely dark.

Gazing up into the darkness I saw myself as a creature driven and derided by vanity; and my eyes burned with anguish and anger.

THE ONES WHO WALK AWAY FROM OMELAS (1973)

Ursula K. LeGuin
b. Berkeley, CA October 1929

With a clamor of bells that set the swallows soaring, the Festival of Summer came to the city Omelas, bright-towered by the sea. The ringing of the boats in harbor sparkled with flags. In the streets between houses with red roofs and painted walls, between old moss-grown gardens and under avenues of trees, past great parks and public buildings, processions moved. Some were decorous: old people in long stiff robes of mauve and gray, grave master workmen, quiet, merry women carrying their babies and chatting as they walked. In other streets the music beat faster, a shimmering of gong and tambourine, and the people went dancing, the procession was a dance. Children dodged in and out, their high calls rising like the swallows' crossing flights over the music and the singing. All the processions wound towards the north side of the city, where on the great water-meadow called the Green Fields boys and girls, naked in the bright air, with mud-stained feet and ankles and long, lithe arms, exercised their restive horses before the race. The horses wore no gear at all but a halter without bit. Their manes were braided with streamers of silver, gold, and green. They flared their nostrils and pranced and boasted to one another; they were vastly excited, the horse being the only animal who has adopted our ceremonies as his own. Far off to the north and west the mountains stood up half encircling Omelas on her bay. The air of morning was so clear that the snow still crowning the Eighteen Peaks burned with white-gold fire across the miles of sunlit air, under the dark blue of the sky. There was just enough wind to make the banners that marked the racecourse snap and flutter now and then. In the silence of the broad green meadows one could hear the music winding throughout the city streets, farther and nearer and ever approaching, a cheerful faint sweetness of the air from time to time trembled and gathered together and broke out into the great joyous clanging of the bells.

Joyous! How is one to tell about joy? How describe the citizens of Omelas?

They were not simple folk, you see, though they were happy. But we do not say the words of cheer much any more. All smiles have become archaic. Given a description such as this one tends to make certain assumptions. Given a description such as this one tends to look next for the King, mounted on a splendid stallion and surrounded by his noble knights, or perhaps in a golden litter borne by great-muscled slaves. But there was no king. They did not use swords, or keep slaves. They were not barbarians, I do not know the rules and laws of their society, but I suspect that they were singularly few. As they did without monarchy and slavery, so they also got on without the stock exchange, the advertisement, the secret police, and the bomb. Yet I repeat that these were not simple folk, not dulcet shepherds, noble savages, bland utopians. There were not less complex than us.

The trouble is that we have a bad habit, encouraged by pedants and sophisticates, of considering happiness as something rather stupid. Only pain is intellectual, only evil interesting. This is the treason of the artist: a refusal to admit the banality of evil and the terrible boredom of pain. If you can't lick 'em, join 'em. If it hurts, repeat it. But to praise despair is to condemn delight, to embrace violence is to lose hold of everything else. We have almost lost hold; we can no longer describe happy man, nor make any celebration of joy. How can I tell you about the people of Omelas? They were not naive and happy children—though their children were, in fact, happy. They were mature, intelligent, passionate adults whose lives were not wretched. O miracle! But I wish I could describe it better. I wish I could convince you. Omelas sounds in my words like a city in a fairy tale, long ago and far away, once upon a time. Perhaps it would be best if you imagined it as your own fancy bids, assuming it will rise to the occasion, for certainly I cannot suit you all. For instance, how about technology? I think that there would be no cars or helicopters in and above the streets; this follows from the fact that the people of Omelas are happy people. Happiness is based on a just discrimination of what is necessary, what is neither necessary nor destructive, and what is destructive. In the middle category, however—that of the unnecessary but undestructive, that of comfort, luxury, exuberance, etc.—they could perfectly well have central heating, subway trains, washing machines, and all kinds of marvelous devices not yet invented here, floating light-sources, fuelless power, a cure for the common cold. Or they could have none of that: it doesn't matter. As you like it. I incline to think that people from towns up and down the coast have been coming to to Omelas during the last days before the Festival on very fast little trains and double-decked trams, and that the trains station of Omelas is actually the handsomest building in town, though plainer than the magnificent Farmers' Market. But even granted trains, I fear that Omelas so far strikes some of you as goody-goody. Smiles, bells, parades, horses, bleh. If so, please add an orgy. If an orgy would help, don't hesitate. Let us not, however, have temples from which issue beautiful nude priests and priestesses already half in ecstasy and ready to copulate with any man or woman, lover or stranger, who desires union with the deep godhead of the blood, although that was my first idea. But really it would be better not to have any temples in Omelas—at least, not manned temples. Religion yes, clergy no. Surely the beautiful nudes can just wander about, offering themselves like divine soufflés to the hunger of the needy and the rapture of the flesh. Let them join the processions. Let tambourines be struck above the copulations, and the glory of desire be proclaimed upon the gongs, and (a not unimportant point) let the offspring of these delightful rituals be beloved and looked after by all. One thing I know there is none of in Omelas is guilt. But what else should there be? I thought at first there were no drugs, but that is puritanical. For those who like it, the faint insistent sweetness of drooz may perfume the ways of the city, drooz which first brings a great lightness and brilliance to the mind and limbs, and then after some hours a dreamy languor, and wonderful visions at last of the very arcane and inmost secrets of the Universe, as well as exciting the pleasure of sex beyond all belief; and it is not habit-forming. For more modest tastes I think there ought to be beer. What else, what else belongs in the joyous city? The sense of victory, surely, the celebration of courage. But as we did without clergy, let us do without soldiers. The joy built upon successful slaughter is not the right kind of joy; it will not do; it is fearful and it is trivial. A boundless and generous contentment, a magnanimous triumph felt not against some outer enemy but in communion with the finest and fairest in the souls of all men everywhere and the splendor of the world's summer: This is what swells the hearts of the people of Omelas, and the victory they celebrate is that of life. I don't think many of them need to take drooz.

Most of the processions have reached the Green Fields by now. A marvelous smell of cooking goes forth from the red and blue tents of the provisioners. The faces of small children are amiably sticky; in the benign gray beard of a man a couple of crumbs of rich pastry are entangled. The youths and girls have mounted their horses and are beginning to group around the starting line of the course. An old woman, small, fat, and laughing, is passing out flowers from a basket, and tall young men wear her flowers in their shining hair. A child of nine or ten sits at the edge of the crowd alone, playing on a wooden flute.

People pause to listen, and they smile, but they do not speak to him, for he never ceases playing and never sees them, his dark eyes wholly rapt in the sweet, thin magic of the tune.

He finishes, and slowly lowers his hands holding the wooden flute.

As if that little private silence were the signal, all at once a trumpet sounds from the pavilion near the starting line: imperious, melancholy, piercing. The horses rear on their slender legs, and some of them neigh in answer. Sober-faced, the young riders stroke the horses' necks and soothe them, whispering, "Quiet, quiet, there my beauty, my hope . . ." They begin to form in rank along the starting line. The crowds along the racecourse are like a field of grass and flowers in the wind. The Festival of Summer has begun.

Do you believe? Do you accept the festival, the city, the joy? No? Then let me describe one more thing.

In a basement under one of the beautiful public buildings of Omelas, or perhaps in the cellar of one of its spacious private homes, there is a room. It has one locked door, and no window. A little light seeps in dustily between cracks in the boards, secondhand from a cobwebbed window somewhere across the cellar. In one corner of the little room a couple of mops, with stiff, clotted, foul-smelling heads, stand near a rusty bucket. The floor is dirt, a little damp to the touch, as cellar dirt usually is.

The room is about three paces long and two wide: a mere broom closet or disused tool room. In the room, a child is sitting. It could be a boy or a girl. It looks about six, but actually is nearly ten. It is feeble-minded. Perhaps it was born defective, or perhaps it has become imbecile through fear, malnutrition, and neglect. It picks its nose and occasionally fumbles vaguely with its toes or genitals, as it sits hunched in the corner farthest from the bucket and the two mops. It is afraid of the mops. It finds them horrible. It shuts its eyes, but it knows the mops are still standing there; and the door is locked; and nobody will come. The door is always locked; and nobody ever comes, except that sometimes—the child has no understanding of time or interval—sometimes the door rattles terribly and opens, and a person, or several people, are there. One of them may come in and kick the child to make it stand up. The others never come close, but peer in at it with frightened, disgusted eyes. The food bowl and the water jug are hastily filled, the door is locked; the eyes disappear. The people at the door never say anything, but the child, who has not always lived in the tool room, and can remember sunlight and its mother's voice, sometimes speaks. "I will be good," it says. "Please let me out. I will be good!" They never answer. The child used to scream for help at night, and cry a good deal, but now it only makes a kind of whining, "eh-haa, eh-haa," and it speaks less and less often. It is so thin there are no calves to its legs; its belly protrudes; it lives on a half-bowl of corn meal and grease a day. It is naked. Its buttocks and thighs are a mass of festered sores, as it sits in its own excrement continually.

They all know it is there, all the people of Omelas. Some of them have come to see it, others are content merely to know it is there. They all know that it has to be there. Some of them understand why, and some do not, but they all understand that their happiness, the beauty of their city, the tenderness of their friendships, the health of their children, the wisdom of their scholars, the skill of their makers, even the abundance of their harvest and the kindly weathers of their skies, depend wholly on this child's abominable misery.

This is usually explained to children when they are between eight and twelve, whenever they seem capable of understanding; and most of those who come to see the child are young people, though often enough an adult comes, or comes back, to see the child. No matter how well the matter has been explained to them, these young spectators are always shocked and sickened at the sight. They feel disgust, which they had thought themselves superior to. They feel anger, outrage, impotence, despite all the explanations. They would like to do something for the child. But there is nothing they can do. If the child were brought up into the sunlight out of that vile place, if it were cleaned and fed and comforted, that would be a good thing, indeed; but if it were done, in that day and hour all the prosperity and beauty and delight of Omelas would wither and be destroyed. Those are the terms. To exchange all the goodness and grace of every life in Omelas for that single, small improvement: to throw away the happiness of thousands for the chance of happiness of one: that would be to let guilt within the walls indeed.

The terms are strict and absolute; there may not even be a kind word spoken to the child.

Often the young people go home in tears, or in a tearless rage, when they have seen the child and faced this terrible paradox. They may brood over it for weeks or years. But as time goes on they begin to realize that even if the child could be released, it would not get much good of its freedom: a little vague pleasure of warmth and food, no real doubt, but little more. It is too degraded and imbecile to know any real joy. It has been afraid too long ever to be free of fear. Its habits are too uncouth for it to respond to humane treatment. Indeed, after so long it would probably be wretched without walls about it to protect it, and darkness for its eyes, and its own excrement to sit in. Their tears at the bitter injustice dry when they begin to perceive the terrible justice of reality, and to accept it. Yet it is their tears and anger, the trying of their generosity and the acceptance of their helplessness, which are perhaps the true source of the splendor of their lives. Theirs is no vapid, irresponsible happiness. They know that they, like the child, are not free. They know compassion. It is the existence of the child, and their knowledge of its existence, that makes possible the nobility of their architecture, the poignancy of their music, the profundity of their science. It is because of the child that they are so gentle with children. They know that if the wretched one were not there sniveling in the dark, the other one, the flute-player, could make no joyful music as the young riders line up in their beauty for the race in the sunlight of the first morning of summer.

Now do you believe them? Are they not more credible? But there is one more thing to tell, and this is quite incredible.

At times one of the adolescent girls or boys who go to see the child does not go home to weep or rage, does not, in fact, go home at all. Sometimes also a man or a woman much older falls silent for a day or two, then leaves home. These people go out into the street, and walk down the street alone. They keep walking, and walk straight out of the city of Omelas, through the beautiful gates. They keep walking across the farmlands of Omelas. Each one goes alone, youth or girl, man or woman.

Night falls; the traveler must pass down village streets, between the houses with yellow-lit windows, and on out into the darkness of the fields. Each alone, they go west or north, towards the mountains. They go on. They leave Omelas, they walk ahead into the darkness, and they do not come back. The place they go towards is a place even less imaginable to most of us than the city of happiness. I cannot describe it at all. It is possible that it does not exist. But they seem to know where they are going, the ones who walk away from Omelas.

BENITO CERENO (1855)

Herman Melville
b. 1819 New York, NY
d. 1891 New York, NY

In the Year 1799, Captain Amasa Delano, of Duxbury in Massachusetts, commanding a large sealer and general trader, lay at anchor with a valuable cargo in the harbor of St. Maria—a small, desert, uninhabited island toward the southern extremity of the long coast of Chile. There he had touched for water.

On the second day, not long after dawn, while lying in his berth, his mate came below, informing him that a strange sail was coming into the bay. Ships were then not so plenty in those waters as now. He rose, dressed, and went on deck.

The morning was one peculiar to that coast. Everything was mute and calm; everything gray. The sea, though undulated into long roods of swells, seemed fixed, and was sleeked at the surface like waved lead that has cooled and set in the smelter's mold. The sky seemed a gray surtout. Flights of troubled gray fowl, kith and kin with flights of troubled gray vapors among which they were mixed, skimmed low and fitfully over the waters, as swallows over meadows before storms. Shadows present, foreshadowing deeper shadows to come.

To Captain Delano's surprise, the stranger, viewed through the glass, showed no colors, though to do so upon entering a haven, however uninhabited in its shores, where but a single other ship might be lying, was the custom among peaceful seamen of all nations. Considering the lawlessness and loneliness of the spot, and the sort of stories at that day associated with those seas, Captain Delano's surprise might have deepened into some uneasiness had he not been a person of a singularly undistrustful good nature, not liable except on extraordinary and repeated incentives, and hardly then, to indulge in personal alarms any way involving the imputation of malign evil in man. Whether, in view of what humanity is capable, such a trait implies, along with a benevolent heart, more than ordinary quickness and accuracy of intellectual perception, may be left to the wise to determine.

But whatever misgivings might have obtruded on first seeing the stranger would almost, in any seaman's mind, have been dissipated by observing that the ship, in navigating into the harbor, was drawing too near the land, a sunken reef making out off her bow. This seemed to prove her a stranger, indeed, not only to the sealer, but the island; consequently she could be no wonted freebooter on that ocean. With no small interest Captain Delano continued to watch her—a proceeding not much facilitated by the vapors partly mantling the hull, through which the far matin light from her cabin streamed equivocally enough; much like the sun—by this time hemisphered on the rim of the horizon, and, apparently, in company with the strange ship entering the harbor—which, wimpled by the same low, creeping clouds, showed not unlike a Lima intrigante's one sinister eye peering across the Plaza from the Indian loophole of her dusk *saya-y-manta*.

It might have been but a deception of the vapors, but the longer the stranger was watched the more singular appeared her maneuvers. Erelong it seemed hard to decide whether she meant to come in or no—what she wanted, or what she was about. The wind, which had breezed up a little during the night, was now extremely light and baffling, which the more increased the apparent uncertainty of her movements.

Surmising at last that it might be a ship in distress, Captain Delano ordered his whaleboat to be dropped, and, much to the wary opposition of his mate, prepared to board her, and, at the least, pilot her in. On the night previous, a fishing party of the seamen had gone a long distance to some detached rocks out of sight from the sealer, and, an hour or two before daybreak, had returned, having set with no small success. Presuming that the stranger might have been long off soundings, the good captain put several baskets of the fish, for presents, into his boat, and so pulled away. From her continuing too near the sunken reef deeming her in danger, calling to his men he made all haste to apprise those on board of their situation. But, some time ere the boat came up, the wind, light though it was, having shifted, had headed the vessel off, as well as partly broken the vapors from about her.

Upon gaining a less remote view, the ship, when made signally visible on the verge of the leaden-hued swells, with the shreds of fog here and there raggedly furring her, appeared like a whitewashed monastery after a thunderstorm, seen perched upon some dun cliff among the Pyrenees. But it was no purely fanciful resemblance which now, for a moment, almost led Captain Delano to think that nothing less than a shipload of monks was before him. Peering over the bulwarks were what really seemed, in the hazy distance, throngs of dark cowls; while, fitfully revealed through the open portholes, other dark moving figures were dimly descried, as of Black Friars pacing the cloisters.

Upon a still nigher approach, this appearance was modified, and the true character of the vessel was plain—a Spanish merchantman of the first class, carrying Negro slaves, amongst other valuable freight, from one colonial port to another. A very large, and, in its time, a very fine vessel, such as in those days were at intervals encountered along that main; sometimes superseded Acapulco treasure ships, or retired frigates of the Spanish king's navy, which, like superannuated Italian palaces, still, under a decline of masters, preserved signs of former state.

As the whaleboat drew more and more nigh, the cause of the peculiar pipe-clayed aspect of the stranger was seen in the slovenly neglect pervading her. The spars, ropes, and great part of the bulwarks looked woolly from long unacquaintance with the scraper, tar, and the brush. Her keel seemed laid, her ribs put together, and she launched, from Ezekiel's Valley of Dry Bones.

In the present business in which she was engaged, the ship's general model and rig appeared to have undergone no material change from their original warlike and Froissart pattern. However, no guns were seen.

The tops were large, and were railed about with what had once been octagonal network, all now in sad disrepair. These tops hung overhead like three ruinous aviaries, in one of which was seen perched, on a ratline, a white noddy, a strange fowl so called from its lethargic, somnambulistic character, being frequently caught by hand at sea. Battered and moldy, the castellated forecastle seemed some ancient turret long ago taken by assault, and then left to decay. Toward the stern, two high-raised quarter galleries—the balustrades here and there covered with dry tindery sea moss—opening out from the unoccupied state cabin, whose deadlights, for all the mild weather, were hermetically closed and calked—these tenantless balconies hung over the sea as if it were the grand Venetian canal. But the principal relic of faded grandeur was the ample oval of the shieldlike sternpiece, intricately carved with the arms of Castile and Leon, medallioned about by groups of mythological or symbolical devices, uppermost and central of which was a dark satyr in a mask holding his foot on the prostrate neck of a writhing figure, likewise masked.

Whether the ship had a figurehead, or only a plain beak, was not quite certain, owing to canvas wrapped about that part, either to protect it while undergoing a refurbishing, or else decently to hide its decay. Rudely painted or chalked, as in a sailor freak, along the forward side of a sort of pedestal below the canvas, was the sentence, SEGUID VUESTRO JEFE ("follow your leader"); while upon the tarnished headboards near by appeared, in stately capitals, once gilt, the ship's name *SAN DOMINICK*, each letter streakingly corroded with tricklings of copper-spike rust; while, like mourning weeds, dark festoons of sea grass slimily swept to and fro over the name with every hearselike roll of the hull.

As, at last, the boat was hooked from the bow along toward the gangway amid-ship, its keel, while yet some inches separated from the hull, harshly grated as on a sunken coral reef. It proved a huge bunch of conglobated barnacles adhering below the water to the side like a wen—a token of baffling airs and long calms passed somewhere in those seas.

Climbing the side, the visitor was at once surrounded by a clamorous throng of whites and blacks, but the latter outnumbering the former more than could have been expected, Negro transportation ship as the stranger in port was. But, in one language, and as with one voice, all poured out a common tale of suffering; in which the Negresses, of whom there were not a few, exceeded the others in their dolorous vehemence. The scurvy, together with the fever, had swept off a great part of their number, more especially the Spaniards. Off Cape Horn they had narrowly escaped shipwreck; then, for days together, they had lain tranced without wind; their provisions were low; their water next to none; their lips that moment were baked.

While Captain Delano was thus made the mark of all eager tongues, his one eager glance took in all faces, with every other object about him.

Always upon first boarding a large and populous ship at sea, especially a foreign one, with a nondescript crew such as Lascars or Manila men, the impression varies in a peculiar way from that produced by first entering a strange house with strange inmates in a strange land. Both house and ship—the one by its walls and blinds, the other by its high bulwarks like ramparts—hoard from view their interiors till the last moment, but in the case of the ship there is this addition: that the living spectacle it contains, upon its sudden and complete disclosure, has, in contrast with the blank ocean which zones it, something of the effect of enchantment. The ship seems unreal; these strange costumes, gestures, and faces but a shadowy tableau just emerged from the deep, which directly must receive back what it gave.

Perhaps it was some such influence, as above is attempted to be described, which, in Captain Delano's mind, heightened whatever, upon a staid scrutiny, might have seemed unusual, especially the conspicuous figures of four elderly grizzled Negroes, their heads like black, doddered willow tops, who, in venerable contrast to the tumult below them, were couched, sphinxlike, one on the starboard cathead, another on the larboard, and the remaining pair face to face on the opposite bulwarks above the mainchains. They each had bits of unstranded old junk in their hands, and, with a sort of stoical self-content, were picking the junk into oakum, a small heap of which lay by their sides. They accompanied the task with a continuous, low, monotonous chant, droning and druling away like so many gray-headed bagpipers playing a funeral march.

The quarter-deck rose into an ample elevated poop, upon the forward verge of which, lifted, like the oakum-pickers, some eight feet above the general throng, sat along in a row, separated by regular spaces, the cross-legged figures of six other blacks, each with a rusty hatchet in his hand, which, with a bit of brick and a rag, he was engaged like a scullion in scouring, while between each two was a small stack of hatchets, their rusted edges turned forward awaiting a like operation. Though occasionally the four oakum-pickers would briefly address some person or persons in the crowd below, yet the six hatchet-polishers neither spoke to others nor breathed a whisper among themselves, but sat intent upon their task, except at intervals, when, with the peculiar love in Negroes of uniting industry with pastime, two and two they sideways clashed their hatchets together, like cymbals, with a barbarous din. All six, unlike the generality, had the raw aspect of unsophisticated Africans.

But that first comprehensive glance which took in those ten figures, with scores less conspicuous, rested but an instant upon them, as, impatient of the hubbub of voices, the visitor turned in quest of whomsoever it might be that commanded the ship.

But as if not unwilling to let nature make known her own case among his suffering charge, or else in despair of restraining it for the time, the Spanish captain, a gentlemanly, reserved-looking, and rather young man to a stranger's eye, dressed with singular richness but bearing plain traces of recent sleepless cares and disquietudes, stood passively by, leaning against the mainmast, at one moment casting a dreary, spiritless look upon his excited people, at the next an unhappy glance toward his visitor. By his side stood a black of small stature, in whose rude face, as occasionally, like a shepherd's dog, he mutely turned it up into the Spaniard's, sorrow and affection were equally blended.

Struggling through the throng, the American advanced to the Spaniard, assuring him of his sympathies, and offering to render whatever assistance might be in his power. To which the Spaniard returned for the present but grave and ceremonious acknowledgments, his national formality dusked by the saturnine mood of ill-health.

But losing no time in mere compliments, Captain Delano, returning to the gangway, had his basket of fish brought up, and as the wind still continued light, so that some hours at least must elapse ere the ship could be brought to the anchorage, he bade his men return to the sealer and fetch back as much water as the whaleboat could carry, with whatever soft bread the steward might have, all the remaining pumpkins on board, with a box of sugar and a dozen of his private bottles of cider.

Not many minutes after the boat's pushing off, to the vexation of all, the wind entirely died away, and, the tide turning, began drifting back the ship helplessly seaward. But trusting this would not long last, Captain Delano sought, with good hopes, to cheer up the strangers, feeling no small satisfaction that, with persons in their condition, he could—thanks to his frequent voyages along the Spanish Main—converse with some freedom in their native tongue.

While left alone with them, he was not long in observing some things tending to heighten his first impressions; but surprise was lost in pity, both for the Spaniards and blacks, alike evidently reduced from scarcity of water and provisions, while long-continued suffering seemed to have brought out the less good-natured qualities of the Negroes, besides at the same time impairing the Spaniard's authority over them. But, under the circumstances, precisely this condition of things was to have been anticipated. In armies, navies, cities, or families, in nature herself, nothing more relaxes good order than misery. Still, Captain Delano was not without the idea that had Benito Cereno been a man of greater energy, misrule would hardly have come to the present pass. But the debility, constitutional or induced by hardships bodily and mental, of the Spanish captain was too obvious to be overlooked. A prey to settled dejection, as if long mocked with hope he would not now indulge it even when it had ceased to be a mock, the prospect of that day, or evening at furthest, lying at anchor, with plenty of water for his people, and a brother captain to counsel and befriend, seemed in no perceptible degree to encourage him. His mind appeared unstrung, if not still more seriously affected. Shut up in these oaken walls, chained to one dull round of command whose unconditionality cloyed him, like some hypochondriac abbot he moved slowly about, at times suddenly pausing, starting, or staring, biting his lip, biting his fingernail, flushing, paling, twitching his beard, with other symptoms of an absent or moody mind. This distempered spirit was lodged, as before hinted, in as distempered a frame. He was rather tall, but seemed never to have been robust, and now with nervous suffering was almost worn to a skeleton. A tendency to some pulmonary complaint appeared to have been lately confirmed. His voice was like that of one with lungs half gone—hoarsely suppressed, a husky whisper. No wonder that, as in this state he tottered about, his private servant apprehensively followed him. Sometimes the Negro gave his master his arm, or took his handkerchief out of his pocket for him; performing these and similar offices with that affectionate zeal which transmutes into something filial or fraternal acts in themselves but menial, and which has gained for the Negro the repute of making the most pleasing body servant in the world; one, too, whom a master need be on no stiffly superior terms with, but may treat with familiar trust—less a servant than a devoted companion.

Marking the noisy indocility of the blacks in general, as well as what seemed the sullen inefficiency of the whites, it was not without humane satisfaction that Captain Delano witnessed the steady good conduct of Babo.

But the good conduct of Babo, hardly more than the ill-behavior of others, seemed to withdraw the half-lunatic Don Benito from his cloudy languor. Not that such precisely was the impression made by the Spaniard on the mind of his visitor. The Spaniard's individual unrest was, for the present, but noted as a conspicuous feature in the ship's general affliction. Still, Captain Delano was not a little concerned at what he could not help taking for the time to be Don Benito's unfriendly indifference towards himself. The Spaniard's manner, too, conveyed a sort of sour and gloomy disdain, which he seemed at no pains to disguise. But this the American in charity ascribed to the harassing effects of sickness, since, in former instances, he had noted that there are peculiar natures on whom prolonged physical suffering seems to cancel every social instinct of kindness, as if, forced to black bread themselves, they deemed it but equity that each person coming nigh them should, indirectly, by some slight or affront, be made to partake of their fare.

But erelong Captain Delano bethought him that, indulgent as he was at the first in judging the Spaniard, he might not after all have exercised charity enough. At bottom it was Don Benito's reserve which displeased him, but the same reserve was shown towards all but his faithful personal attendant. Even the formal reports which, according to sea usage, were, at stated times, made to him by some petty underling, either a white, mulatto, or black, he hardly had patience enough to listen to without betraying contemptuous aversion. His manner upon such occasions was, in its degree, not unlike that which might be supposed to have been his imperial countryman's, Charles V, just previous to the anchoritish retirement of that monarch from the throne.

This splenetic disrelish of his place was evinced in almost every function pertaining to it. Proud as he was moody, he condescended to no personal mandate. Whatever special orders were necessary, their delivery was delegated to his body servant, who in turn transferred them to their ultimate destination, through runners, alert Spanish boys or slave boys, like pages or pilot fish within easy call continually hovering round Don Benito. So that to have beheld this undemonstrative invalid gliding about, apathetic and mute, no landsman could have dreamed that in him was lodged a dictatorship beyond which, while at sea, there was no earthly appeal.

Thus the Spaniard, regarded in his reserve, seemed the involuntary victim of mental disorder. But, in fact, his reserve might, in some degree, have proceeded from design. If so, then here was evinced the unhealthy climax of that icy though conscientious policy more or less adopted by all commanders of large ships, which, except in signal emergencies, obliterates alike the manifestation of sway with every trace of sociality, transforming the man into a block, or rather into a loaded cannon, which, until there is call for thunder, has nothing to say.

Viewing him in this light, it seemed but a natural token of the perverse habit induced by a long course of such hard self-restraint that, notwithstanding the present condition of his ship, the Spaniard should still persist in a demeanor which, however harmless or, it may be, appropriate, in a well-appointed vessel, such as the *San Dominick* might have been at the outset of the voyage, was anything but judicious now. But the Spaniard, perhaps, thought that it was with captains as with gods: reserve, under all events, must still be their cue. But probably this appearance of slumbering dominion might have been but an attempted disguise to conscious imbecility—not deep policy, but shallow device. But be all this as it might, whether Don Benito's manner was designed or not, the more Captain Delano noted its pervading reserve, the less he felt uneasiness at any particular manifestation of that reserve towards himself.

Neither were his thoughts taken up by the captain alone. Wonted to the quiet orderliness of the sealer's comfortable family of a crew, the noisy confusion of the *San Dominick's* suffering host repeatedly challenged his eye. Some prominent breaches, not only of discipline but of decency, were observed. These Captain Delano could not but ascribe, in the main, to the absence of those subordinate deck officers to whom, along with higher duties, is intrusted what may be styled the police department of a populous ship. True, the old oakum-pickers appeared at times to act the part of monitorial constables to their countrymen, the blacks, but though occasionally succeeding in allaying trifling outbreaks now and then between man and man, they could do little or nothing toward establishing general quiet. The *San Dominick* was in the condition of a transatlantic emigrant ship, among whose multitude of living freight are some individuals, doubtless, as little troublesome as crates and bales, but the friendly remonstrances of such with their ruder companions are of not so much avail as the unfriendly arm of the mate. What the *San Dominick* wanted was, what the emigrant ship has, stern superior officers. But on these decks not so much as a fourth mate was to be seen.

The visitor's curiosity was roused to learn the particulars of those mishaps which had brought about such absenteeism, with its consequences, because, though deriving some inkling of the voyage from the wails which at the first moment had greeted him, yet of the details no clear understanding had been had. The best account would, doubtless, be given by the captain. Yet at first the visitor was loath to ask it, unwilling to provoke some distant rebuff. But, plucking up courage, he at last accosted Don Benito, renewing the expression of his benevolent interest, adding that, did he (Captain Delano) but know the particulars of the ship's misfortunes, he would, perhaps be better able in the end to relieve them. Would Don Benito favor him with the whole story.

Don Benito faltered, then, like some somnambulist suddenly interfered with, vacantly stared at his visitor, and ended by looking down on the deck. He maintained this posture so long that Captain Delano, almost equally disconcerted, and involuntarily almost as rude, turned suddenly from him, walking forward to accost one of the Spanish seamen for the desired information. But he had hardly gone five paces, when, with a sort of eagerness, Don Benito invited him back, regretting his momentary absence of mind, and professing readiness to gratify him.

While most part of the story was being given, the two captains stood on the after part of the main deck, a privileged spot, no one being near but the servant.

"It is now a hundred and ninety days," began the Spaniard, in his husky whisper, "that this ship, well officered and well manned, with several cabin passengers—some fifty Spaniards in all—sailed from Buenos Ayres bound to Lima, with a general cargo, hardware, Paraguay tea and the like—and," pointing forward, "that parcel of Negroes, now not more than a hundred and fifty, as you see, but then numbering over three hundred souls. Off Cape Horn we had heavy gales. In one moment, by night, three of my best officers, with fifteen sailors, were lost, with the mainyard, the spar snapping under them in the slings as they sought, with heavers, to beat down the icy sail. To lighten the hull, the heavier sacks of maté were thrown into the sea, with most of the water pipes lashed on deck at the time. And this last necessity it was, combined with the prolonged detentions afterwards experienced, which eventually brought about our chief causes of suffering. When—"

Here there was a sudden fainting attack of his cough, brought on, no doubt, by his mental distress. His servant sustained him, and, drawing a cordial from his pocket, placed it to his lips. He a little revived. But, unwilling to leave him unsupported while yet imperfectly restored, the black with one arm still encircled his master, at the same time keeping his eye fixed on his face, as if to watch for the first sign of complete restoration, or relapse, as the event might prove.

The Spaniard proceeded, but brokenly and obscurely, as one in a dream.

—"Oh, my God! rather than pass through what I have, with joy I would have hailed the most terrible gales; but—"

His cough returned and with increased violence; this subsiding, with reddened lips and closed eyes he fell heavily against his supporter.

"His mind wanders. He was thinking of the plague that followed the gales," plaintively sighed the servant; "my poor, poor master!" wringing one hand, and with the other wiping the mouth. "But be patient, señor," again turning to Captain Delano, "these fits do not last long; master will soon be himself."

Don Benito, reviving, went on; but, as this portion of the story was very brokenly delivered, the substance only will here be set down.

It appeared that after the ship had been many days tossed in storms off the Cape, the scurvy broke out, carrying off numbers of the whites and blacks. When at last they had worked round into the Pacific, their spars and sails were so damaged, and so inadequately handled by the surviving mariners, most of whom were become invalids, that, unable to lay her northerly course by the wind, which was powerful, the unmanageable ship for successive days and nights was blown north-westward, where the breeze suddenly deserted her, in unknown waters to sultry calms. The absence of the water pipes now proved as fatal to life as before their presence had menaced it. Induced, or at least aggravated, by the more than scanty allowance of water, a malignant fever followed the scurvy, with the excessive heat of the lengthened calm making such short work of it as to sweep away, as by billows, whole families of the Africans, and a yet larger number, proportionally, of the Spaniards, including, by a luckless fatality, every remaining officer on board. Consequently, in the smart west winds eventually following the calm, the already rent sails, having to be simply dropped, not furled, at need, had been gradually reduced to the beggars' rags they were now. To procure substitutes for his lost sailors, as well as supplies of water and sails, the captain, at the earliest opportunity, had made for Baldivia, the southernmost civilized port of Chile and South America, but upon nearing the coast the thick weather had prevented him from so much as sighting that harbor. Since which period, almost without a crew, and almost without canvas and almost without water, and at intervals giving its added dead to the sea, the *San Dominick* had been battledored about by contrary winds, inveigled by currents, or grown weedy in calms. Like a man lost in woods, more than once she had doubled upon her own track.

"But throughout these calamities," huskily continued Don Benito, painfully turning in the half-embrace of his servant, "I have to thank those Negroes you see, who, though to your inexperienced eyes appearing unruly, have, indeed, conducted themselves with less of restlessness than even their owner could have thought possible under such circumstances."

Here he again fell faintly back. Again his mind wandered, but he rallied, and less obscurely proceeded.

"Yes, their owner was quite right in assuring me that no fetters would be needed with his blacks; so that while, as is wont in his transportation, those Negroes have always remained upon deck—not thrust below, as in the Guineamen—they have, also, from the beginning, been freely permitted to range within given bounds at their pleasure."

Once more the faintness returned—his mind roved—but, recovering, he resumed:

"But it is Babo here to whom, under God, I owe not only my own preservation, but likewise to him, chiefly, the merit is due of pacifying his more ignorant brethren, when at intervals tempted to murmurings."

"Ah, master," sighed the black, bowing his face, "don't speak of me; Babo is nothing; what Babo has done was but duty."

"Faithful fellow!" cried Captain Delano. "Don Benito, I envy you such a friend; slave I cannot call him."

As master and man stood before him, the black upholding the white, Captain Delano could not but bethink him of the beauty of that relationship which could present such a spectacle of fidelity on the one hand and confidence on the other. The scene was heightened by the contrast in dress, denoting their relative positions. The Spaniard wore a loose Chile jacket of dark velvet; white smallclothes and stockings, with silver buckles at the knee and instep; a high-crowned sombrero of fine grass; a slender sword, silver mounted, hung from a knot in his sash—the last being an almost invariable adjunct, more for utility than ornament, of a South American gentleman's dress to this hour. Excepting when his occasional nervous contortions brought about disarray, there was a certain precision in his attire curiously at variance with the unsightly disorder around, especially in the belittered ghetto, forward of the mainmast, wholly occupied by the blacks.

The servant wore nothing but wide trousers, apparently, from their coarseness and patches, made out of some old topsail; they were clean, and confined at the waist by a bit of unstranded rope, which, with his composed, deprecatory air at times, made him look something like a begging friar of St. Francis.

However unsuitable for the time and place, at least in the blunt-thinking American's eyes, and however strangely surviving in the midst of all his afflictions, the toilette of Don Benito might not, in fashion at least, have gone beyond the style of the day among South Americans of his class. Though on the present voyage sailing from Buenos Ayres, he had avowed himself a native and resident of Chile, whose inhabitants had not so generally adopted the plain coat and once plebeian pantaloons, but, with a becoming modification, adhered to their provincial costume, picturesque as any in the world. Still, relatively to the pale history of the voyage, and his own pale face, there seemed something so incongruous in the Spaniard's apparel as almost to suggest the image of an invalid courtier tottering about London streets in the time of the plague.

The portion of the narrative which perhaps most excited interest, as well as some surprise, considering the latitudes in question, was the long calms spoken of, and more particularly the ship's so long drifting about. Without communicating the opinion, of course, the American could not but impute at least part of the detentions both to clumsy seamanship and faulty navigation. Eying Don Benito's small, yellow hands, he easily inferred that the young captain had not got into command at the hawsehole, but the cabin window; and if so, why wonder at incompetence, in youth, sickness, and gentility united?

But, drowning criticism in compassion, after a fresh repetition of his sympathies, Captain Delano, having heard out his story, not only engaged, as in the first place, to see Don Benito and his people supplied in their immediate bodily needs, but, also now further promised to assist him in procuring a large permanent supply of water, as well as some sails and rigging; and, though it would involve no small embarrassment to himself, yet he would spare three of his best seamen for temporary deck officers, so that without delay the ship might proceed to Conception, there fully to refit for Lima, her destined port.

Such generosity was not without its effect, even upon the invalid. His face lighted up; eager and hectic, he met the honest glance of his visitor. With gratitude he seemed overcome.

"This excitement is bad for master," whispered the servant, taking his arm, and with soothing words gently drawing him aside.

When Don Benito returned, the American was pained to observe that his hopefulness, like the sudden kindling in his cheek, was but febrile and transient.

Erelong, with a joyless mien, looking up towards the poop, the host invited his guest to accompany him there, for the benefit of what little breath of wind might be stirring.

As, during the telling of the story, Captain Delano had once or twice started at the occasional cymbaling of the hatchet-polishers, wondering why such an interruption should be allowed, especially in that part of the ship, and in the ears of an invalid; and moreover, as the hatchets had anything but an attractive look, and the handlers of them still less so, it was, therefore, to tell the truth, not without some lurking reluctance, or even shrinking, it may be, that Captain Delano, with apparent complaisance, acquiesced in his host's invitation. The more so since, with an untimely caprice of punctilio, rendered distressing by his cadaverous aspect, Don Benito, with Castilian bows, solemnly insisted upon his guest's preceding him up the ladder leading to the elevation, where, one on each side of the last step, sat for armorial supporters and sentries two of the ominous file. Gingerly enough stepped good Captain Delano between them, and in the instant of leaving them behind, like one running the gantlet, he felt an apprehensive twitch in the calves of his legs.

But when, facing about, he saw the whole file, like so many organgrinders, still stupidly intent on their work, unmindful of everything beside, he could not but smile at his late fidgety panic.

Presently, while standing with his host looking forward upon the decks below, he was struck by one of those instances of insubordination previously alluded to.

Three black boys, with two Spanish boys, were sitting together on the hatches, scraping a rude wooden platter in which some scanty mess had recently been cooked. Suddenly one of the black boys, enraged at a word dropped by one of his white companions, seized a knife, and, though called to forbear by one of the oakumpickers, struck the lad over the head, inflicting a gash from which blood flowed.

In amazement, Captain Delano inquired what this meant. To which the pale Don Benito dully muttered that it was merely the sport of the lad.

"Pretty serious sport, truly," rejoined Captain Delano. "Had such a thing happened on board the *Bachelor's Delight*, instant punishment would have followed."

At these words the Spaniard turned upon the American one of his sudden, staring, half-lunatic looks, then, relapsing into his torpor, answered, "Doubtless, doubtless, *señor*."

Is it, thought Captain Delano, that this hapless man is one of those paper captains I've known, who by policy wink at what by power they cannot put down? I know no sadder sight than a commander who has little of command but the name.

"I should think, Don Benito," he now said, glancing toward the oakum-picker who had sought to interfere with the boys, "that you would find it advantageous to keep all your blacks employed, especially the younger ones, no matter at what useless task, and no matter what happens to the ship. Why, even with my little band, I find such a course indispensable. I once kept a crew on my quarter-deck thrumming mats for my cabin, when, for three days, I had given up my ship—mats, men, and all—for a speedy loss, owing to the violence of a gale, in which we could do nothing but helplessly drive before it."

"Doubtless, doubtless," muttered Don Benito.

"But," continued Captain Delano, again glancing upon the oakum-pickers and then at the hatchet-polishers, near by, "I see you keep some, at least, of your host employed."

"Yes," was again the vacant response.

"Those old men there, shaking their pows from their pulpits," continued Captain Delano, pointing to the oakum-pickers, "seem to act the part of old dominies to the rest, little heeded as their admonitions are at times. Is this voluntary on their part, Don Benito, or have you appointed them shepherds to your flock of black sheep?"

"What posts they fill, I appointed them," rejoined the Spaniard, in an acrid tone, as if resenting some supposed satiric reflection.

"And these others, these Ashantee conjurers here," continued Captain Delano, rather uneasily eying the brandished steel of the hatchet-polishers, where in spots, it had been brought to a shine, "this seems a curious business they are at, Don Benito?"

"In the gales we met," answered the Spaniard, "what of our general cargo was not thrown overboard was much damaged by the brine. Since coming into calm weather, I have had several cases of knives and hatchets daily brought up for overhauling and cleaning."

"A prudent idea, Don Benito. You are part owner of ship and cargo, I presume; but none of the slaves, perhaps?"

"I am owner of all you see," impatiently returned Don Benito, "except the main company of blacks, who belonged to my late friend, Alexandro Aranda."

As he mentioned this name, his air was heartbroken; his knees shook; his servant supported him.

Thinking he divined the cause of such unusual emotion, to confirm his surmise Captain Delano after a pause said: "And may I ask, Don Benito, whether—since awhile ago you spoke of some cabin passengers—the friend, whose loss so afflicts you, at the outset of the voyage accompanied his blacks?"

"Yes."

"But died of the fever?"

"Died of the fever. Oh, could I but—"

Again quivering, the Spaniard paused.

"Pardon me," said Captain Delano, lowly, "but I think that, by a sympathetic experience, I conjecture, Don Benito, what it is that gives the keener edge to your grief. It was once my hard fortune to lose, at sea, a dear friend, my own brother, then supercargo. Assured of the welfare of his spirit, its departure I could have borne like a man, but that honest eye, that honest hand—both of which had so often met mine—and that warm heart—all, all—like scraps to the dogs—to throw all to the sharks! It was then I vowed never to have for fellow voyager a man I loved, unless, unbeknown to him, I had provided every requisite, in case of a fatality, for embalming his mortal part for interment on shore. Were your friend's remains now on board this ship, Don Benito, not thus strangely would the mention of his name affect you."

"On board this ship?" echoed the Spaniard. Then, with horrified gestures, as directed against some specter, he unconsciously fell into the ready arms of his attendant, who, with a silent appeal toward Captain Delano, seemed beseeching him not again to broach a theme so unspeakably distressing to his master.

This poor fellow now, thought the pained American, is the victim of that sad superstition which associates goblins with the deserted body of man, as ghosts with an abandoned house. How unlike are we made! What to me, in like case, would have been a solemn satisfaction, the bare suggestion, even, terrifies the Spaniard into this trance. Poor Alexandro Aranda! what would you say could you here see your friend—who on former voyages, when you for months were left behind, has, I dare say, often longed and longed for one peep at you—now transported with terror at the least thought of having you anyway nigh him.

At this moment, with a dreary graveyard toll betokening a flaw, the ship's forecastle bell, smote by one of the grizzled oakum-pickers, proclaimed ten o'clock through the leaden calm, when Captain Delano's attention was caught by the moving figure of a gigantic black emerging from the general crowd below and slowly advancing towards the elevated poop. An iron collar was about his neck, from which depended a chain thrice wound round his body, the terminating links padlocked together at a broad band of iron, his girdle.

"How like a mute Atufal moves," murmured the servant.

The black mounted the steps of the poop, and, like a brave prisoner brought up to receive sentence, stood in unquailing muteness before Don Benito, now recovered from his attack.

At the first glimpse of his approach, Don Benito had started; a resentful shadow swept over his face, and, as with the sudden memory of bootless rage, his white lips glued together.

This is some mulish mutineer, thought Captain Delano, surveying, not without a mixture of admiration, the colossal form of the Negro.

"See, he waits your question, master," said the servant.

Thus reminded, Don Benito, nervously averting his glance as if shunning, by anticipation, some rebellious response, in a disconcerted voice, thus spoke:

"Atufal, will you ask my pardon now?"

The black was silent.

"Again, master," murmured the servant, with bitter upbraiding eying his countryman; "again, master; he will bend to master yet."

"Answer," said Don Benito, still averting his glance, "say but the one word, *pardon*, and your chains shall be off."

Upon this, the black, slowly raising both arms, let them lifelessly fall, his links clanking, his head bowed; as much as to say, "No, I am content."

"Go," said Don Benito, with inkept and unknown emotion.

Deliberately as he had come, the black obeyed.

"Excuse me, Don Benito," said Captain Delano, "but this scene surprises me; what means it, pray?"

"It means that that Negro alone, of all the band, has given me peculiar cause of offense. I have put him in chains; I—"

Here he paused; his hand to his head, as if there were a swimming there, or a sudden bewilderment of memory had come over him; but meeting his servant's kindly glance seemed reassured, and proceeded:

"I could not scourge such a form. But I told him he must ask my pardon. As yet he has not. At my command, every two hours he stands before me."

"And how long has this been?"

"Some sixty days."

"And obedient in all else? And respectful?"

"Yes."

"Upon my conscience, then," exclaimed Captain Delano, impulsively, "he has a royal spirit in him, this fellow."

"He may have some right to it," bitterly returned Don Benito, "he says he was king in his own land."

"Yes," said the servant, entering a word, "those slits in Atufal's ears once held wedges of gold; but poor Babo here, in his own land, was only a poor slave; a black man's slave was Babo, who now is the white's."

Somewhat annoyed by these conversational familiarities, Captain Delano turned curiously upon the attendant, then glanced inquiringly at his master; but, as if long wonted to these little informalities, neither master nor man seemed to understand him.

"What, pray, was Atufal's offense, Don Benito?" asked Captain Delano; "if it was not something very serious, take a fool's advice, and, in view of his general docility, as well as in some natural respect for his spirit, remit him his penalty."

"No, no, master never will do that," here murmured the servant to himself, "proud Atufal must first ask master's pardon. The slave there carries the padlock, but master here carries the key."

His attention thus directed, Captain Delano now noticed for the first that, suspended by a slender silken cord from Don Benito's neck, hung a key. At once, from the servant's muttered syllables, divining the key's purpose, he smiled and said: "So, Don Benito—padlock and key—significant symbols, truly."

Biting his lip, Don Benito faltered.

Though the remark of Captain Delano, a man of such native simplicity as to be incapable of satire or irony, had been dropped in playful allusion to the Spaniard's singularly evidenced lordship over the black, yet the hypochondriac seemed some way to have taken it as a malicious reflection upon his confessed inability thus far to break down, at least on a verbal summons, the entrenched will of the slave. Deploring this supposed misconception, yet despairing of correcting it, Captain Delano shifted the subject; but finding his companion more than ever withdrawn, as if still sourly digesting the lees of the presumed affront above mentioned, by and by Captain Delano likewise became less talkative, oppressed, against his own will, by what seemed the secret vindictiveness of the morbidly sensitive Spaniard. But the good sailor, himself of a quite contrary disposition, refrained on his part alike from the appearance as from the feeling of resentment, and if silent, was only so from contagion.

Presently the Spaniard, assisted by his servant, somewhat discourteously crossed over from his guest, a procedure which, sensibly enough, might have been allowed to pass for idle caprice of ill-humor had not master and man, lingering round the corner of the elevated skylight, begun whispering together in low voices. This was unpleasing. And more: the moody air of the Spaniard, which at times had not been without a sort of valetudinarian stateliness, now seemed anything but dignified, while the menial familiarity of the servant lost its original charm of simple-hearted attachment.

In his embarrassment, the visitor turned his face to the other side of the ship. By so doing, his glance accidentally fell on a young Spanish sailor, a coil of rope in his hand, just stepped from the deck to the first round of the mizzen rigging. Perhaps the man would not have been particularly noticed were it not that, during his ascent to one of the yards, he, with a sort of covert intentness, kept his eye fixed on Captain Delano, from whom, presently, it passed, as if by a natural sequence, to the two whisperers.

His own attention thus redirected to that quarter, Captain Delano gave a slight start. From something in Don Benito's manner just then, it seemed as if the visitor had, at least partly, been the subject of the withdrawn consultation going on—a conjecture as little agreeable to the guest as it was flattering to the host.

The singular alternations of courtesy and ill-breeding in the Spanish captain were unaccountable, except on one of two suppositions—innocent lunacy, or wicked imposture.

But the first idea, though it might naturally have occurred to an indifferent observer, and, in some respect, had not hitherto been wholly a stranger to Captain Delano's mind, yet, now that, in an incipient way, he began to regard the stranger's conduct something in the light of an intentional affront, of course the idea of lunacy was virtually vacated. But if not a lunatic, what then? Under the circumstances, would a gentleman, nay, any honest boor, act the part now acted by his host? The man was an impostor. Some low-born adventurer, masquerading as an oceanic grandee, yet so ignorant of the first requisites of mere gentlemanhood as

to be betrayed into the present remarkable indecorum. That strange ceremonious-
ness, too, at other times evinced, seemed not uncharacteristic of one playing a part
above his real level. Benito Cereno—Don Benito Cereno—a sounding name. One,
too, at that period, not unknown, in the surname, to supercargoes and sea captains
trading along the Spanish Main, as belonging to one of the most enterprising and
extensive mercantile families in all those provinces, several members of it having
titles; a sort of Castilian Rothschild, with a noble brother, or cousin, in every great
trading town of South America. The alleged Don Benito was in early manhood,
about twenty-nine or thirty. To assume a sort of roving cadetship in the maritime
affairs of such a house, what more likely scheme for a young knave of talent and
spirit? But the Spaniard was a pale invalid. Never mind. For even to the degree of
simulating mortal disease, the craft of some tricksters had been known to attain. To
think that, under the aspect of infantile weakness, the most savage energies might be
couched—those velvets of the Spaniard but the silky paw to his fangs.

From no train of thought did these fancies come; not from within, but from
without; suddenly, too, and in one throng, like hoarfrost, yet as soon to vanish, as the
mild sun of Captain Delano's good nature regained its meridian.

Glancing over once more towards his host—whose side face, revealed above
the skylight, was now turned towards him—he was struck by the profile, whose
clearness of cut was refined by the thinness incident to ill-health, as well as ennobled
about the chin by the beard. Away with suspicion. He was a true offshoot of a true
hidalgo Cereno.

Relieved by these and other better thoughts, the visitor, lightly humming a
tune, now began indifferently pacing the poop, so as not to betray to Don Benito
that he had at all mistrusted incivility, much less duplicity; for such mistrust would
yet be proved illusory, and by the event, though, for the present, the circumstance
which had provoked that distrust remained unexplained. But when that little mystery should have been cleared up, Captain Delano thought he might extremely
regret it did he allow Don Benito to become aware that he had indulged in ungen-
erous surmises. In short, to the Spaniard's black-letter text, it was best, for a while,
to leave open margin.

Presently, his pale face twitching and overcast, the Spaniard, still supported by
his attendant, moved over towards his guest, when, with even more than his usual
embarrassment, and a strange sort of intriguing intonation in his husky whisper, the
following conversation began:

"*Señor*, may I ask how long you have lain at this isle?"

"Oh, but a day or two, Don Benito."

"And from what port are you last?"

"Canton."

"And there, *señor*, you exchanged your sealskins for teas and silks, I think you
said?"

"Yes. Silks, mostly."

"And the balance you took in specie, perhaps?"

Captain Delano, fidgeting a little, answered, "Yes; some silver; not a very great
deal, though."

"Ah—well. May I ask how many men have you, *señor*?"

Captain Delano slightly started, but answered, "About five-and-twenty, all told."

"And at present, *señor*, all on board, I suppose?"

"All on board, Don Benito," replied the Captain, now with satisfaction.

"And will be tonight, *señor*?"

At this last question, following so many pertinacious ones, for the soul of him Captain Delano could not but look very earnestly at the questioner, who, instead of meeting the glance, with every token of craven discomposure dropped his eyes to the deck; presenting an unworthy contrast to his servant, who, just then, was kneeling at his feet, adjusting a loose shoe buckle, his disengaged face meantime, with humble curiosity, turned openly up into his master's downcast one.

The Spaniard, still with a guilty shuffle, repeated his question:

"And—and will be tonight, *señor*?"

"Yes, for aught I know," returned Captain Delano—"but nay," rallying himself into fearless truth, "some of them talked of going off on another fishing party about midnight."

"Your ships generally go—go more or less armed, I believe, *señor*?"

"Oh, a six-pounder or two, in case of emergency," was the intrepidly indifferent reply, "with a small stock of muskets, sealing spears, and cutlasses, you know."

As he thus responded, Captain Delano again glanced at Don Benito, but the latter's eyes were averted, while, abruptly and awkwardly shifting the subject, he made some peevish allusion to the calm, and then, without apology, once more, with his attendant, withdrew to the opposite bulwarks, where the whispering was resumed.

At this moment, and ere Captain Delano could cast a cool thought upon what had just passed, the young Spanish sailor before mentioned was seen descending from the rigging. In act of stooping over to spring inboard to the deck, his voluminous, unconfined frock, or shirt, of coarse woolen, much spotted with tar, opened out far down the chest, revealing a soiled undergarment of what seemed the finest linen, edged, about the neck, with a narrow blue ribbon, sadly faded and worn. At this moment the young sailor's eye was again fixed on the whisperers, and Captain Delano thought he observed a lurking significance in it, as if silent signs, of some Freemason sort, had that instant been interchanged.

This once more impelled his own glance in the direction of Don Benito, and, as before, he could not but infer that himself formed the subject of the conference. He paused. The sound of the hatchet-polishing fell on his ears. He cast another swift side look at the two. They had the air of conspirators. In connection with the late questionings, and the incident of the young sailor, these things now begat such return of involuntary suspicion that the singular guilelessness of the American could not endure it. Plucking up a gay and humorous expression, he crossed over to the two rapidly, saying: "Ha, Don Benito, your black here seems high in your trust, a sort of privy councilor, in fact."

Upon this, the servant looked up with a good-natured grin, but the master started as from a venomous bite. It was a moment or two before the Spaniard sufficiently recovered himself to reply; which he did, at last, with cold constraint: "Yes, *señor*, I have trust in Babo."

Here Babo, changing his previous grin of mere animal humor into an intelligent smile, not ungratefully eyed his master.

Finding that the Spaniard now stood silent and reserved, as if involuntarily, or purposely giving hint that his guest's proximity was inconvenient just then, Captain Delano, unwilling to appear uncivil even to incivility itself, made some trivial remark and moved off, again and again turning over in his mind the mysterious demeanor of Don Benito Cereno.

He had descended from the poop, and, wrapped in thought, was passing near a dark hatchway leading down into the steerage, when, perceiving motion there, he looked to see what moved. The same instant there was a sparkle in the shadowy hatchway and he saw one of the Spanish sailors, prowling there, hurriedly placing his hand in the bosom of his frock, as if hiding something. Before the man could have been certain who it was that was passing, he slunk below out of sight. But enough was seen of him to make it sure that he was the same young sailor before noticed in the rigging.

What was that which so sparkled? thought Captain Delano. It was no lamp—no match—no live coal. Could it have been a jewel? But how come sailors with jewels?—or with silk-trimmed undershirts either? Has he been robbing the trunks of the dead cabin passengers? But if so he would hardly wear one of the stolen articles on board ship here. Ah, ah—if, now, that was, indeed, a secret sign I saw passing between this suspicious fellow and his captain awhile since; if I could only be certain that, in my uneasiness, my senses did not deceive me, then—

Here, passing from one suspicious thing to another, his mind revolved the strange questions put to him concerning his ship.

By a curious coincidence, as each point was recalled, the black wizards of Ashantee would strike up with their hatchets, as in ominous comment on the white stranger's thoughts. Pressed by such enigmas and portents, it would have been almost against nature had not, even into the least distrustful heart, some ugly misgivings obtruded.

Observing the ship, now helplessly fallen into a current, with enchanted sails drifting with increased rapidity seaward, and noting that, from a lately intercepted projection of the land, the sealer was hidden, the stout mariner began to quake at thoughts which he barely durst confess to himself. Above all, he began to feel a ghostly dread of Don Benito. And yet, when he roused himself, dilated his chest, felt himself strong on his legs, and coolly considered it—what did all these phantoms amount to?

Had the Spaniard any sinister scheme, it must have reference not so much to him (Captain Delano) as to his ship (the *Bachelor's Delight*). Hence the present drifting away of the one ship from the other, instead of favoring any such possible scheme, was, for the time at least, opposed to it. Clearly any suspicion combining such contradictions must need be delusive. Beside, was it not absurd to think of a vessel in distress—a vessel by sickness almost dismanned of her crew—a vessel whose inmates were parched for water—was it not a thousand times absurd that such a craft should, at present, be of a piratical character; or her commander, either for himself or those under him, cherish any desire but for speedy relief and refreshment? But, then, might not general distress, and thirst in particular, be affected? And might not that same undiminished Spanish crew, alleged to have perished off to a remnant, be at that very moment lurking in the hold? On heartbroken pretense of entreating a cup of cold water, fiends in human form had got into lonely dwellings, nor retired until a dark deed had been done. And among the Malay pirates it was no unusual thing to lure ships after them into their treacherous harbors, or entice boarders from a declared enemy at sea, by the spectacle of thinly manned or vacant decks, beneath which prowled a hundred spears with yellow arms ready to upthrust them through the mats. Not that Captain Delano had entirely credited such things. He had heard of them—and now, as stories, they recurred. The present destination of the ship was the anchorage. There she would be near his own vessel. Upon gaining that vicinity, might not the *San Dominick*, like a slumbering volcano, suddenly let loose energies now hid?

He recalled the Spaniard's manner while telling his story. There was a gloomy hesitancy and subterfuge about it. It was just the manner of one making up his tale for evil purposes, as he goes. But if that story was not true, what was the truth? That the ship had unlawfully come into the Spaniard's possession? But in many of its details, especially in reference to the more calamitous parts, such as the fatalities among the seamen, the consequent prolonged beating about, the past sufferings from obstinate calms and still continued suffering from thirst; in all these points, as well as others, Don Benito's story had been corroborated not only by the wailing ejaculations of the indiscriminate multitude, white and black, but likewise—what seemed impossible to be counterfeit—by the very expression and play of every human feature which Captain Delano saw. If Don Benito's story was throughout an invention, then every soul on board, down to the youngest Negress, was his carefully drilled recruit in the plot: an incredible inference. And yet, if there was ground for mistrusting his veracity, that inference was a legitimate one.

But those questions of the Spaniard. There, indeed, one might pause. Did they not seem put with much the same object with which the burglar or assassin, by daytime, reconnoiters the walls of a house? But, with ill purposes to solicit such information openly of the chief person endangered, and so, in effect, setting him on his guard—how unlikely a procedure was that? Absurd, then, to suppose that those questions had been prompted by evil designs. Thus, the same conduct which in this instance had raised the alarm, served to dispel it. In short, scarce any suspicion or uneasiness, however apparently reasonable at the time, which was not now with equally apparent reason dismissed.

At last he began to laugh at his former forebodings, and laugh at the strange ship for, in its aspect, someway siding with them, as it were; and laugh, too, at the odd-looking blacks, particularly those old scissors-grinders, the Ashantees; and those bed-ridden old knitting women, the oakum-pickers; and almost at the dark Spaniard himself, the central hobgoblin of all.

For the rest, whatever in a serious way seemed enigmatical was now good-naturedly explained away by the thought that, for the most part, the poor invalid scarcely knew what he was about; either sulking in black vapors, or putting idle questions without sense or object. Evidently, for the present the man was not fit to be intrusted with the ship. On some benevolent plea withdrawing the command from him, Captain Delano would yet have to send her to Conception, in charge of his second mate, a worthy person and good navigator—a plan not more convenient for the *San Dominick* than for Don Benito; for, relieved from all anxiety, keeping wholly to his cabin, the sick man, under the good nursing of his servant, would, probably, by the end of the passage, be in a measure restored to health, and with that he should also be restored to authority.

Such were the American's thoughts. They were tranquilizing. There was a difference between the idea of Don Benito's darkly preordaining Captain Delano's fate and Captain Delano's lightly arranging Don Benito's. Nevertheless, it was not without something of relief that the good seaman presently perceived his whaleboat in the distance. Its absence had been prolonged by unexpected detention at the sealer's side, as well as its returning trip lengthened by the continual recession of the goal.

The advancing speck was observed by the blacks. Their shouts attracted the attention of Don Benito, who, with a return of courtesy approaching Captain Delano, expressed satisfaction at the coming of some supplies, slight and temporary as they must necessarily prove.

Captain Delano responded, but while doing so, his attention was drawn to something passing on the deck below: among the crowd climbing the landward bulwarks, anxiously watching the coming boat, two blacks, to all appearances accidentally incommoded by one of the sailors, violently pushed him aside, which the sailor someway resenting, they dashed him to the deck, despite the earnest cries of the oakum-pickers.

"Don Benito," said Captain Delano quickly, "do you see what is going on there? Look!"

But, seized by his cough, the Spaniard staggered, with both hands to his face, on the point of falling. Captain Delano would have supported him, but the servant was more alert, who, with one hand sustaining his master, with the other applied the cordial. Don Benito restored, the black withdrew his support, slipping aside a little, but dutifully remaining within call of a whisper. Such discretion was here evinced as quite wiped away, in the visitor's eyes, any blemish of impropriety which might have attached to the attendant from the indecorous conferences before mentioned, showing, too, that if the servant were to blame it might be more the master's fault than his own, since, when left to himself, he could conduct himself thus well.

His glance called away from the spectacle of disorder to the more pleasing one before him, Captain Delano could not avoid again congratulating his host upon possessing such a servant, who, though perhaps a little too forward now and then, must upon the whole be invaluable to one in the invalid's situation.

"Tell me, Don Benito," he added, with a smile—"I should like to have your man here myself—what will you take for him? Would fifty doubloons be any object?"

"Master wouldn't part with Babo for a thousand doubloons," murmured the black, overhearing the offer, and taking it in earnest, and, with the strange vanity of a faithful slave appreciated by his master, scorning to hear so paltry a valuation put upon him by a stranger. But Don Benito, apparently hardly yet completely restored, and again interrupted by his cough, made but some broken reply.

Soon his physical distress became so great, affecting his mind, too, apparently, that, as if to screen the sad spectacle, the servant gently conducted his master below.

Left to himself, the American, to while away the time till his boat should arrive, would have pleasantly accosted some one of the few Spanish seamen he saw, but recalling something that Don Benito had said touching their ill conduct, he refrained, as a shipmaster indisposed to countenance cowardice or unfaithfulness in seamen.

While, with these thoughts, standing with eye directed forward towards that handful of sailors, suddenly he thought that one or two of them returned the glance and with a sort of meaning. He rubbed his eyes and looked again, but again seemed to see the same thing. Under a new form, but more obscure than any previous one, the old suspicions recurred, but, in the absence of Don Benito, with less of panic than before. Despite the bad account given of the sailors, Captain Delano resolved forthwith to accost one of them. Descending the poop, he made his way through the blacks, his movement drawing a queer cry from the oakum-pickers, prompted by whom, the Negroes, twitching each other aside, divided before him, but, as if curious to see what was the object of this deliberate visit to their ghetto, closing in behind in tolerable order, followed the white stranger up. His progress thus proclaimed as by mounted kings-at-arms, and escorted as by a Kaffir guard of honor, Captain Delano, assuming a good-humored, off-handed air, continued to advance; now and then saying a blithe word to the Negroes, and his eye curiously surveying the white faces, here and there sparsely mixed in with the blacks, like stray white pawns venturously involved in the ranks of the chessmen opposed.

While thinking which of them to select for his purpose, he chanced to observe a sailor seated on the deck engaged in tarring the strap of a large block, a circle of blacks squatted round him inquisitively eying the process.

The mean employment of the man was in contrast with something superior in his figure. His hand, black with continually thrusting it into the tarpot held for him by a Negro, seemed not naturally allied to his face, a face which would have been a very fine one but for its haggardness. Whether this haggardness had aught to do with criminality could not be determined, since, as intense heat and cold, though unlike, produce like sensations, so innocence and guilt, when, through casual association with mental pain stamping any visible impress, use one seal—a hacked one.

Not again that this reflection occurred to Captain Delano at the time, charitable man as he was. Rather another idea. Because observing so singular a haggardness combined with a dark eye, averted as in trouble and shame, and then again recalling Don Benito's confessed ill opinion of his crew, insensibly, he was operated upon by certain general notions which, while disconnecting pain and abashment from virtue, invariably link them with vice.

If, indeed, there be any wickedness on board this ship, thought Captain Delano, be sure that man there has fouled his hand in it, even as now he fouls it in the pitch. I don't like to accost him. I will speak to this other, this old Jack here on the windlass.

He advanced to an old Barcelona tar, in ragged red breeches and dirty nightcap, cheeks trenched and bronzed, whiskers dense as thorn hedges. Seated between two sleepy-looking Africans, this mariner, like his younger shipmate, was employed upon some rigging—splicing a cable—the sleepy-looking blacks performing the inferior function of holding the outer parts of the ropes for him.

Upon Captain Delano's approach, the man at once hung his head below its previous level; the one necessary for business. It appeared as if he desired to be thought absorbed with more than common fidelity in his task. Being addressed, he glanced up, but with what seemed a furtive, diffident air, which sat strangely enough on his weather-beaten visage, much as if a grizzly bear, instead of growling and bit-ing, should simper and cast sheep's eyes. He was asked several questions concerning the voyage—questions purposely referring to several particulars in Don Benito's narrative, not previously corroborated by those impulsive cries greeting the visitor on first coming on board. The questions were briefly answered, confirming all that remained to be confirmed of the story. The Negroes about the windlass joined in with the old sailor, but, as they became talkative, he by degrees became mute, and at length quite glum, seemed morosely unwilling to answer more questions, and yet, all the while, this ursine air was somehow mixed with his sheepish one.

Despairing of getting into unembarrassed talk with such a centaur, Captain Delano, after glancing round for a more promising countenance but seeing none, spoke pleasantly to the blacks to make way for him, and so, amid various grins and grimaces, returned to the poop, feeling a little strange at first, he could hardly tell why, but upon the whole with regained confidence in Benito Cereno.

How plainly, thought he, did that old whiskerando yonder betray a conscious-ness of ill desert. No doubt when he saw me coming he dreaded lest I, apprised by his captain of the crew's general misbehavior, came with sharp words for him, and so down with his head. And yet—and yet, now that I think of it, that very old fellow, if I err not, was one of those who seemed so earnestly eying me here a while since. Ah, these currents spin one's head round almost as much as they do the ship. Ha, there now's a pleasant sort of sunny sight; quite sociable, too.

His attention had been drawn to a slumbering Negress, partly disclosed through the lacework of some rigging, lying, with youthful limbs carelessly disposed, under the lee of the bulwarks, like a doe in the shade of a woodland rock. Sprawling at her lapped breasts was her wide-awake fawn, stark naked, its black little body half lifted from the deck, crosswise with its dam's; its hands, like two paws, clambering upon her; its mouth and nose ineffectually rooting to get at the mark; and meantime giving a vexatious half-grunt, blending with the composed snore of the Negress.

The uncommon vigor of the child at length roused the mother. She started up, at a distance facing Captain Delano. But as if not at all concerned at the attitude in which she had been caught, delightedly she caught the child up, with maternal transports, covering it with kisses.

There's naked nature, now, pure tenderness and love, thought Captain Delano, well pleased.

This incident prompted him to remark the other Negresses more particularly than before. He was gratified with their manners: like most uncivilized women, they seemed at once tender of heart and tough of constitution, equally ready to die for their infants or fight for them. Unsophisticated as leopardesses, loving as doves. Ah! thought Captain Delano, these, perhaps, are some of the very women whom Ledyard saw in Africa, and gave such a noble account of.

These natural sights somehow insensibly deepened his confidence and ease. At last he looked to see how his boat was getting on, but it was still pretty remote. He turned to see if Don Benito had returned, but he had not.

To change the scene, as well as to please himself with a leisurely observation of the coming boat, stepping over into the mizzen-chains, he clambered his way into the starboard quarter-gallery—one of those abandoned Venetian-looking water balconies previously mentioned—retreats cut off from the deck. As his foot pressed the half-damp, half-dry sea mosses matting the place, and a chance phantom cat's-paw—an islet of breeze, unheralded, unfollowed—as this ghostly cat's-paw came fanning his cheek; as his glance fell upon the row of small, round, dead-lights—all closed like coppered eyes of the coffined—and the state-cabin door, once connecting with the gallery, even as the deadlights had once looked out upon it, but now calked fast like a sarcophagus lid; and to a purple-black, tarred-over, panel, threshold, and post; and he bethought him of the time when that state cabin and this state balcony had heard the voices of the Spanish king's officers, and the forms of the Lima viceroy's daughters had perhaps leaned where he stood—as these and other images flitted through his mind as the cat's-paw through the calm, gradually he felt rising a dreamy inquietude, like that of one who alone on the prairie feels unrest from the repose of the noon.

He leaned against the carved balustrade, again looking off toward his boat, but found his eye falling upon the ribbon grass, trailing along the ship's water line, straight as a border of green box, and parterres of seaweed, broad ovals and crescents, floating nigh and far, with what seemed long formal alleys between, crossing the terraces of swells, and sweeping round as if leading to the grottoes below. And overhanging all was the balustrade by his arm, which, partly stained with pitch and partly embossed with moss, seemed the charred ruin of some summerhouse in a grand garden long running to waste.

Trying to break one charm, he was but becharmed anew. Though upon the wide sea, he seemed in some far inland country, prisoner in some deserted château, left to stare at empty grounds and peer out at vague roads where never wagon or wayfarer passed.

But these enchantments were a little disenchanted as his eye fell on the corroded mainchains. Of an ancient style, massy and rusty in link, shackle, and bolt, they seemed even more fit for the ship's present business than the one for which she had been built.

Presently he thought something moved nigh the chains. He rubbed his eyes, and looked hard. Groves of rigging were about the chains; and there, peering from behind a great stay, like an Indian from behind a hemlock, a Spanish sailor, a marline-spike in his hand, was seen, who made what seemed an imperfect gesture towards the balcony, but immediately, as if alarmed by some advancing step along the deck within, vanished into the recesses of the hempen forest like a poacher.

What meant this? Something the man had sought to communicate, unbeknown to anyone, even to his captain. Did the secret involve aught unfavorable to his captain? Were those previous misgivings of Captain Delano's about to be verified? Or, in his haunted mood at the moment, had some random, unintentional motion of the man, while busy with the stay as if repairing it, been mistaken for a significant beckoning?

Not unbewildered, again he gazed off for his boat. But it was temporarily hidden by a rocky spur of the isle. As with some eagerness he bent forward, watching for the first shooting view of its beak, the balustrade gave way before him like charcoal. Had he not clutched an outreaching rope he would have fallen into the sea. The crash, though feeble, and the fall, though hollow, of the rotten fragments, must have been overheard. He glanced up. With sober curiosity peering down upon him was one of the old oakum-pickers, slipped from his perch to an outside boom, while below the old Negro, and, invisible to him, reconnoitering from a porthole like a fox from the mouth of its den, crouched the Spanish sailor again. From something suddenly suggested by the man's air, the mad idea now darted into Captain Delano's mind that Don Benito's plea of indisposition, in withdrawing below, was but a pretense: that he was engaged there maturing his plot, of which the sailor, by some means gaining an inkling, had a mind to warn the stranger against, incited, it may be, by gratitude for a kind word on first boarding the ship. Was it from foreseeing some possible interference like this that Don Benito had, beforehand, given such a bad character of his sailors, while praising the Negroes, though, indeed, the former seemed as docile as the latter the contrary? The whites, too, by nature, were the shrewder race. A man with some evil design, would he not be likely to speak well of that stupidity which was blind to his depravity, and malign that intelligence from which it might not be hidden? Not unlikely, perhaps. But if the whites had dark secrets concerning Don Benito, could then Don Benito be any way in complicity with the blacks? But they were too stupid. Besides, who ever heard of a white so far a renegade as to apostatize from his very species almost, by leaguing in against it with Negroes? These difficulties recalled former ones. Lost in their mazes, Captain Delano, who had now regained the deck, was uneasily advancing along it when he observed a new face; an aged sailor seated cross-legged near the main hatchway. His skin was shrunk up with wrinkles like a pelican's empty pouch, his hair frosted, his countenance grave and composed. His hands were full of ropes, which he was working into a large knot. Some blacks were about him obligingly dipping the strands for him, here and there, as the exigencies of the operation demanded.

Captain Delano crossed over to him and stood in silence surveying the knot, his mind, by a not uncongenial transition, passing from its own entanglements to those of the hemp. For intricacy, such a knot he had never seen in an American ship, nor indeed any other. The old man looked like an Egyptian priest making Gordian knots for the temple of Ammon. The knot seemed a combination of double-bowline-knot, treble-crown-knot, back-handed-well-knot, knot-in-and-out-knot, and jamming knot.

At last, puzzled to comprehend the meaning of such a knot, Captain Delano addressed the knotter: "What are you knotting there, my man?"

"The knot," was the brief reply, without looking up.

"So it seems; but what is it for?"

"For someone else to undo," muttered back the old man, plying his fingers harder than ever, the knot being now nearly completed.

While Captain Delano stood watching him, suddenly the old man threw the knot towards him, saying in broken English—the first heard in the ship—something to this effect: "Undo it, cut it, quick." It was said lowly, but with such condensation of rapidity, that the long, slow words in Spanish, which had preceded and followed, almost operated as covers to the brief English between.

For a moment, knot in hand, and knot in head, Captain Delano stood mute, while, without further heeding him, the old man was now intent upon other ropes. Presently there was a slight stir behind Captain Delano. Turning, he saw the chained

Negro, Atufal, standing quietly there. The next moment the old sailor rose, muttering, and, followed by his subordinate Negroes, removed to the forward part of the ship, where in the crowd he disappeared.

An elderly Negro, in a clout like an infant's, and with a pepper-and-salt head and a kind of attorney air, now approached Captain Delano. In tolerable Spanish, and with a good-natured, knowing wink, he informed him that the old knotter was simple-witted, but harmless, often playing his odd tricks. The Negro concluded by begging the knot, for of course the stranger would not care to be troubled with it. Unconsciously, it was handed to him. With a sort of *congé*, the Negro received it, and, turning his back, ferreted into it like a detective custom-house officer after smuggled laces. Soon, with some African words equivalent to pshaw, he tossed the knot overboard.

All this is very queer, thought Captain Delano, with a qualmish sort of emotion; but, as one feeling incipient seasickness, he strove, by ignoring the symptoms, to get rid of the malady. Once more he looked off for his boat. To his delight, it was now again in view, leaving the rocky spur astern.

The sensation here experienced, after at first relieving his uneasiness, with unforeseen efficacy soon began to remove it. The less distant sight of that well-known boat—showing it, not as before, half blended with the haze but with outline defined, so that its individuality, like a man's, was manifest; that boat, *Rover* by name, which, though now in strange seas, had often pressed the beach of Captain Delano's home, and, brought to its threshold for repairs, had familiarly lain there, as a Newfoundland dog; the sight of that household boat evoked a thousand trustful associations, which, contrasted with previous suspicions, filled him not only with lightsome confidence, but somehow with half humorous self-reproaches at his former lack of it.

"What, I, Amasa Delano—Jack of the Beach, as they called me when a lad—I, Amasa, the same that, duck-satchel in hand, used to paddle along the waterside to the schoolhouse made from the old hulk—I, little Jack of the Beach, that used to go berrying with cousin Nat and the rest—I to be murdered here at the ends of the earth on board a haunted pirate ship by a horrible Spaniard? Too nonsensical to think of! Who would murder Amasa Delano? His conscience is clean. There is someone above. Fie, fie, Jack of the Beach! you are a child indeed; a child of the second childhood, old boy; you are beginning to dote and drool, I'm afraid."

Light of heart and foot, he stepped aft, and there was met by Don Benito's servant, who, with a pleasing expression responsive to his own present feelings, informed him that his master had recovered from the effects of his coughing fit, and had just ordered him to go present his compliments to his good guest, Don Amasa, and say that he (Don Benito) would soon have the happiness to rejoin him.

There now, do you mark that? again thought Captain Delano, walking the poop. What a donkey I was. This kind gentleman who here sends me his kind compliments, he, but ten minutes ago, dark-lantern in hand, was dodging round some old grindstone in the hold, sharpening a hatchet for me, I thought. Well, well; these long calms have a morbid effect on the mind, I've often heard, though I never believed it before. Ha! glancing towards the boat, there's *Rover*, a good dog, a white bone in her mouth. A pretty big bone though, seems to me.—What? Yes, she has fallen afoul of the bubbling tide rip there. It sets her the other way, too, for the time. Patience.

It was now about noon, though, from the grayness of everything, it seemed to be getting towards dusk.

The calm was confirmed. In the far distance, away from the influence of land, the leaden ocean seemed laid out and leaded up, its course finished, soul gone, defunct. But the current from landward, where the ship was, increased, silently sweeping her further and further towards the tranced waters beyond.

Still, from his knowledge of those latitudes, cherishing hopes of a breeze, and a fair and fresh one, at any moment, Captain Delano, despite present prospects, buoyantly counted upon bringing the San Dominick safely to anchor ere night. The distance swept over was nothing, since, with a good wind, ten minutes' sailing would retrace more than sixty minutes' drifting. Meantime, one moment turning to mark Rover fighting the tide rip and the next to see Don Benito approaching, he continued walking the poop.

Gradually he felt a vexation arising from the delay of his boat; this soon merged into uneasiness, and at last—his eye falling continually, as from a stage box into the pit, upon the strange crowd before and below him, and by and by recognizing there the face, now composed to indifference, of the Spanish sailor who had seemed to beckon from the mainchains—something of his old trepidations returned.

Ah, thought he, gravely enough, this is like the ague: because it went off, it follows not that it won't come back.

Though ashamed of the relapse, he could not altogether subdue it; and so, exerting his good nature to the utmost, insensibly he came to a compromise.

Yes, this is a strange craft, a strange history, too, and strange folks on board. But—nothing more.

By way of keeping his mind out of mischief till the boat should arrive, he tried to occupy it with turning over and over, in a purely speculative sort of way, some lesser peculiarities of the captain and crew. Among others, four curious points recurred:

First, the affair of the Spanish lad assailed with a knife by the slave boy; an act winked at by Don Benito. Second, the tyranny in Don Benito's treatment of Atufal, the black, as if a child should lead a bull of the Nile by the ring in his nose. Third, the trampling of the sailor by the two Negroes, a piece of insolence passed over without so much as a reprimand. Fourth, the cringing submission to their master of all the ship's underlings, mostly blacks, as if by the least inadvertence they feared to draw down his despotic displeasure.

Coupling these points, they seemed somewhat contradictory. But what then, thought Captain Delano, glancing towards his now nearing boat—what then? Why, Don Benito is a very capricious commander. But he is not the first of the sort I have seen, though it's true he rather exceeds any other. But as a nation—continued he in his reveries—these Spaniards are all an odd set; the very word Spaniard has a curious, conspirator, Guy-Fawkish twang to it. And yet I dare say Spaniards in the main are as good folks as any in Duxbury, Massachusetts. Ah good! At last Rover has come.

As, with its welcome freight, the boat touched the side, the oakumpickers, with venerable gestures, sought to restrain the blacks, who, at the sight of three gurried water casks in its bottom and a pile of wilted pumpkins in its bow, hung over the bulwarks in disorderly raptures.

Don Benito, with his servant, now appeared, his coming, perhaps, hastened by hearing the noise. Of him Captain Delano sought permission to serve out the water, so that all might share alike, and none injure themselves by unfair excess. But sensible, and, on Don Benito's account, kind as this offer was, it was received with what seemed impatience; as if aware that he lacked energy as a commander, Don Benito, with the true jealousy of weakness, resented as an affront any interference. So, at least, Captain Delano inferred.

In another moment the casks were being hoisted in, when some of the eager Negroes accidentally jostled Captain Delano where he stood by the gangway, so that, unmindful of Don Benito, yielding to the impulse of the moment, with good-natured authority he bade the black stand back, to enforce his words making use of a half-mirthful, half-menacing gesture. Instantly the blacks paused, just where they were, each Negro and Negress suspended in his or her posture, exactly as the word had found them—for a few seconds continuing so—while, as between the responsive posts of a telegraph, an unknown syllable ran from man to man among the perched oakum-pickers. While the visitor's attention was fixed by this scene, suddenly the hatchet-polishers half rose, and a rapid cry came from Don Benito.

Thinking that at the signal of the Spaniard he was about to be massacred, Captain Delano would have sprung for his boat, but paused, as the oakum-pickers, dropping down into the crowd with earnest exclamations, forced every white and every Negro back, at the same moment, with gestures friendly and familiar, almost jocose, bidding him, in substance, not be a fool. Simultaneously the hatchet-polishers resumed their seats, quietly as so many tailors, and at once, as if nothing had happened, the work of hoisting in the casks was resumed, whites and blacks singing at the tackle.

Captain Delano glanced towards Don Benito. As he saw his meager form in the act of recovering itself from reclining in the servant's arms, into which the agitated invalid had fallen, he could not but marvel at the panic by which himself had been surprised, on the darting supposition that such a commander, who, upon a legitimate occasion, so trivial too, as it now appeared, could lose all self-command, was, with energetic iniquity, going to bring about his murder.

The casks being on deck, Captain Delano was handed a number of jars and cups by one of the steward's aids, who, in the name of his captain, entreated him to do as he had proposed—dole out the water. He complied, with republican impartiality as to this republican element, which always seeks one level, serving the oldest white no better than the youngest black, excepting, indeed, poor Don Benito, whose condition, if not rank, demanded an extra allowance. To him, in the first place, Captain Delano presented a fair pitcher of the fluid, but, thirsting as he was for it, the Spaniard quaffed not a drop until after several grave bows and salutes, a reciprocation of courtesies which the sight-loving Africans hailed with clapping of hands.

Two of the less wilted pumpkins being reserved for the cabin table, the residue were minced up on the spot for the general regalement. But the soft bread, sugar, and bottled cider Captain Delano would have given the whites alone, and in chief Don Benito, but the latter objected; which disinterestedness not a little pleased the American; and so mouthfuls all around were given alike to whites and blacks, excepting one bottle of cider, which Babo insisted upon setting aside for his master.

Here it may be observed that as, on the first visit of the boat, the American had not permitted his men to board the ship, neither did he now, being unwilling to add to the confusion of the decks.

Not uninfluenced by the peculiar good humor at present prevailing, and for the time oblivious of any but benevolent thought, Captain Delano, who from recent indications counted upon a breeze within an hour or two at furthest, dispatched the boat back to the sealer, with orders for all the hands that could be spared immediately to set about rafting casks to the watering place and filling them. Likewise he bade word be carried to his chief officer that if, against present expectation, the ship was not brought to anchor by sunset, he need be under no concern; for as there was to be a full moon that night, he (Captain Delano) would remain on board ready to play the pilot, come the wind soon or late.

As the two Captains stood together observing the departing boat—the servant, as it happened, having just spied a spot on his master's velvet sleeve, and silently engaged rubbing it out—the American expressed his regrets that the *San Dominick* had no boats, none, at least, but the unseaworthy old hulk of the longboat, which, warped as a camel's skeleton in the desert and almost as bleached, lay pot-wise inverted amidships, one side a little tipped, furnishing a subterranean sort of den for family groups of the blacks, mostly women and small children, who, squatting on old mats below, or perched above in the dark dome on the elevated seats, were described, some distance within, like a social circle of bats sheltering in some friendly cave, at intervals, ebon flights of naked boys and girls three or four years old darting in and out of the den's mouth.

"Had you three or four boats now, Don Benito," said Captain Delano, "I think that, by tugging at the oars, your Negroes here might help along matters some. Did you sail from port without boats, Don Benito?"

"They were stove in the gales, *señor*."

"That was bad. Many men, too, you lost then. Boats and men. Those must have been hard gales, Don Benito."

"Past all speech," cringed the Spaniard.

"Tell me, Don Benito," continued his companion with increased interest, "tell me, were these gales immediately off the pitch of Cape Horn?"

"Cape Horn?—who spoke of Cape Horn?"

"Yourself did, when giving me an account of your voyage," answered Captain Delano, with almost equal astonishment at this eating of his own words, even as he ever seemed eating his own heart, on the part of the Spaniard. "You yourself, Don Benito, spoke of Cape Horn," he emphatically repeated.

The Spaniard turned, in a sort of stooping posture, pausing an instant as one about to make a plunging exchange of elements, as from air to water.

At this moment a messenger boy, a white, hurried by, in the regular performance of his function carrying the last expired half-hour forward to the forecastle from the cabin timepiece, to have it struck at the ship's large bell.

"Master," said the servant, discontinuing his work on the coat sleeve and addressing the rapt Spaniard with a sort of timid apprehensiveness, as one charged with a duty the discharge of which, it was foreseen, would prove irksome to the very person who had imposed it and for whose benefit it was intended, "master told me never mind where he was, or how engaged, always to remind him, to a minute, when shaving time comes. Miguel has gone to strike the half-hour afternoon. It is *now*, master. Will master go into the cuddy?"

"Ah—yes," answered the Spaniard, starting, as from dreams into realities, then, turning upon Captain Delano, he said that erelong he would resume the conversation.

"Then if master means to talk more to Don Amasa," said the servant, "why not let Don Amasa sit by master in the cuddy, and master can talk, and Don Amasa can listen, while Babo here lathers and strops."

"Yes," said Captain Delano, not unpleased with this sociable plan, "yes, Don Benito, unless you had rather not, I will go with you."

"Be it so, *señor*."

As the three passed aft, the American could not but think it another strange instance of his host's capriciousness, this being shaved with such uncommon punctuality in the middle of the day. But he deemed it more than likely that the servant's anxious fidelity had something to do with the matter, inasmuch as the timely interruption served to rally his master from the mood which had evidently been coming upon him.

The place called the cuddy was a light deck cabin formed by the poop, a sort of attic to the large cabin below. Part of it had formerly been the quarters of the officers, but since their death all the partitionings had been thrown down and the whole interior converted into one spacious and airy marine hall; for absence of fine furniture and picturesque disarray of odd appurtenances, somewhat answering to the wide, cluttered hall of some eccentric bachelor squire in the country, who hangs his shooting jacket and tobacco pouch on deer antlers, and keeps his fishing rod, tongs, and walking stick in the same corner.

The similitude was heightened, if not originally suggested, by glimpses of the surrounding sea, since, in one aspect, the country and the ocean seem cousins-german.

The floor of the cuddy was matted. Overhead, four or five old muskets were stuck into horizontal holes along the beams. On one side was a claw-footed old table lashed to the deck, a thumbed missal on it, and over it, a small, meager crucifix attached to the bulkhead. Under the table lay a dented cutlass or two with a hacked harpoon, among some melancholy old rigging, like a heap of poor friars' girdles. There were also two long, sharp-ribbed settees of Malacca cane, black with age, and uncomfortable to look at as inquisitors' racks, with a large, misshapen armchair, which, furnished with a rude barber's crotch at the back, working with a screw, seemed some grotesque engine of torment. A flag locker was in one corner, open, exposing various colored buntings, some rolled up, others half unrolled, still others tumbled. Opposite was a cumbrous washstand of black mahogany, all of one block, with a pedestal like a font, and over it a railed shelf, containing combs, brushes, and other implements of the toilet. A torn hammock of stained grass swung near, the sheets tossed, and the pillow wrinkled up like a brow, as if whoever slept here slept but illy, with alternate visitations of sad thoughts and bad dreams.

The further extremity of the cuddy, overhanging the ship's stern, was pierced with three openings, windows or portholes, according as men or cannon might peer, socially or unsocially, out of them. At present neither men nor cannon were seen, though huge ringbolts and other rusty iron fixtures of the woodwork hinted of twenty-four-pounders.

Glancing towards the hammock as he entered, Captain Delano said, "You sleep here, Don Benito?"

"Yes, *señor*, since we got into mild weather."

"This seems a sort of dormitory, sitting room, sail loft, chapel, armory, and private closet all together, Don Benito," added Captain Delano, looking round.

"Yes, *señor*, events have not been favorable to much order in my arrangements."

Here the servant, napkin on arm, made a motion as if waiting his master's good pleasure. Don Benito signified his readiness, when, seating him in the Malacca armchair, and for the guest's convenience drawing opposite one of the settees, the servant commenced operations by throwing back his master's collar and loosening his cravat.

There is something in the Negro which, in a peculiar way, fits him for avocations about one's person. Most Negroes are natural valets and hairdressers, taking to the comb and brush congenially as to the castanets, and flourishing them apparently with almost equal satisfaction. There is, too, a smooth tact about them in this employment, with a marvelous, noiseless, gliding briskness, not ungraceful in its way, singularly pleasing to behold, and still more so to be the manipulated subject of. And above all is the great gift of good humor. Not the mere grin or laugh is here meant. Those were unsuitable. But a certain easy cheerfulness, harmonious in every glance and gesture, as though God had set the whole Negro to some pleasant tune.

When to this is added the docility arising from the unaspiring contentment of a limited mind, and that susceptibility of blind attachment sometimes inhering in indisputable inferiors, one readily perceives why those hypochondriacs, Johnson and Byron—it may be, something like the hypochondriac Benito Cereno—took to their hearts, almost to the exclusion of the entire white race, their servingmen, the Negroes, Barber and Fletcher. But if there be that in the Negro which exempts him from the inflicted sourness of the morbid or cynical mind, how, in his most prepossessing aspects, must he appear to a benevolent one? When at ease with respect to exterior things, Captain Delano's nature was not only benign, but familiarly and humorously so. At home, he had often taken rare satisfaction in sitting in his door, watching some free man of color at his work or play. If on a voyage he chanced to have a black sailor, invariably he was on chatty and half-gamesome terms with him. In fact, like most men of a good, blithe heart, Captain Delano took to Negroes, not philanthropically, but genially, just as other men to Newfoundland dogs.

Hitherto, the circumstances in which he found the *San Dominick* had repressed the tendency. But in the cuddy, relieved from his former uneasiness, and, for various reasons, more sociably inclined than at any previous period of the day, and seeing the colored servant, napkin on arm, so debonair about his master, in a business so familiar as that of shaving too, all his old weakness for Negroes returned.

Among other things, he was amused with an odd instance of the African love of bright colors and fine shows, in the black's informally taking from the flag locker a great piece of bunting of all hues and lavishly tucking it under his master's chin for an apron.

The mode of shaving among the Spaniards is a little different from what it is with other nations. They have a basin, specifically called a barber's basin, which on one side is scooped out, so as accurately to receive the chin, against which it is closely held in lathering, which is done, not with a brush, but with soap dipped in the water of the basin and rubbed on the face.

In the present instance salt water was used for lack of better, and the parts lathered were only the upper lip and low down under the throat, all the rest being cultivated beard.

The preliminaries being somewhat novel to Captain Delano, he sat curiously eying them, so that no conversation took place, nor, for the present, did Don Benito appear disposed to renew any.

Setting down his basin, the Negro searched among the razors, as for the sharpest, and, having found it, gave it an additional edge by expertly stropping it on the firm, smooth, oily skin of his open palm; he then made a gesture as if to begin, but midway stood suspended for an instant, one hand elevating the razor, the other professionally dabbling among the bubbling suds on the Spaniard's lank neck. Not unaffected by the close sight of the gleaming steel, Don Benito nervously shuddered; his usual ghastliness was heightened by the lather, which lather, again, was intensified in its hue by the contrasting sootiness of the Negro's body. Altogether the scene was somewhat peculiar, at least to Captain Delano, nor, as he saw the two thus postured, could he resist the vagary that in the black he saw a headsman, and in the white a man at the block. But this was one of those antic conceits, appearing and vanishing in a breath, from which, perhaps, the best-regulated mind is not always free.

Meantime the agitation of the Spaniard had a little loosened the bunting from around him, so that one broad fold swept curtainlike over the chair arm to the floor, revealing, amid a profusion of armorial bars and ground colors—black, blue, and yellow—a closed castle in a blood-red field diagonal with a lion rampant in a white.

"The castle and the lion," exclaimed Captain Delano—"why, Don Benito, this is the flag of Spain you use here. It's well it's only I, and not the King, that sees this," he added, with a smile, "but"—turning towards the black—"it's all one, I suppose, so the colors be gay"; which playful remark did not fail somewhat to tickle the Negro.

"Now, master," he said, readjusting the flag, and pressing the head gently further back into the crotch of the chair, "now, master," and the steel glanced nigh the throat.

Again Don Benito faintly shuddered.

"You must not shake so, master. See, Don Amasa, master always shakes when I shave him. And yet master knows I never yet have drawn blood, though it's true if master will shake so I may some of these times. Now master," he continued. "And now, Don Amasa, please go on with your talk about the gale, and all that; master can hear, and, between times, master can answer."

"Ah yes, these gales," said Captain Delano; "but the more I think of your voyage, Don Benito, the more I wonder, not at the gales, terrible as they must have been, but at the disastrous interval following them. For here, by your account, have you been these two months and more getting from Cape Horn to St. Maria, a distance which I myself, with a good wind, have sailed in a few days. True, you had calms, and long ones, but to be becalmed for two months, that is, at least, unusual. Why, Don Benito, had almost any other gentleman told me such a story, I should have been half disposed to a little incredulity."

Here an involuntary expression came over the Spaniard, similar to that just before on the deck, and whether it was the start he gave, or a sudden gawky roll of the hull in the calm, or a momentary unsteadiness of the servant's hand, however it was, just then the razor drew blood, spots of which stained the creamy lather under the throat; immediately the black barber drew back his steel, and, remaining in his professional attitude, back to Captain Delano, and face to Don Benito, held up the trickling razor, saying, with a sort of half humorous sorrow, "See, master—you shook so—here's Babo's first blood."

No sword drawn before James the First of England, no assassination in that timid king's presence, could have produced a more terrified aspect than was now presented by Don Benito.

Poor fellow, thought Captain Delano, so nervous he can't even bear the sight of barber's blood; and this unstrung, sick man, is it credible that I should have imagined he meant to spill all my blood, who can't endure the sight of one little drop of his own? Surely, Amasa Delano, you have been beside yourself this day. Tell it not when you get home, sappy Amasa. Well, well, he looks like a murderer, doesn't he? More like as if himself were to be done for. Well, well, this day's experience shall be a good lesson.

Meantime, while these things were running through the honest seaman's mind, the servant had taken the napkin from his arm, and to Don Benito had said—"But answer Don Amasa, please, master, while I wipe this ugly stuff off the razor, and strop it again."

As he said the words, his face was turned half round, so as to be alike visible to the Spaniard and the American, and seemed, by its expression, to hint that he was desirous, by getting his master to go on with the conversation, considerably to withdraw his attention from the recent annoying accident. As if glad to snatch the offered relief, Don Benito resumed, rehearsing to Captain Delano that, not only were the calms of unusual duration, but the ship had fallen in with obstinate currents, and other things he added, some of which were but repetitions of former statements, to explain how it came to pass that the passage from Cape Horn to St. Maria had been so exceedingly long, now and then mingling with his words incidental praises, less qualified than before, to the blacks, for their general good conduct. These particulars were not given consecutively, the servant, at convenient times, using his razor, and so, between the intervals of shaving, the story and panegyric went on with more than usual huskiness.

To Captain Delano's imagination, now again not wholly at rest, there was something so hollow in the Spaniard's manner, with apparently some reciprocal hollowness in the servant's dusky comment of silence, that the idea flashed across him that possibly master and man, for some unknown purpose, were acting out, both in word and deed, nay, to the very tremor of Don Benito's limbs, some juggling play before him. Neither did the suspicion of collusion lack apparent support, from the fact of those whispered conferences before mentioned. But then, what could be the object of enacting this play of the barber before him? At last, regarding the notion as a whimsey, insensibly suggested, perhaps, by the theatrical aspect of Don Benito in his harlequin ensign, Captain Delano speedily banished it.

The shaving over, the servant bestirred himself with a small bottle of scented waters, pouring a few drops on the head, and then diligently rubbing, the vehemence of the exercise causing the muscles of his face to twitch rather strangely.

His next operation was with comb, scissors, and brush, going round and round, smoothing a curl here, clipping an unruly whisker hair there, giving a graceful sweep to the temple lock, with other impromptu touches evincing the hand of a master, while, like any resigned gentleman in barber's hands, Don Benito bore all much less uneasily, at least, than he had done the razoring; indeed, he sat so pale and rigid now that the Negro seemed a Nubian sculptor finishing off a white statue head.

All being over at last, the standard of Spain removed, tumbled up, and tossed back into the flag locker, the Negro's warm breath blowing away any stray hair which might have lodged down his master's neck, collar and cravat readjusted, a speck of lint whisked off the velvet lapel—all this being done, backing off a little space, and pausing with an expression of subdued self-complacency, the servant for a moment surveyed his master, as, in toilette at least, the creature of his own tasteful hands.

Captain Delano playfully complimented him upon his achievement, at the same time congratulating Don Benito.

But neither sweet waters, nor shampooing, nor fidelity, nor sociality, delighted the Spaniard. Seeing him relapsing into forbidding gloom, and still remaining seated, Captain Delano, thinking that his presence was undesired just then, withdrew, on pretense of seeing whether, as he had prophesied, any signs of a breeze were visible.

Walking forward to the mainmast, he stood awhile thinking over the scene, and not without some undefined misgivings, when he heard a noise near the cuddy, and, turning, saw the Negro, his hand to his cheek. Advancing, Captain Delano perceived that the cheek was bleeding. He was about to ask the cause, when the Negro's wailing soliloquy enlightened him.

"Ah, when will master get better from his sickness; only the sour heart that sour sickness breeds made him serve Babo so, cutting Babo with the razor because, only by accident, Babo had given master one little scratch, and for the first time in so many a day, too. Ah, ah, ah," holding his hand to his face.

Is it possible, thought Captain Delano; was it to wreak in private his Spanish spite against this poor friend of his that Don Benito, by his sullen manner, impelled me to withdraw? Ah this slavery breeds ugly passions in man.—Poor fellow!

He was about to speak in sympathy to the Negro, but with a timid reluctance he now re-entered the cuddy.

Presently master and man came forth, Don Benito leaning on his servant as if nothing had happened.

But a sort of love quarrel, after all, thought Captain Delano.

He accosted Don Benito, and they slowly walked together. They had gone but a few paces, when the steward—a tall, rajah-looking mulatto, Orientally set off with a pagoda turban formed by three or four Madras handkerchiefs wound about his head, tier on tier—approaching with a salaam, announced lunch in the cabin.

On their way thither, the two captains were preceded by the mulatto, who, turning round as he advanced, with continual smiles and bows, ushered them on, a display of elegance which quite completed the insignificance of the small bareheaded Babo, who, as if not unconscious of inferiority, eyed askance the graceful steward. But, in part, Captain Delano imputed his jealous watchfulness to that peculiar feeling which the full-blooded African entertains for the adulterated one. As for the steward, his manner, if not bespeaking much dignity of self-respect, yet evidenced his extreme desire to please, which is doubly meritorious, as at once Christian and Chesterfieldian.

Captain Delano observed with interest that while the complexion of the mulatto was hybrid, his physiognomy was European—classically so.

"Don Benito," whispered he, "I am glad to see this usher-of-the-golden-rod of yours; the sight refutes an ugly remark once made to me by a Barbados planter, that when a mulatto has a regular European face, look out for him; he is a devil. But see, your steward here has features more regular than King George's of England, and yet there he nods, and bows, and smiles, a king, indeed—the king of kind hearts and polite fellows. What a pleasant voice he has, too."

"He has, *señor.*"

"But tell me, has he not, so far as you have known him, always proved a good, worthy fellow?" said Captain Delano, pausing, while with a final genuflexion the steward disappeared into the cabin; "come, for the reason just mentioned, I am curious to know."

"Francesco is a good man," a sort of sluggishly responded Don Benito, like a phlegmatic appreciator, who would neither find fault nor flatter.

"Ah, I thought so. For it were strange indeed, and not very creditable to us whiteskins, if a little of our blood mixed with the African's should, far from improving the latter's quality, have the sad effect of pouring vitriolic acid into black broth—improving the hue, perhaps, but not the wholesomeness."

"Doubtless, doubtless, *señor,* but"—glancing at Babo—"not to speak of Negroes, your planter's remark I have heard applied to the Spanish and Indian intermixtures in our provinces. But I know nothing about the matter," he listlessly added.

And here they entered the cabin.

The lunch was a frugal one. Some of Captain Delano's fresh fish and pumpkins, biscuit and salt beef, the reserved bottle of cider, and the *San Dominick's* last bottle of Canary.

As they entered, Francesco, with two or three colored aids, was hovering over the table giving the last adjustments. Upon perceiving their master they withdrew, Francesco making a smiling *congé*, and the Spaniard, without condescending to notice it, fastidiously remarking to his companion that he relished not superfluous attendance.

Without companions, host and guest sat down, like a childless married couple, at opposite ends of the table, Don Benito waving Captain Delano to his place, and, weak as he was, insisting upon that gentleman being seated before himself.

The Negro placed a rug under Don Benito's feet, and a cushion behind his back, and then stood behind, not his master's chair, but Captain Delano's. At first, this a little surprised the latter. But it was soon evident that; in taking his position, the black was still true to his master, since by facing him he could the more readily anticipate his slightest want.

"This is an uncommonly intelligent fellow of yours, Don Benito," whispered Captain Delano across the table.

"You say true, *señor.*"

During the repast, the guest again reverted to parts of Don Benito's story, begging further particulars here and there. He inquired how it was that the scurvy and fever should have committed such wholesale havoc upon the whites, while destroying less than half of the blacks. As if this question reproduced the whole scene of plague before the Spaniard's eyes, miserably reminding him of his solitude in a cabin where before he had had so many friends and officers round him, his hand shook, his face became hueless, broken words escaped; but directly the same memory of the past seemed replaced by insane terrors of the present. With starting eyes he stared before him at vacancy. For nothing was to be seen but the hand of his servant pushing the Canary over towards him. At length a few sips served partially to restore him. He made random reference to the different constitution of races, enabling one to offer more resistance to certain maladies than another. The thought was new to his companion.

Presently Captain Delano, intending to say something to his host concerning the pecuniary part of the business he had undertaken for him, especially—since he was strictly accountable to his owners—with reference to the new suit of sails, and other things of that sort, and naturally preferring to conduct such affairs in private, was desirous that the servant should withdraw, imagining that Don Benito for a few minutes could dispense with his attendance. He, however, waited awhile, thinking that, as the conversation proceeded, Don Benito, without being prompted, would perceive the propriety of the step.

But it was otherwise. At last catching his host's eye, Captain Delano, with a slight backward gesture of his thumb, whispered, "Don Benito, pardon me, but there is an interference with the full expression of what I have to say to you."

Upon this the Spaniard changed countenance, which was imputed to his resenting the hint, as in some way a reflection upon his servant. After a moment's pause, he assured his guest that the black's remaining with them could be of no disservice; because since losing his officers he had made Babo (whose original office, it now appeared, had been captain of the slaves) not only his constant attendant and companion, but in all things his confidant.

After this, nothing more could be said; though indeed Captain Delano could hardly avoid some little tinge of irritation upon being left ungratified in so inconsiderable a wish, by one, too, for whom he intended such solid services. But it is only his querulousness, thought he, and so, filling his glass, he proceeded to business.

The price of the sails and other matters was fixed upon. But while this was being done, the American observed that, though his original offer of assistance had been hailed with hectic animation, yet now when it was reduced to a business transaction, indifference and apathy were betrayed. Don Benito, in fact, appeared to submit to hearing the details more out of regard to common propriety than from any impression that weighty benefit to himself and his voyage was involved.

Soon his manner became still more reserved. The effort was vain to seek to draw him into social talk. Gnawed by his splenetic mood, he sat twitching his beard, while to little purpose the hand of his servant, mute as that on the wall, slowly pushed over the Canary.

Lunch being over, they sat down on the cushioned transom, the servant placing a pillow behind his master. The long continuance of the calm had now affected the atmosphere. Don Benito sighed heavily, as if for breath.

"Why not adjourn to the cuddy," said Captain Delano; "there is more air there." But the host sat silent and motionless.

Meantime his servant knelt before him with a large fan of feathers. And Francesco, coming in on tiptoes, handed the Negro a little cup of aromatic waters, with which at intervals he chafed his master's brow, smoothing the hair along the temples as a nurse does a child's. He spoke no word. He only rested his eye on his master's, as if, amid all Don Benito's distress, a little to refresh his spirit by the silent sight of fidelity.

Presently the ship's bell sounded two o'clock, and through the cabin windows a slight rippling of the sea was discerned, and from the desired direction.

"There," exclaimed Captain Delano, "I told you so, Don Benito, look!"

He had risen to his feet, speaking in a very animated tone, with a view the more to rouse his companion. But though the crimson curtain of the stern window near him that moment fluttered against his pale cheek, Don Benito seemed to have even less welcome for the breeze than the calm.

Poor fellow, thought Captain Delano, bitter experience has taught him that one ripple does not make a wind, any more than one swallow a summer. But he is mistaken for once. I will get his ship in for him, and prove it.

Briefly alluding to his weak condition, he urged his host to remain quietly where he was, since he (Captain Delano) would with pleasure take upon himself the responsibility of making the best use of the wind.

Upon gaining the deck, Captain Delano started at the unexpected figure of Atufal, monumentally fixed at the threshold, like one of those sculptured porters of black marble guarding the porches of Egyptian tombs.

But this time the start was, perhaps, purely physical. Atufal's presence, singularly attesting docility even in sullenness, was contrasted with that of the hatchet-polishers, who in patience evinced their industry; while both spectacles showed that, lax as Don Benito's general authority might be, still, whenever he chose to exert it, no man so savage or colossal but must, more or less, bow.

Snatching a trumpet which hung from the bulwarks, with a free step Captain Delano advanced to the forward edge of the poop, issuing his orders in his best Spanish. The few sailors and many Negroes, all equally pleased, obediently set about heading the ship towards the harbor.

While giving some directions about setting a lower stunsail, suddenly Captain Delano heard a voice faithfully repeating his orders. Turning, he saw Babo, now for the time acting, under the pilot, his original part of captain of the slaves. This assistance proved valuable. Tattered sails and warped yards were soon brought into some trim. And no brace or halyard was pulled but to the blithe songs of the inspirited Negroes.

Good fellows, thought Captain Delano, a little training would make fine sailors of them. Why see, the very women pull and sing too. These must be some of those Ashantee Negresses that make such capital soldiers, I've heard. But who's at the helm? I must have a good hand there.

He went to see.

The *San Dominick* steered with a cumbrous tiller, with large horizontal pulleys attached. At each pulley end stood a subordinate black, and between them, at the tillerhead, the responsible post, a Spanish seaman, whose countenance evinced his due share in the general hopefulness and confidence at the coming of the breeze.

He proved the same man who had behaved with so shamefaced an air on the windlass.

"Ah—it is you, my man," exclaimed Captain Delano—"well, no more sheep's-eyes now; look straight forward and keep the ship so. Good hand, I trust? And want to get into the harbor, don't you?"

The man assented with an inward chuckle, grasping the tillerhead firmly. Upon this, unperceived by the American, the two blacks eyed the sailor intently.

Finding all right at the helm, the pilot went forward to the forecastle to see how matters stood there.

The ship now had way enough to breast the current. With the approach of evening, the breeze would be sure to freshen.

Having done all that was needed for the present, Captain Delano, giving his last orders to the sailors, turned aft to report affairs to Don Benito in the cabin, perhaps additionally incited to rejoin him by the hope of snatching a moment's private chat while the servant was engaged upon deck.

From opposite sides, there were, beneath the poop, two approaches to the cabin, one further forward than the other, and consequently communicating with a longer passage. Marking the servant still above, Captain Delano, taking the nighest entrance—the one last named, and at whose porch Atufal still stood—hurried on his way, till, arrived at the cabin threshold, he paused an instant, a little to recover from his eagerness. Then, with the words of his intended business upon his lips, he entered. As he advanced toward the seated Spaniard, he heard another footstep, keeping time with his. From the opposite door, a salver in hand, the servant was likewise advancing.

"Confound the faithful fellow," thought Captain Delano; "what a vexatious coincidence."

Possibly the vexation might have been something different, were it not for the brisk confidence inspired by the breeze. But even as it was he felt a slight twinge, from a sudden indefinite association in his mind of Babo with Atufal.

"Don Benito," said he, "I give you joy; the breeze will hold, and will increase. By the way, your tall man and timepiece, Atufal, stands without. By your order, of course?"

Don Benito recoiled, as if at some bland satirical touch delivered with such adroit garnish of apparent good breeding as to present no handle for retort.

He is like one flayed alive, thought Captain Delano; where may one touch him without causing a shrink?

The servant moved before his master, adjusting a cushion; recalled to civility, the Spaniard stiffly replied: "You are right. The slave appears where you saw him, according to my command, which is that if at the given hour I am below he must take his stand and abide my coming."

"Ah now, pardon me, but that is treating the poor fellow like an ex-king indeed. Ah, Don Benito," smiling, "for all the license you permit in some things, I fear lest, at bottom, you are a bitter hard master."

Again Don Benito shrank, and this time, as the good sailor thought, from a genuine twinge of his conscience.

Again conversation became constrained. In vain Captain Delano called attention to the now perceptible motion of the keel gently cleaving the sea; with lackluster eye, Don Benito returned words few and reserved.

By and by, the wind having steadily risen, and still blowing right into the harbor, bore the *San Dominick* swiftly on. Rounding a point of land, the sealer at distance came into open view.

Meantime Captain Delano had again repaired to the deck, remaining there some time. Having at last altered the ship's course so as to give the reef a wide berth, he returned for a few moments below.

I will cheer up my poor friend this time, thought he.

"Better and better, Don Benito," he cried as he blithely re-entered: "there will soon be an end to your cares, at least for a while. For when, after a long, sad voyage, you know, the anchor drops into the haven, all its vast weight seems lifted from the captain's heart. We are getting on famously, Don Benito. My ship is in sight. Look through this side light here; there she is, all a-taunt-o! The *Bachelor's Delight*, my good friend. Ah, how this wind braces one up. Come, you must take a cup of coffee with me this evening. My old steward will give you as fine a cup as ever any sultan tasted. What say you, Don Benito, will you?"

At first, the Spaniard glanced feverishly up, casting a longing look towards the sealer, while, with mute concern, his servant gazed into his face. Suddenly the old ague of coldness returned, and dropping back to his cushions he was silent.

"You do not answer. Come, all day you have been my host; would you have hospitality all on one side?"

"I cannot go," was the response.

"What? it will not fatigue you. The ships will lie together as near as they can without swinging foul. It will be little more than stepping from deck to deck, which is but as from room to room. Come, come, you must not refuse me."

"I cannot go," decisively and repulsively repeated Don Benito.

Renouncing all but the last appearance of courtesy, with a sort of cadaverous sullenness, and biting his thin nails to the quick, he glanced, almost glared, at his guest, as if impatient that a stranger's presence should interfere with the full indulgence of his morbid hour. Meantime the sound of the parted waters came more and more gurglingly and merrily in at the windows; as reproaching him for his dark spleen, as telling him that, sulk as he might, and go mad with it, nature cared not a jot, since whose fault was it, pray?

But the foul mood was now at its depth, as the fair wind at its height.

There was something in the man so far beyond any mere unsociality or sourness previously evinced that even the forbearing good nature of his guest could no longer endure it. Wholly at a loss to account for such demeanor, and deeming sickness with eccentricity, however extreme, no adequate excuse, well satisfied, too, that nothing in his own conduct could justify it, Captain Delano's pride began to be roused. Himself became reserved. But all seemed one to the Spaniard. Quitting him, therefore, Captain Delano once more went to the deck.

The ship was now within less than two miles of the sealer. The whaleboat was seen darting over the interval.

To be brief, the two vessels, thanks to the pilot's skill, erelong in neighborly style lay anchored together.

Before returning to his own vessel, Captain Delano had intended communicating to Don Benito the smaller details of the proposed services to be rendered. But as it was, unwilling anew to subject himself to rebuffs, he resolved, now that he had seen the *San Dominick* safely moored, immediately to quit her, without further allusion to hospitality or business. Indefinitely postponing his ulterior plans, he would regulate his future actions according to future circumstances. His boat was ready to receive him; but his host still tarried below. Well, thought Captain Delano, if he has little breeding, the more need to show mine. He descended to the cabin to bid a ceremonious, and, it may be, tacitly rebukeful adieu. But to his great satisfaction, Don Benito, as if he began to feel the weight of that treatment with which his slighted guest had, not indecorously, retaliated upon him, now, supported by his servant, rose to his feet, and grasping Captain Delano's hand, stood tremulous, too much agitated to speak. But the good augury hence drawn was suddenly dashed by his resuming all his previous reserve with augmented gloom, as, with half-averted eyes, he silently reseated himself on his cushions. With a corresponding return of his own chilled feelings, Captain Delano bowed and withdrew.

He was hardly midway in the narrow corridor, dim as a tunnel, leading from the cabin to the stairs, when a sound, as of the tolling for execution in some jailyard, fell on his ears. It was the echo of the ship's flawed bell striking the hour, drearily reverberated in this subterranean vault. Instantly, by a fatality not to be withstood, his mind, responsive to the portent, swarmed with superstitious suspicions. He paused. In images far swifter than these sentences, the minutest details of all his former distrusts swept through him.

Hitherto, credulous good nature had been too ready to furnish excuses for reasonable fears. Why was the Spaniard, so superfluously punctilious at times, now heedless of common propriety in not accompanying to the side his departing guest? Did indisposition forbid? Indisposition had not forbidden more irksome exertion that day. His last equivocal demeanor recurred. He had risen to his feet, grasped his guest's hand, motioned toward his hat; then, in an instant, all was eclipsed in sinister muteness and gloom. Did this imply one brief repentant relenting at the final moment from some iniquitous plot, followed by remorseless return to it? His last glance seemed to express a calamitous yet acquiescent farewell to Captain Delano forever. Why decline the invitation to visit the sealer that evening? Or was the Spaniard less hardened than the Jew, who refrained not from supping at the board of him whom the same night he meant to betray? What imported all those daylong enigmas and contradictions, except they were intended to mystify, preliminary to some stealthy blow? Atufal, the pretended rebel but punctual shadow, that moment lurked by the threshold without. He seemed a sentry, and more. Who, by his own confession, had stationed him there? Was the Negro now lying in wait?

The Spaniard behind—his creature before: to rush from darkness to light was the involuntary choice.

The next moment, with clenched jaw and hand, he passed Atufal, and stood unharmed in the light. As he saw his trim ship lying peacefully at anchor and almost within ordinary call; as he saw his household boat, with familiar faces in it, patiently rising and falling on the short waves by the *San Dominick's* side; and then, glancing about the decks where he stood, saw the oakum-pickers still gravely plying their fingers, and heard the low, buzzing whistle and industrious hum of the hatchet-polishers still bestirring themselves over their endless occupation; and more than all, as he saw the benign aspect of nature taking her innocent repose in the evening, the screened sun in the quiet camp of the west shining out like the mild light from Abraham's tent—as charmed eye and ear took in all these, with the chained figure of the black, clenched jaw and hand relaxed. Once again he smiled at the phantoms which had mocked him, and felt something like a tinge of remorse that, by harboring them even for a moment, he should by implication have betrayed an atheist doubt of the ever-watchful Providence above.

There was a few minutes' delay, while, in obedience to his orders, the boat was being hooked along to the gangway. During this interval, a sort of saddened satisfaction stole over Captain Delano at thinking of the kindly offices he had that day discharged for a stranger. Ah, thought he, after good actions one's conscience is never ungrateful, however much so the benefited party may be.

Presently his foot, in the first act of descent into the boat, pressed the first round of the side ladder, his face presented inward upon the deck. In the same moment he heard his name courteously sounded, and, to his pleased surprise, saw Don Benito advancing—an unwonted energy in his air, as if, at the last moment, intent upon making amends for his recent discourtesy. With instinctive good feeling, Captain Delano, withdrawing his foot, turned and reciprocally advanced. As he did so, the Spaniard's nervous eagerness increased, but his vital energy failed, so that, the better to support him, the servant, placing his master's hand on his naked shoulder, and gently holding it there, formed himself into a sort of crutch.

When the two captains met, the Spaniard again fervently took the hand of the American, at the same time casting an earnest glance into his eyes, but, as before, too much overcome to speak.

I have done him wrong, self-reproachfully thought Captain Delano; his apparent coldness has deceived me; in no instance has he meant to offend.

Meantime, as if fearful that the continuance of the scene might too much unstring his master, the servant seemed anxious to terminate it. And so, still presenting himself as a crutch, and walking between the two captains, he advanced with them towards the gangway; while still, as if full of kindly contrition, Don Benito would not let go the hand of Captain Delano but retained it in his, across the black's body.

Soon they were standing by the side, looking over into the boat, whose crew turned up their curious eyes. Waiting a moment for the Spaniard to relinquish his hold, the now embarrassed Captain Delano lifted his foot to overstep the threshold of the open gangway, but still Don Benito would not let go his hand. And yet, with an agitated tone, he said, "I can go no further; here I must bid you adieu. Adieu, my dear, dear Don Amasa. Go—go!" suddenly tearing his hand loose, "go, and God guard you better than me, my best friend."

Not unaffected, Captain Delano would now have lingered, but, catching the meekly admonitory eye of the servant, with a hasty farewell he descended into his boat, followed by the continual adieus of Don Benito, standing rooted in the gangway.

Seating himself in the stern, Captain Delano, making a last salute, ordered the boat shoved off. The crew had their oars on end. The bowsmen pushed the boat a sufficient distance for the oars to be lengthwise dropped. The instant that was done, Don Benito sprang over the bulwarks, falling at the feet of Captain Delano; at the same time calling towards his ship, but in tones so frenzied that none in the boat could understand him. But, as if not equally obtuse, three sailors, from three different and distant parts of the ship, splashed into the sea, swimming after their captain, as if intent upon his rescue.

The dismayed officer of the boat eagerly asked what this meant. To which Captain Delano, turning a disdainful smile upon the unaccountable Spaniard, answered that, for his part, he neither knew nor cared; but it seemed as if Don Benito had taken it into his head to produce the impression among his people that the boat wanted to kidnap him. "Or else—give way for your lives," he wildly added, starting at a clattering hubbub in the ship, above which rang the tocsin of the hatchet-polishers, and seizing Don Benito by the throat he added, "this plotting pirate means murder!" Here, in apparent verification of the words, the servant, a dagger in his hand, was seen on the rail overhead, poised, in the act of leaping, as if with desperate fidelity to befriend his master to the last; while, seemingly to aid the black, the three white sailors were trying to clamber into the hampered bow. Meantime, the whole host of Negroes, as if inflamed at the sight of their jeopardized captain, impended in one sooty avalanche over the bulwarks.

All this, with what preceded and what followed, occurred with such involutions of rapidity that past, present, and future seemed one.

Seeing the Negro coming, Captain Delano had flung the Spaniard aside, almost in the very act of clutching him, and, by the unconscious recoil shifting his place, with arms thrown up so promptly grappled the servant in his descent, that with dagger presented at Captain Delano's heart, the black seemed of purpose to have leaped there as to his mark. But the weapon was wrenched away, and the assailant dashed down into the bottom of the boat, which now, with disentangled oars, began to speed through the sea.

At this juncture, the left hand of Captain Delano, on one side, again clutched the half-reclined Don Benito, heedless that he was in a speechless faint, while his right foot, on the other side, ground the prostrate Negro, and his right arm pressed for added speed on the after oar, his eye bent forward, encouraging his men to their utmost.

But here the officer of the boat, who had at last succeeded in beating off the towing sailors, and was now, with face turned aft, assisting the bowsman at his oar, suddenly called to Captain Delano to see what the black was about, while a Portuguese oarsman shouted to him to give heed to what the Spaniard was saying.

Glancing down at his feet, Captain Delano saw the free hand of the servant aiming with a second dagger—a small one, before concealed in his wool—with this he was snakishly writhing up from the boat's bottom at the heart of his master, his countenance lividly vindictive, expressing the centered purpose of his soul; while the Spaniard, half-choked, was vainly shrinking away, with husky words, incoherent to all but the Portuguese.

That moment, across the long-benighted mind of Captain Delano, a flash of revelation swept, illuminating, in unanticipated clearness, his host's whole mysterious demeanor, with every enigmatic event of the day, as well as the entire past voyage of the *San Dominick*. He smote Babo's hand down, but his own heart smote him harder. With infinite pity he withdrew his hold from Don Benito. Not Captain Delano, but Don Benito, the black, in leaping into the boat, had intended to stab.

Both the black's hands were held, as, glancing up towards the *San Dominick*, Captain Delano, now with scales dropped from his eyes, saw the Negroes, not in misrule, not in tumult, not as if frantically concerned for Don Benito, but, with mask torn away, flourishing hatchets and knives in ferocious piratical revolt. Like delirious black dervishes, the six Ashantees danced on the poop. Prevented by their foes from springing into the water, the Spanish boys were hurrying up to the topmost spars, while such of the few Spanish sailors not already in the sea, less alert, were descried, helplessly mixed in, on deck with the blacks.

Meantime Captain Delano hailed his own vessel, ordering the ports up, and the guns run out. But by this time the cable of the *San Dominick* had been cut, and the fag end, in lashing out, whipped away the canvas shroud about the beak, suddenly revealing, as the bleached hull swung round towards the open ocean, death for the figurehead, in a human skeleton, chalky comment on the chalked words below, FOLLOW YOUR LEADER.

At the sight, Don Benito, covering his face, wailed out: "'Tis he, Aranda! my murdered, unburied friend!"

Upon reaching the sealer, calling for ropes, Captain Delano bound the Negro, who made no resistance, and had him hoisted to the deck. He would then have assisted the now almost helpless Don Benito up the side; but Don Benito, wan as he was, refused to move, or he moved, until the Negro should have been first put below out of view. When, presently assured that it was done, he no more shrank from the ascent.

The boat was immediately dispatched back to pick up the three swimming sailors. Meantime, the guns were in readiness, though, owing to the *San Dominick* having glided somewhat astern of the sealer, only the aftermost one could be brought to bear. With this, they fired six times, thinking to cripple the fugitive ship by bringing down her spars, but only a few inconsiderable ropes were shot away. Soon the ship was beyond the gun's range, steering broad out of the bay, the blacks thickly clustering round the bowsprit, one moment with taunting cries towards the whites, the next with upthrown gestures hailing the now dusky moors of ocean—cawing crows escaped from the hand of the fowler.

The first impulse was to slip the cables and give chase. But, upon second thoughts, to pursue with whaleboat and yawl seemed more promising.

Upon inquiring of Don Benito what firearms they had on board the *San Dominick*, Captain Delano was answered that they had none that could be used, because, in the earlier stages of the mutiny, a cabin passenger, since dead, had secretly put out of order the locks of what few muskets there were. But with all his remaining strength Don Benito entreated the Americans not to give chase, either with ship or boat, for the Negroes had already proved themselves such desperadoes that, in case of a present assault, nothing but a total massacre of the whites could be looked for. But, regarding this warning as coming from one whose spirit had been crushed by misery, the American did not give up his design.

The boats were got ready and armed. Captain Delano ordered his men into them. He was going himself when Don Benito grasped his arm.

"What! have you saved my life, *señor*, and are you now going to throw away your own?"

The officers also, for reasons connected with their interests and those of the voyage, and a duty owing to the owners, strongly objected against their commander's going. Weighing their remonstrances a moment, Captain Delano felt bound to remain; appointing his chief mate—an athletic and resolute man, who had been a privateer's man—to head the party. The more to encourage the sailors, they were told that the Spanish captain considered his ship good as lost; that she and her cargo, including some gold and silver, were worth more than a thousand doubloons. Take her, and no small part should be theirs. The sailors replied with a shout.

The fugitives had now almost gained an offing. It was nearly night, but the moon was rising. After hard, prolonged pulling, the boats came up on the ship's quarters, at a suitable distance laying upon their oars to discharge their muskets. Having no bullets to return, the Negroes sent their yells. But upon the second volley, Indianlike, they hurtled their hatchets. One took off a sailor's fingers. Another struck the whaleboat's bow, cutting off the rope there, and remaining stuck in the gunwale like a woodman's ax. Snatching it, quivering, from its lodgment, the mate hurled it back. The returned gauntlet now stuck in the ship's broken quarter-gallery, and so remained.

The Negroes giving too hot a reception, the whites kept a more respectful distance. Hovering now just out of reach of the hurtling hatchets, they, with a view to the close encounter which must soon come, sought to decoy the blacks into entirely disarming themselves of their most murderous weapons in a hand-to-hand fight, by foolishly flinging them, as missiles, short of the mark, into the sea. But, erelong perceiving the stratagem, the Negroes desisted, though not before many of them had to replace their lost hatchets with handspikes, an exchange which, as counted upon, proved, in the end, favorable to the assailants.

Meantime, with a strong wind the ship still clove the water, the boats alternately falling behind and pulling up to discharge fresh volleys.

The fire was mostly directed towards the stern, since there, chiefly, the Negroes at present were clustering. But to kill or maim the Negroes was not the object. To take them, with the ship, was the object. To do it, the ship must be boarded, which could not be done by boats while she was sailing so fast.

A thought now struck the mate. Observing the Spanish boys still aloft, high as they could get, he called to them to descend to the yards, and cut adrift the sails. It was done. About this time, owing to causes hereafter to be shown, two Spaniards, in the dress of sailors and conspicuously showing themselves, were killed, not by volleys, but by deliberate marksman's shots; while, as it afterwards appeared, by one of the general discharges Atufal, the black, and the Spaniard at the helm likewise were killed. What, now, with the loss of the sails and loss of leaders, the ship became unmanageable to the Negroes.

With creaking masts, she came heavily round to the wind, the prow slowly swinging into view of the boats, its skeleton gleaming in the horizontal moonlight and casting a gigantic ribbed shadow upon the water. One extended arm of the ghost seemed beckoning the whites to avenge it.

"Follow your leader!" cried the mate; and, one on each bow, the boats boarded. Sealing-spears and cutlasses crossed hatchets and handspikes. Huddled upon the long-boat amidships, the Negresses raised a wailing chant, whose chorus was the clash of the steel.

For a time, the attack wavered, the Negroes wedging themselves to beat it back, the half-repelled sailors, as yet unable to gain a footing, fighting as troopers in the saddle, one leg sideways flung over the bulwark and one without, plying their cutlasses like carters' whips. But in vain. They were almost overborne, when, rallying themselves into a squad as one man, with a huzzah they sprang inboard, where, entangled, they involuntarily separated again. For a few breaths' space there was a vague, muffled, inner sound, as of submerged swordfish rushing hither and thither through shoals of blackfish. Soon, in a reunited band, and joined by the Spanish seamen, the whites came to the surface, irresistibly driving the Negroes toward the stern. But a barricade of casks and sacks, from side to side, had been thrown up by the mainmast. Here the Negroes faced about, and though scorning peace or truce, yet fain would have had respite. But, without pause overleaping the barrier, the unflagging sailors again closed. Exhausted, the blacks now fought in despair. Their red tongues lolled, wolflike, from their black mouths. But the pale sailors' teeth were set; not a word was spoken, and, in five minutes more, the ship was won.

Nearly a score of the Negroes were killed. Exclusive of those by the balls, many were mangled; their wounds—mostly inflicted by the long-edged sealing-spears, resembling those shaven ones of the English at Preston Pans, made by the poled scythes of the Highlanders. On the other side, none were killed, though several were wounded, some severely, including the mate. The surviving Negroes were temporarily secured, and the ship, towed back into the harbor at midnight, once more lay anchored.

Omitting the incidents and arrangements ensuing, suffice it that, after two days spent in refitting, the ships sailed in company for Conception, in Chile, and thence for Lima, in Peru; where, before the viceregal courts, the whole affair, from the beginning, underwent investigation.

Though, midway on the passage, the ill-fated Spaniard, relaxed from constraint, showed some signs of regaining health with free-will, yet, agreeably to his own fore-boding, shortly before arriving at Lima, he relapsed, finally becoming so reduced as to be carried ashore in arms. Hearing of his story and plight, one of the many religious institutions of the City of Kings opened an hospitable refuge to him, where both physician and priest were his nurses, and a member of the order volunteered to be his one special guardian and consoler, by night and by day.

The following extracts, translated from one of the official Spanish documents, will, it is hoped, shed light on the preceding narrative, as well as, in the first place, reveal the true port of departure and true history of the *San Dominick's* voyage, down to the time of her touching at the island of St. Maria.

But ere the extracts come it may be well to preface them with a remark.

The document selected, from among many others, for partial translation, contains the deposition of Benito Cereno, the first taken in the case. Some disclosures therein were at the time held dubious, for both learned and natural reasons. The tribunal inclined to the opinion that the deponent, not undisturbed in his mind by recent events, raved of some things which could never have happened. But subsequent depositions of the surviving sailors, bearing out the revelations of their captain in several of the strangest particulars, gave credence to the rest. So that the tribunal, in its final decision, rested its capital sentences upon statements which, had they lacked confirmation, it would have deemed it but duty to reject.

I, DON JOSÉ DE ABOS AND PADILLA, His Majesty's Notary for the Royal Revenue, and Register of this Province, and Notary Public of the Holy Crusade of this Bishopric, etc.

Do certify and declare, as much as is requisite in law, that, in the criminal cause commenced the twenty-fourth of the month of September, in the year seventeen hundred and ninety-nine, against the Negroes of the ship *San Dominick*, the following declaration before me was made:

Declaration of the first witness, DON BENITO CERENO.

The same day, and month, and year, His Honor, Doctor Juan Martinez de Rozas, Councilor of the Royal Audience of this Kingdom, and learned in the law of this Intendency, ordered the captain of the ship *San Dominick*, Don Benito Cereno, to appear, which he did in his litter, attended by the monk Infelez, of whom he received the oath, which he took by God, our Lord, and a sign of the Cross, under which he promised to tell the truth of whatever he should know and should be asked; and being interrogated agreeably to the tenor of the act commencing the process, he said that, on the twentieth of May last, he set sail with his ship from the port of Valparaiso, bound to that of Callao, loaded with the produce of the country beside thirty cases of hardware and one hundred and sixty blacks of both sexes, mostly belonging to Don Alexandro Aranda, gentleman, of the city of Mendoza; that the crew of the ship consisted of thirty-six men beside the persons who went as passengers; that the Negroes were in part as follows:

[Here, in the original, follows a list of some fifty names, descriptions, and ages, compiled from certain recovered documents of Aranda's, and also from recollections of the deponent, from which portions only are extracted.]

—One, from about eighteen to nineteen years, named José, and this was the man that waited upon his master, Don Alexandro, and who speaks well the Spanish, having served him four or five years;*** a mulatto, named Francesco, the cabin steward, of a good person and voice, having sung in the Valparaiso churches, native of the province of Buenos Ayres, aged about thirty-five years.*** A smart Negro, named Dago, who had been for many years a gravedigger among the Spaniards, aged forty-six years.*** Four old Negroes, born in Africa, from sixty to seventy, but sound, calkers by trade, whose names are as follows: the first was named Muri, and he was killed (as was also his son named Diamelo); the second, Nacta; the third, Yola, likewise killed; the fourth, Ghofan; and six full-grown Negroes, aged from thirty to forty-five, all raw, and born among the Ashantees—Matiluqui, Yan, Lecbe, Mapenda, Yambaio, Akim; four of whom were killed;*** a powerful Negro named Atufal, who being supposed to have been a chief in Africa, his owner set great store by him.*** And a small Negro of Senegal, but some years among the Spaniards, aged about thirty, which Negro's name was Babo;*** that he does not remember the names of the others, but that still expecting the residue of Don Alexandro's papers will be found, will then take due account of them all, and remit to the court;*** and thirty-nine women and children of all ages.

[*The catalogue over, the deposition goes on*]

That all the Negroes slept upon deck, as is customary in this navigation, and none wore fetters, because the owner, his friend Aranda, told him that they were all tractable; that on the seventh day after leaving port, at three o'clock in the morning, all the Spaniards being asleep except the two officers on the watch, who were the boatswain, Juan Robles, and the carpenter, Juan Bautista Gayete, and the helmsman and his boy, the Negroes revolted suddenly, wounded dangerously the boatswain and the carpenter, and successively killed eighteen men of those who were sleeping upon deck, some with handspikes and hatchets, and others by throwing them alive overboard, after tying them; that of the Spaniards upon deck they left about seven, as he thinks, alive and tied, to maneuver the ship, and three or four more, who hid themselves, remained also alive. Although in the act of revolt the Negroes made themselves masters of the hatchway, six or seven wounded went through it to the cockpit, without any hindrance on their part; that during the act of revolt the mate and another person, whose name he does not recollect, attempted to come up through the hatchway, but, being quickly wounded, were obliged to return to the cabin; that the deponent resolved at break of day to come up the companionway, where the Negro Babo was, being the ringleader, and Atufal, who assisted him, and having spoken to them, exhorted them to cease committing such atrocities, asking them, at the same time what they wanted and intended to do, offering, himself, to obey their commands; that notwithstanding this, they threw, in his presence, three men, alive and tied, overboard; that they told the deponent to come up and that they would not kill him; which having done, the Negro Babo asked him whether there were in those seas any Negro countries where they might be carried, and he answered them, No; that the Negro Babo afterwards told him to carry them to Senegal, or to the neighboring islands of St. Nicholas, and he answered that this was impossible on account of the great distance, the necessity involved of rounding Cape Horn, the bad condition of the vessel, the want of provisions, sails, and water; but that the Negro Babo replied to him he must carry them in anyway, that they would do and conform themselves to everything the deponent should require as to eating and drinking; that after a long conference, being absolutely compelled to please them, for they threatened to kill all the whites if they were not, at all events, carried to Senegal, he told them that what was most wanting for the voyage was water, that they would go near the coast to take it, and thence they would proceed on their course; that the Negro Babo agreed to it, and the deponent steered towards the intermediate ports, hoping to meet some Spanish or foreign vessel that would save them; that within ten or eleven days they saw the land, and continued their course by it in the vicinity of Nasca; that the deponent observed that the Negroes were now restless and mutinous because he did not effect the taking in of water, the Negro Babo having required, with threats, that it should be done, without fail, the following day; he told him he saw plainly that the coast was steep, and the rivers designated in the maps were not to be found, with other reasons suitable to the circumstances, that the best way would be to go to the island of Santa Maria, where they might water easily, it being a solitary island, as the foreigners did; that the deponent did not go to Pisco, that was near, nor make any other port of the coast, because the Negro Babo had intimated to him several times that he would kill all the whites the very moment he should perceive any city, town, or settlement of any kind on the shores to which they should be carried; that having determined to go to the island of Santa Maria, as the deponent had planned, for the purpose of trying whether, on the passage or near the island itself, they could find any vessel that should favor them, or whether he could escape from it in a boat to the neigh-boring coast of Arruco, to adopt the necessary means he immediately changed his course, steering for the island; that the Negroes Babo and Atufal held daily confer-ences, in which they discussed what was necessary for their design of returning to Senegal, whether they were to kill all the Spaniards, and particularly the deponent; that eight days after parting from the coast of Nasca, the deponent being on the watch a little after daybreak, and soon after the Negroes had their meeting, the Negro Babo came to the place where the deponent was and told him that he had determined to kill his master, Don Alexandro Aranda, both because he and his companions could not otherwise be sure of their liberty, and that, to keep the sea-men in subjection, he wanted to prepare a warning of what road they should be made to take did they or any of them oppose him, and that, by means of the death of Don Alexandro, that warning would best be given, but that what this last meant the deponent did not at the time comprehend, nor could not, further than that the death of Don Alexandro was intended; and moreover the Negro Babo proposed to the deponent to call the mate Raneds, who was sleeping in the cabin, before the thing was done, for fear, as the deponent understood it, that the mate, who was a good navigator, should be killed with Don Alexandro and the rest; that the depo-nent, who was the friend from youth of Don Alexandro, prayed and conjured, but all was useless, for the Negro Babo answered him that the thing could not be pre-vented, and that all the Spaniards risked their death if they should attempt to frus-trate his will in this matter or any other; that, in this conflict, the deponent called the mate, Raneds, who was forced to go apart, and immediately the Negro Babo commanded the Ashantee Matiluqui and the Ashantee Lecbe to go and commit the murder; that those two went down with hatchets to the berth of Don Alexandro, that, yet half alive and mangled, they dragged him on deck; that they were going to throw him overboard in that state, but the Negro Babo stopped them, bidding the murder be completed on the deck before him, which was done, when, by his orders, the body was carried below, forward; that nothing more was seen of it by the deponent for three days;*** that Don Alonzo Sidonia, an old man, long resident at Valparaiso, and lately appointed to a civil office in Peru, whither he had taken passage, was at the time sleeping in the berth opposite Don Alexandro's; that awakening at his cries, surprised by them, and at the sight of the Negroes with their bloody hatchets in their hands, he threw himself into the sea through a window which was near him, and was drowned, without it being in the power of the deponent to assist or take him up;*** that a short time after killing Aranda, they brought upon deck his german-cousin, of middle-age, Don Francisco Masa, of Mendoza, and the young Don Joaquín, Marqués de Aramboalaza, then lately from Spain, with his Spanish servant Ponce, and the three young clerks of Aranda, José Mozairi, Lorenzo Bargas, and Hermenegildo Gandix, all of Cádiz; that Don Joaquín and Hermenegildo Gandix, the Negro Babo, for purposes hereafter to appear, preserved alive, but Don Francisco Masa, José Mozairi, and Lorenzo Bargas, with Ponce the servant, beside the boatswain, Juan Robles, the boatswain's mates, Manuel Viscaya and Roderigo Hurta, and four of the sailors the Negro Babo ordered to be thrown alive into the sea, although they made no resistance nor begged for anything else but mercy; that the boatswain, Juan Robles, who knew how to swim, kept the longest above water, making acts of contrition, and, in the last words he uttered, charged this deponent to cause mass to be said for his soul to our Lady of Succor;*** that, during the three days which followed, the deponent, uncertain what fate had befallen the remains of Don Alexandro, frequently asked the Negro Babo where they were, and, if still on board, whether they were to be preserved for interment ashore, entreating him so to order it; that the Negro Babo answered nothing till the fourth day, when, at sunrise, the deponent coming on deck, the Negro Babo showed him a skeleton, which had been substituted for the ship's proper figurehead—the image of Christopher Colón, the discoverer of the New World; that the Negro Babo asked him whose skeleton that was, and whether, from its whiteness, he should not think it a white's, that, upon discovering his face, the Negro Babo, coming close, said words to this effect: "Keep faith with the blacks from here to Senegal, or you shall in spirit, as now in body, follow your leader," pointing to the prow; *** that the same morning the Negro Babo took by succession each Spaniard forward, and asked him whose skeleton that was, and whether, from its whiteness, he should not think it a white's; that each Spaniard covered his face; that then to each the Negro Babo repeated the words in the first place said to the deponent; *** that they (the Spaniards), being then assembled aft, the Negro Babo harangued them, saying that he had now done all; that the deponent (as navigator for the Negroes) might pursue his course, warning him and all of them that they should, soul and body, go the way of Don Alexandro if he saw them (the Spaniards) speak or plot anything against them (the Negroes)— a threat which was repeated every day; that, before the events last mentioned, they had tied the cook to throw him overboard, for it is not known what thing they heard him speak, but finally the Negro Babo spared his life, at the request of the deponent; that a few days after, the deponent, endeavoring not to omit any means to preserve the lives of the remaining whites, spoke to the Negroes of peace and tranquillity, and agreed to draw up a paper, signed by the deponent and the sailors who could write, as also by the Negro Babo, for himself and all the blacks, in which the deponent obliged himself to carry them to Senegal, and they not to kill any more, and he formally to make over to them the ship, with the cargo, with which they were for that time satisfied and quieted. *** But the next day, the more surely to guard against the sailors' escape, the Negro Babo commanded all the boats to be destroyed but the longboat, which was unseaworthy, and another, a cutter in good condition, which, knowing it would yet be wanted for towing the water casks, he had it lowered down into the hold.

★   ★   ★

[*Various particulars of the prolonged and perplexed navigation ensuing here follow, with incidents of a calamitous calm, from which portion one passage is extracted, to wit:*]

—That on the fifth day of the calm, all on board suffering much from the heat and want of water, and five having died in fits, and mad, the Negroes became irritable, and for a chance gesture, which they deemed suspicious—though it was harmless—made by the mate, Raneds, to the deponent in the act of handing a quadrant, they killed him; but that for this they afterwards were sorry, the mate being the only remaining navigator on board, except the deponent.

★   ★   ★

—That omitting other events which daily happened, and which can only serve uselessly to recall past misfortunes and conflicts, after seventy-three days' navigation, reckoned from the time they sailed from Nasca, during which they navigated under a scanty allowance of water, and were afflicted with the calms before mentioned, they at last arrived at the island of Santa Maria, on the seventeenth of the month of August, at about six o'clock in the afternoon, at which hour they cast anchor very near the American ship *Bachelor's Delight*, which lay in the same bay, commanded by the generous Captain Amasa Delano; but at six o'clock in the morning they had already descried the port, and the Negroes became uneasy, as soon as at distance they saw the ship, not having expected to see one there; that the Negro Babo pacified them, assuring them that no fear need be had; that straightway he ordered the figure on the bow to be covered with canvas, as for repairs, and had the decks a little set in order; that for a time the Negro Babo and the Negro Atufal conferred; that the Negro Atufal was for sailing away but the Negro Babo would not, and, by himself, cast about what to do; that at last he came to the deponent, proposing to him to say and do all that the deponent declares to have said and done to the American captain; ******* that the Negro Babo warned him that if he varied in the least, or uttered any word, or gave any look that should give the least intimation of the past events or present state, he would instantly kill him, with all his companions, showing a dagger which he carried hid, saying something which, as he understood it, meant that that dagger would be alert as his eye; that the Negro Babo then announced the plan to all his companions, which pleased them; that he then, the better to disguise the truth, devised many expedients, in some of them uniting deceit and defense; that of this sort was the device of the six Ashantees before named, who were his bravoes; that them he stationed on the break of the poop, as if to clean certain hatchets (in cases, which were part of the cargo), but in reality to use them, and distribute them at need, and at a given word he told them; that, among other devices, was the device of presenting Atufal, his right-hand man, as chained, though in a moment the chains could be dropped; that in every particular he informed the deponent what part he was expected to enact in every device, and what story he was to tell on every occasion, always threatening him with instant death if he varied in the least: that, conscious that many of the Negroes would be turbulent, the Negro Babo appointed the four aged Negroes, who were calkers, to keep what domestic order they could on the decks; that again and again he harangued the Spaniards and his companions, informing them of his intent and of his devices, and of the invented story that this deponent was to tell, charging them lest any of them varied from that story; that these arrangements were made and matured during the interval of two or three hours between their first sighting the ship and the arrival on board of Captain Amasa Delano; that this happened about half-past seven o'clock in the morning, Captain Amasa Delano coming in his boat, and all gladly receiving him; that the deponent, as well as he could force himself, acting then the part of principal owner and a free captain of the ship, told Captain Amasa Delano, when called upon, that he came from Buenos Ayres, bound to Lima, with three hundred Negroes; that off Cape Horn, and in a subsequent fever, many Negroes had died; that also, by similar casualties, all the sea officers and the greatest part of the crew had died.

★ ★ ★

[*And so the deposition goes on, circumstantially recounting the fictitious story dictated to the deponent by Babo, and through the deponent imposed upon Captain Delano, and also recounting the friendly offers of Captain Delano, with other things, but all of which is here omitted. After the fictitious story, etc., the deposition proceeds:*]

★ ★ ★

—that the generous Captain Amasa Delano remained on board all the day, till he left the ship anchored at six o'clock in the evening, deponent speaking to him always of his pretended misfortunes, under the fore-mentioned principles, without having had it in his power to tell a single word or give him the least hint, that he might know the truth and state of things, because the Negro Babo, performing the office of an officious servant with all the appearance of submission of the humble slave, did not leave the deponent one moment; that this was in order to observe the deponent's actions and words, for the Negro Babo understands well the Spanish, and besides, there were thereabout some others who were constantly on the watch, and likewise understood the Spanish; *** that upon one occasion, while deponent was standing on the deck conversing with Amasa Delano, by a secret sign the Negro Babo drew him (the deponent) aside, the act appearing as if originating with the deponent; that then, he being drawn aside, the Negro Babo proposed to him to gain from Amasa Delano full particulars about his ship, and crew, and arms; that the deponent asked "For what?"; that the Negro Babo answered he might conceive; that, grieved at the prospect of what might overtake the generous Captain Amasa Delano, the deponent at first refused to ask the desired questions, and used every argument to induce the Negro Babo to give up this new design; that the Negro Babo showed the point of his dagger; that after the information had been obtained the Negro Babo again drew him aside, telling him that that very night he (the deponent) would be captain of two ships, instead of one, for that, great part of the American's ship's crew going to be absent fishing, the six Ashantees, without anyone else, would easily take it; that at this time he said other things to the same purpose; that no entreaties availed; that, before Amasa Delano's coming on board, no hint had been given touching the capture of the American ship; that to prevent this project the deponent was powerless; *** —that in some things his memory is confused, he cannot distinctly recall every event; *** —that as soon as they had cast anchor at six of the clock in the evening, as has before been stated, the American captain took leave, to return to his vessel; that upon a sudden impulse, which the deponent believes to have come from God and his angels, he, after the farewell had been said, followed the generous Captain Amasa Delano as far as the gunwale, where he stayed, under pretense of taking leave, until Amasa Delano should have been seated in his boat; that, on shoving off, the deponent sprang from the gunwale into the boat, and fell into it, he knows not how, God guarding him; that—

★ ★ ★

[*Here, in the original, follows the account of what further happened at the escape, and how the* San Dominick *was retaken, and of the passage to the coast; including in the recital many expressions of "eternal gratitude" to the "generous Captain Amasa Delano." The deposition then proceeds with recapitulatory remarks, and a partial renumeration of the Negroes, making record of their individual part in the past events, with a view to furnishing, according to command of the court, the data whereon to found the criminal sentences to be pronounced. From this portion is the following;*]

—That he believes that all the Negroes, though not in the first place knowing to the design of revolt, when it was accomplished, approved it. *** That the Negro José, eighteen years old, and in the personal service of Don Alexandro, was the one who communicated the information to the Negro Babo about the state of things in the cabin, before the revolt; that this is known, because, in the preceding midnight, he used to come from his berth, which was under his master's, in the cabin, to the deck where the ringleader and his associates were, and had secret conversations with the Negro Babo, in which he was several times seen by the mate; that, one night, the mate drove him away twice; ** that this same Negro José was the one who, without being commanded to do so by the Negro Babo, as Lecbe and Matiluqui were, stabbed his master, Don Alexandro, after he had been dragged half-lifeless to the deck; ** that the mulatto steward, Francesco, was of the first band of revolters, that he was, in all things, the creature and tool of the Negro Babo; that, to make his court, he, just before a repast in the cabin, proposed to the Negro Babo poisoning a dish for the generous Captain Amasa Delano; this is known and believed, because the Negroes have said it; but that the Negro Babo, having another design, forbade Francesco; ** that the Ashantee Lecbe was one of the worst of them, for that, on the day the ship was retaken, he assisted in the defense of her with a hatchet in each hand, with one of which he wounded in the breast the chief mate of Amasa Delano, in the first act of boarding; this all knew; that, in sight of the deponent, Lecbe struck with a hatchet Don Francisco Masa, when, by the Negro Babo's orders, he was carrying him to throw him overboard alive, beside participating in the murder, before mentioned, of Don Alexandro Aranda and others of the cabin passengers; that, owing to the fury with which the Ashantees fought in the engagement with the boats, but this Lecbe and Yan survived; that Yan was bad as Lecbe; that Yan was the man who, by Babo's command, willingly prepared the skeleton of Don Alexandro, in a way the Negroes afterwards told the deponent, but which he, so long as reason is left him, can never divulge; that Yan and Lecbe were the two who, in a calm by night, riveted the skeleton to the bow; this also the Negroes told him; that the Negro Babo was he who traced the inscription below it; that the Negro Babo was the plotter from first to last; he ordered every murder, and was the helm and keel of the revolt; that Atufal was his lieutenant in all, but Atufal with his own hand committed no murder, nor did the Negro Babo; ** that Atufal was shot, being killed in the fight with the boats, ere boarding; ** that the Negresses, of age, were knowing to the revolt, and testified themselves satisfied at the death of their master, Don Alexandro; that, had the Negroes not restrained them, they would have tortured to death, instead of simply killing, the Spaniards slain by command of the Negro Babo; that the Negresses used their utmost influence to have the deponent made away with; that, in the various acts of murder, they sang songs and danced—not gaily, but solemnly, and before the engagement with the boats, as well as during the action, they sang melancholy songs to the Negroes, and that this melancholy tone was more inflaming than a different one would have been, and was so intended; that all this is believed, because the Negroes have said it. ***—that of the thirty-six men of the crew, exclusive of the passengers (all of whom are now dead), which the deponent had knowledge of, six only remained alive, with four cabin boys and ship boys, not included with the crew;***—that the Negroes broke an arm of one of the cabin boys and gave him strokes with hatchets.

[*Then follow various random disclosures referring to various periods of time. The following are extracted;*]

—That during the presence of Captain Amasa Delano on board, some attempts were made by the sailors, and one by Hermenegildo Gandix, to convey hints to him of the true state of affairs, but that these attempts were ineffectual, owing to fear of incurring death, and, furthermore, owing to the devices which offered contradictions to the true state of affairs, as well as owing to the generosity and piety of Amasa Delano incapable of sounding such wickedness, ***that Luys Galgo, a sailor about sixty years of age, and formerly of the king's navy, was one of those who sought to convey tokens to Captain Amasa Delano; but his intent, though undiscovered, being suspected, he was, on a pretense, made to retire out of sight, and at last into the hold, and there was made away with. This the Negroes have since said; *** that one of the ship boys feeling, from Captain Amasa Delano's presence, some hopes of release, and not having enough prudence, dropped some chance word respecting his expectations, which being overheard and understood by a slave boy with whom he was eating at the time, the latter struck him on the head with a knife, inflicting a bad wound, but of which the boy is now healing; that likewise, not long before the ship was brought to anchor, one of the seamen steering at the time endangered himself by letting the blacks remark some expression in his countenance, arising from a cause similar to the above, but this sailor, by his heedful after conduct, escaped; *** that these statements are made to show the court that from the beginning to the end of the revolt it was impossible for the deponent and his men to act otherwise than they did; ***—that the third clerk, Hermenegildo Gandix, who before had been forced to live among the seamen, wearing a seaman's habit, and in all respects appearing to be one for the time, he, Gandix, was killed by a musket ball fired through mistake from the boats before boarding; having in his fright run up the mizzen rigging, calling to the boats—"don't board," lest upon their boarding the Negroes should kill him; that this inducing the Americans to believe he some way favored the cause of the Negroes, they fired two balls at him, so that he fell wounded from the rigging, and was drowned in the sea; ***—that the young Don Joaquín, Marqués de Aramboalaza, like Hermenegildo Gandix, the third clerk, was degraded to the office and appearance of a common seaman; that upon one occasion when Don Joaquín shrank, the Negro Babo commanded the Ashantee Lecbe to take tar and heat it, and pour it upon Don Joaquín's hands; ***—that Don Joaquín was killed owing to another mistake of the Americans, but one impossible to be avoided, as, upon the approach of the boats, Don Joaquín, with a hatchet tied edge out and upright to his hand, was made by the Negroes to appear on the bulwarks; whereupon, seen with arms in his hands and in a questionable attitude, he was shot for a renegade seaman; ***—that on the person of Don Joaquín was found secreted a jewel, which, by papers that were discovered, proved to have been meant for the shrine of our Lady of Mercy in Lima, a votive offering, beforehand prepared and guarded, to attest his gratitude when he should have landed in Peru, his last destination, for the safe conclusion of his entire voyage from Spain; ***—that the jewel, with the other effects of the late Don Joaquín, is in the custody of the brethren of the Hospital de Sacerdotes, awaiting the disposition of the honorable court; ***—that, owing to the condition of the deponent, as well as the haste in which the boats departed for the attack, the Americans were not forewarned that there were, among the apparent crew, a passenger and one of the clerks disguised by the Negro Babo; ***—that, beside the Negroes killed in the action, some were killed after the capture and reanchoring at night, when shackled to the ringbolts on deck; that these deaths were committed by the sailors, ere they could be prevented.

That so soon as informed of it, Captain Amasa Delano used all his authority, and in particular with his own hand struck down Martínez Gola, who having found a razor in the pocket of an old jacket of his which one of the shackled Negroes had on, was aiming it at the Negro's throat; that the noble Captain Amasa Delano also wrenched from the hand of Bartholomew Barlo a dagger, secreted at the time of the massacre of the whites, with which he was in the act of stabbing a shackled Negro, who, the same day, with another Negro, had thrown him down and jumped upon him; ***—that, for all the events, befalling through so long a time, during which the ship was in the hands of the Negro Babo, he cannot here give account, but that what he has said is the most substantial of what occurs to him at present, and is the truth under the oath which he has taken; which declaration he affirmed and ratified, after hearing it read to him.

He said that he is twenty-nine years of age, and broken in body and mind; that when finally dismissed by the court, he shall not return home to Chile but betake himself to the monastery on Mount Agonia without; and signed with his honor, and crossed himself, and, for the time, departed as he came, in his litter, with the monk Infelez, to the Hospital de Sacerdotes.

BENITO CERENO.

DOCTOR ROZAS.

If the deposition have served as the key to fit into the lock of the complications which precede it, then, as a vault whose door has been flung back, the *San Dominick*'s hull lies open today.

Hitherto the nature of this narrative, besides rendering the intricacies in the beginning unavoidable, has more or less required that many things, instead of being set down in the order of occurrence, should be retrospectively or irregularly given; this last is the case with the following passages, which will conclude the account:

During the long, mild voyage to Lima, there was, as before hinted, a period during which the sufferer a little recovered his health, or, at least in some degree, his tranquility. Ere the decided relapse which came, the two captains had many cordial conversations—their fraternal unreserve in singular contrast with former withdrawments.

Again and again it was repeated how hard it had been to enact the part forced on the Spaniard by Babo.

"Ah, my dear friend," Don Benito once said, "at those very times when you thought me so morose and ungrateful, nay, when, as you now admit, you half thought me plotting your murder, at those very times my heart was frozen; I could not look at you, thinking of what, both on board this ship and your own, hung, from other hands, over my kind benefactor. And as God lives, Don Amasa, I know not whether desire for my own safety alone could have nerved me to that leap into your boat, had it not been for the thought that, did you, unenlightened, return to your ship, you, my best friend, with all who might be with you, stolen upon that night in your hammocks, would never in this world have wakened again. Do but think how you walked this deck, how you sat in this cabin, every inch of ground mined into honeycombs under you. Had I dropped the least hint, made the least advance towards an understanding between us, death explosive death—yours as mine—would have ended the scene."

"True, true," cried Captain Delano, starting, "you have saved my life, Don Benito, more than I yours; saved it, too, against my knowledge and will."

"Nay, my friend," rejoined the Spaniard, courteous even to the point of religion, "God charmed your life, but you saved mine. To think of some things you did— those smilings and chattings, rash pointings and gesturings. For less than these, they slew my mate, Raneds; but you had the Prince of Heaven's safe conduct through all ambuscades."

"Yes, all is owing to Providence, I know: but the temper of my mind that morning was more than commonly pleasant, while the sight of so much suffering, more apparent than real, added to my good-nature, compassion, and charity, happily interweaving the three. Had it been otherwise, doubtless, as you hint, some of my interferences might have ended, unhappily enough. Besides, those feelings I spoke of enabled me to get the better of momentary distrust, at times when acuteness might have cost me my life, without saving another's. Only at the end did my suspicious get the better of me, and you know how wide of the mark they then proved."

"Wide, indeed," said Don Benito, sadly; "you were with me all day; stood with me, sat with me, talked with me, looked at me, ate with me, drank with me; and yet, your last act was to clutch for a monster, not only an innocent man, but the most pitiable of all men. To such degree may malign machinations and deceptions impose. So far may even the best man err in judging the conduct of one with the recesses of whose condition he is not acquainted. But you were forced to it, and you were in time undeceived. Would that, in both respects, it was so ever, and with all men."

"You generalize, Don Benito; and mournfully enough. But the past is passed; why moralize upon it? Forget it. See, you bright sun has forgotten it all, and the blue sea, and the blue sky; these have turned over new leaves."

"Because they have no memory," he dejectedly replied; "because they are not human."

"But these mild trades that now fan your cheek, do they not come with a human-like healing to you? Warm friends, steadfast friends are the trades."

"With their steadfastness they but waft me to my tomb, *señor,*" was the foreboding response.

"You are saved," cried Captain Delano, more and more astonished and pained; "you are saved: what has cast such a shadow upon you?"

"The Negro."

There was silence, while the moody man sat, slowly and unconsciously gathering his mantle about him, as if it were a pall.

There was no more conversation that day.

But if the Spaniard's melancholy sometimes ended in muteness upon topics like the above, there were others upon which he never spoke at all; on which, indeed, all his old reserves were piled. Pass over the worst, and, only to elucidate, let an item or two of these be cited. The dress, so precise and costly, worn by him on the day whose events have been narrated, had not willingly been put on. And that silver-mounted sword, apparent symbol of despotic command, was not, indeed, a sword, but the ghost of one. The scabbard, artificially stiffened, was empty.

As for the black—whose brain, not body, had schemed and led the revolt, with the plot—his slight frame, inadequate to that which it held, had at once yielded to the superior muscular strength of his captor, in the boat. Seeing all was over, he uttered no sound, and could not be forced to. His aspect seemed to say: since I cannot do deeds, I will not speak words. Put in irons in the hold with the rest, he was carried to Lima. During the passage, Don Benito did not visit him. Nor then, nor at any time after, would he look at him. Before the tribunal he refused. When pressed by the judges he fainted. On the testimony of the sailors alone rested the legal identity of Babo.

Some months after, dragged to the gibbet at the tail of a mule, the black met his voiceless end. The body was burned to ashes; but for many days, the head, that hive of subtlety, fixed on a pole in the plaza, met, unabashed, the gazes of the whites, and across the Plaza looked towards St. Bartholomew's church, in whose vaults slept then, as now, the recovered bones of Aranda, and across the Rimac bridge looked towards the monastery, on Mount Agonia without; where, three months after being dismissed by the court, Benito Cereno, borne on the bier, did, indeed, follow his leader.

HOW TO TELL A TRUE
WAR STORY (1990)

Tim O'Brien
b. 1946 Austin, MI

This is true.

I had a buddy in Vietnam. His name was Bob Kiley but everybody called him Rat.

A friend of his gets killed, so about a week later Rat sits down and writes a letter to the guy's sister. Rat tells her what a great brother she had, how strack the guy was, a number one pal and comrade. A real soldier's soldier, Rat says. Then he tells a few stories to make the point, how her brother would always volunteer for stuff nobody else would volunteer for in a million years, dangerous stuff, like doing recon or going out on these really badass night patrols. Stainless steel balls, Rat tells her. The guy was a little crazy, for sure, but crazy in a good way, a real daredevil, because he liked the challenge of it, he liked testing himself, just man against gook. A great, great guy, Rat says.

Anyway, it's a terrific letter, very personal and touching. Rat almost bawls writing it. He gets all teary telling about the good times they had together, how her brother made the war seem almost fun, always raising hell and lighting up villes and bringing smoke to bear every which way. A great sense of humor, too. Like the time at this river when he went fishing with a whole damn crate of hand grenades. Probably the funniest thing in world history, Rat says, all that gore, about twenty zillion dead gook fish. Her brother, he had the right attitude. He knew how to have a good time. On Halloween, this real hot spooky night, the dude paints up his body all different colors and puts on this weird mask and goes out on ambush almost stark naked, just boots and balls and an M-16. A tremendous human being, Rat says. Pretty nutso sometimes, but you could trust him with your life.

And then the letter gets very sad and serious. Rat pours his heart out. He says he loved the guy. He says the guy was his best friend in the world. They were like soul mates, he says, like twins or something, they had a whole lot in common. He tells the guy's sister he'll look her up when the war's over.

So what happens?

Rat mails the letter. He waits two months. The dumb cooze never writes back.

A true war story is never moral. It does not instruct, nor encourage virtue, nor suggest models of proper human behavior, nor restrain men from doing the things they have always done. If a story seems moral, do not believe it. If at the end of a war story you feel uplifted, or if you feel that some small bit of rectitude has been salvaged from the larger waste, then you have been made the victim of a very old and terrible lie. There is no rectitude whatsoever. There is no virtue. As a first rule of thumb, therefore, you can tell a true war story by its absolute and uncompromising allegiance to obscenity and evil. Listen to Rat Kiley. *Cooze*, he says. He does not say *bitch*. He certainly does not say woman, or girl, He says *cooze*. Then he spits and stares. He's nineteen years old—it's too much for him—so he looks at you with those big gentle, killer eyes and says cooze, because his friend is dead, and because it's so incredibly sad and true: she never wrote back.

You can tell a true war story if it embarrasses you. If you don't care for obscenity, you don't care for the truth; if you don't care for the truth, watch how you vote. Send guys to war, they come home talking dirty.

Listen to Rat: "Jesus Christ, man, I write this beautiful fucking letter, I slave over it, and what happens? The dumb cooze never writes back."

The dead guy's name was Curt Lemon. What happened was, we crossed a muddy river and marched west into the mountains, and on the third day we took a break along a trail junction in deep jungle. Right away, Lemon and Rat Kiley started goofing off. They didn't understand about the spookiness. They were kids; they just didn't know. A nature hike, they thought, not even a war, so they went off into the shade of some giant trees—quadruple canopy, no sunlight at all—and they were giggling and calling each other motherfucker and playing a silly game they'd invented. The game involved smoke grenades, which were harmless unless you did stupid things, and what they did was pull out the pin and stand a few feet apart and play catch under the shade of those huge trees. Whoever chickened out was a motherfucker. And if nobody chickened out, the grenade would make a light popping sound and they'd be covered with smoke and they'd laugh and dance around and then do it again.

It's all exactly true.

It happened nearly twenty years ago, but I still remember that trail junction and the giant trees and a soft dripping sound somewhere beyond the trees. I remember the smell of moss. Up in the canopy there were tiny white blossoms, but no sunlight at all, and I remember the shadows spreading out under the trees where Lemon and Rat Kiley were playing catch with smoke grenades. Mitchell Sanders sat flipping his yo-yo. Norman Bowker and Kiowa and Dave Jensen were dozing, or half-dozing, and all around us were those ragged green mountains.

Except for the laughter things were quiet.

At one point, I remember, Mitchell Sanders turned and looked at me, not quite nodding, then after a while he rolled up his yo-yo and moved away.

It's hard to tell what happened next.

They were just goofing. There was a noise, I suppose, which must've been the detonator, so I glanced behind me and watched Lemon step from the shade into bright sunlight. His face was suddenly brown and shining. A handsome kid, really. Sharp gray eyes, lean and narrow-waisted, and when he died it was almost beautiful, the way the sunlight came around him and lifted him up and sucked him high into a tree full of moss and vines and white blossoms.

In any war story, but especially a true one, it's difficult to separate what happened from what seemed to happen. What seems to happen becomes its own happening and has to be told that way. The angles of vision are skewed. When a booby trap explodes, you close your eyes and duck and float outside yourself. When a guy dies, like Lemon, you look away and then look back for a moment and then look away again. The pictures get jumbled; you tend to miss a lot. And then afterward, when you go to tell about it, there is always that surreal seemingness, which makes the story seem untrue, but which in fact represents the hard and exact truth as it seemed.

In many cases a true war story cannot be believed. If you believe it, be skeptical. It's a question of credibility. Often the crazy stuff is true and the normal stuff isn't because the normal stuff is necessary to make you believe the truly incredible craziness.

In other cases you can't even tell a true war story. Sometimes it's just beyond telling.

I heard this one, for example, from Mitchell Sanders. It was near dusk and we were sitting at my foxhole along a wide, muddy river north of Quang Ngai. I remember how peaceful the twilight was. A deep pinkish red spilled out on the river, which moved without sound, and in the morning we would cross the river and march west into the mountains. The occasion was right for a good story.

"God's truth," Mitchell Sanders said. "A six-man patrol goes up into the mountains on a basic listening-post operation. The idea's to spend a week up there, just lie low and listen for enemy movement. They've got a radio along, so if they hear anything suspicious—anything—they're supposed to call in artillery or gunships, whatever it takes. Otherwise they keep strict field discipline. Absolute silence. They just listen."

He glanced at me to make sure I had the scenario. He was playing with his yo-yo, making it dance with short, tight little strokes of the wrist.

His face was blank in the dusk.

"We're talking hardass LP. These six guys, they don't say boo for a solid week. They don't got tongues. *All* ears."

"Right," I said.

"Understand me?"

"Invisible."

Sanders nodded.

"Affirm," he said. "Invisible. So what happens is, these guys get themselves deep in the bush, all camouflaged up, and they lie down and wait and that's all they do, nothing else, they lie there for seven straight days and just listen. And man, I'll tell you—it's spooky. This is mountains. You don't know spooky till you been there. Jungle, sort of, except it's way up in the clouds and there's always this fog-like rain, except it's not raining—everything's all wet and swirly and tangled up and you can't see jack, you can't find your own pecker to piss with. Like you don't even have a body. Serious spooky. You just go with the vapors—the fog sort of takes you in. . . . And the sounds, man. The sounds carry forever. You hear shit nobody should ever hear."

Sanders was quiet for a second, just working the yo-yo, then he smiled at me. "So, after a couple days the guys start hearing this real soft, kind of wacked-out music. Weird echoes and stuff. Like a radio or something, but its not a radio, it's this strange gook music that comes right out of the rocks. Faraway, sort of, but right up close, too. They try to ignore it. But it's a listening post, right? So they listen. And every night they keep hearing this crazyass gook concert. All kinds of chimes and xylophones. I mean, this is wilderness—no way, it can't be real—but there it is, like the mountains are tuned in to Radio Fucking Hanoi. Naturally they get nervous. One guy sticks Juicy Fruit in his ears. Another guy almost flips. Thing is, though, they can't report music. They can't get on the horn and call back to base and say, 'Hey, listen, we need some firepower, we got to blow away this weirdo gook rock band.' They can't do that. It wouldn't go down. So they lie there in the fog and keep their months shut. And what makes it extra bad, see, is the poor dudes can't horse around like normal. Can't joke it away. Can't even talk to each other except maybe in whispers, all hush-hush, and that just revs up the willies. All they do is listen."

Again there was some silence as Mitchell Sanders looked out on the river. The dark was coming on hard now, and off to the west I could see the mountains rising in silhouette, all the mysteries and unknowns.

"This next part," Sanders said quietly, "you won't believe."

"Probably not," I said.

"You won't. And you know why?"

"Why?"

He gave me a tired smile. "Because it happened. Because every word is absolutely dead-on true."

Sanders made a little sound in his throat, like a sigh, as if to say he didn't care if I believed it or not. But he did care. He wanted me to believe, I could tell. He seemed sad, in a way.

"These six guys, they're pretty fried out by now, and one night they start hearing voices. Like at a cocktail party. That's what it sounds like, this big swank gook cocktail party somewhere out there in the fog. Music and chitchat and stuff. It's crazy, I know, but they hear the champagne corks. They hear the actual martini glasses. Real hoity-toity, all very civilized, except this isn't civilization. This is Nam.

"Anyway, the guys try to be cool. They just lie there and groove, but after a while they start hearing—you won't believe this—they hear chamber music. They hear violins and shit. They hear this terrific mama-san soprano. Then after a while they hear gook opera and a glee club and the Haiphong Boys Choir and a barbershop quartet and all kinds of weird chanting and Buddha-Buddha stuff. The whole time, in the background, there's still that cocktail party going on. All these different voices. Not human voices, though. Because it's the mountains. Follow me? The rock—it's *talking*. And the fog, too, and the grass and the goddamn mongooses. Everything talks. The trees talk politics, the monkeys talk religion. The whole country. Vietnam, the place talks.

"The guys can't cope. They lose it. They get on the radio and report enemy movement—a whole army, they say—and they order up the firepower. They get arty and gunships. They call in air strikes. And I'll tell you, they fuckin' crash that cocktail party. All night long, they just smoke those mountains. They make jungle juice. They blow away trees and glee clubs and whatever else there is to blow away. Scorch time. They walk napalm up and down the ridges. They bring in the Cobras and F-4s, they use Willie Peter and HE and incendiaries. It's all fire. They make those mountains bum.

"Around dawn things finally get quiet. Like you never even *heard* quiet before. One of those real thick, real misty days—just clouds and fog, they're off in this special zone—and the mountains are absolutely dead-flat silent. Like Brigadoon— pure vapor, you know? Everything's all sucked up inside the fog. Not a single sound, except they still *hear* it.

"So they pack up and start humping. They head down the mountain, back to base camp, and when they get there they don't say diddly. They don't talk. Not a word, like they're deaf and dumb. Later on this fat bird colonel comes up and asks what the hell happened out there. What'd they hear? Why all the ordnance? The man's ragged out, he gets down tight on their case. I mean, they spent six trillion dollars on firepower, and this fatass colonel wants answers, he wants to know what the fuckin' story is.

"But the guys don't say zip. They just look at him for a while, sort of funnylike, sort of amazed, and the whole war is right there in that stare. It says everything you can't ever say. It says, man, you got wax in your ears. It says, poor bastard, you'll never know—wrong frequency—you don't even want to hear this. Then they salute the fucker and walk away, because certain stories you don't ever tell."

You can tell a true war story by the way it never seems to end. Not then, not ever. Not when Mitchell Sanders stood up and moved off into the dark.

It all happened.

Even now I remember that yo-yo. In a way, I suppose, you had to be there, you had to hear it, but I could tell how desperately Sanders wanted me to believe him, his frustration at not quite getting the details right, not quite pinning down the final and definitive truth.

And I remember sitting at my foxhole that night, watching the shadows of Quang Ngai, thinking about the coming day and how we would cross the river and march west into the mountains, all the ways I might die, all the things I did not understand.

Late in the night Mitchell Sanders touched my shoulder.

"Just came to me," he whispered. "The moral, I mean. Nobody listens. Nobody hears nothing. Like that fatass colonel. The politicians, all the civilian types, what they need is to go out on LP. The vapors, man. Trees and rocks—you got to listen to your enemy."

And then again, in the morning, Sanders came up to me. The platoon was preparing to move out, checking weapons, going through all the little rituals that preceded a day's march. Already the lead squad had crossed the river and was filing off toward the west.

"I got a confession to make," Sanders said. "Last night, man, I had to make up a few things."

"I know that."

"The glee club. There wasn't any glee club."

"Right."

"No opera."

"Forget it, I understand."

"Yeah, but listen, it's still true. Those six guys, they heard wicked sound out there. They heard sound you just plain won't believe."

Sanders pulled on his rucksack, closed his eyes for a moment, then almost smiled at me.

I knew what was coming but I beat him to it.

"All right," I said, "what's the moral?"

"Forget it."

"No, go ahead."

For a long while he was quiet, looking away, and the silence kept stretching out until it was almost embarrassing. Then he shrugged and gave me a stare that lasted all day.

"Hear that quiet, man?" he said. "There's your moral."

In a true war story, if there's a moral at all, it's like the thread that makes the cloth. You can't tease it out. You can't extract the meaning without unraveling the deeper meaning. And in the end, really, there's nothing much to say about a true war story, except maybe "Oh."

True war stories do not generalize. They do not indulge in abstraction or analysis.

For example: War is hell. As a moral declaration the old truism seems perfectly true, and yet because it abstracts, because it generalizes, I can't believe it with my stomach. Nothing turns inside.

It comes down to gut instinct. A true war story, if truly told, makes the stomach believe.

This one does it for me. I've told it before—many times, many versions—but here's what actually happened.

We crossed the river and marched west into the mountains. On the third day, Curt Lemon stepped on a booby-trapped 105 round. He was playing catch with Rat Kiley, laughing, and then he was dead. The trees were thick; it took nearly an hour to cut an LZ for the dustoff.

Later, higher in the mountains, we came across a baby VC water buffalo. What it was doing there I don't know—no farms or paddies—but we chased it down and got a rope around it and led it along to a deserted village where we set for the night. After supper Rat Kiley went over and stroked its nose.

He opened up a can of C rations, pork and beans, but the baby buffalo wasn't interested.

Rat shrugged.

He stepped back and shot it through the right front knee. The animal did not make a sound. It went down hard, then got up again, and Rat took careful aim and shot off an ear. He shot it in the hindquarters and in the little hump at its back. He shot it twice in the flanks. It wasn't to kill; it was just to hurt. He put the rifle muzzle up against the mouth and shot the mouth away. Nobody said much. The whole platoon stood there watching, feeling all kinds of things, but there wasn't a great deal of pity for the baby water buffalo. Lemon was dead. Rat Kiley had lost his best friend in the world. Later in the week he would write a long personal letter to the guy's sister, who would not write back, but for now it was a question of pain. He shot off the tail. He shot away chunks of meat below the ribs. All around us there was the smell of smoke and filth, and deep greenery, and the evening was humid and very hot. Rat went to automatic. He shot randomly, almost casually, quick little spurts in the belly and butt. Then he reloaded, squatted down, and shot it in the left front knee. Again the animal fell hard and tried to get up, but this time it couldn't quite make it. It wobbled and went down sideways. Rat shot it in the nose. He bent forward and whispered something, as if talking to a pet, then he shot it in the throat. All the while the baby buffalo was silent, or almost silent, just a light bubbling sound where the nose had been. It lay very still. Nothing moved except the eyes, which were enormous, the pupils shiny black and dumb.

Rat Kiley was crying. He tried to say something, but then cradled his rifle and went off by himself.

The rest of us stood in a ragged circle around the baby buffalo. For a time no one spoke. We had witnessed something essential, something brand-new and profound, a piece of the world so startling there was not yet a name for it.

Somebody kicked the baby buffalo.

It was still alive, though just barely, just in the eyes.

"Amazing," Dave Jensen said. "My whole life, I never seen anything like it."

"Never?"

"Not hardly. Not once."

Kiowa and Mitchell Sanders picked up the baby buffalo. They hauled it across the open square, hoisted it up, and dumped it in the village well.

Afterward, we sat waiting for Rat to get himself together.

"Amazing," Dave Jensen kept saying.

"For sure."

"A new wrinkle. I never seen it before."

Mitchell Sanders took out his yo-yo.

"'Well, that's Nam," he said, "Garden of Evil. Over here, man, every sin's real fresh and original."

How do you generalize?

War is hell, but that's not the half of it, because war is also mystery and terror and adventure and courage and discovery and holiness and pity and despair and longing and love. War is nasty; war is fun. War is thrilling; war is drudgery. War makes you a man; war makes you dead.

The truths are contradictory. It can be argued, for instance, that war is grotesque. But in truth war is also beauty. For all its horror, you can't help but gape at the awful majesty of combat. You stare out at tracer rounds unwinding through the dark like brilliant red ribbons. You crouch in ambush as a cool, impassive moon rises over the nighttime paddies. You admire the fluid symmetries of troops on the move, the harmonies of sound and shape and proportion, the great sheets of metal-fire streaming down from a gunship, the illumination rounds, the white phosphorous, the purply black glow of napalm, the rocket's red glare. It's not pretty, exactly. It's astonishing. It fills the eye. It commands you. You hate it, yes, but your eyes do not. Like a killer forest fire, like cancer under a microscope, any battle or bombing raid or artillery barrage has the aesthetic purity of absolute moral indifference—a powerful, implacable beauty—and a true war story will tell the truth about this, though the truth is ugly.

To generalize about war is like generalizing about peace. Almost everything is true. Almost nothing is true. At its core, perhaps, war is just another name for death, and yet any soldier will tell you, if he tells the truth, that proximity to death brings with it a corresponding proximity to life. After a fire fight, there is always the immense pleasure of aliveness. The trees are alive. The grass, the soil—everything. All around you things are purely living, and you among them, and the aliveness makes you tremble. You feel an intense, out-of-the-skin awareness of your living self—your truest self, the human being you want to be and then become by the force of wanting it. In the midst of evil you want to be a good man. You want decency. You want justice and courtesy and human concord, things you never knew you wanted. There is a kind of largeness to it; a kind of godliness. Though it's odd, you're never more alive than when you're almost dead. You recognize what's valuable. Freshly, as if for the first time, you love what's best in yourself and in the world, all that might be lost. At the hour of dusk you sit at your foxhole and look out on a wide river turning pinkish red, and at the mountains beyond, and although in the morning you must cross the river and go into the mountains and do terrible things and maybe die, even so, you find yourself studying the fine colors on the river, you feel wonder and awe at the setting of the sun, and you are filled with a hard, aching love for how the world could be and always should be, but now is not.

Mitchell Sanders was right. For the common soldier, at least, war has the feel—the spiritual texture—of a great ghostly fog, thick and permanent. There is no clarity. Everything swirls. The old rules are no longer binding, the old truths no longer true. Right spills over into wrong. Order blends into chaos, love into hate, ugliness into beauty, law into anarchy, civility into savagery. The vapors suck you in. You can't tell where you are, or why you're there, and the only certainty is absolute ambiguity.

In war you lose your sense of the definite, hence your sense of truth itself, and therefore it's safe to say that in a true war story nothing much is ever very true.

Often in a true war story there is not even a point, or else the point doesn't hit you until twenty years later, in your sleep, and you wake up and shake your wife and start telling the story to her, except when you get to the end you've forgotten the point again. And then for a long time you lie there watching the story happen in your head. You listen to your wife's breathing. The war's over. You close your eyes. You smile and think, Christ, what's the *point*?

This one wakes me up.

In the mountains that day, I watched Lemon turn sideways. He laughed and said something to Rat Kiley. Then he took a peculiar half step, moving from shade into bright sunlight, and the booby-trapped 105 round blew him into a tree. The parts were just hanging there, so Norman Bowker and I were ordered to shinny up and peel him off. I remember the white bone of an arm. I remember pieces of skin and something wet and yellow that must've been the intestines. The gore was horrible, and stays with me, but what wakes me up twenty years later is Norman Bowker singing "Lemon Tree" as we threw down the parts.

You can tell a true war story by the questions you ask. Somebody tells a story, let's say, and afterward you ask, "Is it true?" and if the answer matters, you've got your answer.

For example, we've all heard this one. Four guys go down a trail. A grenade sails out. One guy jumps on it and takes the blast and saves his three buddies.

Is it true?

The answer matters.

You'd feel cheated if it never happened. Without the grounding reality, it's just a trite bit of puffery, pure Hollywood, untrue in the way all such stories are untrue. Yet even if it did happen—and maybe it did, anything's possible—even then you know it can't be true, because a true war story does not depend upon that kind of truth. Happeningness is irrelevant. A thing may happen and be a total lie; another thing may not happen and be truer than the truth. For example: Four guys go down a trail. A grenade sails out. One guy jumps on it and takes the blast, but it's a killer grenade and everybody dies anyway. Before they die, though, one of the dead guys says, "The fuck you do that for?" and the jumper says, "Story of my life, man," and the other guy starts to smile but he's dead.

That's a true story that never happened.

Twenty years later, I can still see the sunlight on Lemon's face. I can see him turning, looking back at Rat Kiley, then he laughed and took that curious half-step from shade into sunlight, his face suddenly brown and shining, and when his foot touched down, in that instant, he must've thought it was the sunlight that was killing him. It was not the sunlight. It was a rigged 105 round. But if I could ever get the story right, how the sun seemed to gather around him and pick him up and lift him into a tree, if I could somehow recreate the fatal whiteness of that light, the quick glare, the obvious cause and effect, then you would believe the last thing Lemon believed, which for him must've been the final truth.

Now and then, when I tell this story, someone will come up to me afterward and say she liked it. It's always a woman. Usually it's an older woman of kindly temperament and humane politics. She'll explain that as a rule she hates war stories, she can't understand why people want to wallow in blood and gore. But this one she liked. Sometimes, even, there are little tears. What I should do, she'll say, is put it all behind me. Find new stories to tell.

I won't say it but I'll think it.

I'll picture Rat Kiley's face, his grief, and I'll think, *You dumb cooze.*

Because she wasn't listening.

It wasn't a war story. It was a love story. It was a ghost story.

But you can't say that. All you can do is tell it one more time, patiently, adding and subtracting, making up a few things to get at the real truth. No Mitchell Sanders, you tell her. No Lemon, no Rat Kiley. And it didn't happen in the mountains, it happened in this little village on the Batangan Peninsula, and it was raining like crazy, and one night a guy named Stink Harris woke up screaming with a leech on his tongue. You can tell a true war story if you just keep on telling it.

In the end, of course, a true war story is never about war. It's about the special way that dawn spreads out on a river when you know you must cross the river and march into the mountains and do things you are afraid to do. It's about love and memory. It's about sorrow. It's about sisters who never write back and people who never listen.

Dulce et Decorum Est (1920)

Wilfred Owen
b. 1893 Oswestry, Shropshire, England
d. 1918 Sambre-Oise Canal, France

Bent double, like old beggars under sacks,
Knock-kneed, coughing like hags, we cursed through sludge,
Till on the haunting flares we turned our backs
And towards our distant rest began to trudge.
5   Men marched asleep. Many had lost their boots
But limped on, blood-shod. All went lame; all blind;
Drunk with fatigue; deaf even to the hoots
Of tired, outstripped Five-Nines that dropped behind.
Gas! GAS! Quick, boys!—An ecstasy of fumbling,
Fitting the clumsy helmets just in time;
But someone still was yelling out and stumbling,
And flound'ring like a man in fire or lime . . .
Dim, through the misty panes and thick green light,
As under a green sea, I saw him drowning.
15   In all my dreams, before my helpless sight,
He plunges at me, guttering, choking, drowning.
If in some smothering dreams you too could pace
Behind the wagon that we flung him in,
And watch the white eyes writhing in his face,
20   His hanging face, like a devil's sick of sin;
If you could hear, at every jolt, the blood
Come gargling from the froth-corrupted lungs,
Obscene as cancer, bitter as the cud
Of vile, incurable sores on innocent tongues,—
25   My friend, you would not tell with such high zest
To children ardent for some desperate glory,
The old Lie: Dulce et decorum est
Pro patria mori.

THE PURLOINED LETTER (1845)

Edgar Allen Poe
b. 1809 Boston, MA
d. 1849 Baltimore, MD

Nil sapientiae odiosius acumine nimio.

SENECA

At Paris, just after dark one gusty evening in the autumn of 18—, I was enjoying the twofold luxury of meditation and a meerschaum, in company with my friend, C. Auguste Dupin, in his little back library, or book-closet, *au troisième*, No. 33 *Rue Dunôt, Faubourg St. Germain.* For one hour at least we had maintained a profound silence; while each, to any casual observer, might have seemed intently and exclusively occupied with the curling eddies of smoke that oppressed the atmosphere of the chamber. For myself, however, I was mentally discussing certain topics which had formed matter for conversation between us at an earlier period of the evening; I mean the affair of the Rue Morgue, and the mystery attending the murder of Marie Rogêt. I looked upon it, therefore, as something of a coincidence, when the door of our apartment was thrown open and admitted our old acquaintance, Monsieur G—, the Prefect of the Parisian police.

We gave him a hearty welcome; for there was nearly half as much of the entertaining as of the contemptible about the man, and we had not seen him for several years. We had been sitting in the dark, and Dupin now arose for the purpose of lighting a lamp, but sat down again, without doing so, upon G.'s saying that he had called to consult us, or rather to ask the opinion of my friend, about some official business which had occasioned a great deal of trouble.

"If it is any point requiring reflection," observed Dupin, as he forebore to enkindle the wick, "we shall examine it to better purpose in the dark."

"That is another of your odd notions," said the Prefect, who had the fashion of calling every thing "odd" that was beyond his comprehension, and thus lived amid an absolute legion of "oddities."

"Very true," said Dupin, as he supplied his visitor with a pipe, and rolled toward him a comfortable chair.

"And what is the difficulty now?" I asked. "Nothing more in the assassination way I hope?"

"Oh, no; nothing of that nature. The fact is, the business is *very* simple indeed, and I make no doubt that we can manage it sufficiently well ourselves; but then I thought Dupin would like to hear the details of it, because it is so excessively *odd*."

"Simple and odd," said Dupin.

"Why, yes; and not exactly that either. The fact is, we have all been a good deal puzzled because the affair *is* so simple, and yet baffles us altogether."

"Perhaps it is the very simplicity of the thing which puts you at fault," said my friend.

"What nonsense you *do* talk!" replied the Prefect, laughing heartily.

"Perhaps the mystery is a little *too* plain," said Dupin.

"Oh, good heavens! who ever heard of such an idea?"

"A little *too* self-evident."

"Ha! ha! ha!—ha! ha! ha!—ho! ho! ho!" roared our visitor, profoundly amused, "oh, Dupin, you will be the death of me yet!"

"And what, after all, *is* the matter on hand?" I asked.

"Why, I will tell you," replied the Prefect, as he gave a long, steady, and contemplative puff, and settled himself in his chair. "I will tell you in a few words; but, before I begin, let me caution you that this is an affair demanding the greatest secrecy, and that I should most probably lose the position I now hold, were it known that I confided it to any one."

"Proceed," said I.

"Or not," said Dupin.

"Well, then; I have received personal information, from a very high quarter, that a certain document of the last importance has been purloined from the royal apartments. The individual who purloined it is known; this beyond a doubt; he was seen to take it. It is known, also, that it still remains in his possession."

"How is this known?" asked Dupin.

"It is clearly inferred," replied the Prefect, "from the nature of the document, and from the non-appearance of certain results which would at once arise from its passing *out* of the robber's possession;—that is to say, from his employing it as he must design in the end to employ it."

"Be a little more explicit," I said.

"Well, I may venture so far as to say that the paper gives its holder a certain power in a certain quarter where such power is immensely valuable." The Prefect was fond of the cant of diplomacy.

"Still I do not quite understand," said Dupin.

"No? Well, the disclosure of the document to a third person, who shall be nameless, would bring in question the honor of a personage of most exalted station; and this fact gives the holder of the document an ascendancy over the illustrious personage whose honor and peace are so jeopardized."

"But this ascendancy," I interposed, "would depend upon the robber's knowledge of the loser's knowledge of the robber. Who would dare—"

"The thief," said G., "is the Minister D——, who dares all things, those unbecoming as well as those becoming a man. The method of the theft was not less ingenious than bold. The document in question—a letter, to be frank—had been received by the personage robbed while alone in the royal *boudoir*. During its perusal she was suddenly interrupted by the entrance of the other exalted personage from whom especially it was her wish to conceal it. After a hurried and vain endeavor to thrust it in a drawer, she was forced to place it, open as it was, upon a table. The address, however, was uppermost, and, the contents thus unexposed, the letter escaped notice. At this juncture enters the Minister D——. His lynx eye immediately perceives the paper, recognizes the handwriting of the address, observes the confusion of the personage addressed, and fathoms her secret. After some business transactions, hurried through in his ordinary manner, he produces a letter somewhat similar to the one in question, opens it, pretends to read it, and then places it in close juxtaposition to the other. Again he converses, for some fifteen minutes, upon the public affairs. At length, in taking leave, he takes also from the table the letter to which he had no claim. Its rightful owner saw, but, of course, dared not call attention to the act, in the presence of the third personage who stood at her elbow. The minister decamped; leaving his own letter—one of no importance—upon the table."

"Here, then," said Dupin to me, "you have precisely what you demand to make the ascendancy complete—the robber's knowledge of the loser's knowledge of the robber."

"Yes," replied the Prefect; "and the power thus attained has, for some months past, been wielded, for political purposes, to a very dangerous extent. The personage robbed is more thoroughly convinced, every day, of the necessity of reclaiming her letter. But this, of course, cannot be done openly. In fine, driven to despair, she has committed the matter to me."

"Than whom," said Dupin, amid a perfect whirlwind of smoke, "no more sagacious agent could, I suppose, be desired, or even imagined."

"You flatter me," replied the Prefect; "but it is possible that some such opinion may have been entertained."

"It is clear," said I, "as you observe, that the letter is still in the possession of the minister; since it is this possession, and not any employment of the letter, which bestows the power. With the employment the power departs."

"True," said G.; "and upon this conviction I proceeded. My first care was to make thorough search of the minister's hotel; and here my chief embarrassment lay in the necessity of searching without his knowledge. Beyond all things, I have been warned of the danger which would result from giving him reason to suspect our design."

"But," said I, "you are quite *au fait* in these investigations. The Parisian police have done this thing often before."

"Oh, yes; and for this reason I did not despair. The habits of the minister gave me, too, a great advantage. He is frequently absent from home all night. His servants are by no means numerous. They sleep at a distance from their master's apartment, and, being chiefly Neapolitans, are readily made drunk. I have keys, as you know, with which I can open any chamber or cabinet in Paris. For three months a night has not passed, during the greater part of which I have not been engaged, personally, in ransacking the D—Hotel. My honor is interested, and, to mention a great secret, the reward is enormous. So I did not abandon the search until I had become fully satisfied that the thief is a more astute man than myself. I fancy that I have investigated every nook and corner of the premises in which it is possible that the paper can be concealed."

"But is it not possible," I suggested, "that although the letter may be in possession of the minister, as it unquestionably is, he may have concealed it elsewhere than upon his own premises?"

"This is barely possible," said Dupin. "The present peculiar condition of affairs at court, and especially of those intrigues in which D—is known to be involved, would render the instant availability of the document—its susceptibility of being produced at a moment's notice—a point of nearly equal importance with its possession."

"Its susceptibility of being produced?" said I.

"That is to say, of being *destroyed*," said Dupin.

"True," I observed; "the paper is clearly then upon the premises. As for its being upon the person of the minister, we may consider that as out of the question."

"Entirely," said the Prefect. "He has been twice waylaid, as if by footpads, and his person rigorously searched under my own inspection."

"You might have spared yourself this trouble," said Dupin. "D—, I presume, is not altogether a fool, and, if not, must have anticipated these waylayings, as a matter of course."

"Not *altogether* a fool," said G., "but then he is a poet, which I take to be only one remove from a fool."

"True," said Dupin, after a long and thoughtful whiff from his meerschaum, "although I have been guilty of certain doggerel myself."

"Suppose you detail," said I, "the particulars of your search."

"Why, the fact is, we took our time, and we searched *everywhere*. I have had long experience in these affairs. I took the entire building, room by room; devoting the nights of a whole week to each. We examined, first, the furniture of each apartment. We opened every possible drawer; and I presume you know that, to a properly trained police agent, such a thing as a 'secret' drawer is impossible. Any man is a dolt who permits a 'secret' drawer to escape him in a search of this kind. The thing is *so* plain. There is a certain amount of bulk—of space—to be accounted for in every cabinet. Then we have accurate rules. The fiftieth part of a line could not escape us. After the cabinets we took the chairs. The cushions we probed with the fine long needles you have seen me employ. From the tables we removed the tops."

"Why so?"

"Sometimes the top of a table, or other similarly arranged piece of furniture, is removed by the person wishing to conceal an article; then the leg is excavated, the article deposited within the cavity, and the top replaced. The bottoms and tops of bedposts are employed in the same way."

"But could not the cavity be detected by sounding?" I asked.

"By no means, if, when the article is deposited, a sufficient wadding of cotton be placed around it. Besides, in our case, we were obliged to proceed without noise."

"But you could not have removed—you could not have taken to pieces *all* articles of furniture in which it would have been possible to make a deposit in the manner you mention. A letter may be compressed into a thin spiral roll, not differing much in shape or bulk from a large knitting-needle, and in this form it might be inserted into the rung of a chair, for example. You did not take to pieces all the chairs?"

"Certainly not; but we did better—we examined the rungs of every chair in the hotel, and, indeed, the jointings of every description of furniture, by the aid of a most powerful microscope. Had there been any traces of recent disturbance we should not have failed to detect it instantly. A single grain of gimlet-dust, for example, would have been as obvious as an apple. Any disorder in the gluing—any unusual gaping in the joints—would have sufficed to insure detection."

"I presume you looked to the mirrors, between the boards and the plates, and you probed the beds and the bedclothes, as well as the curtains and carpets."

"That of course; and when we had absolutely completed every particle of the furniture in this way, then we examined the house itself. We divided its entire surface into compartments, which we numbered, so that none might be missed then we scrutinized each individual square inch throughout the premises, including the two houses immediately adjoining, with the microscope, as before."

"The two houses adjoining!" I exclaimed; "you must have had a great deal of trouble."

"We had; but the reward offered is prodigious."

"You include the *grounds* about the houses?"

"All the grounds are paved with brick. They gave us comparatively little trouble. We examined the moss between the bricks, and found it undisturbed."

"You looked among D—'s papers, of course, and into the books of the library?"

"Certainly; we opened every package and parcel; we not only opened every book, but we turned over every leaf in each volume, not contenting ourselves with a mere shake, according to the fashion of some of our police officers. We also measured the thickness of every book-*cover*, with the most accurate admeasurement, and applied to each the most jealous scrutiny of the microscope. Had any of the bindings been recently meddled with, it would have been utterly impossible that the fact should have escaped observation. Some five or six volumes, just from the hands of the binder, we carefully probed, longitudinally, with the needles."

"You explored the floors beneath the carpets?"

"Beyond doubt. We removed every carpet, and examined the boards with the microscope."

"And the paper on the walls?"

"Yes."

"You looked into the cellars?"

"We did."

"Then," I said, "you have been making a miscalculation, and the letter is *not* upon the premises, as you suppose."

"I fear you are right there," said the Prefect. "And now, Dupin, what would you advise me to do?"

"To make a thorough research of the premises."

"That is absolutely needless," replied G—. "I am not more sure that I breathe than I am that the letter is not at the hotel."

"I have no better advice to give you," said Dupin. "You have, of course, an accurate description of the letter?"

"Oh, yes!"—And here the Prefect, producing a memorandum-book, proceeded to read aloud a minute account of the internal, and especially of the external appearance of the missing document. Soon after finishing the perusal of this description, he took his departure, more entirely depressed in spirits than I had ever known the good gentleman before.

In about a month afterward he paid us another visit, and found us occupied very nearly as before. He took a pipe and a chair and entered into some ordinary conversation. At length I said:

"Well, but G—, what of the purloined letter? I presume you have at last made up your mind that there is no such thing as overreaching the Minister?"

"Confound him, say I—yes; I made the re-examination, however, as Dupin suggested—but it was all labor lost, as I knew it would be."

"How much was the reward offered, did you say?" asked Dupin.

"Why, a very great deal—a *very* liberal reward—I don't like to say how much, precisely; but one thing I *will* say, that I wouldn't mind giving my individual check for fifty thousand francs to any one who could obtain me that letter. The fact is, it is becoming of more and more importance every day; and the reward has been lately doubled. If it were trebled, however, I could do no more than I have done."

"Why, yes," said Dupin, drawlingly between the whiffs of his meerschaum. "I really—think, G—, you have not exerted yourself—to the utmost in this matter. You might—do a little more, I think, eh?"

"How?—in what way?"

"Why—puff, puff—you might—puff, puff—employ counsel in the matter, eh?—puff, puff, puff. Do you remember the story they tell of Abernethy?"

"No; hang Abernethy!"

"To be sure! hang him and welcome. But, once upon a time, a certain rich miser conceived the design of sponging upon this Abernethy for a medical opinion. Getting up, for this purpose, an ordinary conversation in a private company, he insinuated his case to the physician, as that of an imaginary individual.

"'We will suppose,' said the miser, 'that his symptoms are such and such; now, doctor, what would *you* have directed him to take?'

"'Take!' said Abernethy, 'why, take *advice*, to be sure.'"

"But," said the Prefect, a little discomposed, "I am *perfectly* willing to take advice, and to pay for it. I would *really* give fifty thousand francs to any one who would aid me in the matter."

"In that case," replied Dupin, opening a drawer, and producing a check-book, "you may as well fill me up a check for the amount mentioned. When you have signed it, I will hand you the letter."

I was astounded. The Prefect appeared absolutely thunderstricken. For some minutes he remained speechless and motionless, looking incredulously at my friend with open mouth, and eyes that seemed starting from their sockets; then apparently recovering himself in some measure, he seized a pen, and after several pauses and vacant stares, finally filled up and signed a check for fifty thousand francs, and handed it across the table to Dupin. The latter examined it carefully and deposited it in his pocket-book, then, unlocking an *escritoire*, took thence a letter and gave it to the Prefect. This functionary grasped it in a perfect agony of joy, opened it with a trembling hand, cast a rapid glance at its contents, and then scrambling and struggling to the door, rushed at length unceremoniously from the room and from the house, without having uttered a syllable since Dupin had requested him to fill up the check.

When he had gone, my friend entered into some explanations.

"The Parisian police," he said, "are exceedingly able in their way. They are persevering, ingenious, cunning, and thoroughly versed in the knowledge which their duties seem chiefly to demand. Thus, when G—detailed to us his mode of searching the premises at the Hotel D—, I felt entire confidence in his having made a satisfactory investigation—so far as his labors extended."

"So far as his labors extended?" said I.

"Yes," said Dupin. "The measures adopted were not only the best of their kind, but carried out to absolute perfection. Had the letter been deposited within the range of their search, these fellows would, beyond a question, have found it."

I merely laughed—but he seemed quite serious in all that he said.

"The measures then," he continued, "were good in their kind, and well executed; their defect lay in their being inapplicable to the case and to the man. A certain set of highly ingenious resources are, with the Prefect, a sort of Procrustean bed, to which he forcibly adapts his designs. But he perpetually errs by being too deep or too shallow for the matter in hand; and many a schoolboy is a better reasoner than he. I knew one about eight years of age, whose success at guessing in the game of 'even and odd' attracted universal admiration. This game is simple, and is played with marbles. One player holds in his hand a number of these toys, and demands of another whether that number is even or odd. If the guess is right, the guesser wins one; if wrong, he loses one. The boy to whom I allude won all the marbles of the school. Of course he had some principle of guessing; and this lay in mere observation and admeasurement of the astuteness of his opponents. For example an arrant simpleton is his opponent, and, holding up his closed hand, asks, 'Are they even or odd?' Our schoolboy replies, Odd,' and loses; but upon the second trial he wins, for he then says to himself, 'The simpleton had them even upon the first trial, and his amount of cunning is just sufficient to make him have them odd upon the second; I will therefore guess odd';—he guesses odd, and wins. Now, with a simpleton a degree above the first, he would have reasoned thus: 'This fellow finds that in the first instance I guessed odd, and, in the second, he will propose to himself, upon the first impulse, a simple variation from even to odd, as did the first simpleton; but then a second thought will suggest that this is too simple a variation, and finally he will decide upon putting it even as before. I will therefore guess even';—he guesses even, and wins. Now this mode of reasoning in the schoolboy, whom his fellows termed 'lucky,'—what, in its last analysis, is it?"

"It is merely," I said, "an identification of the reasoner's intellect with that of his opponent."

"It is," said Dupin; "and, upon inquiring of the boy by what means he effected the *thorough* identification in which his success consisted, I received answer as follows: 'When I wish to find out how wise, or how stupid, or how good, or how wicked is any one, or what are his thoughts at the moment, I fashion the expression of my face, as accurately as possible, in accordance with the expression of his, and then wait to see what thoughts or sentiments arise in my mind or heart, as if to match or correspond with the expression.' This response of the schoolboy lies at the bottom of all the spurious profundity which has been attributed to Rochefoucault, to La Bougive, to Machiavelli, and to Campanella."

"And the identification," I said, "of the reasoner's intellect with that of his opponent, depends, if I understand you aright, upon the accuracy with which the opponent's intellect is admeasured."

"For its practical value it depends upon this," replied Dupin; "and the Prefect and his cohort fail so frequently, first by default of his identification, and, secondly, by ill-admeasurement, or rather through non-admeasurement, of the intellect with which they are engaged. They consider only their *own* ideas of ingenuity; and, in searching for anything hidden advert only to the modes in which *they* would have hidden it. They are right in this much—that their own ingenuity is a faithful representative of that of the *mass*; but when the cunning of the individual felon is diverse in character from their own, the felon foils them, of course. This always happens when it is above their own, and very usually when it is below. They have no variation of principle in their investigations; at best, when urged by some unusual emergency—by some extraordinary reward—they extend or exaggerate their old modes of *practice*, without touching their principles. What, for example, in this case of D—, has been done to vary the principle of action? What is all this boring, and probing, and sounding, and scrutinizing with the microscope, and dividing the surface of the building into registered square inches—what is it all but an exaggeration *of the application* of the one principle or set of principles of search, which are based upon the one set of notions regarding human ingenuity, to which the Prefect, in the long routine of his duty, has been accustomed? Do you not see he has taken it for granted that *all* men proceed to conceal a letter—not exactly in a gimlet-hole bored in a chair-leg, but, at least, in *some* out-of-the-way hole or corner suggested by the same tenor of thought which would urge a man to secrete a letter in a gimlet-hole bored in a chair-leg? And do you not see also that such *recherchés* nooks for concealment are adapted only for ordinary occasions, and would be adopted only by ordinary intellects; for, in all cases of concealment, a disposal of the article concealed—a disposal of it in this *recherché* manner,—is in the very first instance, presumable and presumed; and thus its discovery depends, not at all upon the acumen, but altogether upon the mere care, patience, and determination of the seekers; and where the case is of importance—or, what amounts to the same thing in the political eyes, when the reward is of magnitude,—the qualities in question have *never* been known to fail. You will now understand what I meant in suggesting that, had the purloined letter been hidden anywhere within the limits of the Prefect's examination—in other words, had the principle of its concealment been comprehended within the principles of the Prefect—its discovery would have been a matter altogether beyond question. This functionary, however, has been thoroughly mystified; and the remote source of his defeat lies in the supposition that the Minister is a fool, because he has acquired renown as a poet. All fools are poets; this the Prefect feels; and he is merely guilty of a *non distributio medii* in thence inferring that all poets are fools."

"But is this really the poet?" I asked. "There are two brothers, I know; and both have attained reputation in letters. The minister I believe has written learnedly on the Differential Calculus. He is a mathematician, and no poet."

"You are mistaken; I know him well; he is both. As poet *and* mathematician, he would reason well; as mere mathematician, he could not have reasoned at all, and thus would have been at the mercy of the Prefect."

"You surprise me," I said, "by these opinions, which have been contradicted by the voice of the world. You do not mean to set at naught the well-digested idea of centuries. The mathematical reason has long been regarded as *the* reason *par excellence.*"

"'*Il-y a parier,*'" replied Dupin, quoting from Chamfort, "'*que toute idée pub- lique, toute convention reçue, est une sottise, car elle a convenue au plus grand nombre.*' The mathematicians, I grant you, have done their best to promulgate the popular error to which you allude, and which is none the less an error for its promulgation as truth. With an art worthy a better cause, for example, they have insinuated the term 'analysis' into application to algebra. The French are the originators of this particu- lar deception; but if a term is of any importance—if words derive any value from applicability—then 'analysis' conveys 'algebra' about as much as, in Latin, '*ambitus*' implies 'ambition,' '*religio*' 'religion,' or '*homines honesti*' a set of *honorable* men."

"You have a quarrel on hand, I see," said I, "with some of the algebraists of Paris; but proceed."

"I dispute the availability, and thus the value, of that reason which is cultivated in any especial form other than the abstractly logical. I dispute in particular, the reason educed by mathematical study. The mathematics are the science of form and quantity; mathematical reasoning is merely logic applied to observation upon form and quantity. The great error lies in supposing that even the truths of what is called *pure* algebra are abstract or general truths. And this error is so egregious that I am confounded at the universality with which it has been received. Math- ematical axioms are *not* axioms of general truth. What is true of *relation*—of form and quantity—is often grossly false in regard to morals, for example. In this latter science it is very usually *untrue* that the aggregated parts are equal to the whole. In chemistry also the axiom fails. In the consideration of motive it fails; for two motives, each of a given value, have not, necessarily, a value when united, equal to the sum of their values apart. There are numerous other mathematical truths which are only truths within the limits of *relation*. But the mathematician argues from his *finite truths*, through habit, as if they were of an absolutely general applicability—as the world indeed imagines them to be. Bryant, in his very learned 'Mythology,' mentions an analogous source of error, when he says that 'although the Pagan fables are not believed, yet we forget ourselves continually, and make inferences from them as existing realities.' With the algebraists, however, who are Pagans themselves, the 'Pagan fables' *are* believed, and the inferences are made, not so much through lapse of memory as through an unaccountable addling of the brains. In short, I never yet encountered the mere mathematician who could be trusted out of equal roots, or one who did not clandestinely hold it as a point of his faith that $x^2 + px$ was absolutely and unconditionally equal to q. Say to one of these gentlemen, by way of experiment, if you please, that you believe occasions may occur where $x^2 + px$ is not altogether equal to q, and, having made him understand what you mean, get out of his reach as speedily as convenient, for, beyond doubt, he will endeavor to knock you down.

"I mean to say," continued Dupin, while I merely laughed at his last observations, "that if the Minister had been no more than a mathematician, the Prefect would have been under no necessity of giving me this check. I knew him, however, as both mathematician and poet, and my measures were adapted to his capacity, with reference to the circumstances by which he was surrounded. I knew him as a courtier, too, and as a bold *intriguant*. Such a man, I considered, could not fail to be aware of the ordinary political modes of action. He could not have failed to anticipate—and events have proved that he did not fail to anticipate—the way-layings to which he was subjected. He must have foreseen, I reflected, the secret investigations of his premises. His frequent absences from home at night, which were hailed by the Prefect as certain aids to his success, I regarded only as *ruses*, to afford opportunity for thorough search to the police, and thus the sooner to impress them with the conviction to which G——, in fact, did finally arrive—the conviction that the letter was not upon the premises. I felt, also, that the whole train of thought, which I was at some pains in detailing to you just now, concerning the invariable principle of political action in searches for articles concealed—I felt that this whole train of thought would necessarily pass through the mind of the Minister. It would imperatively lead him to despise all the ordinary *nooks* of concealment. *He* could not, I reflected, be so weak as not to see that the most intricate and remote recess of his hotel would be as open as his commonest closets to the eyes, to the probes, to the gimlets, and to the microscopes of the Prefect. I saw, in fine, that he would be driven, as a matter of course, to *simplicity*, if not deliberately induced to it as a matter of choice. You will remember, perhaps, how desperately the Prefect laughed when I suggested, upon our first interview, that it was just possible this mystery troubled him so much on account of its being so *very* self-evident."

"Yes," said I, "I remember his merriment well. I really thought he would have fallen into convulsions."

"The material world," continued Dupin, "abounds with very strict analogies to the immaterial; and thus some color of truth has been given to the rhetorical dogma, that metaphor, or simile, may be made to strengthen an argument as well as to embellish a description. The principle of the *vis inertiae*, for example, seems to be identical in physics and metaphysics. It is not more true in the former, that a large body is with more difficulty set in motion than a smaller one, and that its subsequent *momentum* is commensurate with this difficulty, than it is, in the latter, that intellects of the vaster capacity, while more forcible, more constant, and more eventful in their movements than those of inferior grade, are yet the less readily moved, and more embarrassed, and full of hesitation in the first few steps of their progress. Again: have you ever noticed which of the street signs, over the shop doors, are the most attractive of attention?"

"I have never given the matter a thought," I said.

"There is a game of puzzles," he resumed, "which is played upon a map. One party playing requires another to find a given word—the name of town, river, state, or empire—any word, in short, upon the motley and perplexed surface of the chart. A novice in the game generally seeks to embarrass his opponents by giving them the most minutely lettered names; but the adept selects such words as stretch, in large characters, from one end of the chart to the other. These, like the over-largely lettered signs and placards of the street, escape observation by dint of being excessively obvious; and here the physical oversight is precisely analogous with the moral inapprehension by which the intellect suffers to pass unnoticed those considerations which are too obtrusively and too palpably self-evident. But this is a point, it appears, somewhat above or beneath the understanding of the Prefect. He never once thought it probable, or possible, that the Minister had deposited the letter immediately beneath the nose of the whole world by way of best preventing any portion of that world from perceiving it.

"But the more I reflected upon the daring, dashing, and discriminating ingenuity of D—; upon the fact that the document must always have been *at hand*, if he intended to use it to good purpose; and upon the decisive evidence, obtained by the Prefect, that it was not hidden within the limits of that dignitary's ordinary search—the more satisfied I became that, to conceal this letter, the Minister had resorted to the comprehensive and sagacious expedient of not attempting to conceal it at all.

"Full of these ideas, I prepared myself with a pair of green spectacles, and called one fine morning quite by accident, at the Ministerial hotel. I found D—at home, yawning, lounging, and dawdling, as usual, and pretending to be in the last extremity of *ennui*. He is, perhaps, the most really energetic human being now alive—but that is only when nobody sees him.

"To be even with him, I complained of my weak eyes, and lamented the necessity of the spectacles, under cover of which I cautiously and thoroughly surveyed the apartment, while seemingly intent only upon the conversation of my host.

"I paid especial attention to a large writing-table near which he sat, and upon which lay confusedly, some miscellaneous letters and other papers, with one or two musical instruments and a few books. Here, however, after a long and very deliberate scrutiny, I saw nothing to excite particular suspicion.

"At length my eyes, in going the circuit of the room, fell upon a trumpery filigree card-rack of pasteboard, that hung dangling by a dirty blue ribbon, from a little brass knob just beneath the middle of the mantel-piece. In this rack, which had three or four compartments, were five or six visiting cards and a solitary letter. This last was much soiled and crumpled. It was torn nearly in two, across the middle—as if a design, in the first instance, to tear it entirely up as worthless, had been altered or stayed in the second. It had a large black seal, bearing the D—cipher *very* conspicuously, and was addressed, in a diminutive female hand, to D—, the minister, himself. It was thrust carelessly, and even, as it seemed, contemptuously, into one of the upper divisions of the rack.

"No sooner had I glanced at this letter than I concluded it to be that of which I was in search. To be sure, it was, to all appearance, radically different from the one of which the Prefect had read us so minutely a description. Here the seal was large and black, with the D—cipher; there it was small and red, with the ducal arms of the S—family. Here, the address, to the Minister, was diminutive and feminine; there the superscription, to a certain royal personage, was markedly bold and decided; the size alone formed a point of correspondence. But, then, the *radicalness* of these differences, which was excessive; the dirt; the soiled and torn condition of the paper, so inconsistent with the *true* methodical habits of D—, and so suggestive of a design to delude the beholder into an idea of the worthlessness of the document;—these things, together with the hyperobtrusive situation of this document, full in the view of every visitor, and thus exactly in accordance with the conclusions to which I had previously arrived: these things, I say, were strongly corroborative of suspicion, in one who came with the intention to suspect.

"I protracted my visit as long as possible, and, while I maintained a most animated discussion with the Minister, upon a topic which I knew well had never failed to interest and excite him, I kept my attention really riveted upon the letter. In this examination, I committed to memory its external appearance and arrangement in the rack; and also fell, at length, upon a discovery which set at rest whatever trivial doubt I might have entertained. In scrutinizing the edges of the paper, I observed them to be more *chafed* than seemed necessary. They presented the *broken* appearance which is manifested when a stiff paper, having been once folded and pressed with a folder, is refolded in a reversed direction, in the same creases or edges which had formed the original fold. This discovery was sufficient. It was clear to me that the letter had been turned as a glove, inside out, re-directed and re-sealed. I bade the Minister good-morning, and took my departure at once, leaving a gold snuff-box upon the table.

"The next morning I called for the snuff-box, when we resumed, quite eagerly, the conversation of the preceding day. While thus engaged, however, a loud report, as if of a pistol, was heard immediately beneath the windows of the hotel, and was succeeded by a series of fearful screams, and the shoutings of a mob. D—rushed to a casement, threw it open, and looked out. In the meantime I stepped to the card-rack, took the letter, put it in my pocket, and replaced it by a *fac-simile*, (so far as regards externals) which I had carefully prepared at my lodgings—imitating the D—cipher, very readily, by means of a seal formed of bread.

"The disturbance in the street had been occasioned by the frantic behavior of a man with a musket. He had fired it among a crowd of women and children. It proved, however, to have been without ball, and the fellow was suffered to go his way as a lunatic or a drunkard. When he had gone, D—came from the window, whither I had followed him immediately upon securing the object in view. Soon afterward I bade him farewell. The pretended lunatic was a man in my own pay."

"But what purpose had you," I asked, "in replacing the letter by a *fac-simile*? Would it not have been better at the first visit, to have seized it openly, and departed?"

"D—," replied Dupin, "is a desperate man, and a man of nerve. His hotel, too, is not without attendants devoted to his interests. Had I made the wild attempt you suggest, I might never have left the Ministerial presence alive. The good people of Paris might have heard of me no more. But I had an object apart from these considerations. You know my political prepossessions. In this matter, I act as a partisan of the lady concerned. For eighteen months the Minister has had her in his power. She has now him in hers—since, being unaware that the letter is not in his possession, he will proceed with his exactions as if it was. Thus will he inevitably commit himself, at once, to his political destruction. His downfall, too, will not be more precipitate than awkward. It is all very well to talk about the *facilis descensus Averni*; but in all kinds of climbing, as Catalani said of singing, it is far more easy to get up than to come down. In the present instance I have no sympathy—at least no pity—for him who descends. He is that *monstrum horrendum*, an unprincipled man of genius. I confess, however, that I should like very well to know the precise character of his thoughts, when, being defied by her whom the Prefect terms 'a certain personage,' he is reduced to opening the letter which I left for him in the card-rack."

"How? did you put any thing particular in it?"

"Why—it did not seem altogether right to leave the interior blank—that would have been insulting. D—, at Vienna once, did me an evil turn, which I told him, quite good-humoredly, that I should remember. So, as I knew he would feel some curiosity in regard to the identity of the person who had outwitted him; I thought it a pity not to give him a clew. He is well acquainted with my MS., and I just copied into the middle of the blank sheet the words—

—Un dessein si funeste,
S'iln'est digne d'Atrée, est digne de Thyeste.
They are to be found in Crébillon's 'Atrée.'"

Selection from A Narrative of the Captivity and Restoration of Mrs. Mary Rowlandson (1682)

Mary White Rowlandson
b. 1637 Somerset, England
d. 1711 Wethersfield, Connecticut

PREFACE TO THE READER

It was on Tuesday, Feb. 1, 1675, in the afternoon, when the *Narrhagansets* Quarters (in or toward the *Nipmug* Country, whither they were now retired for fear of the *English* Army, lying in their own Country) were the second time beaten up by the Forces of the United Colonies, who thereupon soon betook themselves to flight, and were all the next day pursued by the *English*, some overtaken and destroyed. But on Thursday, Feb. 3, the *English*, having now been six days' on their March from their Headquarters in Wickford, in the Narrhaganset Country, toward and after the enemy, and Provision grown exceeding short; insomuch that they were fain to kill some Horses for the supply, especially of their *Indian* Friends, they were necessitated to consider what was best to be done; and about noon (having hitherto followed the Chase as hard as they might) a Council was called, and though some few were of another mind, yet it was concluded, by far the greater part of the Council of War, that the Army should desist the pursuit, and retire; the forces of Plimouth and the Bay to the next town of the Bay, and Connecticut forces to their own next towns, which determination was immediately put in execution: The consequent whereof, as it was not difficult to be foreseen by those that knew the causeless enmity of these *Barbarians* against the *English*, and the malicious and revengeful spirit of these Heathen; so it soon proved dismal.

The *Narrhagansets* were now driven quite from their own Country, and all their Provisions there hoarded up, to which they durst not at present return, and being so numerous as they were, soon devoured those to whom they went, whereby both the one and the other were now reduced to extreme straits, and so necessitated to take the first and best opportunity for supply, and very glad no doubt of such an opportunity as this, to provide for themselves, and make spoile of the *English* at once; and seeing themselves thus discharged of their pursuers, and a little refreshed after their flight, the very next week, on Thursday, Feb. 10, they fell with a mighty force and fury upon Lancaster. which small Town, remote from aid of others, and not being Garrison'd as it might, the Army being now come in, and as the time indeed required (the design of the *Indians* against that place being known to the English some time before) was not able to make effectual resistance; but notwithstanding the utmost endeavour of the Inhabitants, most of the buildings were turned into ashes, many People (Men, Women, and Children) slain, and others captivated. The most solemn and remarkable part of this Tragedy may that justly be reputed which fell upon the Family of that Reverend Servant of God, Mr Joseph Rowlandson, the faithful Pastor of the Church of Christ in that place, who, being gone down to the Council of the Massachusets, to seek aid for the defence of the place, at his return found the Town in flames or smoke, his own-house being set on fire by the Enemy, through the disadvantage of a defective Fortification, and all in it consumed; his precious yoke-fellow, and dear Children, wounded and captivated (as the issue evidenced, and the following Narrative declares) by these cruel and barbarous Salvages. A sad Catastrophe! Thus all things come alike to all: None knows either love or hatred by all that is before him. 'Tis no new thing for God's precious ones to drink as deep as others, of the Cup of common Calamity: take just *Lot* (yet captivated) for instance, beside others. But it is not my business to dilate on these things, but only in few words introductively to preface to the following script, which is a Narrative of the wonderfully awful, wise, holy, powerful, and gracious providence of God, toward that worthy and precious Gentlewoman, the dear Consort of the said Reverend Mr Rowlandson, and her Children with her, as in casting of her into such a waterless pit, so in preserving, supporting, and carrying through so many such extream hazards, unspeakable difficulties and disconsolateness, and at last delivering her out of them all, and her surviving Children also. It was a strange and amazing dispensation that the Lord should so afflict his precious Servant, and Hand-maid: It was as strange, if not more, that he should so bear up the spirits of his Servant under such bereavements, and of his Hand-maid under such Captivity, travels, and hardships (much too hard for flesh and blood) as he did, and at length deliver and restore. But he was their Saviour, who hath said, *When thou passes through the Waters, I will be with thee; and through the Rivers, they shall not overflow thee: when thou walkest through the Fire; thou shalt not be burnt, nor shall the flame kindle upon thee,* Isai. xliii ver. 3; and again, *He woundeth, and his hands make whole; he shall deliver thee in six troubles, yea, in seven there shall no evil touch thee: In Famine he shall redeem thee from death; and in War from the power of the sword,* Job v. 18, 19, 20. Methinks this dispensation doth bear some resemblance to those of *Joseph, David,* and *Daniel,* yea, and of the three children too, the stories whereof do represent us with the excellent textures of divine providence, curious pieces of divine work: And truly so doth this, and therefore not to be forgotten, but worthy to be exhibited to, and viewed and pondered by all, that disclain not to consider the operation of his hands.

The works of the Lord (not only of Creation, but of Providence also, especially those that do more peculiarly concern his dear ones, that are as the apple of his eye, as the signet upon his hand, the delight of his eyes, and the object of his tenderest care) are great, sought out of all those that have pleasure therein; and of these, verily, this is none of the least.

This Narrative was Penned by this Gentlewoman her self, to be to her a *Memorandum* of God's dealing with her, that she might never forget, but remember the same, and the several circumstances thereof, all the daies of her life. A pious scope, which deserves both commendation and imitation. Some Friends having obtained a sight of it, could not be so much affected with the many passages of working providence discovered therein, as to judge it worthy of publick view, and altogether unmeet that such works of God should be hid from present and future Generations; and therefore though this Gentlewoman's modesty would not thrust it into the press yet her gratitude unto God, made her not hardly perswadable to let it pass, that God might have his due glory, and others benefit by it as well as her selfe.

I hope by this time none will cast any reflection upon this Gentlewoman, on the score of this publication of her Affliction and Deliverance. If any should, doubtless they may be reckoned with the nine Lepers, of whom it is said, *Were there not ten cleansed? where are the nine?* but one returning to give God thanks. Let such further know, that this was a dispensation of publick note and of Universal concernment; and so much the more, by how much the nearer this Gentlewoman stood related to that faithful Servant of God, whose capacity and employment was publick, in the House of God, and his Name on that account of a very sweet savour in the Churches of Christ. Who is there of a true Christian spirit, that did not look upon himself much concerned in this bereavement, this Captivity in the time thereof, and in this deliverance when it came, yea, more than in many others? And how many are there to whom, so concerned, it will doubtless be a very acceptable thing, to see the way of God with this Gentlewoman in the aforesaid dispensation, thus laid out and pourtrayed before their eyes.

To conclude, Whatever any coy phantasies may deem, yet it highly concerns those that have so deeply tasted how good the Lord is, to enquire with *David, What shall I render to the Lord for all his benefits to me?* Psal. cxvi. 12. He thinks nothing too great: yea, being sensible of his own disproportion to the due praises of God, he calls in help: *O magnifie the Lord with me, let us exalt his Name together, Psal.* xxxiv. 3. And it is but reason that our praises should hold proportion with our prayers; and that as many have helped together by prayer for the obtaining of this mercy, so praises should be returned by many on this behalf; and forasmuch as not the general but particular knowledge of things makes deepest impression upon the affections, this Narrative particularizing the several passages of this providence, will not a little conduce thereunto: and therefore holy David, in order to the attainment of that end, accounts himself concerned to declare what God had done for his Soul, *Psal.* lxyi. 16. *Come and hear, all ye that fear God, and I will declare what God hath done for my Soul,* i.e. *for his Life.* See ver. 9, 10. *He holdeth our soul in life, and suffers not our feet to be moved; for thou our God hast proved us: thou hast tried us, as silver is tried.* Life-mercies are heart-affecting mercies; of great impression and force, to enlarge pious hearts in the praises of God, so that such know not how but to talk of God's acts, and to speak of and publish his wonderful works. Deep troubles, when the waters come in unto the Soul, are wont to produce vows: Vows must be paid: *It is better not vow, than to vow and not pay.* I may say, that as none knows what it is to fight and pursue such an enemy as this, but they that have fought and pursued them: so none can imagine, what it is to be captivated, and enslaved to such Atheistical, proud, wild, cruel, barbarous, brutish, (in one word,) diabolical Creatures as these, the worst of the heathen; nor what difficulties, hardships, hazards, sorrows, anxieties, and perplexities, do unavoidably wait upon such a condition, but those that have tried it. No serious spirit then (especially knowing any thing of this Gentlewoman's Piety) can imagine but that the vows of God are upon her. Excuse her then if she come thus into the publick, to pay those Vows. Come and hear what she hath to say.

I am confident that no Friend of divine Providence, will ever repent his time and pains spent in reading over these sheets, but will judge them worth perusing again and again.

Here *Reader*, you may see an instance of the Sovereignty of God, who doth what he will with his own as well as others; and who may say to him, *what dost thou?* here you may see an instance of the Faith and Patience of the Saints, under the most heart-sinking Tryals; here you may see, the Promises are breasts full of Consolation, when all the World besides is empty, and gives nothing but sorrow. That God is indeed the supream Lord of the World: ruling the most unruly, weakening the most cruel and salvage: granting his People mercy in the sight of the most unmerciful: curbing the lusts of the most filthy, holding the hands of the violent, delivering the prey from the mighty, and gathering together the out-casts of Israel. Once and again, you have heard, but here you may see, that power belongeth unto God: that our God is the God of Salvation: and to him belong the issues from Death. That our God is in the Heavens, and doth whatever pleases him. Here you have *Samson's* riddle exemplified, and that great promise, *Rom.* viii. 28, verified: *Out of the Eater comes forth meat, and sweetness out of the strong;* The worst of evils working together for the best good. How evident is it that the Lord hath made this Gentlewoman a gainer by all this Affliction, that she can say, 'tis good for her, yea better that she hath been, than she should not have been, thus afflicted.

Oh how doth God shine forth in such things as these!

Reader, if thou gettest no good by such a Declaration as this, the fault must needs be thine own. Read, therefore, peruse, ponder, and from hence lay up something from the experience of another, against thine own turn comes: that so thou also through patience and consolation of the Scripture mayest have hope.

Per Amicum

On the tenth of February 1675, Came the Indians with great numbers upon Lancaster; Their first coming was about Sun-rising; hearing the noise of some Guns, we looked out; several Houses were burning, and the Smoke ascending to Heaven. There were five persons taken in one house, the Father, and the Mother and a sucking Child, they knockt on the head; the other two they took and carried away alive. There were two others, who being out of their Garison upon some occasion were set upon; one was knockt on the head, the other escaped: Another their was who running along was shot and wounded, and fell down; he begged of them his life, promising them Money (as they told me) but they would not hearken to him but knockt him in head, and stript him naked, and split open his Bowels. Another seeing many of the Indians about his Barn, ventured and went out, but was quickly shot down. There were three others belonging to the same Garison who were killed; the Indians getting up upon the roof of the Barn, had advantage to shoot down upon them over their Fortification. Thus these murtherous wretches went on, burning, and destroying before them.

At length they came and beset our own house, and quickly it was the dolefullest day that ever mine eyes saw. The House stood upon the edg of a hill; some of the Indians got behind the hill, others into the Barn, and others behind any thing that could shelter them; from all which places they shot against the House, so that the Bullets seemed to fly like hail; and quickly they wounded one man among us; then another, and then a third, About two hours (according to my observation, in that amazing time) they had been about the house before they prevailed to fire it (which they did with Flax and Hemp, which they brought out of the Barn, and there being no defence about the House, only two Flankers at two opposite corners and one of them not finished) they fired it once and one ventured out and quenched it, but they quickly fired it again, and that took. Now is the dreadfull hour come, that I have often heard of (in time of War, as it was the case of others) but now mine eyes see it. Some in our house were fighting for their lives, others wallowing in their blood, the House on fire over our heads, and the bloody Heathen ready to knock us on the head, if we stirred out. Now might we hear Mothers and Children crying out for themselves; and one another, Lord, What shall we do? Then I took my Children (and one of my sisters, hers) to go forth and leave the house: but as soon as we came to the dore and appeared, the Indians shot so thick that the bullets rattled against the House, as if one had taken an handfull of stones and threw them, so that we were fain to give back. We had six stout Dogs belonging to our Garrison, but none of them would stir, though another time, if any Indian had come to the door, they were ready to fly upon him and tear him down. The Lord hereby would make us the more acknowledge his hand, and to see that our help is always in him. But out we must go, the fire increasing, and coming along behind us, roaring, and the Indians gaping before us with their Guns, Spears and Hatchets to devour us. No sooner were we out of the House, but my Brother in Law (being before wounded, in defending the house, in or near the throat) fell down dead, wherat the Indians scornfully shouted, and hallowed, and were presently upon him, stripping off his cloaths, the bulletts flying thick, one went through my side, and the same (as would seem) through the bowels and hand of dear Child in my arms. One of my elder Sisters Children, named William, had then his Leg broken, which the Indians perceiving, they knockt him on head. Thus were we butchered by those merciless Heathen, standing amazed, with the blood running down to our heels. My eldest Sister being yet in the House, and seeing those wofull sights, the Infidels haling Mothers one way, and Children another, and some wallowing in their blood: and her elder Son telling her that her Son William was dead, and my self was wounded, she said, And, Lord, let me dy with them; which was no sooner said, but she was struck with a Bullet, and fell down dead over the threshold. I hope she is reaping the fruit of her good labours, being faithfull to the service of God in her place. In her younger years she lay under much trouble upon spiritual accounts, till it pleased God to make that precious Scripture take hold of her heart, 2 Cor. 12.9. *And he said unto me; my Grace is sufficient for thee.* More then twenty years after I have heard her tell how sweet and comfortable that place was to her. But to return: The Indians laid hold of us, pulling me one way, and the Children another, and said, Come go along with us; I told them they would kill me: they answered, If I were willing to go along with them, they would not hurt me.

Oh the dolefull sight that now was to behold at this House! *Come, behold the works of the Lord, what dissolations he had made in the Earth.* Of thirty seven persons who were in this one House, none escaped either present death, or a bitter captivity, save only one, who might say as he, Job. 1. 15. *And I only am escaped alone to tell the News.* There were twelve killed, some shot, some stab'd with their Spears, some knock'd down with their Hatchets. When we are in prosperity, Oh the little that we think of such dreadfull sights, and to see our dear Friends, and Relations ly bleeding out their heart-blood upon the ground. There was one who was chopt into the head with a Hatchet, and stript naked, and yet was crawling up and down. It is a solemn sight to see so many Christians lying in their blood, some here, and some there, like a company of Sheep torn by Wolves, All of them stript naked by a company of hell-hounds, roaring, singing, ranting and insulting, as if they would have torn our very hearts out; yet the Lord by his Almighty power preserved a number of us from death, for there were twenty-four of us taken alive and carried Captive.

I had often before this said, that if the Indians should come, I should chuse rather to be killed by them then taken alive but when it came to the tryal my mind changed; their glittering weapons so daunted my spirit, that I chose rather to go along with those (as I may say) ravenous Beasts, then that moment to end my dayes; and that I may the better declare what happened to me during that grievous Captivity, I shall particularly speak of the severall Removes we had up and down the Wilderness.

THE FIRST REMOVE

Now away we must go with those Barbarous Creatures, with our bodies wounded and bleeding, and our hearts no less than our bodies. About a mile we went that night, up upon a hill within sight of the Town, where they intended to lodge. There was hard by a vacant house (deserted by the English before, for fear of the Indians). I asked them whither I might not lodge in the house that night to which they answered, what will you love English men still? this was the dolefullest night that ever my eyes saw. Oh the roaring, and singing and danceing, and yelling of those black creatures in the night, which made the place a lively resemblance of hell. And as miserable was the wast that was there made, of Horses, Cattle, Sheep, Swine, Calves, Lambs, Roasting Pigs, and Fowl (which they had plundered in the Town) some roasting, some lying and burning, and some boyling to feed our merciless Enemies; who were joyful enough though we were disconsolate. To add to the dolefulness of the former day, and the dismalness of the present night: my thoughts ran upon my losses and sad bereaved condition. All was gone, my Husband gone (at least separated from me, he being in the Bay, and to add to my grief, the Indians told me they would kill him as he came homeward) my Children gone, my Relations and Friends gone, our House and home and all our comforts within door, and without, all was gone, (except my life) and I knew not but the next moment that might go too. There remained nothing to me but one poor wounded Babe, and it seemed at present worse than death that it was in such a pitiful condition, bespeaking Compassion, and I had no refreshing for it, nor suitable things to revive it. Little do many think what is the savageness and bruitishness of this barbarous Enemy, I even those that seem to profess more than others among them, when the English have fallen into their hands.

Those seven that were killed at Lancaster the summer before upon a Sabbath day, and the one that was afterward killed upon a week day, were slain and mangled in a barbarous manner, by one-ey'd John and Marlborough's Praying Indians, which Capt. Mosely brought to Boston, as the Indians told me.

THE SECOND REMOVE

But now, the next morning, I must turn my back upon the Town, and travel with them into the vast and desolate Wilderness, I knew not whither. It is not my tongue, or pen can express the sorrows of my heart, and bitterness of my spirit, that I had at this departure: but God was with me, in a wonderfull manner, carrying me along, and bearing up my spirit, that it did not quite fail. One of the Indians carried my poor wounded Babe upon a horse, I went moaning all along, I shall dy, I shall dy. I went on foot after it, with sorrow that cannot be exprest. At length I took it off the horse, and carried it in my armes till my strength failed, and I fell down with it: Then they set me upon a horse with my wounded Child in my lap, and there being no furniture upon the horse back, as we were going down a steep hill, we both fell over the horses head, at which they like inhumane creatures laught, and rejoyced to see it, though I thought we should there have ended our dayes, as overcome with so many difficulties. But the Lord renewed my strength still, and carried me along, that I might see more of his Power; yea, so much that I could never have thought of, had I not experienced it.

After this it quickly began to snow, and when night came on, they stopt: and now down I must sit in the snow, by a little fire, and a few boughs behind me, with my sick Child in my lap; and calling much for water, being now (through the wound) fallen into a violent Fever. My own wound also growing so stiff, that I could scarce sit down or rise up; yet so it must be, that I must sit all this cold winter night upon the cold snowy ground, with my sick Child in my armes, looking that every hour would be the last of its life; and having no Christian friend near me, either to comfort or help me. Oh, I may see the wonderfull power of God, that my Spirit did not utterly sink under my affliction: still the Lord upheld me with his gracious and mercifull Spirit, and we were both alive to see the light of the next morning.

THE THIRD REMOVE

The morning being come, they prepared to go on their way. One of the Indians got up upon a horse, and they set me up behind him, with my poor sick Babe in my lap. A very wearisome and tedious day I had of it; what with my own wound, and my Childs being so exceeding sick, and in a lamentable condition with her wound. It may be easily judged what a poor feeble condition we were in, there being not the least crumb of refreshing that came within either of our mouths, from Wednesday night to Saturday night, except only a little cold water. This day in the afternoon, about an hour by Sun, we came to the place where they intended, *viz* an Indian

Town, called Wenimesset, Norward of Quabaug When we were come, Oh the number of Pagans (now merciless enemies) that there came about me, that I may say as David, Psal. 27. 13, *I had fainted, unless I had believed,* etc. The next day was the Sabbath: I then remembered how careless I had been of Gods holy time, how many Sabbaths I had lost and mispent, and how evily I had walked in Gods sight; which lay so close unto my spirit, that it was easie for me to see how righteous it was with God to cut off the thread of my life, and cast me out of his presence for ever. Yet the Lord still shewed mercy to me, and upheld me; and as he wounded me with one hand, so he healed me with the other. This day there came to me one Robbert Pepper (a man belonging to Roxbury) who was taken in Captain Beers his Fight, and had been now a considerable time with the Indians; and up with them almost as far as Albany, to see king Philip, as he told me, and was now very lately come into these parts. Hearing, I say, that I was in this Indian Town, he obtained leave to come and see me. He told me, he himself was wounded in the leg at Captain Beers his Fight; and was not able some time to go, but as they carried him, and as he took Oaken leaves and laid to his wound, and through the blessing of God he was able to travel again. Then I took Oaken leaves and laid to my side, and with the blessing of God it cured me also; yet before the cure was wrought, I may say, as it is in Psal. 38.5, 6. *My wounds stink and are corrupt, I am troubled, I am bowed down greatly, I go mourning all the day long.* I sat much alone with a poor wounded Child in my lap, which moaned night and day, having nothing to revive the body, or cheer the spirits of her, but in stead of that, sometimes one Indian would come and tell me one hour, that your Master will knock your Child in the head, and then a second, and then a third, your Master will quickly knock your Child in the head.

This was the comfort I had from them, miserable comforters are ye all, as he said. Thus nine dayes I sat upon my knees, with my Babe in my lap, till my flesh was raw again; my Child being even ready to depart this sorrowfull world, they bade me carry it out to another Wigwam (I suppose because they would not be troubled with such spectacles) Whither I went with a very heavy heart, and down I sat with the picture of death in my lap. About two houres in the night, my sweet Babe like a Lambe departed this life, on Feb. 18, 1675. It being about six yeares, and five months old. It was nine dayes from the first wounding, in this miserable condition, without any refreshing of one nature or other, except a little cold water. I cannot, but take notice, how at another time I could not bear to be in the room where any dead person was, but now the case is changed; I must and could ly down by my dead Babe, side by side all the night after. I have thought since of the wonderfull goodness of God to me, in preserving me in the use of my reason and senses, in that distressed time, that I did not use wicked and violent means to end my own miserable life. In the morning, when they understood that my child was dead they sent for me home to my Masters Wigwam: (by my Master in this writing, must be understood Quanopin, who was a Saggamore, and married King Phillips wives Sister; not that he first took me, but I was sold to him by another Narrhaganset Indian, who took me when first I came out of the Garison). I went to take up my dead child in my arms to carry it with me, but they bid me let it alone: there was no resisting, but goe I must and leave it. When I had been at my masters wigwam, I took the first opportunity I could get, to go look after my dead child: when I came I askt them what they had done with it? then they told me it was upon the hill: then they went and shewed me where it was, where I saw the ground was newly digged, and there they told me they had buried it: There I left that Child in the Wilderness, and must commit it, and my self also in this Wilderness-condition, to him who is above all. God having taken away this dear Child, I went to see my daughter Mary, who was at this same Indian town, at a Wigwam not very far off, though we had little liberty or opportunity to see one another. She was about ten years old, and taken from the door at first by a Praying Ind and afterward sold for a gun. When I came in sight, she would fall a weeping; at which they were provoked, and would not let me come near her, but bade me be gone; which was a heart-cutting word to me. I had one Child dead, another in the Wilderness, I knew nor where, the third they would not let me come near to: *Me* (as he said) *have ye bereaved of my Children, Joseph is not, and Simeon is not, and ye will take Benjamin also, all these things are against me.* I could not sit still in this condition, but kept walking from one place to another. And as I was going along, my heart was even overwhelm'd with the thoughts of my condition, and that I should have Children, and a Nation which I knew not ruled over them. Whereupon I earnestly entreated the Lord, that he would consider my low estate, and shew me a token for good, and if it were his blessed will, some sign and hope of some relief. And indeed quickly the Lord answered, in some measure, my poor prayers: for as I was going up and down mourning and lamenting my condition, my Son came to me, and asked me how I did; I had not seen him before, since the destruction of the Town, and I knew not where he was, till I was informed by himself, that he was amongst a smaller percel of Indians, whose place was about six miles off; with tears in his eyes, he asked me whether his Sister Sarah was dead; and told me he had seen his Sister Mary; and prayed me, that I would not be troubled in reference to himself. The occasion of his coming to see me at this time, was this: There was, as I said, about six miles from us, a small Plantation of Indians, where it seems he had been during his Captivity; and at this time, there were some Forces of the Ind. gathered out of our company, and some also from them (among whom was my Sons master) to go to assault and burn Medfield: In this time of the absence of his master, his dame brought him to see me. I took this to be some gracious answer to my earnest and unfeigned desire. The next day, *viz* to this, the Indians returned from Medfield, all the company, for those that belonged to the other smal company, came thorough the Town that now we were at. But before they came to us, Oh! the outragious roaring and hooping that there was: They began their din about a mile before they came to us. By their noise and hooping they signified how many they had destroyed (which was at that time twenty three.) Those that were with us at home, were gathered together as soon as they heard the hooping, and every time that the other went over their number, these at home gave a shout, that the very Earth rung again: And thus they continued till those that had been upon the expedition were come up to the Sagamores Wigwam; and then, Oh, the hideous insulting and triumphing that there was over some Englishmens scalps that they had taken (as their manner is) and brought with them, I cannot but take notice of the wonderfull mercy of God to me in those afflictions, in sending me a Bible. One of the Indians that came from Medfield fight, had brought some plunder, came to me, and asked me, if I would have a Bible, he had got one in his Basket. I was glad of it, and asked him, whether he thought the Indians would let me read? he answered, yes: So I took the Bible, and in that melancholy time, it came into my mind to read first the 28. Chap. of Deut.; which I did, and when I had read it, my dark heart wrought on this manner, That there was no mercy for me, that the blessing were gone, and the curses come in their room, and that I had lost my opportunity. But the Lord helped me still to go on reading till I came to Chap. 30 the seven first verses, where I found; there was mercy promised again, if we would return to him by repentance; and though we were scatered from one end of the Earth to the other, yet the Lord would gather us together, and turn all those curses upon our Enemies. I do not desire to live to forget this Scripture, and what comfort it was to me. . . .

THE FOURTH REMOVE

Heart-aking thoughts here I had about my poor Children, who were scattered up and down among the wild beasts of the forrest: My head was light and dissey (either through hunger or hard lodging, or trouble or altogether): my knees feeble, my body raw by sitting double night and day, that I cannot express to man the affliction that lay upon my Spirit, but the Lord helped me at that time to express it to himself. I opened my Bible to read, and the Lord brought that precious Scripture to me, Jer. 31. 16. *Thus saith the Lord, refrain thy voice from weeping, and thine eyes from tears, for thy work shall be rewarded, and they shall come again from the land of the Enemy.* This was a sweet Cordial to me, when I was ready to faint, many and many a time have I sat down, and weept sweetly over this Scripture. At this place we continued about four dayes.

THE FIFTH REMOVE

The occasion (as I thought) of their moving at this time, was, the English Army, it being near and following them: For they went, as if they had gone for their lives, for some considerable way, and then they made a stop, and chose some of their stoutest men, and sent them back to hold the English Army in play whilst the rest escaped: And then, like Jehu, they marched on furiously, with their old, and with their young: some carried their old decrepit mothers, some carried one, and some another. Four of them carried a great Indian upon a Bier; but going through a thick Wood with him, they were hindered, and could make no hast; whereupon they took him upon their backs, and carried him, one at a time, till they came to Bacquaug River. Upon a Friday, a little after noon we came to this River. When all the company was come up, and were gathered together, I thought to count the number of them, but they were so many, and being somewhat in motion, it was beyond my skil. In this travel, because of my wound, I was somewhat favoured in my load; I carried only my knitting work and two quarts of parched meal. Being very faint I asked my mistriss to give me one spoonfull of the meal, but she would not give me a taste. They quickly fell to cutting dry trees, to make Rafts to carry them over the river: and soon my turn came to go over: By the advantage of some brush which they had laid upon the Raft to sit upon, I did not wet my foot (which many of themselves at the other end were mid-leg deep) which cannot but be acknowledged as a favour of God to my weakned body, it being a very cold time. I was not before acquainted with such kind of doings or dangers. *When thou passeth through the waters I will be with thee, and through the Rivers they shall not overflow thee*, Isai. 43.2. A certain number of us got over the River that night, but it was the night after the Sabbath before all the company was got over. On the Saturday they boyled an old Horses leg which they had got, and so we drank of the broth, as soon as they thought it was ready, and when it was almost all gone, they filled it up again.

The first week of my being among them, I hardly ate any thing; the second week, I found my stomach grow very faint for want of something; and yet it was very hard to get down their filthy trash: but the third week, though I could think how formerly my stomach would turn against this or that, and I could starve and dy before I could eat such things, yet they were sweet and savoury to my taste. I was at this time knitting a pair of white cotton stockins for my mistriss; and had not yet wrought upon a Sabbath day, when the Sabbath came they bade me go to work; I told them it was the Sabbath day, and desired them to let me rest, and told them I would do as much more to morrow; to which they answered me, they would break my face. And here I cannot but take notice of the strange providence of God in preserving the heathen: They were many hundreds, old and young, some sick, and some lame, many had Papooses at their backs, the greatest number at this time with us, were Squaws, and they travelled with all they had, bag and baggage, and yet they got over this River aforesaid; and on Munday they set their Wigwams on fire, and away they went: On that very day came the English Army after them to this River, and saw the smoak of their Wigwams, and yet this River put a stop to them. God did not give them courage or activity to go over after us; we were not ready for so great a mercy as victory and deliverance; if we had been, God would have found out a way for the English to have passed this River, as well as for the Indians with their Squaws and Children, and all their Luggage. *Oh that my People had hearkened to me, and Israel had walked in my ways, I should soon have subdued their Enemies, and turned my hand against their Adversaries*, Psal. 81: 13.14.

THE EIGHTH REMOVE

On the morrow morning we must go over the River, *i.e.* Connecticot, to meet with King Philip; two Cannoos ful, they had carried over, the next Turn I my self was to go; but as my foot was upon the Cannoo to step in, there was a sudden out-cry among them, and I must step back; and instead of going over the River, I must go four or five miles up the River farther Northward. Some of the Indians ran one way, and some another. The cause of this rout was, as I thought, their espying some English Scouts, who were thereabout. In this travel up the River, about noon the Company made a stop, and sate down; some to eat, and others to rest them. As I sate amongst them, musing of things past, my Son Joseph unexpectedly came to me: we asked of each others welfare, bemoaning our dolefull condition, and the change that had come upon uss. We had Husband and Father, and Children, and Sisters, and Friends, and Relations, and House, and Home, and many Comforts of this Life: but now we may say, as Job, *Naked came I out of my Mothers Womb, and naked shall I return: The Lord gave, and the Lord hath taken away, Blessed be the Name of the Lord*. I asked him whither he would read; he told me, he earnestly desired it, I gave him my Bible, and he lighted upon that comfortable Scripture, Psal. 118. 17, 18. *I shall not dy but live, and declare the works of the Lord: the Lord hath chastened me sore, yet he hath not given me over to death*. Look here, Mother (says he) did you read this? And here I may take occasion to mention one principall ground of my setting forth these Lines: even as the Psalmist says, To declare the Works of the Lord, and his wonderfull Power in carrying us along, preserving us in the Wilderness, while under the Enemies hand, and returning of us in safety again, And His goodness in bringing to my hand so many comfortable and suitable Scriptures in my distress. But to Return, We travelled on till night; and in the morning, we must go over the River to Philip's Crew. When I was in the Cannoo, I could not but be amazed at the numerous crew of Pagans that were on the Bank on the other side. When I came ashore, they gathered all about me, I sitting alone in the midst: I observed they asked one another questions, and laughed, and rejoyced over their Gains and Victories. Then my heart began to fail: and I fell a weeping which was the first time to my remembrance, that I wept before them. Although I had met with so much Affliction, and my heart was many times ready to break, yet could I not shed one tear in their sight: but rather had been all this while in a maze, and like one astonished: but now I may say as, Psal. 137. 1. *By the Rivers of Babylon, there we sate down: yea, we wept when we remembered Zion*. There one of them asked me, why I wept, I could hardly tell what to say: yet I answered, they would kill me: No, said he, none will hurt you. Then came one of them and gave me two spoon-fulls of Meal to comfort me; and another gave me half a pint of Pease; which was more worth than many Bushels at another time. Then I went to see King Philip, he bade me come in and sit down, and asked me whether I woold smoke it (a usual Complement nowadayes amongst Saints and Sinners) but this no way suited me. For though I had formerly used Tobacco, yet I had left it ever since I was first taken. It seems to be a Bait, the Devil layes to make men loose their precious time: I remember with shame, how formerly, when I had taken two or three pipes, I was presently ready for another, such a bewitching thing it is. But I thank God, he has now given me power over it; surely there are many who may be better imployed than to ly sucking a stinking Tobacco-pipe.

Now the Indians gather their Forces to go against North-Hampton: over-night one went about yelling and hooting to give notice of the design. Whereupon they fell to boyling of Ground-nuts, and parching of Corn (as many as had it) for their Provision: and in the morning away they went. During my abode in this place, Philip spake to me to make a shirt for his boy, which I did, for which he gave me a shilling: I offered the mony to my master, but he bade me keep it: and with it I bought a piece of Horse flesh. Afterwards he asked me to make a Cap for his boy, for which he invited me to Dinner. I went, and he gave me a Pancake, about as big as two fingers; it was made of parched wheat, beaten, and fryed in Bears grease, but I thought I never tasted pleasanter meat in my life. . . .

THE TWELFTH REMOVE

It was upon a Sabbath-day-morning, that they prepared for their Travel. This morning I asked my master whither he would sell me to my Husband; he answered me

Nux, which did much rejoyce my spirit. My mistriss, before we went, was gone to the burial of a Papoos, and returning, she found me sitting and reading in my Bible; she snatched it hastily out of my hand, and threw it out of doors; I ran out and catcht it up, and put it into my pocket, and never let her see it afterward. Then they packed up their things to be gone, and gave me my load: I complained it was too heavy, whereupon she gave me a slap in the face, and bade me go; I lifted up my heart to God, hoping the Redemption was not far off: and the rather because their insolency grew worse and worse.

But the thoughts of my going homeward (for so we bent our course) much cheared my Spirit, and made my burden seem light, and almost nothing at all. But (to my amazement and great perplexity) the scale was soon turned: for when we had gone a little way, on a sudden my mistriss gives out, she would go no further, but turn back again, and said, I must go back again with her, and she called her *Sannup*, and would have had him gone back also, but he would not, but said, He would go on, and come to us again in three dayes. My Spirit was upon this, I confess, very impatient, and almost outragious. I thought I could as well have dyed as went back: I cannot declare the trouble that I was in about it; but yet back again I must go. As soon as I had an opportunity, I took my Bible to read, and that quieting Scripture came to my hand, Psal. 46. 10. *Be still, and know that I am God.* Which stilled my spirit for the present: But a sore time of tryal, I concluded, I had to go through, My master being gone, who seemed to me the best friend that I had of an Indian, both in cold and hunger, and quickly so it proved. Down I sat, with my heart as full as it could hold, and yet so hungry that I could not sit neither: but going out to see what I could find, and walking among the Trees, I found six Acorns, and two Ches-nuts, which were some refreshment to me. Towards Night I gathered me some sticks for my own comfort, that I might not ly a-cold: but when we came to ly down they bade me go out, and ly some-where-else, for they had company (they said) come in more than their own: I told them, I could not tell where to go, they bade me go look; I told them, if I went to another Wigwam they would be angry, and send me home again. Then one of the Company drew his sword, and told me he would run me thorough if I did not go presently. Then was I fain to stoop to this rude fellow, and to go out in the night, I knew not whither. Mine eyes have seen that fellow afterwards walking up and down Boston, under the appearance of a Friend-Indian, and severall others of the like Cut. I went to one Wigwam, and they told me they had no room. Then I went to another, and they said the same; at last an old Indian bade me come to him, and his Squaw gave me some Ground-nuts; she gave me also something to lay under my head, and a good fire we had: and through the good providence of God, I had a comfortable lodging that night. In the morning, another Indian bade me come at night, and he would give me six Ground-nuts, which I did. We were at this place and time about two miles from Connecticut River. We went in the morning to gather Ground-nuts, to the River, and went back again that night. I went with a good load at my back (for they when they went, though but a little way, would carry all their trumpery with them) I told them the skin was off my back, but I had no other comforting answer from them than this, That it would be no matter if my head were off too.

THE THIRTEENTH REMOVE

Instead of going toward the Bay, which was that I desired, I must go with them five or six miles down the River into a mighty Thicket of Brush: where we abode almost a fortnight. Here one asked me to make a shirt for her Papoos, for which she gave me a mess of Broth, which was thickened with meal made of the Bark of a Tree, and to make it the better, she had put into it about a handful of Pease, and a few roasted Ground-nuts. I had not seen my son a pritty while, and here was an Indian of whom I made inquiry after him, and asked him when he saw him: he answered me, that such a time his master roasted him, and that himself did eat of piece of him, as big as his two fingers, and that he was very good meat: But the Lord upheld my Spirit, under this discouragement; and I considered their horrible addictedness to lying, and that there is not one of them that makes the least conscience of speaking of truth. In this place, on a cold night, as I lay by the fire, I removed a stick that kept the heat from me, a Squaw moved it down again, at which I lookt up, and she threw a handfull of ashes in mine eyes; I thought I should have been quite blinded, and have never seen more: but lying down, the water run out of my eyes, and carried the dirt with it, that by the morning, I recovered my sight again. Yet upon this, and the like occasions, I hope it is not too much to say with Job, *Have pitty upon me, have pitty upon me, O ye my Friends, for the Hand of the Lord has touched me.* And here I cannot but remember how many times sitting in their Wigwams, and musing on things past, I should suddenly leap up and run out, as if I had been at home, forgetting where I was, and what my condition was: But when I was without, and saw nothing but Wilderness, and Woods, and a company of barbarous heathens, my mind quickly returned to me, which made me think of that, spoken concerning Sampson, who said, *I will go out and shake my self as at other times, but he wist not that the Lord was departed from him.* About this time I began to think that all my hopes of Restoration would come to nothing. I thought of the English Army, and hoped for their coming, and being taken by them, but that failed. I hoped to be carried to Albany, as the Indians had discoursed before, but that failed also. I thought of being sold to my Husband, as my master spake, but in stead of that, my master himself was gone, and left behind; so that my Spirit was now quite ready to sink. I asked them to let me go out and pick up some sticks, that I might get alone, And poure out my heart unto the Lord. Then also I took my Bible to read, but I found no comfort here neither, which many times I was wont to find: So easie a thing it is with God to dry up the Streames of Scripture-comfort from us. Yet I can say, that in all my sorrows and afflictions, God did not leave me to have my impatience work towards himself, as if his wayes were unrighteous. But I knew that he laid upon me less then I deserved. Afterward, before this dolefull time ended with me, I was turning the leaves of my Bible, and the Lord brought to me some Scriptures, which did a little revive me, as that Isai. 55. 8, *For my thoughts are not your thoughts, neither are your wayes my ways, saith the Lord.* And also that, Psal. 37. 5, *Commit thy way unto the Lord, trust also in him, and be shal bring it to pass.* About this time they came yelping from Hadly, where they had killed three English men, and brought one Captive with them, *viz.* Thomas Read. They all gathered about the poor Man, asking him many Questions. I desired also to go and see him; and when I came, he was crying bitterly, supposing they would quickly kill him. Whereupon I asked one of them, whether they intended to kill him; he answered me, they would not: He being a little cheared with that, I asked him about the wel-fare of my Husband, he told me he saw him such a time in the Bay, and he was well, but very melancholly. By which I certainly understood (thought I suspected it before) that whatsoever the Indians told me respecting him was vanity and lies. Some of them told me, he was dead, and they had killed him: some said he was Married again, and that the Governour wished him to Marry; and told him he should have his choice, and that all perswaded I was dead. So like were these barbarous creatures to him who was a lyer from the beginning.

As I was sitting once in the Wigwam here, Phillips Maid came in with the Child in her arms, and asked me to give her a piece of my Apron, to make a flap for it, I told her I would not: then my Mistriss bad me give it, but still I said no: the maid told me if I would not give her a piece, she would tear a piece off it: I told her I would tear her Coat then, with that my Mistriss rises up, and takes up a stick big enough to have killed me, and struck at me with it, but I stept out, and she struck the stick into the Mat of the Wigwam. But while she was-pulling of it out, I ran to the Maid and gave her all my Apron, and so that storm went over.

Hearing that my Son was come to this place, I went to see him, and told him his Father was well, but melancholly: he told me he was as much grieved for his Father as for himself; I wondered at his speech, for I thought I had enough upon my spirit in reference to my self, to make me mindless of my Husband and every one else: they being safe among their Friends. He told me also, that a while before, his Master (together with other Indians) where going to the French for Powder; but by the way the Mohawks met with them, and killed four of their Company which made the rest turn back again, for it might have been worse with him, had he been sold to the French, than it proved to be in his remaining with the Indians.

I went to see an English Youth in this place, one John Gillberd of Springfield. I found him lying without dores, upon the ground; I asked him how he did? he told me he was very sick of a flux, with eating so much blood: They had turned him out of the Wigwam, and with him an Indian Papoos, almost dead, (whose Parents had been killed) in a bitter cold day, without fire or clothes: the young man himself had nothing on, but his shirt and wastcoat. This sight was enough to melt a heart of flint. There they lay quivering in the Cold, the youth round like a dog; the Papoos stretcht out, with his eyes and nose and mouth full of dirt, and yet alive, and groaning. I advised John to go and get to some fire: he told me he could not stand, but I perswaded him still, lest he should ly there and die: and with much adoe I got him to a fire, and went my self home. As soon as I was got home, his Masters Daughter came after me, to know what I had done with the English man, I told her I had got him to a fire in such a place. Now had I need to pray Pauls Prayer, 2 Thess. 3. 2. *That we may be delivered from unreasonable and wicked men.* For her satisfaction I went along with her, and brought her to him; but before I got home again, it was noised about, that I was running away and getting the English youth, along with me; that as soon as I came in, they began to rant and domineer: asking me Where I had been, and what I had been doing? and saying they would knock him on the head: I told them, I had been seeing the English Youth, and that I would not run away, they told me

I lyed; and taking up a Hatchet, they came to me, and said they would knock me down if I stirred out again; and so confined me to the Wigwam. Now may I say with David, 2 Sam. 24. 14. *I am in a great strait.* If I keep in, I must dy with hunger, and if I go out, I must be knockt in head. This distressed condition held that day, and half the next; And then the Lord remembred me, whose mercyes are great. Then came an Indian to me with a pair of stockings that were too big for him, and he would have me ravel them out, and knit them fit for him. I shewed my self willing, and bid him ask my mistriss if I might go along with him a little way; she said yes, I might, but I was not a little refresht with that news, that I had my liberty again. Then I went along with him, and he gave me some roasted Ground-nuts, which did again revive my feeble stomach.

Being got out of her sight, I had time and liberty again to look into my Bible: Which was my Guid by day, and my Pillow by night. Now that comfortable Scripture presented it self to me, Isa. 54. 7. *For a smal moment have I forsaken thee, but with great mercies will I gather thee.* Thus the Lord carried me along from one time to another, and made good to me this precious promise, and many others. Then my Son came to see me, and I asked his master to let him stay a while with me, that I might comb his head, and look over him, for he was almost overcome with lice. He told me, when I had done, that he was very hungry, but I had nothing to relieve him; but bid him go into the Wigwams as he went along, and see if he could get anything among them. Which he did, and it seems tarried a little too long; for his Master was angry with him, and beat him, and then sold him. Then he came running to tell me he had a new Master, and that he had given him some Groundnuts already. Then I went along with him to his new Master who told me he loved him: and he should not want. So his Master carried him away, and I never saw him afterward, till I saw him at Pascataqua in Portsmouth.

That night they bade me go out of the Wigwam again: my Mistrisses Papoos was sick, and it died that night, and there was one benefit in it, that there was more room. I went to a Wigwam, and they bade me come in, and gave me a skin to ly upon, and a mess of Venson and Ground-nuts, which was a choice Dish among them. On the morrow they buried the Papoos, and afterward, both morning and evening, there came a company to mourn and howle with her: though I confess, I could not much condole with them. Many sorrowfull dayes I had in this place: often getting alone; *like a Crane, or a Swallow; so did I chatter: I did mourn as a Dove, mine eyes ail with looking upward. Oh, Lord, I am oppressed; undertake for me,* Isa. 38. 14. I could tell the Lord as Hezeckiah, ver. 3. *Remember now O Lord, I beseech thee, how I have walked before thee in truth.* Now had I time to examine all my wayes: my Conscience did not accuse me of un-righteousness toward one or other: yet I saw now in my walk with God, I had been a careless creature. As David said, *Against thee, thee only have I sinned.* and I might say with the poor Publican, *God be merciful unto me a sinner.* On the Sabbath-dayes, I could look upon the Sun and think how People were going to the house of God, to have their Souls refresht; and then home, and their bodies also but I was destitute of both; and might say as the poor Prodigal, *he would fain have filled his belly with the husks that the Swine did eat, and no man gave unto him.* Luke 15. 16. For I must say with him, *Father I have sinned against Heaven, and in thy sight;* ver. 21. I remembred how on the night before and after the Sabbath, when my Family was about me, and Relations and Neighbours with us, we would pray and sing, and then have a comfortable Bed to ly down on: but in stead of all this, I had only a little Swill for the body, and then like a Swine, must ly down on the ground. I cannot express to man the sorrow that lay upon my Spirit, the Lord knows it. Yet that comfortable Scripture would often come to my mind, *For a small moment have I forsaken thee, but with great mercies will I gather thee.*

THE FIFTEENTH REMOVE

We went on our travel, I having got one handful of Ground nuts for my support that day they gave me my load, and I went on cheerfully, (with the thoughts of going homeward) having my burden more on my back than my spirit; we came to Baquaug River again that day, near which we abode a few days. Sometimes one of them would give me a Pipe, another a little Tobacco, another a little Salt; which I would change for a little Victuals. I cannot but think what a Wolvish appetite persons have in a starving condition; for many times, when they gave me that which was hot, I was so greedy, that I should burn my mouth, that it would trouble me hours after; and yet I should quickly do the same again. And after I was thoroughly hungry, I was never again satisfied; for though sometimes it fell out that I got enough, and did eat till I could eat no more, yet I was as unsatisfied as I was when I began. And now could I see that Scripture verified, (there being many Scriptures which we do not take notice of, or understand, till we are afflicted,) *Mic.* vi. 14, *Thou shalt eat and not be satisfied.* Now might I see more than ever before, the miseries that sin hath brought upon us. Many times I should be ready to run out against the Heathen, but that Scripture would quiet me again, *Amos* iii. 6, *Shall there be evil in the City and the Lord hath not done it?* The Lord help me to make a right improvement of his word, and that I might learn that great lesson, *Mic.* vi. 8, 9; *He hath shewed thee, O Man, what is good; and what doth the Lord require of thee but to do justly, and love mercy, and walk humbly with thy God? Hear ye the rod, and who hath appointed it.*

THE EIGHTEENTH REMOVE

We took up our packs, and along we went; but a wearsome day I had of it. As we went along I saw an *English-man* stript naked, and lying dead upon the ground, but knew not who it was. Then we came to another Indian Town, where we stayed all night: In this Town there were four *English Children*, Captives: and one of them my own Sister's: I went to see how she did, and she was well, considering her Captive condition. I would have tarried that night with her, but they that owned her would not suffer it. Then I went to another Wigwam, where they were boiling Corn and Beans, which was a lovely sight to see; but I could not get a taste thereof. Then I went into another Wigwam, where there were two of the *English Children*. The Squaw was boiling horses feet; then she cut me off a little piece, and gave one of the *English Children* a piece also: Being very hungry, I had quickly eat up mine; but the Child could not bite it, it was so tough and sinewy, but lay sucking, gnawing, chewing, and slobbering it in the mouth and hand; then I took it of the Child, and eat it myself; and savoury it was to my taste.

That I may say as *Job,* chap. vi. 7, *The things that my Soul refused to touch are as my sorrowful meat.* Thus the Lord made that pleasant and refreshing which another time would have been an Abomination. Then I went home to my Mistress's Wigwam; and they told me I disgraced my Master with begging; and if I did so any more they would knock me on the head: I told them, they had as good knock me on the head as starve me to death.

THE NINETEENTH REMOVE

They said, when we went out, that we must travel to Wachuset this day. But a bitter weary day I had of it, travelling now three dayes together, without resting any day between. At last, after many weary steps, I saw Wachuset hills, but many miles off. Then we came to a great Swamp, through which we travelled, up to the knees in mud and water, which was heavy going to one tyred before. Being almost spent, I thought I should have sunk down at last, and never gat out; but I may say, as in Psal. 94. 18, *When my foot slipped, thy mercy, O Lord, held me up.* Going along, having indeed my life, but little spirit, Philip, who was in the Company, came up and took me by the hand, and said, Two weeks more and you shal be Mistress again. I asked him, if he spake true? he answered, Yes, and quickly you shal come to your master again; who had been gone from us three weeks. After many weary steps we came to Wachuset, where he was: and glad I was to see him. He asked me, When I washt me? I told him not this month, then he fetcht me some water himself, and bid me wash, and gave me the Glass to see how I lookt; and bid his Squaw give me something to eat: so she gave me a mess of Beans and meat, and a little Ground-nut Cake. I was wonderfully revived with this favour shewed me, Psal. 106. 46, *He made them also to be pittied, of all those that carried them Captives.*

My master had three Squaws, living sometimes with one, and sometimes with another one, this old Squaw, at whose Wigwam I was, and with whom my Master had been those three weeks. Another was Wattimore, with whom I had lived and served all this while: A severe and proud Dame she was, bestowing every day in dressing her self neat as much time as any of the Gentry of the land: powdering her hair, and painting her face, going with Neck-laces, with Jewels in her ears, and Bracelets upon her hands: When she had dressed her self, her work was to make Girdles of Wampom and Beads. The third Squaw was a younger one, by whom he had two Papooses. By that time I was refresht by the old Squaw, with whom my master was, Wettimores Maid came to call me home, at which I fell a weeping. Then the old Squaw told me, to encourage me, that if I wanted victuals, I should come to her, and that I should ly there in her Wigwam. Then I went with the maid, and quickly came again and lodged there. The Squaw laid a Mat under me, and a good Rugg over me; the first time I had any such kindness shewed me. I understood that Wettimore thought, that if she should let me go and serve with the old Squaw, she would be in danger to loose, not only my service, but the redemption-pay also. And I was not a little glad to hear this; being by it raised in my hopes, that in Gods due time there would be an end of this sorrowfull hour. Then came an Indian, and asked me to knit him three pair of Stockins, for which I had a Hat, and a silk Handker-chief. Then another asked me to make her a shift, for which she gave me an Apron.

Then came Tom and Peter, with the second Letter from the Council, about the Captives. Though they were Indians, I gat them by the hand, and burst out into tears; my heart was so full that I could not speak to them; but recovering my self, I asked them how my husband did, and all my friends and acquaintance? they said, They are all very well but melancholy. They brought me two Biskets, and a pound of Tobacco. The Tobacco I quickly gave away; when it was all gone, one asked me to give him a pipe of Tobacco, I told him it was all gone; then began he to rant and threaten: I told him when my Husband came I would give him some: Hang him Rogue (says he) I will knock out his brains, if he comes here. And then again, in the same breath they would say, That if there should come an hundred without Guns, they would do them no hurt. So unstable and like mad men they were. So that fearing the worst, I durst not send to my Husband, though there were some thoughts of his coming to Redeem and fetch me, not knowing what might follow. For there was little more trust to them then to the master they served. When the Letter was come, the Saggamores met to consult about the Captives, and called me to them to enquire how much my husband would give to redeem me, when I came I sate down among them, as I was wont to do, as their manner is: Then they bade me stand up, and said, they were the General Court. They bid me speak what I thought he would give. Now knowing that all we had was destroyed by the Indians, I was in a great strait: I thought if I should speak of but a little, it would be slighted, and hinder the matter; if of a great sum, I knew not where it would be procured: yet at a venture, I said. Twenty pounds, yet desired them to take less; but they would not hear of that, but sent that message to Boston, that for Twenty pounds I should be redeemed. It was a Praying-Indian that wrote their Letter for them. There was another Praying Indian, who told me, that he had a brother, that would not eat Horse; his conscience was so tender and scrupulous (though as large as hell, for the destruction of poor Christians). Then he said, he read that Scripture to him, 2 Kings, 6.25. *There was a famine in Samaria, and behold they beseiged it, untill an Asses head was sold for fourscore pieces of silver, and the fourth part of a Kab of Doves dung, for five pieces of silver.* He expounded this place to his brother, and shewed him that it was lawfull to eat that in a Famine which is not at another time. And now, says he, he will eat Horse with any Indian of them all. There was another Praying-Indian, who when he had done all the mischief that he could, betrayed his own Father into the English hands, thereby to purchase his own life. Another Praying-Indian was at Sudbury-fight, though, as he deserved, he was afterward hanged for it. There was another Praying Indian, so wicked and cruel, as to wear a string about his neck, strung with *Christian* Fingers. Another Praying *Indian*, when they went to *Sudbury* Fight, went with them, and his Squaw also with him, with her Papoos at her back: before they went to that Fight, they got a company together to *Powaw:* the manner was as followeth. There was one that kneeled upon a *Deerskin,* with the Company round him in a Ring, who kneeled, striking upon the Ground with their hands, and with sticks, and muttering or humming with their Mouths. Besides him who kneeled in the ring, there also stood one with a Gun in his hand: Then he on the Deer-skin made a speech and all manifested assent to it; and so they did many times together. Then they bade him with the Gun go out of the ring, which he did; but when he was out they called him in again; but he seemed to make a stand; then they called the more earnestly, till he returned again. Then they all sang. Then they gave him two Guns, in either hand one. And so he on the Deer-skin began again; and at the end of every Sentence in his speaking, they all assented, humming or muttering with their Mouthes, and striking upon the Ground with the Hands. Then they bade him with the two Guns go out of the Ring again; which he did a little way. Then they called him in again, but he made a stand, so they called him with greater earnestness: but he stood reeling and wavering, as if he knew not whether he should stand or fall, or which way to go. Then they called him with exceeding great vehemency, all of them, one and another: after a little while, he turned in, staggering as he went, with his Arms stretched out; in either hand a Gun. As soon as he came in, they all sang and rejoyced exceedingly a while. And then he upon the Deer skin, made another speech, unto which they all assented in a rejoycing manner; and so they ended their business, and forthwith went to *Sudbury* Fight. To my thinking they went without any scruple but that they should prosper and gain the Victory. And they went out not so rejoycing, but that they came home with as great a Victory. For they said they had killed two Captains, and almost an hundred men. One *Englishman* they brought alive with them; and he said, it was too true, for they had made sad work at Sudbury, as indeed it proved. Yet they came home without that rejoycing and triumphing over their victory, which they were wont to shew at other times, but rather like Dogs (as they say) which have lost their ears. Yet I could not perceive that it was for their own loss of men: They said, they had not lost above five or six: and I missed none, except in one Wigwam. When they went, they acted as if the Devil had told them that they should gain the victory: and now they acted, as if the Devil had told them they should have a fall. Whither it were so or no, I cannot tell, but so it proved, for quickly they began to fall, and so held on that Summer, till they came to utter ruine.

THE TWENTIETH REMOVE

It was their usual manner to remove, when they had done any mischief, lest they should be found out: and so they did at this time. We went about three or four miles, and there they build a great. Wigwam, big enough to hold an hundred Indians, which they did in preparation to a great day of Dancing. They would say now amongest themselves, that the Governour would be so angry for his loss at Sudbury, that he would send no more about the Captives, which made me grieve and tremble. My Sister being not far from the place where we now were, and hearing that I was here, desired her master to let her come and see me, and he was willing to it, and would go with her: but she being ready before him, told him she would go before, and was come within a Mile or two of the place; Then he overtook her, and began to rant as if he had been mad; and made her go back again in the Rain; so that I never saw her till I saw her in Charlestown. But the Lord requited many of their ill doings, for this Indian her Master, was hanged afterward at Boston. The Indians now began to come from all quarters; against their merry dancing day. Among some of them came one Goodwife Kettle. I told her my heart was so heavy that it was ready to break: so is mine too said she, but yet said, I hope we shall hear some good news shortly. I could hear how earnestly my Sister desired to see me, and I as earnestly desired to see her: and yet neither of us could get an opportunity. My Daughter was also now about a mile off, and I had not seen her in nine or ten weeks, as I had not seen my Sister since our first taking. I earnestly desired them to let me go and see them yea, I intreated begged, and perswaded them, but to let me see my Daughter; and yet so hard hearted were they, that they would not suffer it. They made use of their tyrannical power whilst they had it: but through the Lords wonderfull mercy, their time was now but short.

On a Sabbath day, the Sun being about an hour high in the afternoon, came Mr. John Hoar (the Council permitting him, and his own forward spirit inclining him) together with the two fore mentioned Indians, Tom and Peter, with their third Letter from the Council. When they came near, I was abroad: though I saw them not, they presently called me in, and bade me sit down and not stir. Then they catched up their Guns, and away they ran, as if an Enemy had been at hand; and the Guns went off apace. I manifested some great trouble, and they asked me what was the matter? I told them, I thought they had killed the English man (for they had in the mean time informed me that an English-man was come) they said, No; They shot over his Horse and under, and before his Horse; and they pusht him this way and that way, at their pleasure: shewing what they could do: Then they let them come to their Wigwams. I begged of them to let me see the English-man, but they would not. But there was I fain to sit their pleasure. When they had talked their fill with him, they suffered me to go to him. We asked each other of our welfare, and how my Husband did, and all my Friends? He told me they were all well, and would be glad to see me. Amongst other things which my Husband sent me, there came a pound of Tobacco: which I sold for nine shillings in Money for many of the Indians for want of Tobacco, smoaked Hemlock, and Ground-Ivy. It was a great mistake in any, who thought I sent for Tobacco: for through the favour of God, that desire was overcome. I now asked them, whither I should go home with Mr. Hoar? They answered No, one and another of them and it being night, we lay down with that answer; in the morning, Mr. Hoar invited the Saggamores to Dinner; but when we went to get it ready, we found that they had stollen the greatest part of the Provision Mr. Hoar had brought, out of his Bags, in the night. And we may see the wonderfull power of God, in that one passage, in that when there was such a great number of the Indians together, and so greedy of a little good food; and no English there, but Mr. Hoar and my self, that there they did not knock us in the head, and take what we had: there being not only some Provision, but also Trading cloth, a part of the twenty pounds agreed upon. But instead of doing us any mischief, they seemed to be ashamed of the fact, and said, it were some Matchit Indian that did it. Oh, that we could believe that there is not thing too hard for God! God shewed his Power over the Heathen in this, as he did over the hungry Lyons when Daniel was cast into the Den. Mr. Hoar called them betime to Dinner, but they ate very little, they being so busie in dressing themselves, and getting ready for their Dance: which was carried on by eight of them four Men and four Squaws: My master and mistress being two. He was dressed in his Holland shirt, with great Laces sewed at the tail of it, he had his silver Buttons, his white Stockins, his Garters were hung round with Shillings, and he had Girdles of Wampom upon his head and shoulders. She had a Kersey Coat, and covered with Girdles of Wampom from the Loins upward: her armes from her elbows to her hands were covered with Bracelets; there were handfulls of Necklaces about her neck, and severall sorts of Jewels in her ears. She had fine red Stokins and white Shoos, her hair powdered and face painted Red, that was alwayes before Black. And all the Dancers were after the same manner. There were two other singing and knocking on a Kettle for their musick. They keept hopping up and down one after another, with a Kettle of water in the midst, standing warm upon some Embers, to drink of when they were dry. They held on till it was almost night, throwing out Wampom to the standers by. At night I asked them again, if I should go home? They all as one said No, except my Husband would come for me. When we were lain down, my Master went out of the Wigwam, and by and by sent in an Indian called James the Printer who told Mr. Hoar, that my Master would let me go home tomorrow, if he would let him have one pint of Liquors. Then Mr. Hoar called his own Indians, Tom and Peter, and bid them go and see whither he would promise it before them three: and if he would, he should have it; which he did, and he had it. Then Philip smelling the business cal'd me to him, and asked me what I would give him, to tell me some good news, and speak a good word for me. I told him, I could not tell what to give him, I would any thing I had, and asked him what he would have? He said, two Coats and twenty shillings in Mony, and half a bushel of seed Corn, and some Tobacco. I thanked him for his love: but I knew the good news as well as the crafty Fox. My Master after he had had his drink, quickly came ranting into the Wigwam again, and called for Mr. Hoar, drinking to him, and saying, He was a good man: and then again he would say, Hang him Rogue: Being almost drunk, he would drink to him, and yet presently say he should be hanged. Then he called for me. I trembled to hear him, yet I was fain to go to him, and he drank to me, shewing no incivility. He was the first Indian I saw drunk all the while that I was amongst them. At last his Squaw ran out, and he after her, round the Wigwam, with his mony jingling at his knees: But she escaped him: But having an old Squaw he ran to her: and so through the Lords mercy, we were no more troubled that night. Yet I had not a comfortable nights rest: for I think I can say; I did not sleep for three nights together. The night before the Letter came from the Council, I could not rest, I was so full of feares and troubles, God many times leaving us most in the dark, when deliverance is nearest: yea, at this time I could not rest night nor day. The next night I was overjoyed, Mr. Hoar being come, and that with such good tidings. The third night I was even swallowed up with the thoughts of things, *viz.* that ever I should go home again; and that I must go, leaving my Children behind me in the Wilderness; so that sleep was now almost departed from mine eyes.

On Tuesday morning they called their General Court (as they call it) to consult and determine, whether I should go home or no: And they all as one man did seemingly consent to it, that I should go home; except Philip, who would not come among them.

But before I go any further, I would take leave to mention a few remarkable passages of providence, which I took special notice of in my afflicted time.

1.   Of the fair opportunity lost in the long March, a little after the Fort-fight, when our English Army was so numerous, and in pursuit of the Enemy, and so near as to take several and destroy them: and the Enemy in such distress for food; that our men might track them by their rooting in the

earth for Ground-nuts, whilest they were flying for their lives. I say, that then our Army should want Provision, and be forced to leave their pursuit and return homeward; and the very next week the Enemy came upon our Town, like Bears bereft of their whelps, or so many ravenous Wolves, rending us and our Lambs to death. But what shall I say? God seemed to leave his People to themselves, and order all things for his own holy ends. *Shal there be evil in the City and the Lord bath not done it? They are not grieved for the affliction of Joseph, therefore shal they go Captive, with the first that go Captive.* It is the Lords doing, and it should be marvelous in our eyes.

2. I cannot but remember how the Indians derided the slowness, and dulness of the English Army, in its setting out. For after the desolations at Lancaster and Medfield, as I went along with them, they asked me when I thought the English Army would come after them? I told them I could not tell: It may be they will come in May, said they. Thus did they scoffe at us, as if the English would be a quarter of a year getting ready.

3. Which also I have hinted before, when the English Army with new supplies were sent forth to pursue after the enemy, and they understanding it, fled before them till they came to Baquaug River, where they forthwith went over safely; that that River should be impassable to the English. I can but admire to see the wonderfull providence of God in preserving the heathen for farther affliction to our poor Countrey. They could go in great numbers over, but the English must stop. God had an over-ruling hand in all those things.

4. It was thought, if their Corn were cut down, they would starve and dy with hunger and all their Corn that could be found, was destroyed, and they driven from that little they had in store, into the Woods in the midst of Winter; and yet how to admiration did the Lord preserve them for his holy ends, and the destruction of many still amongst the English! strangely did the Lord provide for them; that I did not see (all the time I was among them) one Man, Woman, or Child, die with hunger.

Though many times they would eat that, that a Hog or a Dog would hardly touch; yet by that God strengthned them to be a scourge to his People.

The chief and commonest food was Ground-nuts: They eat also Nuts and Acorns, Harty-choaks, Lilly roots, Ground-beans, and several other weeds and roots, that I know not.

They would pick up old bones, and cut them to pieces at the joynts, and if they were full of wormes and magots, they would scald them over the fire to make the vermine come out, and then boile them, and drink up the Liquor, and then beat the great ends of them in a Morter, and so eat them. They would eat Horses guts, and ears, and all sorts of wild Birds which they could catch: also Bear, Vennison, Beaver, Tortois, Frogs, Squirrels, Dogs, Skunks, Rattle-snakes; yea, the very Bark of Trees; besides all sorts of creatures, and provision which they plundered from the English. I can but stand in admiration to see the wonderful power of God, in providing for such a vast number of our Enemies in the Wilderness, where there was nothing to be seen, but from hand to mouth. Many times in a morning, the generality of them would eat up all they had, and yet have some further supply against they wanted.

It is said, Psal. 81. 13, 14. *Oh, that my People had hearkned to me, and Israel had walked in my wayes, I should soon have subdued their Enemies, and turned my hand against their Adversaries.* But now our perverse and evil carriages in the sight of the Lord, have so offended him, that instead of turning his hand against them, the Lord feeds and nourishes them up to be a scourge to the whole Land.

5.   Another thing that I would observe is, the strange providence of God, in turning things about when the Indians was at the highest, and the English at the lowest. I was with the Enemy eleven weeks and five dayes, and not one Week passed without the fury of the Enemy, and some desolation by fire and sword upon one place or other. They mourned (with their black faces) for their own lossess, yet triumphed and rejoyced in their inhumane, and many times devilish cruelty to the English. They would boast much of their Victories; saying, that in two hours time they had destroyed such a Captain, and his Company at such a place; and such a Captain and his Company in such a place; and such a Captain and his Company in such a place: and boast how many Towns they had destroyed, and then scoffe, and say. They had done them a good turn, to send them to Heaven so soon. Again, they would say. This Summer that they would knock all the Rogues in the head, or drive them into the Sea, or make them flie the Countrey thinking surely, Agag-like, *The bitterness of Death is past.* Now the Heathen begins to think all is their own, and the poor Christians hopes to fail (as to man) and now their eyes are more to God, and their hearts sigh heaven-ward: and to say in good earnest, *Help Lord, or we perish:* When the Lord had brought his people to this, that they saw no help in any thing but himself: then he takes the quarrel into his own hand: and though they had made a pit, in their own imaginations, as deep as hell for the Christians that Summer, yet the Lord hurll'd them selves into it. And the Lord had not so many wayes before to preserve them, but now he hath as many to destroy them.

But to return again to my going home, where we may see a remarkable change of Providence. At first they were all against it, except my Husband would come for me; but afterwards they assented to it, and seemed much to rejoyce in it, some askt me to send them some Bread, others some Tobacco, others shaking me by the hand, offering me a Hood and Scarfe to ride in, not one moving hand or tongue against it. Thus hath the Lord answered my poor desire, and the many earnest requests of others put up unto God for me. In my travels an Indian came to me, and told me, if I were willing, he and his Squaw would run away, and go home along with me: I told him No. I was not willing to run away, but desired to wait Gods time, that I might go home quietly, and without fear. And now God hath granted me my desire. O the wonderfull power of God that I have seen, and the experience that I have had. I have been in the midst of those roaring Lyons, and Salvage Bears, that feared neither God, nor Man, nor the Devil, by night and day, alone and in company sleeping all sorts together, and yet not one of them ever offered me the least abuse of unchastity to me, in word or action. Though some are ready to say, I speak it for my own credit; But I speak it in the presence of God, and to his Glory. Gods Power is as great now, and as sufficient to save, as when he preserved Daniel in the Lions Den or the three Children in the fiery Furnace. I may well say as his Psal. 107.12, *Oh give thanks unto the Lord for he is good, for his mercy endureth for ever.* Let the Redeemed of the Lord say so, whom he hath redeemed from the hand of the Enemy, especially that I should come away in the midst of so many hundreds of Enemies quietly and peacably, and not a Dog moving his tongue. So I took my leave of them, and in coming along my heart melted into tears, more then all the while I was with them, and I was almost swallowed up with the thoughts that ever I should go home again. About the Sun going down, Mr. Hoar, and my self, and the two Indians came to Lancaster, and a solemn sight it was to me. There had I lived many comfortable years amongst my Relations and Neighbours, and now not one Christian to be seen, nor one house left standing. We went on to a Farm house that was yet standing, where we lay all night: and a comfortable lodging we had, though nothing but straw to ly on. The Lord preserved us in safety that night, and raised us up again in the morning, and carried us along that before noon we came to Concord. Now was I full of joy, and yet not without sorrow: joy to see such a lovely sight, so many Christians together, and some of them my Neighbours: There I met with my Brother, and my Brother in Law, who asked me, if I knew where his Wife was? Poor heart! he had helped to bury her, and knew it not; she being shot down by the house was partly burnt: so that those who were at Boston at the desolation of the Town, and came back afterward, and buried the dead, did not know her. Yet I was not without sorrow, to think how many were looking and longing, and my own Children amongst the rest, to enjoy that deliverance that I had now received, and I did not know whither ever I should see them again. Being recruited with food and raiment we went to Boston that day, where I met with my dear. Husband, but the thoughts of our dean Children, one being dead, and the other we could not tell where, abated our comfort each to other. I was not before so much hem'd in with the merciless and cruel Heathen, but now as much with pittiful, tender-hearted and compassionate Christians. In that poor, and destressed, and beggerly condition I was received in, I was kindly entertained in severall Houses: so much love I received from several (some of whom I knew, and others I knew not) that I am not capable to declare it. But the Lord knows them all by name. The Lord reward them seven fold into their bosoms of his spirituals, for their temporals. The twenty pounds the price of my redemption was raised by some Boston Gentlemen, and Mrs. Usher, whose bounty and religious charity, I would not forget to make mention of. Then Mr. Thomas Shepard of Charlstown received us into his House, where we continued eleven weeks; and a Father and Mother they were to us. And many more tender-hearted Friends we met with in that place. We were now in the midst of love, yet not without much and frequent heaviness of heart for our poor Children, and other Relations, who were still in affliction. The week following, after my coming in, the Governour and Council sent forth to the Indians again and that not without success; for they brought in my Sister, and Good-wife Kettler. Their not knowing where our Children were, was a sore tryal to us still and yet we were not without secret hopes that we should see them again. That which was dead lay heavier upon my spirit, than those which were alive and amongst the Heathen; thinking how it suffered with its wounds, and I was no way able to relieve it; and how it was buried by the Heathen in the Wilderness from among all Christians. We were hurried up and down in our thoughts, sometime we should hear a report that they were gone this way, and sometimes that; and that they were come in, in this place or that. We kept enquiring and listning to hear concerning them, but no certain news as yet. About this time the Council had ordered a day a publick. Thanks-giving: though I thought I had still cause of mourning, and being unsettled in our minds, we thought we would ride toward the Eastward, to see if we could hear any thing concerning our Children. And as we were riding along (God is the wise disposer of all things) between Ipswich and Rowly we met with Mr. William Hubbard, who told us that our Son Joseph was come in to Major Waldrens, and another with him, which was my Sisters Son. I asked him how he knew it? He said, the Major himself told him so. So along we went till we came to Newbury; and their Minister being absent, they desired my Husband to Preach the Thanks giving for them; but he was not willing to stay there that night, but would go over to Salisbury, to hear further, and come again in the morning; which he did, and Preached there that day. At night, when he had done, one came and told him that his Daughter was come in at Providence; Here was mercy on both hands: Now hath God fulfiled that precious Scripture which was such a comfort to me in my distressed condition. When my heart was ready to sink into the Earth (my Children being gone I could not tell whither) and my knees trembled under me, And I was walking through the valley of the shadow of Death: Then the Lord brought, and now has fulfilled that reviving word unto me: *Thus saith the Lord, Refrain thy voice from weeping, and thine eyes from tears, for thy Work shall be rewarded, saith the Lord, and they sall come again from the Land of the Enemy.* Now we were between them, the one on the East, and the other on the West: Our Son being nearest, we went to him first, to Portsmouth, where we met with him, and with the Major also: who told us he had done what he could, but could not redeem him under seven pounds; which the good People thereabouts were pleased to pay. The Lord reward the Major, and all the rest, though unknown to me, for their labour of Love. My Sisters Son was redeemed for four pounds, which the Council gave order for the payment of. Having now received one of our Children, we hastened toward the other; going back through Newbury, my Husband preached there on the Sabbath-day: for which they rewarded him many fold.

On Muriday we came to Charlstown, where we heard that the Governour of Road-Island had sent over for our Daughter, to take care of her, being now within his Jurisdiction: which should not pass without our acknowledgments. But she being nearer Rehoboth than Road-Island, Mr. Newman went over, and took care of hen and brought her to his own House. And the goodness of God was admirable to us in our low estate, in that he raised up passionate. Friends on every side to us, when we had nothing to recompance any for their love. The Indians were now gone that way, that it was apprehended dangerous to go to her: But the Carts which carried Provision to the English Army, being guarded, brought her with them to Dorchester, where we received her safe: blessed be the Lord for it, For great is his Power, and he can do whatsoever seemeth him good. Her coming in was after this manner: She was travelling one day with the Indians, with her basket at her back; the company of Indians were got before her, and gone out of sight, all except one Squaw; she followed the Squaw till night, and then both of them lay down, having nothing over them but the heavens, and under them but the earth. Thus she travelled three dayes together, not knowing whither she was going: having nothing to eat or drink but water, and green Hirtle-berries. At last they came into Providence, where she was kindly entertained by several of that Town. The Indians often said, that I should never have her under twenty pounds: But now the Lord hath brought her in upon free-cost, and given her to me the second time. The Lord make us a blessing indeed, each to others. Now have I seen that Scripture also fulfilled, Deut. 30:4, 7. *If any of thine be driven out to the outmost parts of heaven, from thence will the Lord thy God gather thee, and from thence will be fetch thee. And the Lord thy God will put all these curses upon thine enemies, and on them which hate thee, which persecuted thee.* Thus hath the Lord brought me and mine out of that horrible pit, and hath set us in the midst of tender hearted and compassionate Christians. It is the desire of my soul, that we may walk worthy of the mercies received, and which we are receiving.

Our Family being now gathered together (those of us that were living) the South Church in Boston hired an House for us. Then we removed from Mr. Shepards, those cordial Friends, and went to Boston, where we continued about three quarters of a year: Still the Lord went along with us, and provided graciously for us. I thought it somewhat strange to set up House-keeping with bare walls; but as Solomon says, *Mony answers all things,* and that we had through the benevolence of Christian-friends, some in this Town, and some in that, and others. And some from England, that in a little time we might look, and see the House furnished with love. The Lord hath been exceeding good to us in our low estate, in that when we had neither house nor home, nor other necessaries; the Lord so moved the hearts of these and those towards us, that we wanted neither food, nor raiment for our selves or ours, Prov. 18. 24. *There is a Friend which sticketh closer than a Brother.* And how many such Friends have we found, and now living amongst? And truly such a Friend have we found him to be unto us, in whose house we lived, *viz.* Mr. James Whitcomb, a Friend unto us near hand, and afar off.

I can remember the time, when I used to sleep quietly without workings in my thoughts, whole nights together, but now it is other wayes with me. When all are fast about me, and no eye open, but his who ever waketh, my thoughts are upon things past, upon the awfull dispensation of the Lord towards us; upon his wonderfull power and might, in carrying of us through so many difficulties, in returning us in safety, and suffering none to hurt us. I remember in the night season, how the other day I was in the midst of thousands of enemies, and nothing but death before me. It is then hard work to perswade my self, that ever I should be satisfied with bread again. But now we are fed with the finest of the Wheat, and as I may say, With honey out of the rock. In stead of the Husk, we have the fatted Calf. The thoughts of these things in the particulars of them, and of the love and goodness of God towards us, make it true of me, what David said of himself, Psal. 6.5. *I watered my Couch with my tears.* Oh! the wonderfull power of God that mine eyes have seen, affording matter enough for my thoughts to run in, that when others are sleeping mine eyes are weeping.

I have seen the extrem vanity of this World: One hour I have been in health, and wealth, wanting nothing. But the next hour in sickness and wounds, and death, having nothing but sorrow and affliction.

Before I knew what affliction meant, I was ready sometimes to wish for it. When I lived in prosperity, having the comforts of the World about me, my relations by me, my Heart chearfull, and taking little care for any thing and yet seeing many, whom I preferred before my self, under many tryals and afflictions, in sickness, weakness, poverty, losses, crosses, and cares of the World, I should be sometimes jealous least I should have my portion in this life, and that Scripture would come to my mind. Heb. 12.6 *For whom the Lord loveth he chasteneth, and scourgeth every Son whom he receiveth*. But now I see the Lord had his time to scourge and chasten me. The portion of some is to have their afflictions by drops, now one drop and then another; but the dregs of the Cup, the Wine of astonishment, like a sweeping rain that leaveth no food, did the Lord prepare to be my portion. Affliction I wanted, and affliction. I had, full measure (I thought) pressed down and running over; yet I see, when God calls a Person to any thing, and through never so many difficulties, yet he is fully able to carry them through and make them see, and say they have been gainers thereby. And I hope I can say in some measure, As David did, *It is good for me that I have been afflicted*. The Lord hath shewed me the vanity of these outward things. That they are the Vanity of vanities, and vexation of spirit; that they are but a shadow, a blast, a bubble, and things of no continuance. That we must rely on God himself, and our whole dependance must be upon him. If trouble from smaller matters begin to arise in me, I have something at hand to check my self with, and say, why am I troubled? It was but the other day that if I had had the world, I would have given it for my freedom, or to have been a Servant to a Christian. I have learned to look beyond present and smaller troubles, and to be quieted under them, as Moses said, Exod. 14. 13. *Stand still and see the salvation of the Lord*.

SEASON'S GREETINGS TO OUR FRIENDS AND FAMILY!!! (1994)

David Sedaris
b. 1956 Binghamton, NY

Many of you, our friends and family, are probably taken aback by this, our annual holiday newsletter. You've read of our recent tragedy in the newspapers and were no doubt thinking that, what with all of their sudden legal woes and "hassles," the Dunbar clan might just stick their heads in the sand and avoid this upcoming holiday season altogether!!

You're saying, "There's no way the Dunbar family can grieve their terrible loss *and* carry on the traditions of the season. No family is *that* strong," you're thinking to yourselves.

Well, think again!!!!!!!!!!!!

While this past year has certainly dealt our family a heavy hand of sorrow and tribulation, we have (so far!) weathered the storm and shall continue to do so! Our tree is standing tall in the living room, the stockings are hung, and we are eagerly awaiting the arrival of a certain portly gentleman who goes by the name "Saint Nick"!!!!!!!!!!!!

Our trusty PC printed out our wish lists weeks ago and now we're cranking it up again to wish you and yours The Merriest of Christmas Seasons from the entire Dunbar family: Clifford, Jocelyn, Kevin, Jacki, Kyle, and Khe Sahn!!!!!

Some of you are probably reading this and scratching your heads over the name "Khe Sahn." "That certainly doesn't fit with the rest of the family names," you're saying to yourself. "What, did those crazy Dunbars get themselves a Siamese cat?"

You're close.

To those of you who live in a cave and haven't heard the news, allow us to introduce Khe Sahn Dunbar who, at the age of twenty-two, happens to be the newest member of our family.

Surprised?

JOIN THE CLUB!!!!!!!

It appears that Clifford, husband of yours truly and father to our three natural children, accidentally planted the seeds for Khe Sahn twenty-two years ago during his stint in . . . where else?

VIETNAM!!!!

This was, of course, years before Clifford and I were married. At the time of his enlistment we were pre-engaged and the long period of separation took its toll on both of us. I corresponded regularly. (I wrote him every single day, even when I couldn't think of anything interesting. His letters were much less frequent but I saved all four of them!)

While I had both the time and inclination to put my feelings into envelopes, Clifford, along with thousands of other American soldiers, had no such luxury. While the rest of us were watching the evening news in our safe and comfortable homes, he was *making* the evening news, standing waist high in a stagnant foxhole. The hazards and the torments of war are something that, luckily, most of us cannot begin to imagine and, for that, we should all count our blessings.

Clifford Dunbar, twenty-two years ago, a young man in a war-torn country, made a mistake. A terrible, heinous mistake. A stupid, thoughtless, permanent mistake with dreadful, haunting consequences.

But who are you, who are any of us, to judge him for it? Especially now, with Christmas at our heels. Who are we to judge?

When his tour of duty ended Clifford returned home, where, after making the second biggest mistake of his life (I am referring to his brief eight-month "marriage" to Doll Babcock), he and I were reunited. We lived, you might remember, in that tiny apartment over on Halsey Street. Clifford had just begun his satisfying career at Sampson Interlock and I was working part-time, accounting for Hershel Beck when . . . along came the children!!!!!! We struggled and saved and eventually (finally!!) bought our house on Tiffany Circle, number 714, where the Dunbar clan remains nested to this very day!!!!

It was here, 714 Tiffany Circle, where I first encountered Khe Sahn, who arrived at our door on (as fate would have it) Halloween!!!

I recall mistaking her for a Trick-or-Treater! She wore, I remember, a skirt the size of a beer cozy, a short, furry jacket, and, on her face, enough rough, eye shadow, and lipstick to paint our entire house, inside and out. She's a very small person and I mistook her for a child, a child masquerading as a prostitute. I handed her a fistful of chocolate nougats, hoping that, like the other children, she would quickly move on to the next house.

But Khe Sahn was no Trick-or-Treater.

I started to close the door but was interrupted by her interpreter, a very feminine-looking man carrying an attaché case. He introduced himself in English and then turned to Khe Sahn, speaking a language I have sadly come to recognize as Vietnamese. While our language flows from our mouths, the Vietnamese language sounds as though it is being forced from the speaker by a series of heavy and merciless blows to the stomach. The words themselves are the sounds of pain. Khe Sahn responded to the interpreter, her voice as high-pitched and relentless as a car alarm. The two of them stood on my doorstep, screeching away in Vietnamese while I stood by, frightened and confused.

I am still, to this day, frightened and confused. Very much so. It is frightening that, after all this time, a full-grown bastard (I use that word technically) can cross the seas and make herself comfortable in my home, all with the blessing of our government. Twenty-two years ago Uncle Sam couldn't stand the Vietnamese. Now he's dressing them like prostitutes and moving them into our houses!!!! Out of nowhere this young woman has entered our lives with the force and mystery of the Swine Flu and there appears to be nothing we can do about it. Out of nowhere this land mine knocks upon our door and we are expected to recognize her as our child!!!!????????

Clifford likes to say that the Dunbar children inherited their mother's looks and their father's brains. It's true: Kevin, Jackelyn, and Kyle are all just as good-looking as they can possibly be! And smart? Well, they're smart enough, smart like their father, with the exception of our oldest son, Kevin. After graduating Moody High with honors, Kevin is currently enrolled in his third year at Feeny State, majoring in chemical engineering. He's made the honor roll every semester and there seems to be no stopping him!!! A year and a half left to go and already the job offers are pouring in!

We love you, Kevin!!!!!!!!!!!!!!!!!!!

We sometimes like to joke that when God handed out brains to the Dunbar kids He saw Kevin standing first in line and awarded him the whole sack!!! What the other children lack in brains they seem to make up for in one way or another. They have qualities and personalities and make observations, unlike Khe Sahn, who seems to believe she can coast through life on her looks alone!! She hasn't got the ambition God gave a sparrow! She arrived in this house six weeks ago speaking only the words "Daddy," "Shiny," and "Five dollar now."

Quite a vocabulary!!!!!!!!!!

While an industrious person might buckle down and seriously study the language of her newly adopted country, Khe Sahn appeared to be in no hurry whatsoever. When asked a simple question such as, "Why don't you go back where you came from?" she would touch my hand and launch into a spasm of Vietnamese drivel—as if I were the outsider, expected to learn *her* language! We were visited several times by Lonnie Tipit, that "interpreter," that "man" who accompanied Khe Sahn on her first visit. Mr. Tipit seemed to feel that the Dunbar door was open for him anytime, day or night. He'd drop by (most often during the supper hours) and, between helpings of *my* home-cooked meals (thank you very much), "touch base" with his "friend," Khe Sahn. "I don't think she's getting enough exposure to the community," he would say. "Why don't you start taking her around town, to church get-togethers and local events?" Well, that was easy for *him* to say! I told him, I said, "*You* try taking a girl in a halter top to a confirmation class. *You* take her to the Autumn Craft Caravan and watch her snatch every shiny object that catches her eye. I've learned my lesson already." Then he and Khe Sahn would confer in Vietnamese and he would listen, his eyes fixed upon me as if I were a witch he had once read about in books but did not recognize without a smoldering kettle and a broom. Oh, I knew that look!

Lonnie Tipit went so far as to suggest that we hire him as Khe Sahn's English tutor at, get this, seventeen dollars an hour!!!!!!!!!!! Seventeen dollars an hour so she can learn to lisp and twitter and flutter her hands like two small birds? NO, THANK YOU!!!!!!! Oh, I saw right through Lonnie Tipit. While he pretended to care for Khe Sahn I understood that his true interest was in my son Kyle. "How's the schoolwork coming, Kyle? Working hard or hardly working?" and "Say, Kyle, what do you think about this new sister of yours? Is she the greatest or what?"

It wasn't difficult to see through Lonnie Tipit. He wanted one thing and one thing only. "If not me, then I can suggest another tutor," he said. Someone like who? Someone like him? Regardless of who the English teacher was, I am not in the habit of throwing my money away. And that, my friends, is what it would have amounted to. Why not hire an expensive private tutor to teach the squirrels to speak in French! It would be no more ridiculous than teaching Khe Sahn English. A person has to *want* to learn. I know that. Apparently, back in Ho Chi Minh City, Her Majesty was treated like a queen and sees no reason to change her ways!!!! Her Highness rises at around noon, wolfs down a fish or two (all she eats is fish and chicken breasts), and settles herself before the makeup mirror, waiting for her father to return home from work. At the sound of his car in the driveway she perks up and races to the door like a spaniel, panting and wagging her tail to beat the band! Suddenly she is eager to please and attempt conversation!! Well, I don't know how they behave in Vietnam, but in the United States it is not customary for a half-dressed daughter to offer her father a five-dollar massage!!! After having spent an exhausting day attempting to communicate a list of simple chores, I would stand in amazement at Khe Sahn's sudden grasp of English when faced with my husband.

"Daddy happy five dollar shiny now, OK?"

"You big feet friendly with ABC Khe Sahn. You Big Bird Daddy Grover."

Apparently she had picked up a few words while watching "Sesame Street."

"Daddy special special funky fresh jam party commercial free jam."

She began listening to the radio.

Khe Sahn treats our youngest son, Kyle, with complete indifference, which is probably a blessing in disguise. This entire episode has been very difficult for Kyle, who, at age fifteen, tends to be the artistic loner of the family. He keeps to himself, spending many hours in his bedroom, where he burns incense, listens to music, and carves gnomes out of soap. Kyle is very good-looking and talented and we are looking forward to the day when he sets aside his jackknife and bar of Irish Spring and begins "carving out" a future rather than a shriveled troll! He is at that very difficult age but we pray he will grow out of it and follow his brother's footsteps to success before it is too late. Hopefully, the disasters of his sister, Jackelyn, will open his eyes to the hazards of drugs, the calamity of a thoughtless, premature marriage, and the heartaches of parenthood!

We had, of course, warned our daughter against marrying Timothy Speaks. We warned, threatened, cautioned, advised, what have you—but it did no good as a young girl, with all the evidence before her, sees only what she *wants* to see. The marriage was bad enough but the news of her pregnancy struck her father and me with the force of a hurricane.

Timothy Speaks, the father of our grandchild? How could it be????

Timothy Speaks, who had so many pierced holes in his ears you could have torn the lobe right off, effortlessly ripped it loose the same way you might separate a stamp from a sheet.

Timothy Speaks, who had his back and neck tattooed with brilliant flames. His neck!!!

We told Jacki, "One of these days he's going to have to grow up and find a job, and when he does, those employers are going to wonder why he's wearing a turtleneck under his business suit. People with tattooed necks do not, as a rule, hold down high-paying jobs," we said.

She ran back to Timothy repeating our warning. . . . Lo and behold, two days later, *she* showed up with a tattooed neck as well!!!!! They even made plans to have their baby tattooed!!!! A tattoo, on an infant!!!!!!!!!!!

Timothy Speaks held our daughter in a web of madness that threatened to ensnare the entire Dunbar family. It was as if he held her under a perverse spell, convincing her, little by little, to destroy the lives of those around her.

The Jackelyn Dunbar-Speaks who lived with Timothy in that squalid "space" on West Vericose Avenue bore no resemblance to the beautiful girl pictured in our photo albums. The sensitive and considerate daughter we once knew became, under his fierce coaching, a mean-spirited, unreliable, and pregnant ghost who eventually gave birth to a ticking time bomb!!!!!

We, of course, saw it coming. The child, born September tenth under the influence of drugs, spent the first two months of his life in the critical care unit of St. Joe's Hospital. (At a whopping cost and guess who paid the bill for *that* one?) Faced with the concrete responsibility of fatherhood, Timothy Speaks abandoned his sick wife and child. Suddenly. Gone. Poof!

Surprised?

We saw it coming and are happy to report that, as of this writing, we have no idea where he is or what he is up to. (We could guess, but why bother.)

We have all read the studies and understand that a drug-addicted baby faces a difficult, uphill battle in terms of living a normal life. This child, having been given the legal name "Satan Speaks" would, we felt, have a harder time than most. We were lucky enough to get Jacki into a fine treatment center on the condition that the child remain here with us until which time (if ever) she is able to assume responsibility for him. The child arrived at our home on November tenth and shortly thereafter, following her initial withdrawal, Jacki granted us permission to address it as "Don." Don, a nice, simple name.

The name change enabled us to look upon the baby without having to consider the terrible specter of his father, Timothy Speaks. It made a difference, believe me.

While I could not describe him as being a "normal" baby, taking care of young Don gave me a great deal of pleasure. Terribly insistent, prone to hideous rashes, a twenty-four-hour round-the-clock screamer, he was our grandchild and we loved him. Knowing that he would physically grow to adulthood while maintaining the attention span of a common housefly did not, in the least bit, diminish our feelings for him.

Clifford would sometimes joke that Don was a "Crack Baby" because he woke us at the crack of dawn!

I would then take the opportunity to mention that Khe Sahn was something of a "Crack Baby" herself, wandering around our house all hours of the day and night wearing nothing but a pair of hot pants and a glorified sports bra. Most nights, the dinnertime napkin in her lap provided more coverage than she was accustomed to!!! Clifford suggested that I buy her a few decent dresses and a couple pairs of jeans and I tried, oh, how I tried! I sat with her, leafing through catalogs, and watched as she pawed the expensive designer outfits. I walked with her through Cut Throat's and Discount Plus and watched as she turned up her nose at their sensibly priced clothing. I don't know about you, but in *this* family the children are rewarded for hard work. Call me old-fashioned but if you want a fifty-dollar sweater you have to prove that you deserve it! If I've said it once I've said it a thousand times: "A family is not a charitable organization." Khe Sahn wanted something for nothing and I buttoned my purse and said the most difficult word a parent can say, "No!" I made her several outfits, sewed them with my own hands, two floor-length dresses, beautiful burlap dresses, but did she wear them? Of course not!!!

She continued in her usual fashion, trotting about the house in her underwear! When the winter winds began to blow she took to draping herself in a bed blanket, huddling beside the fireplace. While her "Poor Little Match Girl" routine might win a Tony Award on Broadway it did nothing for this ticket holder!

She carried on, following at Clifford's heels, until Thanksgiving Day, when she was introduced to our son Kevin, home for the holiday. One look at Kevin and it was "Clifford? Clifford who?" as far as Khe Sahn was concerned. One look at our handsome son and the "Shivering Victim" dropped her blanket and showed her true colors. It is a fact that she appeared at our Thanksgiving table wearing nothing but a string bikini!!!!!!!!!

"Not in *my* house," said yours truly! When I demanded she change into one of the dresses I had sewn for her, Khe Sahn frowned into her cranberry sauce, pretending not to understand. Clifford and Kevin tried to convince me that, in Vietnam, it is customary for the women to wear swimsuits on Thanksgiving Day but I still don't believe a word of it. Since when do the Vietnamese observe Thanksgiving? What do those people have to be thankful for.

She ruined our holiday dinner with her giggling, coy games. She sat beside Kevin until, insisting she had seen a spider in her chair, she moved into his lap!! "You new funky master jam party mix silly fresh spider five dollar Big Bird."

Those of you who know Kevin understand that, while he is an absolute whip at some things, he is terribly naive at others. Tall and good-looking, easy with a smile and a kind word, Kevin has been the target of many a huntress. He is both smart and foolish: it is his gift and his weakness, bound together, constantly struggling for control. He has always had more than his fair share of opportunists, both at Moody High and Feeny State. Always the gentleman, he treated the young ladies like glass, which, looking back, was appropriate because you could see through each and every one of them. When he asked to bring a date home for Thanksgiving I said I thought it was a bad idea as we were all under more than enough stress already. Looking back, I wish he *had* brought a date, as it might have dampened the sky-high hopes and aspirations of Khe Sahn, his half-sister!!!!!!!!!!

"Me no big big potato spoon fork tomorrow? Kevin have big big shiny face like hand of chicken soon with funky crazy Sesame Street jammy jam."

I could barely choke down my meal and found myself counting the minutes before Kevin, the greatest joy of our lives, called an end to the private English lesson he gave Khe Sahn in her bedroom, got into his car, and returned to Feeny State.

As I mentioned before, Kevin has always been a very caring person, always going out of his way to lend a hand or comfort a stranger. Being as that is his nature, he returned to school and, evidently, began phoning Khe Sahn, sometimes speaking with the aid of a Vietnamese student who acted as an interpreter. He was, in his own way, foolishly trying to make her feel welcome and adjust to life in her new, highly advanced country. He even went out of his way to drive all the way home in order to take her out and introduce her to the ways of nightlife in this, her adopted land. That is the Kevin we all know and love, always trying to help a person less intelligent than himself, bending over backwards to coax a smile!

Unfortunately, Khe Sahn misinterpreted his interest as a declaration of romantic concern. She took to "manning" the telephone twenty-four hours a day, hovering above it and regarding it as though it were a living creature. Whenever (God forbid!) someone called for Clifford, Kyle, or me, she would simply hang up!!!!

How's *that* for an answering service!!!!!!!!!!!!!!!

Eventually, recognizing that her behavior bordered on madness, I had a word with her.

"HE'S NOT FOR YOU," I yelled. (I have been criticized for yelling, told that it doesn't serve any real purpose when speaking to a foreigner, but at least it gets their attention!) "HE'S MY SON IN COLLEGE. MY SON ON THE DEAN'S LIST, NOT FOR YOU."

She was perched beside the telephone with a curling iron in her hand. At the sound of my voice she instinctively turned her attention elsewhere.

"BOTH MY SON AND MY HUSBAND ARE OFF-LIMITS AS FAR AS YOU'RE CONCERNED, DO YOU UNDERSTAND? THEY ARE EACH RELATED TO YOU IN ONE WAY OR ANOTHER AND THAT MAKES IT WRONG. AUTOMATICALLY WRONG. BAD, BAD, WRONG! WRONG AND BAD TOGETHER FOR THE KHE SAHN TO BE WITH JOCELYN'S SON OR HUSBAND. BAD AND WRONG. DO YOU UNDERSTAND WHAT I AM SAYING NOW?"

She looked up for a moment or two before returning her attention to the electrical cord.

I gave up. Trying to explain moral principles to Khe Sahn was like reviewing a standard 1040 tax form with a house cat! She understands only what she chooses to understand. Say the word "shopping" and, quicker than you can blink, she's sitting in the front seat of the car! Try a more complicated word such as "sweep" or "iron" and she shrugs her shoulders and retreats to the bedroom.

"VACUUM," I would say. "VACUUM THE CARPET."

In response she would jangle her bracelet or observe her fingernails.

In a desperate attempt to make myself understood I would pull out the vacuum cleaner and demonstrate.

"LOOK AT JOCELYN. JOCELYN VACUUMS THE CARPET. LA LA LA!! IT IS MUCH FUN TO VACUUM. IT IS AN ENJOYMENT AND A PLEA-SURE TO CLEAN MY HOME WITH A VACUUM. LA LA LA!!"

I tried to convey it as a rewarding exercise but, by the time I finally sparked her interest I was finished with the job.

As I said earlier, Khe Sahn understands only what she wants to understand. Looking back, I suppose I had no valid reason to trust her sudden willingness to lend a hand but, on the day in question, I was nearing the end of my rope.

We were approaching Christmas, December sixteenth, when I made the thoughtless mistake of asking her to watch the child while I ran some errands. With a needy, shriveled newborn baby, a teenaged son, and a twenty-two-year-old, half-dressed "step-daughter" in my house, my hands were full from one moment to the next, twenty-eight hours a day!!!! It was nine days before Christmas and, busy as I was, I hadn't bought a single gift. (Santa, where are you????????)

On that early afternoon Kyle was in school, Clifford was at the office, and Khe Sahn was seated beside the telephone, picking at a leftover baked fish with her bare hands.

"WATCH THE BABY," I said. "WATCH DON, THE BABY, WHILE I GO OUT."

She considered her greasy fingers.

"YOU WATCH BABY DON WHILE JOCELYN GOES SHOPPING FOR SPECIAL PRESENT FOR THE KHE SAHN!" I said. "HO, HO, HO, SPECIAL CHRISTMAS FOR THE KHE SAHN. HO, HO!"

At the mention of the word "shopping" she perked up and gave me her full attention. Having heard the radio and watched TV, she understood Christmas as an opportunity to receive gifts and was in the habit of poring over the mail-order catalogs and expressing her desires with the words "Ho, Ho, Ho."

I clearly remember my choice of words on that cold and cloudy December afternoon. I did not say "baby-sit," fearing that she might take me at my word and literally sit upon the baby.

"WATCH THE BABY," I said to that twenty-two-year-old adult on the afternoon of December sixteenth.

"WATCH THE BABY," I said as we climbed the stairs toward the bedroom that she and Don shared. Khe Sahn had been sleeping in Kevin's vacant bedroom until, following her Thanksgiving high jinks, I decided to move her into the nursery with Don.

"WATCH THE BABY," I repeated as we stood over the crib and observed the wailing infant. I picked him up and rocked him gently as he struggled in my arms. "WATCH BABY."

"Watch Baby," Khe Sahn responded, holding out her arms to accept him. "Watch Baby for Jocelyn get shop special HO, HO, HO, Khe Sahn fresh shiny."

"Exactly," I said, laying a hand on her shoulder.

How foolish I was to have honestly believed that she was finally catching on! I was, at that moment in time, convinced of her sincerity. I was big enough to set aside all of the trouble she had visited upon our household and give her another chance! "That is all behind us now," I said to myself, watching her cradle the wailing child.

Oh, what a fool I was!!!!!!!!!!!!!

Leaving the house and driving toward White Paw Center I felt a sense of relief I had not known in quite a while. This was the first time in weeks I had allowed myself a moment alone and, with six Dunbar wish lists burning a hole in my pocket, I intended to make the most of it!!!

I can't account for every moment of my afternoon. Never did it occur to me that I would one day be called upon to do so but, that being the case, I will report what I remember. I can comfortably testify that, on the afternoon of December sixteenth, I visited the White Paw Shopping Center, where I spent a brief amount of time in The Slack Heap, searching for a gift for Kyle. I found what he wanted but not in his size. I then left The Slack Heap and walked over to—&—, where I bought a—for my daughter Jacki. (I'm not going to ruin anyone's Christmas surprises here. Why should I?) I stuck my head inside Turtleneck Crossing and searched for candles at Wax and Wane. I bought a gift for Clifford at—, and I suppose I browsed. There are close to a hundred shops at the White Paw Center and you'll have to forgive me if I can't provide a detailed list of how long I spent in this or that store. I shopped until I grew wary of the time. On the way home I stopped at The Food Carnival and bought a few items. It was getting dark, perhaps four-thirty, when I pulled into the driveway of our home on Tiffany Circle. I collected my packages from the car and entered my home, where I was immediately struck by the eerie silence. "This doesn't feel right to me," I remember saying to myself. It was an intuition, a mother's intuition, that unexplainable language of the senses. I laid down my bags and was startled by the sound they made—the crisp noise of paper bags settling against the floor. The problem was that I could hear the sound at all! Normally I would have heard nothing over the chronic bleating of Baby Don and the incessant blaring radio of Khe Sahn.

"Something is wrong," I said to myself. "Something is terribly, terribly wrong."

Before calling out for Khe Sahn or checking on the baby I instinctively phoned the police. I then stood there, stock-still in the living room, staring at my shopping bags until they arrived (twenty-seven minutes later!!).

At the sound of the squad car in the driveway, Khe Sahn made an entrance, parading down the stairs in a black lace half-slip and a choker made from the cuff of Kevin's old choir robe.

"WHERE IS THE BABY?" I asked her. "WHERE IS DON?"

Accompanied by the police we went upstairs into the nursery and stood beside the empty crib.

"WHERE IS MY GRANDCHILD, DON? WHAT HAVE YOU DONE TO THE BABY?"

Khe Sahn, of course, said nothing. It is part of her act to tug at her hemline and feign shyness when first confronted by strangers. We left her standing there while the police and I began our search. We combed the entire house, the officers and I, before finally finding the helpless baby in the laundry room, warm but lifeless in the dryer.

The autopsy later revealed that Don had also been subjected to a wash cycle—hot wash, cold rinse. He died long before the spin cycle, which is, I suppose, the only blessing to be had in this entire ugly episode. I am still, to this day, haunted by the mental picture of my grandchild undergoing such brutality. The relentless pounding he received during his forty-five minutes in the dryer is something I would rather not think about. The thought of it visits me like a nightmare! It comes repeatedly to my mind and I put my hands to my head, desperately trying to drive it away. One wishes for an only grandchild to run and play, to graduate from college, to marry and succeed, not to . . . (see, I can't even say it!!!!!!).

The shock and horror that followed Don's death are something I would rather not recount: Calling our children to report the news, watching the baby's body, small as a loaf of bread, as it was zipped into a heavy plastic bag—these images have nothing to do with the merriment of Christmas, and I hope my mention of them will not dampen your spirits at this, the most special and glittering time of the year.

The evening of December sixteenth was a very dark hour for the Dunbar family. At least with Khe Sahn in police custody we could grieve privately, consoling ourselves with the belief that justice had been carried out.

How foolish we were!!!!!!!!!!!!

The bitter tears were still wet upon our faces when the police returned to Tiffany Circle, where they began their ruthless questioning of Yours Truly!!!!!!!!!!!!! Through the aid of an interpreter, Khe Sahn had spent a sleepless night at police headquarters, constructing a story of unspeakable lies and betrayal! While I am not at liberty to discuss her exact testimony, allow me to voice my disappointment that anyone (let alone the police!) would even *think* of taking Khe Sahn's word over my own. How could I have placed a helpless child in the washing machine? Even if I were cruel enough to do such a thing, when would I have found the time? I was out shopping.

You may have read that our so-called "neighbor" Cherise Clarmont-Shea reported that she witnessed me leaving my home at around one-fifteen on the afternoon of December sixteenth and then, twenty minutes later, allegedly park my car on the far corner of Tiffany and Papageorge and, in her words, "creep" through her backyard and in through my basement door!!!!!! Cherise Clarmont-Shea certainly understands the meaning of the word *creep*, doesn't she? She's been married to one for so long that she has turned into something of a creep herself!! How many times have I opened the door to Cherise, her face swollen and mustard-colored, suffering another of her husband's violent slugfests! She's been smacked in the face so many times she's lucky if she can see anything through those swollen eyes of hers! If the makeup she applies is any indication of her vision, then I believe it is safe to say she can't see two inches in front of her, much less testify to the identity of someone she might think she's seen crossing her yard. She's on pills, everyone knows that. She's desperate for attention and I might pity her under different circumstances. I did not return home early and creep through the Shea's unkept backyard, but even if I had, what possible motive would I have had? Why would I, as certain people have been suggesting, want to murder my own grandchild? This is madness, pure and simple. It reminds me of a recurring nightmare I often have wherein I am desperately trying to defend myself against a heavily armed hand puppet. The grotesque puppet angrily accuses me of spray-painting slogans on his car. I have, of course, done no such thing. "This is insane, preposterous," I think to myself. "This makes no sense," I say, all the while eyeing the loaded weapon in his small hands and praying for this nightmare to end. Cherise Clarmont-Shea has no more sense than a hand puppet. She has three names! And the others who have made statements against me, Chaz Staples and Vivian Taps, they were both at home during a weekday afternoon doing guess what while their spouses were hard at work. What are *they* hiding? I feel it is of utmost importance to consider the source.

These charges are ridiculous, yet I must take them seriously as my very life may be at stake! Listening to a taped translation of Khe Sahn's police statement, the Dunbar family has come to fully understand the meaning of the words "controlling," "vindictive," "manipulative," "greedy," and, in a spiritual sense, "ugly."

Not exactly the words one wishes to toss about during the Christmas season!!!!!!!!

A hearing has been set for December twenty-seventh and, knowing how disappointed you, our friends, might feel at being left out, I have included the time and address at the bottom of this letter. The hearing is an opportunity during which you might convey your belated Christmas spirit through deed and action. Given the opportunity to defend *your* character I would not hesitate and I know you must feel the exact same way toward me. That heartfelt concern, that desire to stand by your friends and family, is the very foundation upon which we celebrate the Christmas season, isn't it?

While this year's Dunbar Christmas will be seasoned with loss and sadness, we plan to proceed, as best we can, toward that day of days, December twenty-seventh—1:45 P.M. at The White Paw County Courthouse, room 412.

I will be calling to remind you of that information and look forward to discussing the festive bounty of your holiday season.

Until that time we wish the best to you and yours.

Merry Christmas,

The Dunbars

OTHELLO THE MOOR OF VENICE (1604)

William Shakespeare
b. 1564 Stratford-upon-Avon, England
d. 1616 Stratford-upon-Avon, England

THE NAMES OF THE ACTORS

Othello, the Moor
Brabantio, [a Venetian senator,] father to Desdemona
Cassio, an honorable lieutenant [to Othello]
Iago, [Othello's ancient,] a villain
Roderigo, a gulled gentleman
Duke of Venice
Senators [of Venice]
Montano, governor of Cyprus
Lodovico and Gratiano, [kinsmen to Brabantio,] two noble Venetians
Sailors
Clowns
Desdemona, wife to Othello
Emilia, wife to Iago
Bianca, a courtesan
[Messenger, Herald, Officers, Venetian Gentlemen, Musicians, Attendants

SCENE: *Venice and Cyprus]*

ACT I

SCENE I: *A street in Venice.*

> *Enter Roderigo and Iago.*
> *Roderigo:* Tush, never tell me! I take it much unkindly
> That thou, Iago, who hast had my purse

As if the strings were thine, shouldst know of this
Iago: 'Sblood, but you'll not hear me!
5   If ever I did dream of such a matter,
Abhor me.
Roderigo: Thou told'st me thou didst hold him in thy hate.
Iago: Despise me if I do not. Three great ones of the city,
In personal suit to make me his lieutenant,
10   Off-capped to him; and, by the faith of man,
I know my price; I am worth no worse a place.
But he, as loving his own pride and purposes,
Evades them with a bombast circumstance.
Horribly stuffed with epithets of war;
15   [And, in conclusion,]
Nonsuits my mediators; for, "Certes," says he,
"I have already chose my officer."
And what was he?
Forsooth, a great arithmetician,
20   One Michael Cassio, a Florentine
(A fellow almost damned in a fair wife)
That never set a squadron in the field,
Nor the division of a battle knows
More than a spinster; unless the bookish theoric,
25   Wherein the togèd consuls can propose
As masterly as he. Mere prattle without practice
Is all his soldiership. But he, sir, had th' election;
And I (of whom his eyes had seen the proof
At Rhodes, at Cyprus, and on other grounds
30   Christian and heathen) must be belee'd and calmed
By debitor and creditor; this counter-caster,
He, in good time, must his lieutenant be,
And I—God bless the mark!—his Moorship's ancient.
Roderigo: By heaven, I rather would have been his hangman.
35   *Iago:* Why, there's no remedy; 'tis the curse of service.
Preferment goes by letter and affection,
And not by old gradation, where each second
Stood heir to th' first. Now, sir, be judge yourself,
Whether I in any just term am affined
To love the Moor.
40   *Roderigo:* I would not follow him then.
Iago: O, sir, content you;
I follow him to serve my turn upon him.
We cannot all be masters, nor all masters
Cannot be truly followed. You shall mark
45   Many a duteous and knee-crooking knave
That, doting on his own obsequious bondage,
Wears out his time, much like his master's ass,

For naught but provender; and when he's old, cashiered.
Whip me such honest knaves! Others there are
50   Who, trimmed in forms and visages of duty,
Keep yet their hearts attending on themselves;
And, throwing but shows of service on their lords,
Do well thrive by them, and when they have lined their coats,
Do themselves homage. These fellows have some soul;
55   And such a one do I profess myself. For, sir,
It is as sure as you are Roderigo,
Were I the Moor, I would not be Iago.
In following him, I follow but myself;
Heaven is my judge, not I for love and duty,
60   But seeming so, for my peculiar end;
For when my outward action doth demonstrate
The native act and figure of my heart
In compliment extern, 'tis not long after
But I will wear my heart upon my sleeve
65   For daws to peck at; I am not what I am.
Roderigo: What a full fortune does the thick-lips owe
If he can carry't thus!
Iago: Call up her father,
Rouse him. Make after him, poison his delight,
Proclaim him in the streets. Incense her kinsmen,
70   And though he in a fertile climate dwell,
Plague him with flies; though that his joy be joy,
Yet throw such changes of vexation on't
As it may lose some color.
Roderigo: Here is her father's house. I'll call aloud.
75 *Iago:*   Do, with like timorous accent and dire yell
As when, by night and negligence, the fire
Is spied in populous cities.
Roderigo: What, ho, Brabantio! Signior Brabantio, ho!
Iago: Awake! What, ho, Brabantio! Thieves! thieves! thieves!
80   Look to your house, your daughter, and your bags!
Thieves! thieves!
Brabantio at a window.
Brabantio (above):   What is the reason of this terrible summons?
What is the matter there?
Roderigo: Signior, is all your family within?
Iago: Are your doors locked?
85 *Brabantio:*   Why, wherefore ask you this?
Iago: Zounds, sir, y' are robbed! For shame, put on your gown!
Your heart is burst; you have lost half your soul.
Even now, now, very now, an old black ram
Is tupping your white ewe. Arise, arise!
90   Awake the snorting citizens with the bell.

Or else the devil will make a grandsire of you.
Arise, I say!

Brabantio: What, have you lost your wits?

Roderigo: Most reverend signior, do you know my voice?

95   *Brabantio:*   Not I. What are you?

Roderigo: My name is Roderigo.

Brabantio: The worser welcome!
I have charged thee not to haunt about my doors.
In honest plainness thou hast heard me say
My daughter is not for thee; and now, in madness,

100   Being full of supper and distemp'ring draughts,
Upon malicious knavery dost thou come
To start my quiet.

Roderigo: Sir, sir, sir—

Brabantio: But thou must needs be sure

105   My spirit and my place have in them power
To make this bitter to thee.

Roderigo: Patience, good sir.

Brabantio: What tell'st thou me of robbing? This is Venice;
My house is not a grange.

Roderigo: Most grave Brabantio,
In simple and pure soul I come to you.

110   *Iago:*   Zounds, sir, you are one of those that will not serve God if the devil bid
you. Because we come to do you service, and you think we are ruffians, you'll
have your daughter covered with a Barbary horse; you'll have your nephews
neigh to you; you'll have coursers for cousins, and gennets for germans.

115   *Brabantio:*   What profane wretch art thou?

Iago: I am one, sir, that comes to tell you your daughter and the Moor are
now making the beast with two backs.

Brabantio: Thou are a villain.

Iago: You are—a senator.

Brabantio: This thou shalt answer. I know thee, Roderigo.

120   *Roderigo:*   Sir, I will answer anything. But I beseech you,
If't be your pleasure and most wise consent,
As partly I find it is, that your fair daughter,
At this odd-even and dull watch o' th' night,
Transported, with no worse nor better guard

125   But with a knave of common hire, a gondolier,
To the gross clasps of a lascivious Moor—
If this be known to you, and your allowance,
We then have done you bold and saucy wrongs;
But if you know not this, my manners tell me

130   We have your wrong rebuke. Do not believe
That, from the sense of all civility,
I thus would play and trifle with your reverence.
Your daughter, if you have not given her leave,

I say again, hath made a gross revolt,
135   Tying her duty, beauty, wit, and fortunes
       In an extravagant and wheeling stranger
       Of here and everywhere. Straight satisfy yourself.
       If she be in her chamber, or your house,
       Let loose on me the justice of the state
       For thus deluding you.
140 *Brabantio:*   Strike on the tinder, ho!
       Give me a taper! Call up all my people!
       This accident is not unlike my dream.
       Belief of it oppresses me already.
       Light, I say! light!   *Exit [above].*
     Iago: Farewell, for I must leave you.
145   It seems not meet, nor wholesome to my place,
       To be produced—as, if I stay, I shall—
       Against the Moor. For I do know the state,
       However this may gall him with some check,
       Cannot with safety cast him; for he's embarked
150   With such loud reason to the Cyprus wars,
       Which even now stand in act, that for their souls
       Another of his fathom they have none
       To lead their business; in which regard,
       Though I do hate him as I do hell-pains,
       Yet, for necessity of present life,
155   I must show out a flag and sign of love,
       Which is indeed but sign. That you shall surely find him,
       Lead to the Sagittary the raised search;
       And there will I be with him. So farewell.   *Exit.*
       Enter [below] Brabantio in his nightgown, and Servants with torches.
160 *Brabantio:*   It is too true an evil. Gone she is;
       And what's to come of my despisèd time
       Is naught but bitterness. Now, Roderigo,
       Where didst thou see her?—O unhappy girl!—
       With the Moor, say'st thou?—Who would be a father?—
       How didst thou know 'twas she! — O, she deceives me
       Past thought!—What said she to you?—Get moe tapers!
       Raise all my kindred!—Are they married, think you?
     Roderigo: Truly I think they are.
     Brabantio: O heaven! How got she out? O treason of the blood!
170   Fathers, from hence trust not your daughters' minds
       By what you see them act. Is there not charms
       By which the property of youth and maidhood
       May be abused? Have you not read, Roderigo,
       Of some such thing?
     Roderigo: Yes, sir, I have indeed.
175 *Brabantio:*   Call up my brother.—O, would you had had her!—

Some one way, some another.—Do you know
Where we may apprehend her and the Moor?
Roderigo: I think I can discover him, if you please
To get good guard and go along with me.
180   *Brabantio:*   I pray you lead on. At every house I'll call;
I may command at most.—Get weapons, ho!
And raise some special officers of night.—
On, good Roderigo; I'll deserve your pains.   *Exeunt.*

Scene II: *Before the lodgings of Othello.*

Enter Othello, Iago, and Attendants with torches.
Iago: Though in the trade of war I have slain men,
Yet do I hold it very stuff o' th' conscience
To do no contrived murther. I lack iniquity
Sometimes to do me service. Nine or ten times
5   I had thought t' have yerked him here under the ribs.
Othello: 'Tis better as it is.
Iago: Nay, but he prated,
And spoke such scurvy and provoking terms
Against your honor
That with the little godliness I have
10   I did full hard forbear him. But I pray you, sir,
Are you fast married? Be assured of this,
That the magnifico is much beloved,
And hath in his effect a voice potential
As double as the Duke's. He will divorce you,
15   Or put upon you what restraint and grievance
The law, with all his might to enforce it on,
Will give him cable.
Othello: Let him do his spite.
My services which I have done the signiory
Shall out-tongue his complaints. 'Tis yet to know—
20   Which, when I know that boasting is an honor,
I shall promulgate—I fetch my life and being
From men of royal siege; and my demerits
May speak unbonneted to as proud a fortune
25   As this that I have reached. For know, Iago,
But that I love the gentle Desdemona,
I would not my unhoused free condition
Put into circumscription and confine
For the sea's worth. But look what lights come yond?
Iago: Those are the raisèd father and his friends.
You were best go in.
30   *Othello:*   Not I; I must be found.
My parts, my title, and my perfect soul

Shall manifest me rightly. Is it they?

Iago: By Janus, I think no.

Enter Cassio, with torches, Officers.

Othello: The servants of the Duke, and my lieutenant.

35   The goodness of the night upon you, friends!
   What is the news?

Cassio: The Duke does greet you, general;
   And he requires your haste-post-haste appearance
   Even on the instant.

Othello: What's the matter, think you?

Cassio: Something from Cyprus, as I may divine.

40   It is a business of some heat. The galleys
   Have sent a dozen sequent messengers
   This very night at one another's heels,
   And many of the consuls, raised and met,
   Are at the Duke's already. You have been hotly called for;

45   When, being not at your lodging to be found,
   The Senate hath sent about three several quests
   To search you out.

Othello: 'Tis well I am found by you.
   I will but spend a word here in the house,
   And go with you.   *[Exit]*

Cassio: Ancient, what makes he here?

50   *Iago:*   Faith, he to-night hath boarded a land carack.
   If it prove lawful prize, he's made for ever.

Cassio: I do not understand.

Iago: He's married.

Cassio: To who?

   [Enter Othello.]

Iago: Marry, to—Come, captain, will you go?

Othello: Have with you.

Cassio: Here comes another troop to seek for you.

   Enter Brabantio, Roderigo, and others with lights and weapons.

55   *Iago:*   It is Brabantio. General, be advised.
   He comes to bad intent.

Othello: Holla! stand there!

Roderigo: Signior, it is the Moor.

Brabantio: Down with him, thief!

   [They draw on both sides.]

Iago: You, Roderigo! Come, sir, I am for you.

Othello: Keep up your bright swords, for the dew will rust them.

60   Good signior, you shall more command with years
   Than with your weapons.

Brabantio: O thou foul thief, where hast thou stowed my daughter?
   Damned as thou art, thou hast enchanted her!
   For I'll refer me to all things of sense,

65 If she in chains of magic were not bound,
 Whether a maid so tender, fair, and happy,
 So opposite to marriage that she shunned.
 The wealthy curlèd darlings of our nation,
 Would ever have, t'incur a general mock,
70 Run from her guardage to the sooty bosom
 Of such a thing as thou—to fear, not to delight.
 Judge me the world if 'tis not gross in sense
 That thou hast practiced on her with foul charms,
 Abused her delicate youth with drugs or minerals
75 That weaken motion. I'll have't disputed on;
 'Tis probable, and palpable to thinking.
 I therefore apprehend and do attach thee
 For an abuser of the world, a practicer
 Of arts inhibited and out of warrant.
80 Lay hold upon him. If he do resist,
 Subdue him at his peril.
Othello: Hold your hands,
 Both you of my inclining and the rest.
 Were it my cue to fight, I should have known it
 Without a prompter. Where will you that I go
 To answer this your charge?
85 *Brabantio:* To prison, till fit time
 Of law and course of direct session
 Call thee to answer.
Othello: What if I do obey?
 How may the Duke be therewith satisfied,
 Whose messengers are here about my side
90 Upon some present business of the state
 To bring me to him?
Officer: 'Tis true, most worthy signior.
 The Duke's in council, and your noble self
 I am sure is sent for.
Brabantio: How? The Duke in council?
 In this time of the night? Bring him away.
95 Mine's not an idle cause. The Duke himself,
 Or any of my brothers of the state,
 Cannot but feel this wrong as 'twere their own;
 For if such actions may have passage free,
 Bondslaves and pagans shall our statesmen be.   *Exeunt.*

SCENE III: *The Venetian Senate Chamber.*

Enter Duke and Senators, set at a table, with lights and Attendants.
Duke: There is no composition in these news
 That gives them credit.

1. Senator: Indeed they are disproportioned.
     My letters say a hundred and seven galleys.
Duke: And mine a hundred forty.
2. Senator: And mine two hundred.
5   But though they jump not on a just account—
     As in these cases where the aim reports
     'Tis oft with difference—yet do they all confirm
     A Turkish fleet, and bearing up to Cyprus.
Duke: Nay, it is possible enough to judgment.
     I do not so secure me in the error
10   But the main article I do approve
     In fearful sense.
Sailor (within):   What, ho! what, ho! what, ho!
Officer: A messenger from the galleys.
     Enter Sailor.
Duke: Now, what's the business?
15 *Sailor:*   The Turkish preparation makes for Rhodes.
     So was I bid report here to the state
     By Signior Angelo.
Duke: How say you by this change?
1. Senator: This cannot be
     By no assay of reason. 'Tis a pageant
     To keep us in false gaze. When we consider
20   Th' importancy of Cyprus to the Turk,
     And let ourselves again but understand
     That, as it more concerns the Turk than Rhodes,
     So may he with more facile question bear it,
     For that it stands not in such warlike brace,
25   But altogether lacks th' abilities
     That Rhodes is dressed in—if we make thought of this,
     We must not think the Turk is so unskillful
     To leave that latest which concerns him first,
     Neglecting an attempt of ease and gain
30   To wake and wage a danger profitless.
Duke: Nay, in all confidence, he's not for Rhodes.
Officer: Here is more news.
     Enter a Messenger.
Messenger: The Ottomites, reverend and gracious,
     Steering with due course toward the isle of Rhodes,
35   Have there injointed them with an after fleet.
1. Senator: Ay, so I thought. How many, as you guess?
Messenger: Of thirty sail; and now they do restem
     Their backward course, bearing with frank appearance
     Their purposes toward Cyprus, Signior Montano,
40   Your trusty and most valiant servitor,
     With his free duty recommends you thus,

And prays you to believe him.

Duke: 'Tis certain then for Cyprus.

Marcus Luccicos, is not he in town?

1. Senator: He's now in Florence.

45 *Duke:* Write from us to him; post, post-haste dispatch.

1. Senator: Here comes Brabantio and the valiant Moor.

Enter Brabantio, Othello, Cassio, Iago, Roderigo, and Officers.

Duke: Valiant Othello, we must straight employ you

Against the general enemy Ottoman.   *[To Brabantio.]*

50 I did not see you. Welcome, gentle signior.

We lacked your counsel and your help to-night.

Brabantio: So did I yours. Good your grace, pardon me.

Neither my place, nor aught I heard of business,

Hath raised me from my bed; nor doth the general care

55 Take hold on me; for my particular grief

Is of so floodgate and o'erbearing nature

That it engluts and swallows other sorrows,

And it is still itself.

Duke: Why, what's the matter?

Brabantio: My daughter! O, my daughter!

All: Dead?

Brabantio: Ay, to me.

60 She is abused, stol'n from me, and corrupted

By spells and medicines bought of mountebanks;

For nature so prepost'rously to err,

Being not deficient, blind, or lame of sense,

Sans witchcraft could not.

65 *Duke:* Whoe'er he be that in this foul proceeding

Hath thus beguiled your daughter of herself,

And you of her, the bloody book of law

You shall yourself read in the bitter letter

After your own sense; yea, though our proper son

70 Stood in your action.

Brabantio: Humbly I thank your grace.

Here is the man—this Moor, whom now, it seems,

Your special mandate for the state affairs

Hath hither brought.

All: We are very sorry for't.

Duke [to Othello]: What, in your own part, can you say to this?

75 *Brabantio:* Nothing, but this is so.

Othello: Most potent, grave, and reverend signiors;

My very noble, and approved good masters,

That I have ta'en away this old man's daughter,

It is most true; true I have married her.

80 The very head and front of my offending

Hath this extent, no more. Rude am I in my speech,

And little blessed with the soft phrase of peace;
For since these arms of mine had seven years' pith
Till now some nine moons wasted, they have used
85 Their dearest action in the tented field;
And little of this great world can I speak
More than pertains to feats of broil and battle;
And therefore little shall I grace my cause
In speaking for myself. Yet, by your gracious patience,
90 I will a round unvarnished tale deliver
Of my whole course of love—what drugs, what charms,
What conjuration, and what mighty magic
(For such proceeding am I charged withal)
I won his daughter.
Brabantio: A maiden never bold;
95 Of spirit so still and quiet that her motion
Blushed at herself; and she—in spite of nature,
Of years, of country, credit, everything—
To fall in love with what she feared to look on!
It is a judgment maimed and most imperfect
100 That will confess perfection so could err
Against all rules of nature, and must be driven
To find out practices of cunning hell
Why this should be. I therefore vouch again
That with some mixtures pow'rful o'er the blood,
105 Or with some dram, conjured to this effect,
He wrought upon her.
Duke: To vouch this is no proof,
Without more certain and more overt test
Than these thin habits and poor likelihoods
Of modern seeming do prefer against him.
110 *I. Senator:*   But, Othello, speak.
Did you by indirect and forcèd courses
Subdue and poison this young maid's affections?
Or came it by request, and such fair question
As soul to soul affordeth?
Othello: I do beseech you,
115 Send for the lady to the Sagittary
And let her speak of me before her father.
If you do find me foul in her report,
The trust, the office, I do hold of you
Not only take away, but let your sentence
Even fall upon my life.
120 *Duke:*   Fetch Desdemona hither.
Othello: Ancient, conduct them; you best know the place.
Exit [Iago, with] two or three [Attendants].
And till she come, as truly as to heaven

I do confess the vices of my blood,
125 So justly to your grave ears I'll present
How I did thrive in this fair lady's love,
And she in mine.
Duke: Say it, Othello.
Othello: Her father loved me, oft invited me;
Still questioned me the story of my life
130 From year to year—the battles, sieges, fortunes
That I have passed.
I ran it through, even from my boyish days
To th' very moment that he bade me tell it.
Wherein I spoke of most disastrous chances,
135 Of moving accidents by flood and field;
Of hairbreadth scapes i' th' imminent deadly breach;
Of being taken by the insolent foe
And sold to slavery; of my redemption thence
And portance in my travels' history;
140 Wherein of anters vast and deserts idle,
Rough quarries, rocks, and hills whose heads touch heaven,
It was my hint to speak—such was the process;
And of the Cannibals that each other eat,
The Anthropophagi, and men whose heads
145 Do grow beneath their shoulders. This to hear
Would Desdemona seriously incline;
But still the house affairs would draw her thence;
Which ever as she could with haste dispatch,
She'ld come again, and with a greedy ear.
150 Devour up my discourse. Which I observing,
Took once a pliant hour, and found good means
To draw from her a prayer of earnest heart
That I would all my pilgrimage dilate,
Whereof by parcels she had something heard,
155 But not intentively. I did consent,
And often did beguile her of her tears
When I did speak of some distressful stroke
That my youth suffered. My story being done,
She gave me for my pains a world of sighs.
160 She swore, i' faith, 'twas strange, 'twas passing strange;
'Twas pitiful, 'twas wondrous pitiful.
She wished she had not heard it; yet she wished
That heaven had made her such a man. She thanked me;
And bade me, if I had a friend that loved her,
165 I should but teach him how to tell my story,
And that would woo her. Upon this hint I spake.
She loved me for the dangers I had passed,
And I loved her that she did pity them.

This only is the witchcraft I have used.
170   Here comes the lady. Let her witness it.
          Enter Desdemona, Iago, Attendants.
     Duke: I think this tale would win my daughter too.
          Good Brabantio,
          Take up this mangled matter at the best.
          Men do their broken weapons rather use
          Than their bare hands.
175 *Brabantio:*   I pray you hear her speak.
          If she confess that she was half the wooer,
          Destruction on my head if my bad blame
          Light on the man! Come hither, gentle mistress.
          Do you perceive in all this noble company
          Where most you owe obedience?
180 *Desdemona:*   My noble father,
          I do perceive here a divided duty.
          To you I am bound for life and education;
          My life and education both do learn me
          How to respect you: you are the lord of duty;
185   I am hitherto your daughter. But here's my husband;
          And so much duty as my mother showed
          To you, preferring you before her father,
          So much I challenge that I may profess
          Due to the Moor my lord.
     Brabantio: God be with you! I have done.
190   Please it your grace, on to the state affairs.
          I had rather to adopt a child than get it.
          Come hither, Moor.
          I here do give thee that with all my heart
          Which, but thou hast already, with all my heart
195   I would keep from thee. For your sake, jewel,
          I am glad at soul I have no other child;
          For thy escape would teach me tyranny,
          To hang clogs on them. I have done, my lord.
     Duke: Let me speak like yourself and lay a sentence
200   Which, as a grise or step, may help these lovers
          [Into your favor.]
          When remedies are past, the griefs are ended
          By seeing the worst, which late on hopes depended.
          To mourn a mischief that is past and gone
205   Is the next way to draw new mischief on.
          What cannot be preserved when fortune takes,
          Patience her injury a mock'ry makes.
          The robbed that smiles steals something from the thief;
          He robs himself that spends a bootless grief.
210 *Brabantio:*   So let the Turk of Cyprus us beguile:

We lose it not so long as we can smile.
He bears the sentence well that nothing bears
But the free comfort which from thence he hears;
But he bears both the sentence and the sorrow
215   That to pay grief must of poor patience borrow.
These sentences, to sugar, or to gall,
Being strong on both sides, are equivocal.
But words are words. I never yet did hear
That the bruisèd heart was piercèd through the ear.
220   Beseech you, now to the affairs of state.

Duke: The Turk with a most mighty preparation makes for Cyprus. Othello, the fortitude of the place is best known to you; and though we have there a substitute of most allowed sufficiency, yet opinion, a more sovereign mistress of effects, throws a more safer voice on you. You must therefore be
225   content to slubber the gloss of your new fortunes with this more stubborn and boist'rous expedition.

Othello: The tyrant custom, most grave senators,
Hath made the flinty and steel couch of war
My thrice-driven bed of down. I do agnize
230   A natural and prompt alacrity
I find in hardness; and do undertake
These present wars against the Ottomites.
Most humbly, therefore, bending to your state,
I crave fit disposition for my wife,
235   Due reference of place, and exhibition,
With such accommodation and besort
As levels with her breeding.

Duke: If you please,
Be't at her father's.

Brabantio: I will not have it so.

Othello: Nor I.

240 *Desdemona:* Nor I. I would not there reside,
To put my father in impatient thoughts
By being in his eye. Most gracious Duke,
To my unfolding lend your prosperous ear,
And let me find a charter in your voice,
245   T' assist my simpleness.

Duke: What would you, Desdemona?

Desdemona: That I did love the Moor to live with him,
My downright violence, and storm of fortunes,
May trumpet to the world. My heart's subdued
250   Even to the very quality of my lord.
I saw Othello's visage in his mind,
And to his honors and his valiant parts
Did I my soul and fortunes consecrate.
So that, dear lords, if I be left behind,

255   A moth of peace, and he go to the war,
      The rites for which I love him are bereft me,
      And I a heavy interim shall support
      By his dear absence. Let me go with him.
Othello: Let her have your voice.
260   Vouch with me, heaven, I therefore beg it not
      To please the palate of my appetite,
      Not to comply with heat—the young affects.
      In me defunct—and proper satisfaction;
      But to be free and bounteous to her mind;
265   And heaven defend your good souls that you think
      I will your serious and great business scant
      When she is with me. No, when light-winged toys
      Of feathered Cupid seel with wanton dullness
      My speculative and officed instruments,
270   That my disports corrupt and taint my business,
      Let housewives make a skillet of my helm,
      And all indign and base adversities
      Make head against my estimation!
Duke: Be it as you shall privately determine,
275   Either for her stay or going. Th' affair cries haste,
      And speed must answer it.
I. Senator: You must away to-night.
Othello: With all my heart.
Duke: At nine i' th' morning here we'll meet again.
      Othello, leave some officer behind,
280   And he shall our commission bring to you,
      With such things else of quality and respect
      As doth import you.
Othello: So please your grace, my ancient;
      A man he is of honesty and trust
      To his conveyance I assign my wife,
285   With what else needful your good grace shall think
      To be sent after me.
Duke: Let it be so.
      Good night to every one.
      [To Brabantio.] And, noble signior,
      If virtue no delighted beauty lack,
      Your son-in-law is far more fair than black.
290   *I. Senator:*   Adieu, brave Moor. Use Desdemona well.
Brabantio: Look to her, Moor, if thou hast eyes to see:
      She has deceived her father, and may thee.
                    Exeunt [Duke, Senators, Officers, etc.].
Othello: My life upon her faith!—Honest Iago,
      My Desdemona must I leave to thee.
295   I prithee let thy wife attend on her,

And bring them after in the best advantage.
Come, Desdemona. I have but an hour
Of love, of worldly matters and direction,
To spend with thee. We must obey the time.

Exit Moor and Desdemona.

300   *Roderigo:*   Iago,—

Iago: What say'st thou, noble heart?

Roderigo: What will I do, think'st thou?

Iago: Why, go to bed and sleep.

Roderigo: I will incontinently drown myself.

305   *Iago:*   If thou dost, I shall never love thee after. Why, thou silly gentleman!

Roderigo: It is silliness to live when to live is torment; and then have we a prescription to die when death is our physician.

Iago: O villainous! I have looked upon the world for four times seven years; and since I could distinguish betwixt a benefit and an injury, I never found

310   man that knew how to love himself. Ere I would say I would drown myself for the love of a guinea hen, I would change my humanity with a baboon.

Roderigo: What should I do? I confess it is my shame to be so fond, but it is not in my virtue to amend it.

315   *Iago:*   Virtue? a fig! 'Tis in ourselves that we are thus or thus. Our bodies are our gardens, to which our wills are gardeners; so that if we will plant nettles or sow lettuce, set hyssop and weed up thyme, supply it with one gender of herbs or distract it with many—either to have it sterile with idleness or manured with industry—why, the power and corrigible authority of this

320   lies in our wills. If the balance of our lives had not one scale of reason to poise another of sensuality, the blood and baseness of our natures would conduct us to most preposterous conclusions. But we have reason to cool our raging motions, our carnal strings, our unbitted lusts; whereof I take

325   this that you call love to be a sect or scion.

Roderigo: It cannot be.

Iago: It is merely a lust of the blood and a permission of the will. Come, be a man! Drown thyself? Drown cats and blind puppies! I have professed me thy friend, and I confess me knit to thy deserving with cables of per-

330   durable toughness. I could never better stead thee than now. Put money in thy purse. Follow thou the wars; defeat thy favor with an usurped beard. I say, put money in thy purse. It cannot be that Desdemona should long continue her love to the Moor—put money in thy purse— nor he his to her. It was a violent commencement in her, and thou shalt see an

335   answerable sequestration—put but money in thy purse. These Moors are changeable in their wills—fill thy purse with money. The food that to him now is as luscious as locusts shall be to him shortly as bitter as coloquintida. She must change for youth: when she is sated with his body, she will find the error of her choice. [She must have change, she

340   must.] Therefore put money in thy purse. If thou wilt needs damn thyself, do it a more delicate way than drowning. Make all the money thou canst. If sanctimony and a frail vow betwixt an erring barbarian and a

supersubtle Venetian be not too hard for my wits and all the tribe of hell,
thou shalt enjoy her. Therefore make money. A pox of drowning thyself!

345 'Tis clean out of the way. Seek thou rather to be hanged in compassing
thy joy than to be drowned and go without her.

Roderigo: Wilt thou be fast to my hopes, if I depend on the issue?

Iago: Thou art sure of me. Go, make money. I have told thee often, and I retell
thee again and again, I hate the Moor. My cause is hearted; thine hath

350 no less reason. Let us be conjunctive in our revenge against him. If thou
canst cuckold him, thou dost thyself a pleasure, me a sport. There are many
events in the womb of time; which will be delivered. Traverse, go, provide
thy money! We will have more of this tomorrow. Adieu.

355 *Roderigo:* Where shall we meet i' th' morning?

Iago: At my lodging.

Roderigo: I'll be with thee betimes.

Iago: Go to, farewell—Do you hear, Roderigo?

[*Roderigo:* What say you?

360 *Iago:* No more of drowning, do you hear?

Roderigo: I am changed.

Iago: Go to, farewell. Put money enough in your purse.]

Roderigo: I'll sell all my land.   *Exit.*

Iago: Thus do I ever make my fool my purse;

365 For I mine own gained knowledge should profane
If I would time expend with such a snipe
But for my sport and profit. I hate the Moor;
And it is thought abroad that 'twixt my sheets
H'as done my office. I know not if 't be true;

370 But I, for mere suspicion in that kind,
Will do as if for surety. He holds me well;
The better shall my purpose work on him.
Cassio's a proper man. Let me see now:
To get his place, and to plume up my will

375 In double knavery—How, how?—Let's see:—
After some time, to abuse Othello's ears
That he is too familiar with his wife.
He hath a person and a smooth dispose
To be suspected—framed to make women false.

380 The Moor is of a free and open nature
That thinks men honest that but seem to be so;
And will as tenderly be led by th' nose
As asses are.
I have 't! It is engend'red! Hell and night

385 Must bring this monstrous birth to the world's light.   *Exit.*

ACT II

SCENE I: *An open place in Cyprus, near the harbor.*

Enter Montano and two Gentlemen.

Montano: What from the cape can you discern at sea?

1. Gentleman: Nothing at all: it is a high-wrought flood.
I cannot 'twixt the heaven and the main
Descry a sail.

5 *Montano:* Methinks the wind hath spoke aloud at land;
A fuller blast ne'er shook our battlements.
If it hath ruffianed so upon the sea,
What ribs of oak, when mountains melt on them,
Can hold the mortise? What shall we hear of this?

10 *2. Gentleman:* A segregation of the Turkish fleet.
For do but stand upon the foaming shore,
The chidden billow seems to pelt the clouds;
The wind-shaked surge, with high and monstrous mane,
Seems to cast water on the burning Bear

15 And quench the Guards of th' ever-fixèd pole.
I never did like molestation view
On the enchafèd flood.

Montano: If that the Turkish fleet
Be not ensheltered and embayed, they are drowned;
It is impossible to bear it out.

Enter a third Gentleman.

20 *3. Gentleman:* News, lads! Our wars are done.
The desperate tempest hath so banged the Turks
That their designment halts. A noble ship of Venice
Hath seen a grievous wrack and sufferance
On most part of their fleet.

Montano: How? Is this true?

25 *3. Gentleman:* The ship is here put in,
A Veronesa; Michael Cassio,
Lieutenant to the warlike Moor Othello,
Is come on shore; the Moor himself at sea,
And is in full commission here for Cyprus.

30 *Montano:* I am glad on't. 'Tis a worthy governor.

3. Gentleman: But his same Cassio, though he speak of comfort
Touching the Turkish loss, yet he looks sadly
And prays the Moor be safe, for they were parted
With foul and violent tempest.

Montano: Pray heaven he be;

35 For I have served him, and the man commands
Like a full soldier. Let's to the seaside, ho!
As well to see the vessel that's come in
As to throw out our eyes for brave Othello,
Even till we make the main and th' aerial blue
An indistinct regard.

40 *3. Gentleman:* Come, let's do so;

For every minute is expectancy
Of more arrivance.
Enter Cassio.
Cassio: Thanks, you the valiant of this warlike isle,
That so approve the Moor! O, let the heavens
45 Give him defense against the elements,
For I have lost him on a dangerous sea!
Montano: Is he well shipped?
Cassio: His bark is stoutly timbered, and his pilot
Of very expert and approved allowance;
50 Therefore my hopes, not surfeited to death,
Stand in bold cure.
(Within.) A sail, a sail, a sail! *Enter a messenger.*
Cassio: What noise?
Messenger: The town is empty; on the brow o' th' sea
Stand ranks of people, and they cry "A sail!"
55 *Cassio:* My hopes do shape him for the governor.
A shot.
2. Gentleman: They do discharge their shot of courtesy:
Our friends at least.
Cassio: I pray you, sir, go forth
And give us truth who 'tis that is arrived.
2. Gentleman: I shall.   *Exit.*
60 *Montano:* But, good lieutenant, is your general wived?
Cassio: Most fortunately. He hath achieved a maid
That paragons description and wild fame;
One that excels the quirks of blazoning pens,
And in th' essential vesture of creation
Does tire the ingener.
Enter Second Gentleman.
65 How now? Who has put in?
2. Gentleman: 'Tis one Iago, ancient to the general.
Cassio: H'as had most favorable and happy speed:
Tempests themselves, high seas, and howling winds,
The guttered rocks and congregated sands,
70 Traitors ensteeped to clog the guiltless keel,
As having sense of beauty, do omit
Their mortal natures, letting go safely by
The divine Desdemona.
Montano: What is she?
Cassio: She that I spake of, our great captain's captain,
75 Left in the conduct of the bold Iago,
Whose footing here anticipates our thoughts
A se'nnight's speed. Great Jove, Othello guard,
And swell his sail with thine own pow'rful breath,
That he may bless this bay with his tall ship,

80   Make love's quick pants in Desdemona's arms,
        Give renewed fire to our extincted spirits,
        [And bring all Cyprus comfort!]
        Enter Desdemona, Iago, Roderigo, and Emilia [with Attendants].
        O, behold!
        The riches of the ship is come on shore!
        You men of Cyprus, let her have your knees.
85   Hail to thee, lady! and the grace of heaven,
        Before, behind thee, and on every hand,
        Enwheel thee round!
  Desdemona: I thank you, valiant Cassio.
        What tidings can you tell me of my lord?
  Cassio: He is not yet arrived; nor know I aught
90   But that he's well and will be shortly here.
  Desdemona: O but I fear! How lost you company?
  Cassio: The great contention of the sea and skies
        Parted our fellowship.
        (Within.) A sail, a sail! *[A shot]*
        But hark. A sail!
  2. Gentleman: They give their greeting to the citadel;
        This likewise is a friend.
95   *Cassio:*   See for the news.

                                                      [Exit Gentleman.]

        Good ancient, you are welcome.
        [To Emilia.] Welcome, mistress.—
        Let it not gall your patience, good Iago,
        That I extend my manners. 'Tis my breeding
        That gives me this bold show of courtesy.
        [Kisses Emilia.]
100   *Iago:*   Sir, would she give you so much of her lips
        As of her tongue she oft bestows on me,
        You would have enough.
  Desdemona: Alas, she has no speech!
  Iago: In faith, too much.
        I find it still when I have list to sleep.
105   Marry, before your ladyship, I grant,
        She puts her tongue a little in her heart
        And chides with thinking.
  Emilia: You have little cause to say so.
  Iago: Come on, come on! You are pictures out of doors,
110   Bells in your parlors, wildcats in your kitchens,
        Saints in your injuries, devils being offended,
        Players in your housewifery, and housewives in your beds.
  Desdemona: O, fie upon thee, slanderer!
  Iago: Nay, it is true, or else I am a Turk:

115   You rise to play, and go to bed to work.

       Emilia: You shall not write my praise.

       Iago: No, let me not.

       Desdemona: What wouldst thou write of me, if thou shouldst praise me?

       Iago: O gentle lady, do not put me to't,

          For I am nothing if not critical.

120   *Desdemona:* Come on, assay.—There's one gone to the harbor?

       Iago: Ay, madam.

       Desdemona: I am not merry; but I do beguile

          The thing I am by seeming otherwise.—

          Come, how wouldst thou praise me?

125   *Iago:* I am about it; but indeed my invention

          Comes from my pate as birdlime does from frieze—

          It plucks out brains and all. But my Muse labors,

          And thus she is delivered:

          If she be fair and wise, fairness and wit—

130   The one's for use, the other useth it.

       Desdemona: Well praised! How if she be black and witty?

       Iago: If she be black, and thereto have a wit,

          She'll find a white that shall her blackness fit.

       Desdemona: Worse and worse!

135   *Emilia:* How if fair and foolish?

       Iago: She never yet was foolish that was fair,

          For even her folly helped her to an heir.

       Desdemona: These are old fond paradoxes to make fools laugh i' th' alehouse.

          What miserable praise hast thou for her that's foul and foolish?

140   *Iago:* There's none so foul, and foolish thereunto,

          But does foul pranks which fair and wise ones do.

       Desdemona: O heavy ignorance! Thou praisest the worst best. But what

          praise couldst thou bestow on a deserving woman indeed—one that

          in the authority of her merit did justly put on the vouch of very

145   malice itself?

       Iago: She that was ever fair, and never proud;

          Had tongue at will, and yet was never loud;

          Never lacked gold, and yet went never gay;

          Fled from her wish, and yet said "Now I may";

150   She that, being ang'red, her revenge being nigh,

          Bade her wrong stay, and her displeasure fly;

          She that in wisdom never was so frail

          To change the cod's head for the salmon's tail;

          She that could think, and ne'er disclose her mind;

155   See suitors following, and not look behind;

          She was a wight (if ever such wight were)—

       Desdemona: To do what?

       Iago: To suckle fools and chronicle small beer.

Desdemona: O most lame and impotent conclusion! Do not learn of him,
160   Emilia, though he be thy husband. How say you, Cassio? Is he not a most
profane and liberal counsellor?

Cassio: He speaks home, madam. You may relish him more in the soldier than
in the scholar.

Iago [aside]:   He takes her by the palm. Ay, well said, whisper! With as little a
165   web as this will I ensnare as great a fly as Cassio. Ay, smile upon her, do!
I will gyve thee in thine own courtship.—You say true; 'tis so, indeed! —If
such tricks as these strip you out of your lieutenantry, it had been better
you had not kissed your three fingers so oft—which now again you are
most apt to play the sir in. Very good! well kissed! an excellent courtesy!
170   'Tis so, indeed. Yet again your fingers to your lips? Would they were clyster
pipes for your sake! *(Trumpet within.)*
The Moor! I know his trumpet.

Cassio: 'Tis truly so.

Desdemona: Let's meet him and receive him.

175   *Cassio:*   Lo, where he comes.
Enter Othello and Attendants.

Othello: O my fair warrior!

Desdemona: My dear Othello!

Othello: It gives me wonder great as my content
To see you here before me. O my soul's joy!
If after every tempest come such calms,
180   May the winds blow till they have wakened death!
And let the laboring bark climb hills of seas
Olympus-high, and duck again as low
As hell's from heaven! If it were now to die,
'Twere now to be most happy; for I fear
185   My soul hath her content so absolute
That not another comfort like to this
Succeeds in unknown fate.

Desdemona: The heavens forbid
But that our loves and comforts should increase
Even as our days do grow.

Othello: Amen to that, sweet powers!
190   I cannot speak enough of this content;
It stops me here; it is too much of joy.
And this, and this, the greatest discords be
They kiss.
That e'er our hearts shall make!

Iago [aside]:   O, you are well tuned now!
But I'll set down the pegs that make this music,
As honest as I am.

195   *Othello:*   Come, let us to the castle.
News, friends! Our wars are done; the Turks are drowned.
How does my old acquaintance of this isle?—

Honey, you shall be well desired in Cyprus;
I have found great love amongst them. O my sweet,
200   I prattle out of fashion, and I dote
In mine own comforts. I prithee, good Iago,
Go to the bay and disembark my coffers.
Bring thou the master to the citadel;
He is a good one, and his worthiness
205   Does challenge much respect.—Come, Desdemona,
Once more well met at Cyprus.

Exit Othello [with all but Iago and Roderigo].

Iago [to an Attendant, who goes out]:   Do thou meet me presently at the harbor.
[To Roderigo.] Come hither. If thou be'st valiant (as they say base men being
in love have then a nobility in their natures more than is native to them), list
210   me. The lieutenant to-night watches on the court of guard. First, I must tell
thee this: Desdemona is directly in love with him.

Roderigo: With him? Why, 'tis not possible.

Iago: Lay thy finger thus, and let thy soul be instructed. Mark me with what
215   violence she first loved the Moor, but for bragging and telling her fantastical
lies; and will she love him still for prating? Let not thy discreet heart think it.
Her eye must be fed; and what delight shall she have to look on the devil?
When the blood is made dull with the act of sport, there should be, again
to inflame it and to give satiety a fresh appetite, loveliness in favor, sympathy
220   in years, manners, and beauties; all which the Moor is defective in. Now for
want of these required conveniences, her delicate tenderness will find itself
abused, begin to heave the gorge, disrelish and abhor the Moor. Very nature
will instruct her in it and compel her to some second choice. Now, sir, this
granted—as it is a most pregnant and unforced position—who stands so
225   eminent in the degree of this fortune as Cassio does? A knave very voluble;
no further conscionable than in putting on the mere form of civil and
humane seeming for the better compassing of his salt and most hidden loose
affection? Why, none! Why, none! A slipper and subtle knave; a finder-out
230   of occasions; that has an eye can stamp and counterfeit advantages, though
true advantage never present itself; a devilish knave! Besides, the knave is
handsome, young, and hath all those requisites in him that folly and green
minds look after. A pestilent complete knave! and the woman hath found
him already.

235   *Roderigo:*   I cannot believe that in her; she's full of most blessed condition.

Iago: Blessed fig's-end! The wine she drinks is made of grapes. If she had been
blessed, she would never have loved the Moor. Blessed pudding! Didst thou
not see her paddle with the palm of his hand? Didst not mark that?

240   *Roderigo:*   Yes, that I did; but that was but courtesy.

Iago: Lechery, by this hand! an index and obscure prologue to the history of
lust and foul thoughts. They met so near with their lips that their breaths
embraced together. Villainous thoughts, Roderigo! When these mutualities
so marshal the way, hard at hand comes the master and main exercise, th'
245   incorporate conclusion. Pish! But, sir, be you ruled by me: I have brought

you from Venice. Watch you to-night; for the command, I'll lay't upon you.
Cassio knows you not. I'll not be far from you: do you find some occasion to
anger Cassio, either by speaking too loud, or tainting his discipline, or from
250   what other course you please which the time shall more favorably minister.

Roderigo: Well.

Iago: Sir, he's rash and very sudden in choler, and haply with his truncheon
may strike at you. Provoke him that he may; for even out of that will
I cause these of Cyprus to mutiny; whose qualification shall come into no
255   true taste again but by the displanting of Cassio. So shall you have a shorter
journey to your desires by the means I shall then have to prefer them; and
the impediment most profitably removed without the which there were no
expectation of our prosperity.

Roderigo: I will do this if you can bring it to any opportunity.

260 *Iago:* I warrant thee. Meet me by and by at the citadel; I must fetch his necessaries ashore. Farewell.

Roderigo: Adieu.   *Exit.*

Iago: That Cassio loves her, I do well believe't;
That she loves him, 'tis apt and of great credit.
265   The Moor, howbeit that I endure him not,
Is of a constant, loving, noble nature,
And I dare think he'll prove to Desdemona
A most dear husband. Now I do love her too;
Not out of absolute lust, though peradventure
270   I stand accountant for as great a sin,
But partly led to diet my revenge,
For that I do suspect the lusty Moor
Hath leaped into my seat; the thought whereof
Doth, like a poisonous mineral, gnaw my inwards;
275   And nothing can or shall content my soul
Till I am evened with him, wife for wife;
Or failing so, yet that I put the Moor
At least into a jealousy so strong
That judgment cannot cure. Which thing to do,
280   If this poor trash of Venice, whom I trash
For his quick hunting, stand the putting on,
I'll have our Michael Cassio on the hip,
Abuse him to the Moor in the rank garb
(For I fear Cassio with my nightcap too),
285   Make the Moor thank me, love me, and reward me
For making him egregiously an ass
And practicing upon his peace and quiet
Even to madness. 'Tis here, but yet confused:
Knavery's plain face is never seen till used.   *Exit.*

SCENE II: *A street in Cyprus.*

Enter Othello's Herald, with a proclamation.

Herald: It is Othello's pleasure, our noble and valiant general, that, upon certain tidings now arrived, importing the mere perdition of the Turkish fleet,
every man put himself into triumph; some to dance, some to make bonfires,
each man to what sport and revels his addiction leads him. For, besides these
5   beneficial news, it is the celebration of his nuptial. So much was his pleasure
should be proclaimed. All offices are open, and there is full liberty of feasting
from the present hour of five till the bell have told eleven. Heaven bless the
isle of Cyprus and our noble general Othello! *Exit.*

SCENE III: *The Cyprian Castle.*

Enter Othello, Desdemona, Cassio, and Attendants.
Othello: Good Michael, look you to the guard to-night.
Let's teach ourselves that honorable stop,
Not to outsport discretion.
Cassio: Iago hath direction what to do;
5   But not withstanding, with my personal eye
Will I look to't.
Othello: Iago is most honest.
Michael, good night. To-morrow with your earliest
Let me have speech with you.
[To Desdemona.] Come, my dear love.
The purchase made, the fruits are to ensue;
10   That profit's yet to come 'tween me and you.—
Good night.
                    Exit [Othello with Desdemona and Attendants].
Enter Iago.
Cassio: Welcome, Iago. We must to the watch.
Iago: Not this hour, lieutenant; 'tis not yet ten o' th' clock. Our general cast
us thus early for the love of his Desdemona; who let us not therefore
15   blame. He hath not yet made wanton the night with her, and she is sport
for Jove.
Cassio: She's a most exquisite lady.
Iago: And, I'll warrant her, full of game.
Cassio: Indeed, she's a most fresh and delicate creature.
20 *Iago:*   What an eye she has! Methinks it sounds a parley to provocation.
Cassio: An inviting eye; and yet methinks right modest.
Iago: And when she speaks, is it not an alarum to love?
Cassio: She is indeed perfection.
Iago: Well, happiness to their sheets! Come, lieutenant, I have a stoup of wine,
25   and here without are a brace of Cyprus gallants that would fain have a
measure to the health of black Othello.
Cassio: Not to-night, good Iago. I have very poor and unhappy brains for
drinking; I could well wish courtesy would invent some other custom of
entertainment.
30 *Iago:*   O, they are our friends. But one cup! I'll drink for you.

Cassio: I have drunk but one cup to-night, and that was craftily qualified too; and behold what innovation it makes here. I am unfortunate in the infirmity and dare not task my weakness with any more.

Iago: What, man! 'Tis a night of revels: the gallants desire it.

35   *Cassio:*   Where are they?

Iago: Here at the door; I pray you call them in.

Cassio: I'll do't, but it dislikes me.   *Exit.*

Iago: If I can fasten but one cup upon him
            With that which he hath drunk to-night already,
40   He'll be as full of quarrel and offense
            As my young mistress' dog. Now my sick fool Roderigo,
            Whom love hath turned almost the wrong side out,
            To Desdemona hath to-night caroused
            Potations pottle-deep; and he's to watch.
45   Three lads of Cyprus—noble swelling spirits,
            That hold their honors in a wary distance,
            The very elements of this warlike isle—
            Have I to-night flustered with flowing cups,
            And they watch too. Now, 'mongst this flock of drunkards
50   Am I to put our Cassio in some action
            That may offend the isle.
            Enter Cassio, Montano, and Gentlemen [; Servants following with wine].
            But here they come.
            If consequence do but approve my dream,
            My boat sails freely, both with wind and stream.

Cassio: 'Fore God, they have given me a rouse already.

55   *Montano:*   Good faith, a little one; not past a pint, as I am a soldier.

Iago: Some wine, ho!
            [Sings.] And let me the canakin clink, clink;
            And let me the canakin clink
            A soldier's a man;
60   A life's but a span,
            Why then, let a soldier drink.
            Some wine, boys!

Cassio: 'Fore God, an excellent song!

Iago: I learned it in England, where indeed they are most potent in potting.
            Your Dane, your German, and your swag-bellied Hollander—Drink, ho!—
65   are nothing to your English.

Cassio: Is your Englishman so expert in his drinking?

Iago: Why, he drinks you with facility your Dane dead drunk; he sweats not
            to overthrow your Almain; he gives your Hollander a vomit ere the next
70   pottle can be filled.

Cassio: To the health of our general!

Montano: I am for it, lieutenant, and I'll do you justice.

Iago: O sweet England!

75   *[Sings.]* King Stephen was a worthy peer;

His breeches cost him but a crown;
He held 'em sixpence all too dear,
With that he called the tailor lown.
He was a wight of high renown,
And thou art but of low degree.
80   'Tis pride that pulls the country down;
Then take thine auld cloak about thee.
Some wine, ho!

Cassio: 'Fore God, this is a more exquisite song than the other.

Iago: Will you hear't again?

Cassio: No, for I hold him to be unworthy of his place that does those
85   things. Well, God's above all; and there be souls must be saved, and there
be souls must not be saved.

Iago: It's true, good lieutenant.

Cassio: For mine own part—no offense to the general, nor any man of quality—
85   I hope to be saved.

Iago: And so do I too, lieutenant.

Cassio: Ay, but, by your leave, not before me. The lieutenant is to be saved before
the ancient. Let's have no more of this; let's to our affairs.— God forgive us
our sins!—Gentlemen, let's look to our business. Do not think, gentlemen,
95   I am drunk. This is my ancient; this is my right hand, and this is my left. I am
not drunk now. I can stand well enough, and I speak well enough.

All: Excellent well!

Cassio: Why, very well then. You must not think then that I am drunk.

Exit.

100   *Montano:*   To th' platform, masters. Come, let's set the watch.

Iago: You see this fellow that is gone before.
He's a soldier fit to stand by Caesar
And give direction; and do but see his vice.
'Tis to his virtue a just equinox,
105   The one as long as th' other. 'Tis pity of him.
I fear the trust Othello puts him in,
On some odd time of his infirmity,
Will shake this island.

Montano: But is he often thus?

Iago: 'Tis evermore his prologue to his sleep:
110   He'll watch the horologe a double set
If drink rock not his cradle.

Montano: It were well
The general were put in mind of it.
Perhaps he sees it not, or his good nature
Prizes the virtue that appears in Cassio
115   And looks not on his evils. Is not this true?

Enter Roderigo.

Iago [aside to him.]:   How now, Roderigo?
I pray you after the lieutenant, go!

Exit Roderigo.

Montano: And 'tis great pity that the noble Moor
          Should hazard such a place as his own second
120   With one of an ingraft infirmity.
          It were an honest action to say
          So to the Moor.
Iago: Not I, for this fair island!
          I do love Cassio well and would do much
          To cure him of this evil.
          (Within.) Help! help!
125   But hark! What noise?
          Enter Cassio, driving in Roderigo.
Cassio: Zounds, you rogue! you rascal!
Montano: What's the matter, lieutenant?
Cassio: A knave to teach me my duty?
          I'll beat the knave into a twiggen bottle.
Roderigo: Beat me?
Cassio: Dost thou prate, rogue? *[Strikes him.]*
Montano: Nay, good lieutenant!

                                                            [Stays him.]

          I pray you, sir, hold your hand.
130   *Cassio:*   Let me go, sir,
          Or I'll knock you o'er the mazzard.
Montano: Come, come, you're drunk!
Cassio: Drunk?
          They fight.
Iago [aside to Roderigo]:   Away, I say! Go out and cry a mutiny!

                                                            Exit Roderigo.

          Nay, good lieutenant. God's will, gentlemen!
135   Help, ho!—lieutenant—sir—Montano—sir—
          Help, masters!—Here's a goodly watch indeed!
          A bell rung.
          Who's that which rings the bell? Diablo, ho!
          The town will rise. God's will, lieutenant, hold!
          You'll be shamed for ever.
          Enter Othello and Gentlemen with weapons.
Othello: What is the matter here?
140   *Montano:*   Zounds, I bleed still. I am hurt to th' death.
          He dies!
Othello: Hold for your lives!
Iago: Hold, hold! Lieutenant—sir—Montano—gentlemen!
          Have you forgot all sense of place and duty?
145   Hold! The general speaks to you. Hold, for shame!
Othello: Why, how now ho? From whence ariseth this?
          Are we turned Turks, and to ourselves do that
          Which heaven hath forbid the Ottomites?
          For Christian shame put by this barbarous brawl!

150   He that stirs next to carve for his own rage.
              Holds his soul light; he dies upon his motion.
              Silence that dreadful bell! It frights the isle
              From her propriety. What is the matter, masters?
              Honest Iago, that looks dead with grieving,
155   Speak. Who began this? On thy love, I charge thee.
      Iago: I do not know. Friends all, but now, even now,
              In quarter, and in terms like bride and groom
              Devesting them for bed; and then, but now—
              As if some planet had unwitted men—
160   Swords out, and tilting one at other's breast
              In opposition bloody. I cannot speak
              Any beginning to this peevish odds,
              And would in action glorious I had lost
              Those legs that brought me to a part of it!
165   *Othello:*   How comes it, Michael, you are thus forgot?
     Cassio: I pray you pardon me; I cannot speak.
    Othello: Worthy Montano, you were wont to be civil;
              The gravity and stillness of your youth
              The world hath noted, and your name is great
170   In months of wisest censure. What's the matter
              That you unlace your reputation thus
              And spend your rich opinion for the name
              Of a night-brawler? Give me answer to it.
    Montano: Worthy Othello, I am hurt to danger.
175   Your officer, Iago, can inform you,
              While I spare speech, which something now offends me,
              Of all that I do know; nor know I aught
              By me that's said or done amiss this night,
180   Unless self-charity be sometimes a vice,
              And to defend ourselves it be a sin
              When violence assails us.
    Othello: Now, by heaven,
              My blood begins my safer guides to rule,
              And passion, having my best judgment collied,
              Assays to lead the way. If I once stir
185   Or do but lift this arm, the best of you
              Shall sink in my rebuke. Give me to know
              How this foul rout began, who set it on;
              And he that is approved in this offense,
190   Though he had twinned with me, both at a birth,
              Shall lose me. What! in a town of war,
              Yet wild, the people's hearts brimful of fear,
              To manage private and domestic quarrel?
              In night, and on the court and guard of safety?
              'Tis monstrous. Iago, who began't?

195   *Montano:* If partially affined, or leagued in office,
        Thou dost deliver more or less than truth,
        Thou art no soldier.
      Iago: Touch me not so near.
        I had rather have this tongue cut from my mouth
        Than it should do offense to Michael Cassio;
200   Yet I persuade myself, to speak the truth
        Shall nothing wrong him. This it is, general.
        Montano and myself being in speech,
        There comes a fellow crying out for help,
        And Cassio following him with determined sword
205   To execute upon him. Sir, this gentleman
        Steps in to Cassio and entreats his pause.
        Myself the crying fellow did pursue,
        Lest by his clamor—as it so fell out—
        The town might fall in fright. He, swift of foot,
210   Outran my purpose; and I returned then rather
        For that I heard the clink and fall of swords,
        And Cassio high in oath; which till to-night
        I ne'er might say before. When I came back—
        For this was brief—I found them close together
215   At blow and thrust, even as again they were
        When you yourself did part them.
        More of this matter cannot I report;
        But men are men; the best sometimes forget.
        Though Cassio did some little wrong to him,
220   As men in rage strike those that wish them best,
        Yet surely Cassio I believe received
        From him that fled some strange indignity,
        Which patience could not pass.
      Othello: I know, Iago,
        Thy honesty and love doth mince this matter,
225   Making it light to Cassio. Cassio, I love thee;
        But never more be officer of mine.
        Enter Desdemona, attended.
        Look if my gentle love be not raised up!
        I'll make thee an example.
      Desdemona: What's the matter?
      Othello: All's well now, sweeting; come away to bed.
        [To Montano.]
230   Sir, for your hurts, myself will be your surgeon.
        Lead him off.
        [Montano is led off.]
        Iago, look with care about the town
        And silence those whom this vile brawl distracted.
        Come, Desdemona; 'tis the soldiers' life

235   To have their balmy slumbers waked with strife.

           Exit [with all but Iago and Cassio].

Iago: What, are you hurt, lieutenant?

Cassio: Ay, past all surgery.

Iago: Marry, God forbid!

Cassio: Reputation, reputation, reputation! O, I have lost my reputation!
240   I have lost the immortal part of myself, and what remains is bestial. My
   reputation, Iago, my reputation!

Iago: As I am an honest man, I thought you had received some bodily wound.
   There is more sense in that than in reputation. Reputation is an idle and
   most false imposition; oft got without merit and lost without deserving.
245   You have lost no reputation at all unless you repute yourself such a loser.
   What, man! there are ways to recover the general again. You are but now
   cast in his mood—a punishment more in policy than in malice, even so
   as one would beat his offenseless dog to affright an imperious lion. Sue to
   him again, and he's yours.

250 *Cassio:* I will rather sue to be despised than to deceive so good a commander
   with so slight, so drunken, and so indiscreet an officer. Drunk! and speak
   parrot! and squabble! swagger! swear! and discourse fustian with one's own
   shadow! O thou invisible spirit of wine, if thou hast no name to be known
   by, let us call thee devil!

255 *Iago:* What was he that you followed with your sword? What had he done to you?

Cassio: I know not.

Iago: Is't possible?

Cassio: I remember a mass of things, but nothing distinctly; a quarrel, but
260   nothing wherefore. O God, that men should put an enemy in their mouths
   to steal away their brains! that we should with joy, pleasance, revel, and
   applause transform ourselves into beasts!

Iago: Why, but you are now well enough. How came you thus recovered?

Cassio: It hath pleased the devil drunkenness to give place to the devil wrath.
265   One unperfectness shows me another, to make me frankly despise myself.

Iago: Come, you are too severe a moraler. As the time, the place, and the condition
   of this country stands, I could heartily wish this had not so befall'n; but since it
   is as it is, mend it for your own good.

Cassio: I will ask him for my place again: he shall tell me I am a drunkard!
   Had I as many mouths as Hydra, such an answer would stop them all. To
   be now a sensible man, by and by a fool, and presently a beast! O strange!
270   Every inordinate cup is unblest, and the ingredient is a devil.

Iago: Come, come, good wine is a good familiar creature if it be well used.
275   Exclaim no more against it. And, good lieutenant, I think you think I love you.

Cassio: I have well approved it, sir. I drunk!

Iago: You or any man living may be drunk at some time, man. I'll tell you what
   you shall do. Our general's wife is now the general. I may say so in this
   respect, for that he hath devoted and given up himself to the contemplation,
   mark, and denotement of her parts and graces. Confess yourself freely to
   her; importune her help to put you in your place again. She is of so free, so

280 kind, so apt, so blessed a disposition she holds it a vice in her goodness not
to do more than she is requested. This broken joint between you and her
husband entreat her to splinter; and my fortunes against any lay worth nam-
285 ing, this crack of your love shall grow stronger than it was before.

Cassio: You advise me well.

Iago: I protest, in the sincerity of love and honest kindness.

Cassio: I think it freely; and betimes in the morning will I beseech the virtuous Desdemona to undertake for me. I am desperate of my fortunes if they
290 check me here.

Iago: You are in the right. Good night, lieutenant; I must to the watch.

Cassio: Good night, honest Iago. *Exit Cassio.*

295 *Iago:*   And what's he then that says I play the villain,
When this advice is free I give and honest,
Probal to thinking, and indeed the course
To win the Moor again? For 'tis most easy
Th' inclining Desdemona to subdue
300 In an honest suit; she's framed as fruitful
As the free elements. And then for her
To win the Moor—were't to renounce his baptism,
All seals and symbols of redeemèd sin—
His soul is so enfettered to her love
305 That she may make, unmake, do what she list,
Even as her appetite shall play the god
With his weak function. How am I then a villain
To counsel Cassio to this parallel course,
Directly to his good? Divinity of hell!
310 When devils will the blackest sins put on,
They do suggest at first with heavenly shows,
As I do now. For whiles this honest fool
Plies Desdemona to repair his fortunes,
And she for him pleads strongly to the Moor,
I'll pour this pestilence into his ear,
315 That she repeals him for her body's lust;
And by how much she strives to do him good,
She shall undo her credit with the Moor.
So will I turn her virtue into pitch,
320 And out of her own goodness make the net
That shall enmesh them all.
Enter Roderigo.
How, now, Roderigo?

Roderigo: I do follow here in the chase, not like a hound that hunts, but one that
fills up the cry. My money is almost spent; I have been tonight exceedingly
well cudgelled; and I think the issue will be—I shall have so much experience
for my pains; and so, with no money at all, and a little more wit, return again
325 to Venice.

Iago: How poor are they that have not patience!

What wound did ever heal but by degrees?
Thou know'st we work by wit, and not by witchcraft;
And wit depends on dilatory time.
330   Doesn't not go well? Cassio hath beaten thee,
And thou by that small hurt hast cashiered Cassio.
Though other things grow fair against the sun,
Yet fruits that blossom first will first be ripe.
Content thyself awhile. By the mass, 'tis morning!
Pleasure and action make the hours seem short.
Retire thee; go where thou art billeted.
Away, I say! Thou shalt know more hereafter.
Nay, get thee gone!   *Exit Roderigo.*
Two things are to be done:
340   My wife must move for Cassio to her mistress;
I'll set her on;
Myself the while to draw the Moor apart
And bring him jump when he may Cassio find
Soliciting his wife. Ay, that's the way!
345   Dull no device by coldness and delay.   *Exit.*

ACT III

Scene I: *Before the chamber of Othello and Desdemona.*

Enter Cassio, with Musicians and the Clown.

Cassio: Masters, play here, I will content your pains:
Something that's brief; and bid "Good morrow, general."
[They play.]

Clown: Why, masters, ha' your instruments been in Naples, that they speak i'
th' nose thus?

5   *Musician:*   How, sir, how?

Clown: Are these, I pray you, called wind instruments?

Musician: Ay, marry, are they, sir.

Clown: O, thereby hangs a tail.

Musician: Whereby hangs a tail, sir?

10   *Clown:*   Marry, sir, by many a wind instrument that I know. But, masters, here's
money for you; and the general so likes your music that he desires you, for
love's sake, to make no more noise with it.

Musician: Well, sir, we will not.

Clown: If you have any music that may not be heard, to't again: but, as they
15   say, to hear music the general does not greatly care.

Musician: We have none such, sir.

Clown: Then put up your pipes in your bag, for I'll away. Go, vanish into air,
away!   *Exit Musician [with his fellows].*

Cassio: Dost thou hear, my honest friend?

20   *Clown:*   No, I hear not your honest friend. I hear you.

Cassio: Prithee keep up thy quillets. There's a poor piece of gold for thee. If the gentlewoman that attends the general's wife be stirring, tell her there's one Cassio entreats her a little favor of speech. Wilt thou do this?

25   *Clown:*   She is stirring sir. If she will stir hither, I shall seem to notify unto her.

Cassio: [Do, good my friend.]   *Exit Clown.*

    Enter Iago.

    In happy time, Iago.

Iago: You have not been abed then?

Cassio: Why, no; the day had broke

30   Before we parted. I have made bold, Iago,
    To send in to your wife: my suit to her
    Is that she will to virtuous Desdemona
    Procure me some access.

Iago: I'll send her to you presently;
    And I'll devise a mean to draw the Moor

35   Out of the way, that your converse and business
    May be more free.

Cassio: I humbly thank you for't.   *Exit [Iago].*
    I never knew
    A Florentine more kind and honest.

    Enter Emilia.

Emilia: Good morrow, good lieutenant. I am sorry

40   For your displeasure: but all will sure be well.
    The general and his wife are talking of it,
    And she speaks for you stoutly. The Moor replied
    That he you hurt is of great fame in Cyprus
    And great affinity, and that in wholesome wisdom

45   He might not but refuse you; but he protests he loves you,
    And needs no other suitor but his likings
    [To take the safest occasion by the front]
    To bring you in again.

Cassio: Yet I beseech you,
    If you think fit, or that it may be done,

50   Give me advantage of some brief discourse
    With Desdemona alone.

Emilia: Pray you come in.
    I will bestow you where you shall have time
    To speak your bosom freely.

Cassio: I am much bound to you.   *Exeunt.*

SCENE II: *The castle.*

    Enter Othello, Iago, and Gentlemen.

Othello: These letters give, Iago, to the pilot
    And by him do my duties to the Senate.
    That done, I will be walking on the works;

Repair there to me.

Iago: Well, my good lord, I'll do't.

5   *Othello:*   This fortification, gentlemen, shall we see't?

Gentlemen: We'll wait upon your lordship.   *Exeunt.*

SCENE III: *The castle grounds.*

Enter Desdemona, Cassio, and Emilia.

Desdemona: Be thou assured, good Cassio, I will do
All my abilities in thy behalf.

Emilia: Good madam, do. I warrant it grieves my husband
As if the cause were his.

5   *Desdemona:*   O, that's an honest fellow. Do not doubt, Cassio,
But I will have my lord and you again
As friendly as you were.

Cassio: Bounteous madam,
Whatever shall become of Michael Cassio,
He's never anything but your true servant.

10   *Desdemona:*   I know't; I thank you. You do love my lord;
You have known him long; and be you well assured
He shall in strangeness stand no farther off
Than in a politic distance.

Cassio: Ay, but, lady,
That policy may either last so long,

15   Or feed upon such nice and waterish diet,
Or breed itself so out of circumstance,
That, I being absent, and my place supplied,
My general will forget my love and service.

Desdemona: Do not doubt that; before Emilia here

20   I give thee warrant of thy place. Assure thee,
If I do vow a friendship, I'll perform it
To the last article. My lord shall never rest;
I'll watch him tame and talk him out of patience;
His bed shall seem a school, his board a shrift;

25   I'll intermingle everything he does
With Cassio's suit. Therefore be merry, Cassio,
For thy solicitor shall rather die
Than give thy cause away.

Enter Othello and Iago [at a distance].

Emilia: Madam, here comes my lord.

30   *Cassio:*   Madam, I'll take my leave.

Desdemona: Why, stay, and hear me speak.

Cassio: Madam, not now: I am very ill at ease,
Unfit for mine own purposes.

Desdemona: Well, do your discretion.   *Exit Cassio.*

Iago: Ha! I like not that.

35   *Othello:* What dost thou say?
         Iago: Nothing, my lord; or if—I know not what.
         Othello: Was not that Cassio parted from my wife?
         Iago: Cassio, my lord? No, sure, I cannot think it,
            That he would steal away so guilty-like,
            Seeing your coming.
40   *Othello:* I do believe 'twas he.
         Desdemona: How now, my lord?
            I have been talking with a suitor here,
            A man that languishes in your displeasure.
         Othello: What is't you mean?
45   *Desdemona:* Why, your lieutenant, Cassio. Good my lord,
            If I have any grace or power to move you,
            His present reconciliation take;
            For if he be not one that truly loves you,
            That errs in ignorance, and not in cunning,
            I have no judgment in an honest face,
50   I prithee call him back.
         Othello: Went he hence now?
         Desdemona: Yes, faith; so humbled
            That he hath left part of his grief with me
            To suffer with him. Good love, call him back.
55   *Othello:* Not now, sweet Desdemon; some other time.
         Desdemona: But shall't be shortly?
         Othello: The sooner, sweet, for you.
         Desdemona: Shall't be to-night at supper?
         Othello: No, not to-night.
         Desdemona: Tomorrow dinner then?
         Othello: I shall not dine at home;
            I meet the captains at the citadel.
60   *Desdemona:* Why then, tomorrow night, or Tuesday morn,
            On Tuesday noon or night, or Wednesday morn.
            I prithee name the time, but let it not
            Exceed three days. I' faith, he's penitent;
            And yet his trespass, in our common reason
65   (Save that, they say, the wars must make examples
            Out of their best), is not almost a fault
            T' incur a private check. When shall he come?
            Tell me, Othello. I wonder in my soul
            What you could ask me that I should deny
70   Or stand so mamm'ring on. What? Michael Cassio,
            That came a-wooing with you, and so many a time,
            When I have spoke of you dispraisingly,
            Hath ta'en your part—to have so much to do
            To bring him in? By'r Lady, I could do much—
75   *Othello:* Prithee no more. Let him come when he will!

        I will deny thee nothing.

Desdemona: Why, this is not a boon;
        'Tis as I should entreat you wear your gloves,
        Or feed on nourishing dishes, or keep you warm,
        Or sue to you to do a peculiar profit
80   To your own person. Nay, when I have a suit
        Wherein I mean to touch your love indeed,
        It shall be full of poise and difficult weight,
        And fearful to be granted.

Othello: I will deny thee nothing!
        Whereon I do beseech thee grant me this,
85   To leave me but a little to myself.

Desdemona: Shall I deny you? No. Farewell, my lord.

Othello: Farewell, my Desdemon: I'll come to thee straight.

Desdemona: Emilia, come.—Be as your fancies teach you;
        Whate'er you be, I am obedient. *Exit [with Emilia].*

90   *Othello:*   Excellent wretch! Perdition catch my soul
        But I do love thee! and when I love thee not,
        Chaos is come again.

Iago: My noble lord—

Othello: What dost thou say, Iago?

Iago: Did Michael Cassio, when you wooed my lady,
95   Know of your love?

Othello: He did, from first to last. Why dost thou ask?

Iago: But for a satisfaction of my thought;
        No further harm.

Othello: Why of thy thought, Iago?

Iago: I did not think he had been acquainted with her.

100   *Othello:*   O, yes, and went between us very oft.

Iago: Indeed?

Othello: Indeed? Ay, indeed! Discern'st thou aught in that?
        Is he not honest?

Iago: Honest, my lord?

Othello: Honest. Ay, honest.

Iago: My lord, for aught I know.

Othello: What dost thou think?

Iago: Think, my lord?

105   *Othello:*   Think, my lord?
        By heaven, he echoes me,
        As if there were some monster in his thought
        Too hideous to be shown. Thou dost mean something:
        I heard thee say even now, thou lik'st not that,
110   When Cassio left my wife. What didst not like?
        And when I told thee he was of my counsel
        In my whole course of wooing, thou cried'st "Indeed?"
        And didst contract and purse thy brow together,

As if thou then hadst shut up in thy brain
115   Some horrible conceit. If thou dost love me,
Show me thy thought

Iago: My lord, you know I love you.

Othello: I think thou dost;
And, for I know thou'rt full of love and honesty
And weigh'st thy words before thou giv'st them breath,
120   Therefore these stops of thine fright me the more;
For such things in a false disloyal knave
Are tricks of custom; but in a man that's just
They are close dilations, working from the heart
That passion cannot rule.

Iago: For Michael Cassio,
125   I dare be sworn I think that he is honest.

Othello: I think so too.

Iago: Men should be what they seem;
Or those that be not, would they might seem none!

Othello: Certain, men should be what they seem.

Iago: Why then, I think Cassio's an honest man.
130   *Othello:*   Nay, yet there's more in this.
I prithee speak to me as to thy thinkings,
As thou dost ruminate, and give thy worst of thoughts
The worst of words.

Iago: Good my lord, pardon me:
Though I am bound to every act of duty,
135   I am not bound to that all slaves are free to.
Utter my thoughts? Why, say they are vile and false,
As where's that palace whereinto foul things
Sometimes intrude not? Who has a breast so pure
But some uncleanly apprehensions
140   Keep leets and law days, and in Sessions sit
With meditations lawful?

Othello: Thou dost conspire against thy friend, Iago,
If thou but think'st him wronged, and mak'st his ear
A stranger to thy thoughts.

Iago: I do beseech you—
145   Though I perchance am vicious in my guess
(As I confess it is my nature's plague
To spy into abuses, and oft my jealousy
Shapes faults that are not), that your wisdom yet
From one that so imperfectly conjects
150   Would take no notice, nor build yourself a trouble
Out of his scattering and unsure observance.
It were not for your quiet nor your good,
Nor for my manhood, honesty, and wisdom,
To let you know my thoughts.

Othello: What dost thou mean?

155   *Iago:*   Good name in man and woman, dear my lord,
Is the immediate jewel of their souls.
Who steals my purse steals trash; 'tis something, nothing;
'Twas mine, 'tis his, and has been slave to thousands;
But he that filches from me my good name

160   Robs me of that which not enriches him
And makes me poor indeed.

Othello: By heaven, I'll know thy thoughts!

Iago: You cannot, if my heart were in your hand;
Nor shall not whilst 'tis in my custody.

Othello: Ha!

Iago: O, beware, my lord, of jealousy!

165   It is the green-eyed monster, which doth mock
The meat it feeds on. That cuckold lives in bliss
Who, certain of his fate, loves not his wronger;
But O, what damnèd minutes tells he o'er

170   Who dotes, yet doubts—suspects, yet strongly loves!

Othello: O misery!

Iago: Poor and content is rich, and rich enough;
But riches fineless is as poor as winter
To him that ever fears he shall be poor.

175   Good God, the souls of all my tribe defend
From jealousy!

Othello: Why, why is this?
Think'st thou I'ld make a life of jealousy,
To follow still the changes of the moon
With fresh suspicions? No! To be once in doubt

180   Is once to be resolved. Exchange me for a goat
When I shall turn the business of my soul
To such exsufflicate and blown surmises,
Matching this inference. 'Tis not to make me jealous
To say my wife is fair, feeds well, loves company,

185   Is free of speech, sings, plays, and dances;
Where virtue is, these are more virtuous.
Nor from mine own weak merits will I draw
The smallest fear or doubt of her revolt,
For she had eyes, and chose me. No, Iago;

190   I'll see before I doubt; when I doubt, prove;
And on the proof there is no more but this—
Away at once with love or jealousy!

Iago: I am glad of this; for now I shall have reason
To show the love and duty that I bear you

195   With franker spirit. Therefore, as I am bound,
Receive it from me. I speak not yet of proof.
Look at your wife; observe her well with Cassio;

Wear your eyes thus, not jealous nor secure;
I would not have your free and noble nature,
200   Out of self-bounty, be abused. Look to't.
I know our country disposition well:
In Venice they do let God see the pranks
They dare not show their husbands; their best conscience
Is not to leave't undone, but keep't unknown.
205 *Othello:* Dost thou say so?
     Iago: She did deceive her father, marrying you;
And when she seemed to shake and fear your looks,
She loved them most.
     Othello: And so she did.
     Iago: Why, go to then!
She that, so young, could give out such a seeming
210   To seel her father's eyes up close as oak—
He thought 'twas witchcraft—but I am much to blame.
I humbly do beseech you of your pardon
For too much loving you.
     Othello: I am bound to thee for ever.
     Iago: I see this hath a little dashed your spirits.
     Othello: Not a jot, not a jot.
215 *Iago:* I' faith, I fear it has.
I hope you will consider what is spoke
Comes from my love. But I do see y' are moved.
I am to pray you not to strain my speech
To grosser issues nor to larger reach
220   Than to suspicion.
     Othello: I will not.
     Iago: Should you do so, my lord,
My speech should fall into such vile success
As my thoughts aim not at. Cassio's my worthy friend—
My lord, I see y' are moved.
     Othello: No, not much moved:
225   I do not think but Desdemona's honest.
     Iago: Long live she so! and long live you to think so!
     Othello: And yet, how nature erring from itself—
     Iago: Ay, there's the point! as (to be bold with you)
Not to affect many proposèd matches
230   Of her own clime, complexion, and degree,
Whereto we see in all things nature tends—
Foh! one may smell in such a will most rank,
Foul disproportions, thought unnatural—
But pardon me—I do not in position.
235   Distinctly speak of her; though I may fear
Her will, recoiling to her better judgment,
May fall to match you with her country forms,

And happily repent.

Othello: Farewell, farewell!
    If more thou dost perceive, let me know more:
240   Set on thy wife to observe. Leave me, Iago.

Iago: My lord, I take my leave. *[Going.]*

Othello: Why did I marry? This honest creature doubtless
    Sees and knows more, much more, than he unfolds.

Iago [returns]:   My lord, I would I might entreat your honor
245   To scan this thing no further: leave it to time.
    Although 'tis fit that Cassio have his place,
    For sure he fills it up with great ability,
    Yet, if you please to hold off a while,
    You shall by that perceive him and his means.
250   Note if your lady strain his entertainment
    With any strong or vehement importunity;
    Much will be seen in that. In the mean time
    Let me be thought too busy in my fears
    (As worthy cause I have to fear I am)
255   And hold her free, I do beseech your honor.

Othello: Fear not my government.

Iago: I once more take my leave. *Exit.*

Othello: This fellow's of exceeding honesty,
    And knows all qualities, with a learned spirit
260   Of human dealings. If I do prove her haggard,
    Though that her jesses were my dear heartstrings,
    I'd whistle her off and let her down the wind
    To prey at fortune. Haply, for I am black
    And have not those soft parts of conversation
265   That chamberers have, or for I am declined
    Into the vale of years—yet that's not much—
    She's gone. I am abused, and my relief
    Must be to loathe her. O curse of marriage,
    That we can call these delicate creatures ours,
270   And not their appetites! I had rather be a toad
    And live upon the vapor of a dungeon
    Than keep a corner in the thing I love
    For others' uses. Yet 'tis the plague of great ones;
    Prerogatived are they less than the base.
275   'Tis destiny unshunnable, like death.
    Even then this forkèd plague is fated to us
    When we do quicken. Look where she comes.

Enter Desdemona and Emilia.

    If she be false, O, then heaven mocks itself!
    I'll not believe't.

Desdemona: How now, my dear Othello?
280   Your dinner, and the generous islanders

By you invited, do attend your presence.
Othello: I am to blame.
Desdemona: Why do you speak so faintly?
Are you not well?
Othello: I have a pain upon my forehead, here.
285   *Desdemona:*   Faith, that's with watching; 'twill away again.
Let me but bind it hard, within this hour
It will be well.
Othello: Your napkin is too little;
[*He pushes the handkerchief from him, and it falls unnoticed.*]
Let it alone. Come, I'll go in with you.
Desdemona: I am very sorry that you are not well.   *Exit [with Othello]:*
290   *Emilia:*   I am glad I have found this napkin;
This was her first remembrance from the Moor,
My wayward husband hath a hundred times
Wooed me to steal it; but she so loves the token
(For he conjured her she should ever keep it)
295   That she reserves it evermore about her
To kiss and talk to. I'll have the work ta'en out
And give't Iago.
What he will do with it heaven knows, not I;
I nothing but to please his fantasy.
Enter Iago.
300   *Iago:*   How now? What do you here alone?
Emilia: Do not you chide; I have a thing for you.
Iago: A thing for me? It is a common thing—
Emilia: Ha?
Iago: To have a foolish wife.
305   *Emilia:*   O, is that all? What will you give me now
For that same handkerchief?
Iago: What handkerchief?
Emilia: What handkerchief!
Why, that the Moor first gave to Desdemona;
That which so often you did bid me steal.
310   *Iago:*   Hast stol'n it from her?
Emilia: No, faith; she let it drop by negligence,
And to th' advantage, I, being here, took't up.
Look, here it is.
Iago: A good wench! Give it me.
Emilia: What will you do with't, that you have been so earnest
To have me filch it?
315   *Iago:*   Why, what is that to you?
[*Snatches it.*]
Emilia: If it be not for some purpose of import,
Give't me again. Poor lady, she'll run mad
When she shall lack it.

Iago: Be not acknown on't; I have use for it.
320   Go, leave me.   *Exit Emilia.*
         I will in Cassio's lodgings lose this napkin
         And let him find it. Trifles light as air
         Are to the jealous confirmations strong
         As proofs of holy writ. This may do something.
325   The Moor already changes with my poison:
         Dangerous conceits are in their nature poisons,
         Which at the first are scarce found to distaste,
         But with a little act upon the blood
         Burn like the mines of sulphur.
         Enter Othello.
         I did say so.
330   Look where he comes! Not poppy nor mandragora,
         Nor all the drowsy syrups of the world,
         Shall ever med'cine thee to that sweet sleep
         Which thou owedst yesterday.
Othello: Ha! ha! false to me?
Iago: Why, how now, general? No more of that!
335 *Othello:*   Avaunt! be gone! Thou hast set me on the rack.
         I swear 'tis better to be much abused
         Than but to know't a little.
Iago: How now, my lord?
Othello: What sense had I of her stol'n hours of lust?
         I saw't not, thought it not, it harmed not me;
340   I slept the next night well, fed well, was free and merry;
         I found not Cassio's kisses on her lips
         He that is robbed, not wanting what is stol'n,
         Let him not know't, and he's not robbed at all.
Iago: I am sorry to hear this.
345 *Othello:*   I had been happy if the general camp,
         Pioneers and all, had tasted her sweet body,
         So I had nothing known. O, now for ever
         Farewell the tranquil mind! farewell content!
         Farewell the plumèd troop, and the big wars
350   That make ambition virtue! O, farewell!
         Farewell the neighing steed and the shrill trump,
         The spirit-stirring drum, th' ear-piercing fife,
         The royal banner, and all quality,
         Pride, pomp, and circumstance of glorious war!
355   And O you mortal engines whose rude throats
         Th' immortal Jove's dread clamors counterfeit,
         Farewell! Othello's occupation's gone!
Iago: Is't possible, my lord?
Othello: Villain, be sure thou prove my love a whore!
360   Be sure of it; give me the ocular proof;

Or, by the worth of mine eternal soul,
Thou hadst been better have been born a dog
Than answer my waked wrath!

Iago: Is't come to this?

Othello: Make me to see't; or at the least so prove it
365   That the probation bear no hinge nor loop
To hang a doubt on—or woe upon thy life!

Iago: My noble lord—

Othello: If thou dost slander her and torture me,
Never pray more; abandon all remorse;
370   On horror's head horrors accumulate;
Do deeds to make heaven weep, all earth amazed;
For nothing canst thou to damnation add
Greater than that.

Iago: O grace! O heaven forgive me!
Are you a man? Have you a soul or sense?—
375   God b' wi' you! take mine office. O wretched fool,
That liv'st to make thine honesty a vice!
O monstrous world! Take note, take note, O world,
To be direct and honest is not safe.
I thank you for this profit; and from hence
380   I'll love no friend, sith love breeds such offense.

Othello: Nay, stay. Thou shouldst be honest.

Iago: I should be wise; for honesty's a fool
And loses that it works for.

Othello: By the world,
I think my wife be honest, and think she is not;
385   I think that thou art just, and think thou art not.
I'll have some proof. Her name, that was as fresh
As Dian's visage, is now begrimed and black
As mine own face. If there be cords, or knives,
Poison, or fire, or suffocating streams,
390   I'll not endure it. Would I were satisfied!

Iago: I see, sir, you are eaten up with passion:
I do repent me that I put it to you.
You would be satisfied?

Othello: Would? Nay, I will.

Iago: And may; but how? how satisfied, my lord?
395   Would you, the supervisor, grossly gape on?
Behold her topped?

Othello: Death and damnation! O!

Iago: It were a tedious difficulty, I think,
To bring them to that prospect. Damn them then,
If ever mortal eyes do see them bolster
400   More than their own! What then? How then?
What shall I say? Where's satisfaction?

It is impossible you should see this,
Were they as prime as goats, as hot as monkeys,
As salt as wolves in pride, and fools as gross
405   As ignorance made drunk. But yet, I say,
If imputation and strong circumstances
Which lead directly to the door of truth
Will give you satisfaction, you may haven't.
Othello: Give me a living reason she's disloyal.
410   *Iago:*   I do not like the office.
But sith I am ent'red in this cause so far,
Pricked to't by foolish honesty and love,
I will go on. I lay with Cassio lately,
And being troubled with a raging tooth,
415   I could not sleep.
There are a kind of men so loose of soul
That in their sleeps will mutter their affairs.
One of this kind is Cassio.
In sleep I heard him say, "Sweet Desdemona,
420   Let us be wary, let us hide our loves!"
And then, sir, would he gripe and wring my hand,
Cry "O sweet creature!" and then kiss me hard,
As if he plucked up kisses by the roots
That grew upon my lips; then laid his leg
425   Over my thigh, and sighed, and kissed, and then
Cried "Cursèd fate that gave thee to the Moor!"
Othello: O monstrous! monstrous!
Iago: Nay, this was but his dream.
Othello: But this denoted a foregone conclusion;
'Tis a shrewd doubt, though it be but a dream.
430   *Iago:*   And this may help to thicken other proofs
That do demonstrate thinly.
Othello: I'll tear her all to pieces!
Iago: Nay, but be wise. Yet we see nothing done;
She may be honest yet. Tell me but this—
Have you not sometimes seen a handkerchief
435   Spotted with strawberries in your wife's hand?
Othello: I gave her such a one; 'twas my first gift.
Iago: I know not that; but such a handkerchief—
I am sure it was your wife's—did I to-day
See Cassio wipe his beard with.
Othello: If it be that—
440   *Iago:*   If it be that, or any that was hers,
It speaks against her with the other proofs.
Othello: O, that the slave had forty thousand lives!
One is too poor, too weak for my revenge.
Now do I see 'tis true. Look here, Iago:

445 All my fond love thus do I blow to heaven.
'Tis gone.
Arise, black vengeance, from the hollow hell!
Yield up, O love, thy crown and hearted throne
To tyrannous hate! Swell, bosom, with thy fraught,
For 'tis of aspics' tongues!

450 *Iago:* Yet be content.
Othello: O, blood, blood, blood!
Iago: Patience, I say. Your mind perhaps may change.
Othello: Never, Iago. Like to the Pontic sea,
Whose icy current and compulsive course

455 Ne'er feels retiring ebb, but keeps due on
To the Propontic and the Hellespont,
Even so my bloody thoughts, with violent pace,
Shall ne'er look back, ne'er ebb to humble love,
Till that a capable and wide revenge
Swallow them up.

460 (He kneels.) Now, by yond marble heaven,
In the due reverence of a sacred vow
I here engage my words.
Iago: Do not rise yet.
(Iago kneels.)
Witness, you ever-burning lights above,
You elements that clip us round about,

465 Witness that here Iago doth give up
The execution of his wit, hands, heart
To wronged Othello's service! Let him command,
And to obey shall be in me remorse,
What bloody business ever.
[They rise.]
Othello: I greet thy love,

470 Not with vain thanks but with acceptance bounteous,
And will upon the instant put thee to't.
Within these three days let me hear thee say
That Cassio's not alive.
Iago: My friend is dead; 'tis done at your request.

475 But let her live.
Othello: Damn her, lewd minx! O, damn her! damn her!
Come, go with me apart. I will withdraw
To furnish me with some swift means of death
For the fair devil. Now art thou my lieutenant.

480 *Iago:* I am your own forever.   *Exeunt.*

Scene IV: *The environs of the castle.*

Enter Desdemona, Emilia, and Clown.

Desdemona: Do you know, sirrah, where Lieutenant Cassio lies?

Clown: I dare not say he lies anywhere.

Desdemona: Why, man?

Clown: He's a soldier, and for me to say a soldier lies is stabbing.

5   *Desdemona:*   Go to. Where lodges he?

Clown: To tell you where he lodges is to tell you where I lie.

Desdemona: Can anything be made of this?

Clown: I know not where he lodges; and for me to devise a lodging, and say
he lies here or he lies there, were to lie in mine own throat.

10   *Desdemona:*   Can you enquire him out, and be edified by report?

Clown: I will catechize the world for him; that is, make questions, and by
them answer.

Desdemona: Seek him, bid him come hither. Tell him I have moved my lord
on his behalf and hope all will be well.

Clown: To do this is within the compass of man's wit, and therefore I'll attempt

15   the doing of it.   *Exit.*

Desdemona: Where should I lose that handkerchief, Emilia?

Emilia: I know not, madam.

Desdemona: Believe me, I had rather have lost my purse

20   Full of crusadoes; and but my noble Moor
Is true of mind, and made of no such baseness
As jealous creatures are, it were enough
To put him to ill thinking.

Emilia: Is he not jealous?

Desdemona: Who? he? I think the sun where he was born
Drew all such humors from him.

Enter Othello.

25   *Emilia:*   Look where he comes.

Desdemona: I will not leave him now till Cassio
Be called to him—How is't with you, my lord?

Othello: Well, my good lady. *[Aside.]* O, hardness to dissemble!—
How do you, Desdemona?

Desdemona: Well, my good lord.

30   *Othello:*   Give me your hand. This hand is moist, my lady.

Desdemona: It yet hath felt no age nor known no sorrow.

Othello: This argues fruitfulness and liberal heart.
Hot, hot, and moist. This hand of yours requires
A sequester from liberty, fasting and prayer,

35   Much castigation, exercise devout; 35
For here's a young and sweating devil here
That commonly rebels. 'Tis a good hand,
A frank one.

Desdemona: You may, indeed, say so;

40   For 'twas that hand that gave away my heart.

Othello: A liberal hand! The hearts of old gave hands;
But our new heraldry is hands, not hearts.

Desdemona: I cannot speak of this. Come now, your promise!

Othello: What promise, chuck?

45 *Desdemona:* I have sent to bid Cassio come speak with you.

Othello: I have a salt and sorry rheum offends me.
Lend me thy handkerchief.

Desdemona: Here, my lord.

Othello: That which I gave you.

Desdemona: I have it not about me.

Othello: Not?

Desdemona: No, faith, my lord.

Othello: That's a fault.

50 That handkerchief
Did an Egyptian to my mother give.
She was a charmer, and could almost read
The thoughts of people. She told her, while she kept it,
'Twould make her amiable and subdue my father

55 Entirely to her love; but if she lost it
Or made a gift of it, my father's eye
Should hold her loathèd, and his spirits should hunt
After new fancies. She, dying, gave it me,
And bid me, when my fate would have me wive;

60 To give it her. I did so; and take heed on't;
Make it a darling like your precious eye.
To lose't or give't away were such perdition
As nothing else could match.

Desdemona: Is't possible?

Othello: 'Tis true. There's magic in the web of it.

65 A sibyl that had numb'red in the world
The sun to course two hundred compasses,
In her prophetic fury sewed the work;
The worms were hallowed that did breed the silk;
And it was dyed in mummy which the skillful
Conserved of maidens' hearts.

70 *Desdemona:* I' faith? Is't true?

Othello: Most veritable. Therefore look to't well.

Desdemona: Then would to God that I had never seen't!

Othello: Ha! Wherefore?

Desdemona: Why do you speak so startingly and rash?

75 *Othello:* Is't lost? Is't gone? Speak, is it out o' th' way?

Desdemona: Heaven bless us!

Othello: Say you?

Desdemona: It is not lost. But what an if it were?

Othello: How?

Desdemona: I say it is not lost.

80 *Othello:* Fetch't, let me see't!

Desdemona: Why, so I can, sir; but I will not now.

This is a trick to put me from my suit:
Pray you let Cassio be received again.
Othello: Fetch me the handkerchief! My mind misgives.

85   *Desdemona:*   Come, come!
You'll never meet a more sufficient man.
Othello: The handkerchief!
[*Desdemona:*   I pray talk me of Cassio.
Othello: The handkerchief!]
Desdemona: A man that all his time
Hath founded his good fortunes on your love,

90   Shared dangers with you—
Othello: The handkerchief!
Desdemona: I' faith, you are to blame.
Othello: Zounds!   *Exit Othello.*
Emilia: Is not this man jealous?

95   *Desdemona:*   I ne'er saw this before.
Sure there's some wonder in this handkerchief;
I am most unhappy in the loss of it.
Emilia: 'Tis not a year or two shows us a man.
They are all but stomachs, and we all but food;

100   They eat us hungerly, and when they are full,
They belch us.
Enter Iago and Cassio.
Look you—Cassio and my husband!
Iago: There is no other way; 'tis she must do't.
And lo the happiness! Go and importune her.
Desdemona: How now, good Cassio? What's the news with you?

105   *Cassio:*   Madam, my former suit. I do beseech you
That by your virtuous means I may again
Exist, and be a member of his love
Whom I with all the office of my heart
Entirely honor. I would not be delayed.

110   If my offense be of such mortal kind
That neither service past, nor present sorrows,
Nor purposed merit in futurity,
Can ransom me into his love again,
But to know so must be my benefit.

115   So shall I clothe me in a forced content,
And shut myself up in some other course,
To fortune's alms.
Desdemona: Alas, thrice-gentle Cassio!
My advocation is not now in tune.
My lord is not my lord; nor should I know him,

120   Were he in favor as in humor altered.
So help me every spirit sanctified
As I have spoken for you all my best

And stood within the blank of his displeasure
For my free speech! You must a while be patient.
125   What I can do I will; and more I will
Than for myself I dare. Let that suffice you.
Iago: Is my lord angry?
Emilia: He went hence but now,
And certainly in strange unquietness.
Iago: Can he be angry? I have seen the cannon
130   When it hath blown his ranks into the air
And, like the devil, from his very arm
Puffed his own brother—and is he angry?
Something of moment then. I will go meet him.
There's matter in't indeed if he be angry.
Desdemona: I prithee do so.   *Exit [Iago].*
135   Something sure of state,
Either from Venice or some unhatched practice
Made demonstrable here in Cyprus to him,
Hath puddled his clear spirit; and in such cases
Men's natures wrangle with inferior things,
140   Though great ones are their object. 'Tis even so;
For let our finger ache, and it endues
Our other, healthful members even to a sense
Of pain. Nay, we must think men are not gods,
Nor of them look for such observancy
145   As fits the bridal. Beshrew me much, Emilia,
I was, unhandsome warrior as I am,
Arraigning his unkindness with my soul;
But now I find I had suborned the witness,
And he's indicted falsely.
150   *Emilia:*   Pray heaven it be state matters, as you think,
And no conception nor no jealous toy
Concerning you.
Desdemona: Alas the day! I never gave him cause.
Emilia: But jealous souls will not be answered so;
155   They are not ever jealous for the cause,
But jealous for they're jealous. 'Tis a monster
Begot upon itself, born on itself.
Desdemona: Heaven keep that monster from Othello's mind!
Emilia: Lady, amen.
160   *Desdemona:*   I will go seek him. Cassio, walk here about:
If I do find him fit, I'll move your suit
And seek to effect it to my uttermost.
Cassio: I humbly thank your ladyship.
                                    Exeunt Desdemona and Emilia.
Enter Bianca.
Bianca: Save you, friend Cassio!

Cassio: What make you from home?

165   How is't with you, my most fair Bianca?

I' faith, sweet love, I was coming to your house.

Bianca: And I was going to your lodging, Cassio.

What, keep a week away? seven days and nights?

Eightscore eight hours? and lovers' absent hours,

170   More tedious than the dial eightscore times?

O weary reck'ning!

Cassio: Pardon me, Bianca:

I have this while with leaden thoughts been pressed;

But I shall in a more continuate time

Strike off this score of absence. Sweet Bianca,

[Gives her Desdemona's handkerchief.]

Take me this work out.

175   *Bianca:*   O Cassio, whence came this?

This is some token from a newer friend.

To the felt absence now I feel a cause.

Is't come to this? Well, well.

Cassio: Go to, woman!

Throw your vile guesses in the devil's teeth,

180   From whence you have them. You are jealous now

That this is from some mistress, some remembrance.

No, by my faith, Bianca.

Bianca: Why, whose is it?

Cassio: I know not, sweet; I found it in my chamber.

I like the work well; ere it be demanded,

185   As like enough it will, I'd have it copied.

Take it and do't, and leave me for this time.

Bianca: Leave you? Wherefore?

Cassio: I do attend here on the general

And think it no addition, nor my wish,

To have him see me womaned.

190   *Bianca:*   Why, I pray you?

Cassio: Not that I love you not.

Bianca: But that you do not love me!

I pray you bring me on the way a little,

And say if I shall see you soon at night.

Cassio: 'Tis but a little way that I can bring you,

195   For I attend here; but I'll see you soon.

Bianca: 'Tis very good. I must be circumstanced.   *Exeunt.*

ACT IV

SCENE I: *The environs of the castle.*

Enter Othello and Iago.

Iago: Will you think so?

Othello: Think so, Iago?

Iago: What,
  To kiss in private?

Othello: An unauthorized kiss.

Iago: Or to be naked with her friend in bed
  An hour or more, not meaning any harm?

5 *Othello:*   Naked in bed, Iago, and not mean harm?
  It is hypocrisy against the devil.
  They that mean virtuously, and yet do so,
  The devil their virtue tempts, and they tempt heaven.

10 *Iago:*   So they do nothing, 'tis a venial slip.
  But if I give my wife a handkerchief—

Othello: What then?

Iago: Why, then 'tis hers, my lord; and being hers,
  She may, I think, bestow't on any man.

Othello: She is protectress of her honor too;

15   May she give that?

Iago: Her honor is an essence that's not seen;
  They have it very oft that have it not.
  But for the handkerchief—

Othello: By heaven, I would most gladly have forgot it!

20   Thou said'st—O, it comes o'er my memory
  As doth the raven o'er the infected house,
  Boding to all!—he had my handkerchief.

Iago: Ay, what of that?

Othello: That's not so good now.

Iago: What
  If I had said I had seen him do you wrong?

25   Or heard him say—as knaves be such abroad
  Who having, by their own importunate suit,
  Or voluntary dotage of some mistress,
  Convincèd or supplied them, cannot choose
  But they must blab—

Othello: Hath he said anything?

30 *Iago:*   He hath, my lord; but be you well assured,
  No more than he'll unswear.

Othello: What hath he said?

Iago: Faith, that he did—I know not what he did.

Othello: What? what?

Iago: Lie—

Othello: With her?

Iago: With her, on her; what you will.

Othello: Lie with her? lie on her?—We say lie on her when they belie her.—
  Lie with her! Zounds, that's fulsome.—Handkerchief—confessions—
  handkerchief!—To confess, and be hanged for his labor—first to behanged,

and then to confess! I tremble at it. Nature would not invest herself in
40   such shadowing passion without some instruction. It is not words that
shakes me thus.—Pish! Noses, ears, and lips? Is't possible?—Confess?—
Handkerchief?—O devil!
(Falls in a trance.)
Iago: Work on,
My med'cine, work! Thus credulous fools are caught,

Shakespeare / Othello the Moor of Venice

45   And many worthy and chaste dames even thus,
All guiltless, meet reproach.—What, ho! my lord!
My lord, I say! Othello!
Enter Cassio. How now, Cassio?
Cassio: What's the matter?
Iago: My lord is fall'n into an epilepsy.
50   This is his second fit; he had one yesterday.
Cassio: Rub him about the temples.
Iago: No, forbear.
The lethargy must have his quiet course.
If not, he foams at mouth, and by and by
Breaks out to savage madness. Look, he stirs.
55   Do you withdraw yourself a little while.
He will recover straight. When he is gone,
I would on great occasion speak with you.   *[Exit Cassio.]*
How is it, general? Have you not hurt your head?
Othello: Dost thou mock me?
Iago: I mock you? No, by heaven.
60   Would you would bear your fortune like a man!
Othello: A hornèd man's a monster and a beast.
Iago: There's many a beast then in a populous city,
And many a civil monster.
Othello: Did he confess it?
Iago: Good sir, be a man.
65   Think every bearded fellow that's but yoked
May draw with you. There's millions now alive
That nightly lie in those unproper beds
Which they dare swear peculiar: your case is better.
70   O, 'tis the spite of hell, the fiend's arch-mock,
To lip a wanton in a secure couch,
And to suppose her chaste! No, let me know;
And knowing what I am, I know what she shall be.
Othello: O, thou art wise! 'Tis certain.
Iago: Stand you awhile apart;
Confine yourself but in a patient list.
75   Whilst you were here, o'erwhelmèd with your grief—
A passion most unsuiting such a man—
Cassio came hither. I shifted him away

And laid good 'scuse upon your ecstasy;
Bade him anon return, and here speak with me;
80   The which he promised. Do but encave yourself
And mark the fleers, the gibes, and notable scorns
That dwell in every region of his face;
For I will make him tell the tale anew—
Where, how, how oft, how long ago, and when
85   He hath, and is again to cope your wife.
I say, but mark his gesture. Marry, patience!
Or I shall say y'are all in all in spleen,
And nothing of a man.
Othello: Dost thou hear, Iago?
I will be found most cunning in my patience;
But—dost thou hear?—most bloody.
90   *Iago:*   That's not amiss:
But yet keep time in all. Will you withdraw?

[Othello retires.]

Now will I question Cassio of Bianca,
A huswife that by selling her desires
Buys herself bread and clothes. It is a creature
95   That dotes on Cassio, as 'tis the strumpet's plague
To beguile many and be beguiled by one.
He, when he hears of her, cannot refrain
From the excess of laughter. Here he comes.
Enter Cassio.
As he shall smile, Othello shall go mad;
And his unbookish jealousy must conster
Poor Cassio's smiles, gestures, and light behavior
Quite in the wrong. How do you now, lieutenant?
Cassio: The worser that you give me the addition
Whose want even kills me.
105   *Iago:*   Ply Desdemona well, and you are sure on't.
Now, if this suit lay in Bianca's power,
How quickly should you speed!
Cassio: Alas, poor caitiff!
Othello: Look how he laughs already!
Iago: I never knew a woman love man so.
110   *Cassio:*   Alas, poor rogue! I think, i' faith, she loves me.
Othello: Now he denies it faintly, and laughs it out.
Iago: Do you hear, Cassio?
Othello: Now he importunes him
To tell it o'er. Go to! Well said, well said!
Iago: She gives out that you shall marry her.
Do you intend it?
Cassio: Ha, ha, ha!
Othello: Do you triumph, Roman? Do you triumph?

Cassio: I marry her? What, a customer? Prithee bear some charity to my wit; do not think it so unwholesome. Ha, ha, ha!

120   *Othello:*   So, so, so, so! They laugh that win!

Iago: Faith, the cry goes that you shall marry her.

Cassio: Prithee say true.

Iago: I am a very villain else.

Othello: Have you scored me? Well.

125   *Cassio:*   This is the monkey's own giving out. She is persuaded I will marry her out of her own love and flattery, not out of my promise.

Othello: Iago beckons me; now he begins the story.

Cassio: She was here even now; she haunts me in every place. I was t' other day talking on the sea bank with certain Venetians, and thither comes the

130   bauble, and, by this hand, she falls me thus about my neck—

Othello: Crying "O dear Cassio!" as it were. His gesture imports it.

Cassio: So hangs, and lolls, and weeps upon me; so shakes and pulls me! Ha, ha, ha!

Othello: Now he tells how she plucked him to my chamber. O, I see that nose

135   of yours, but not that dog I shall throw it to.

Cassio: Well, I must leave her company.

Enter Bianca.

Iago: Before me! Look where she comes.

Cassio: 'Tis such another fitchew! marry, a perfumed one. What do you mean by this haunting of me?

140   *Bianca:*   Let the devil and his dam haunt you! What did you mean by that same handkerchief you gave me even now? I was a fine fool to take it. I must take out the whole work? A likely piece of work that you should find it in your chamber and know not who left it there! This is some minx's token, and I must take out the work? There! Give it your hobby-horse. Wheresoever

145   you had it, I'll take out no work on 't.

Cassio: How now, my sweet Bianca? How now? how now?

Othello: By heaven, that should be my handkerchief!

Bianca: An you'll come to supper to-night, you may; an you will not, come when you are next prepared for.   *Exit.*

150   *Iago:*   After her, after her!

Cassio: Faith, I must; she'll rail in the street else.

Iago: Will you sup there?

Cassio: Yes, I intend so.

Iago: Well, I may chance to see you; for I would very fain speak with you.

155   *Cassio:*   Prithee come. Will you?

Iago: Go to! say no more.   *Exit Cassio.*

Othello [comes forward]:   How shall I murder him, Iago?

Iago: Did you perceive how he laughed at his vice?

Othello: O Iago!

160   *Iago:*   And did you see the handkerchief?

Othello: Was that mine?

Iago: Your, by this hand! And to see how he prizes the foolish woman your wife! She gave it him, and he hath giv'n it his whore.

Othello: I would have him nine years a-killing—A fine woman! a fair woman!
165 a sweet woman!

Iago: Nay, you must forget that.

Othello: Ay, let her rot, and perish, and be damned to-night; for she shall not live. No, my heart is turned to stone; I strike it, and it hurts my hand. O, the world hath not a sweeter creature! She might lie by an emperor's side and
170 command him tasks.

Iago: Nay, that's not your way.

Othello: Hang her! I do but say what she is. So delicate with her needle! an admirable musician! O, she will sing the savageness out of a bear! Of so high and plenteous wit and invention—

175 *Iago:* She's the worse for all this.

Othello: O, a thousand thousand times! And then, of so gentle a condition!

Iago: Ay, too gentle.

Othello: Nay, that's certain. But yet the pity of it, Iago! O Iago, the pity of it, Iago!

180 *Iago:* If you are so fond over her iniquity, give her patent to offend; for if it touch not you, it comes near nobody.

Othello: I will chop her into messes! Cuckold me!

Iago: O, 'tis foul in her.

Othello: With mine officer!

185 *Iago:* That's fouler.

Othello: Get me some poison, Iago, this night. I'll not expostulate with her, lest her body and beauty unprovide my mind again. This night, Iago!

Iago: Do it not with poison. Strangle her in her bed, even the bed she hath contaminated.

190 *Othello:* Good, good! The justice of it pleases. Very good!

Iago: And for Cassio, let me be his undertaker; you shall hear more by midnight.

Othello: Excellent good!

  A trumpet.

  What trumpet is that same?

Iago: I warrant something from Venice.

  Enter Lodovico, Desdemona, and Attendants.

195 'Tis Lodovico.

  This comes from the Duke; and see, your wife is with him.

Lodovico: God save you, worthy general!

Othello: With all my heart, sir.

Lodovico: The Duke and senators of Venice greet you.

  [Gives him a letter.]

Othello: I kiss the instrument of their pleasures.

  [Opens the letter and reads.]

200 *Desdemona:* And what's the news, good cousin Lodovico?

Iago: I am very glad to see you, signior.

Welcome to Cyprus.
Lodovico: I thank you. How does Lieutenant Cassio?
Iago: Lives, sir.
Desdemona: Cousin, there's fall'n between him and my lord
205   An unkind breach; but you shall make all well.
Othello: Are you sure of that?
Desdemona: My lord?
Othello [reads]:   "This fail you not to do, as you will—"
Lodovico: He did not call; he's busy in the paper.
210   Is there division 'twixt thy lord and Cassio?
Desdemona: A most unhappy one. I would do much
         T' atone them, for the love I bear to Cassio.
Othello: Fire and brimstone!
Desdemona: My lord?
Othello: Are you wise?
Desdemona: What, is he angry?
Lodovico: May be the letter moved him;
215   For, as I think, they do command him home,
         Deputing Cassio in his government.
Desdemona: By my troth, I am glad on't.
Othello: Indeed?
Desdemona: My lord?
Othello: I am glad to see you mad.
Desdemona: Why, sweet Othello—
Othello: Devil!
         [Strikes her.]
220   *Desdemona:*   I have not deserved this.
Lodovico: My lord, this would not be believed in Venice,
         Though I should swear I saw't. 'Tis very much.
         Make her amends; she weeps.
Othello: O devil, devil!
         If that the earth could teem with woman's tears,
225   Each drop she falls would prove a crocodile.
         Out of my sight!
Desdemona: I will not stay to offend you.   *[Going.]*
Lodovico: Truly, an obedient lady.
         I do beseech your lordship call her back.
Othello: Mistress!
Desdemona: My lord?
230   *Othello:*   What would you with her, sir?
Lodovico: Who? I, my lord?
Othello: Ay! You did wish that I would make her turn.
         Sir, she can turn, and turn, and yet go on
         And turn again; and she can weep, sir, weep;
235   And she's obedient; as you say, obedient,
         Very obedient.—Proceed you in your tears.—

Concerning this, sir—O well-painted passion!—
I am commanded home.—Get you away;
I'll send for you anon.—Sir, I obey the mandate
240   And will return to Venice.—Hence, avaunt!

[Exit Desdemona.]

Cassio shall have my place. And, sir, to-night
I do entreat that we may sup together.
You are welcome, sir, to Cyprus—Goats and monkeys!

Exit.

Lodovico: Is this the noble Moor whom our full Senate
245   Call all in all sufficient? Is this the nature
Whom passion could not shake? whose solid virtue
The shot of accident nor dart of chance
Could neither graze nor pierce?
Iago: He is much changed.
Lodovico: Are his wits safe? Is he not light of brain?
250 *Iago:* He's that he is; I may not breathe my censure.
What he might be—if what he might he is not—
I would to heaven he were!
Lodovico: What, strike his wife?
Iago: Faith, that was not so well; yet would I knew
That stroke would prove the worst!
Lodovico: Is it his use?
255   Or did the letters work upon his blood
And new-create this fault?
Iago: Alas, alas!
It is not honesty in me to speak
What I have seen and known. You shall observe him,
And his own courses will denote him so
260   That I may save my speech. Do but go after
And mark how he continues.
Lodovico: I am sorry that I am deceived in him.

Exeunt.

SCENE II: *Within the castle.*

Enter Othello and Emilia.
Othello: You have seen nothing then?
Emilia: Nor ever heard, nor ever did suspect.
Othello: Yes, you have seen Cassio and she together.
Emilia: But then I saw no harm, and then I heard
5   Each syllable that breath made up between them.
Othello: What, did they never whisper?
Emilia: Never, my lord.
Othello: Nor send you out o' th' way?
Emilia: Never.
Othello: To fetch her fan, her gloves, her mask, nor nothing?

10   *Emilia:*   Never, my lord.

     Othello: That's strange.

     Emilia: I durst, my lord, to wager she is honest,

        Lay down my soul at stake. If you think other,

        Remove your thought; it doth abuse your bosom.

15   If any wretch have put this in your head,

        Let heaven requite it with the serpent's curse!

        For if she be not honest, chaste, and true,

        There's no man happy; the purest of their wives

        Is foul as slander.

     Othello: Bid her come hither. Go.   *Exit Emilia.*

20   She says enough; yet she's a simple bawd

        That cannot say as much. This is a subtle whore,

        A closet lock and key of villainous secrets;

        And yet she'll kneel and pray; I have seen her do't.

     Enter Desdemona and Emilia.

     Desdemona: My lord, what is your will?

     Othello: Pray, chuck, come hither.

     Desdemona: What is your pleasure?

25   *Othello:*   Let me see your eyes.

        Look in my face.

     Desdemona: What horrible fancy's this?

     Othello [to Emilia]:   Some of your function, mistress.

        Leave procreants alone and shut the door;

        Cough or cry hem if anybody come.

30   Your mystery, your mystery! Nay, dispatch!

                                   Exit Emilia.

     Desdemona: Upon my knees, what doth your speech import?

        I understand a fury in your words,

        [But not the words.]

     Othello: Why, what art thou?

     Desdemona: Your wife, my lord; your true

        And loyal wife.

35   *Othello:*   Come, swear it, damn thyself;

        Lest, being like one of heaven, the devils themselves

        Should fear to seize thee. Therefore be double-damned—

        Swear thou art honest.

     Desdemona: Heaven doth truly know it.

     Othello: Heaven truly knows that thou art false as hell.

40   *Desdemona:*   To whom, my lord? With whom? How am I false?

     Othello: Ah, Desdemona! away! away! away!

     Desdemona: Alas the heavy day! Why do you weep?

        Am I the motive of these tears, my lord?

        If haply you my father do suspect

45   An instrument of this your calling back,

        Lay not your blame on me. If you have lost him,

Why, I have lost him too.
Othello: Had it pleased heaven
   To try me with affliction, had they rained
   All kinds of sores and shames on my bare head,
50 Steeped me in poverty to the very lips,
   Given to captivity me and my utmost hopes,
   I should have found in some place of my soul
   A drop of patience. But, alas, to make me
   A fixèd figure for the time of scorn
55 To point his slow unmoving finger at!
   Yet could I bear that too; well, very well.
   But there where I have garnered up my heart,
   Where either I must live or bear no life,
   The fountain from the which my current runs
60 Or else dries up—to be discarded thence,
   Or keep it as a cistern for foul toads
   To knot and gender in — turn thy complexion there,
   Patience, thou young and rose-lipped cherubin!
   Ay, there look grim as hell!
65 *Desdemona:*   I hope my noble lord esteems me honest.
  Othello: O, ay; as summer flies are in the shambles,
   That quicken even with blowing. O thou weed,
   Who art so lovely fair, and smell'st so sweet,
   That the sense aches at thee, would thou hadst ne'er been born!
70 *Desdemona:*   Alas, what ignorant sin have I committed?
  Othello: Was this fair paper, this most goodly book,
   Made to write "whore" upon? What committed?
   Committed? O thou public commoner!
   I should make very forges of my cheeks
75 That would to cinders burn up modesty,
   Did I but speak thy deeds. What committed?
   Heaven stops the nose at it, and the moon winks;
   The bawdy wind, that kisses all it meets,
   Is hushed within the hollow mine of earth
80 And will not hear it. What committed?
   Impudent strumpet!
 Desdemona: By heaven, you do me wrong!
 Othello: Are not you a strumpet?
 Desdemona: No, as I am a Christian!
   If to preserve this vessel for my lord
   From any other foul unlawful touch
85 Be not to be a strumpet, I am none.
 Othello: What, not a whore?
 Desdemona: No, as I shall be saved!
 Othello: Is't possible?
 Desdemona: O, heaven forgive us!

Othello: I cry you mercy then.
 I took you for that cunning whore of Venice

90 That married with Othello.—*[Calling.]* You, mistress,
 That have the office opposite to Saint Peter
 And keep the gate of hell!
 Enter Emilia.
 You, you, ay, you!
 We have done our course; there's money for your pains:
 I pray you turn the key, and keep our counsel.   *Exit.*

95 *Emilia:*   Alas, what does this gentleman conceive?
 How do you, madam? How do you, my good lady?
Desdemona: Faith, half asleep.
Emilia: Good madam, what's the matter with my lord?
Desdemona: With who?

100 *Emilia:*   Why, with my lord, madam.
Desdemona: Who is thy lord?
Emilia: He that is yours, sweet lady.
Desdemona: I have none. Do not talk to me, Emilia.
 I cannot weep; nor answer have I none
 But what should go by water. Prithee to-night

105 Lay on my bed my wedding sheets, remember;
 And call thy husband hither.
Emilia: Here's a change indeed! *Exit.*
Desdemona: 'Tis meet I should be used so, very meet.
 How have I been behaved, that he might stick
 The small'st opinion on my least misuse?
 Enter Iago and Emilia.

110 *Iago:*   What is your pleasure, madam? How is't with you?
Desdemona: I cannot tell. Those that do teach young babes
 Do it with gentle means and easy tasks:
 He might have chid me so; for, in good faith,
 I am a child to chiding.
Iago: What is the matter, lady?

115 *Emilia:*   Alas, Iago, my lord hath so bewhored her,
 Thrown such despite and heavy terms upon her
 As true hearts cannot bear.
Desdemona: Am I that name, Iago?
Iago: What name, fair lady?
Desdemona: Such as she said my lord did say I was.
Emilia: He called her whore. A beggar in his drink
 Could not have laid such terms upon his callet.
Iago: Why did he so?
Desdemona: I do not know; I am sure I am none such.
Iago: Do not weep, do not weep. Alas the day!

125 *Emilia:*   Hath she forsook so many noble matches,
 Her father and her country, and her friends,

To be called whore? Would it not make one weep?
Desdemona: It is my wretched fortune.
Iago: Beshrew him for't!
  How comes this trick upon him?
Desdemona: Nay, heaven doth know.
130   *Emilia:*   I will be hanged if some eternal villain,
  Some busy and insinuating rogue,
  Some cogging, cozening slave, to get some office,
  Have not devised this slander. I'll be hanged else.
Iago: Fie, there is no such man! It is impossible.
135   *Desdemona:*   If any such there be, heaven pardon him!
  Emilia: A halter pardon him! and hell gnaw his bones!
    Why should he call her whore? Who keeps her company?
    What place? what time? what form? what likelihood?
    The Moor's abused by some most villainous knave,
140   Some base notorious knave, some scurvy fellow.
    O heaven, that such companions thou 'dst unfold,
    And put in every honest hand a whip
    To lash the rascals naked through the world
    Even from the east to th' west!
  Iago: Speak within door.
145   *Emilia:*   O, fie upon them! Some such squire he was
    That turned your wit the seamy side without
    And made you to suspect me with the Moor.
  Iago: You are a fool. Go to.
  Desdemona: Alas, Iago,
    What shall I do to win my lord again?
150   Good friend, go to him; for, by this light of heaven,
    I know not how I lost him. Here I kneel:
    If e'er my will did trespass 'gainst his love
    Either in discourse of thought or actual deed,
    Or that mine eyes, mine ears, or any sense
155   Delighted them in any other form,
    Or that I do not yet, and ever did,
    And ever will (though he do shake me off
    To beggarly divorcement) love him dearly,
    Comfort forswear me! Unkindness may do much;
160   And his unkindness may defeat my life,
    But never taint my love. I cannot say "whore."
    It does abhor me now I speak the word;
    To do the act that might the addition earn
    Not the world's mass of vanity could make me.
165   *Iago:*   I pray you be content. 'Tis but his humor.
    The business of the state does him offense,
    [And he does chide with you.]
  Desdemona: If 'twere no other—

Iago: 'Tis but so, I warrant.

[*Trumpets within.*]

Hark how these instruments summon you to supper.

The messengers of Venice stay the meat:

170   Go in, and weep not. All things shall be well.

Exeunt Desdemona and Emilia.

Enter Roderigo.

How now, Roderigo?

Roderigo: I do not find that thou deal'st justly with me.

Iago: What in the contrary?

175   *Roderigo:*   Every day thou daff'st me with some device, Iago, and rather, as it seems to me now, keep'st from me all conveniency than suppliest me with the least advantage of hope. I will indeed no longer endure it; nor am I yet persuaded to put up in peace what already I have foolishly suffered.

180   *Iago:*   Will you hear me, Roderigo?

Roderigo: Faith, I have heard too much; for your words and performances are no kin together.

Iago: You charge me most unjustly.

Roderigo: With naught but truth. I have wasted myself out of my means.

185   The jewels you have had from me to deliver to Desdemona would half have corrupted a votarist. You have told me she hath received them, and returned me expectations and comforts of sudden respect and acquaintance; but I find none.

Iago: Well, go to; very well.

190   *Roderigo:*   Very well! go to! I cannot go to, man; nor 'tis not very well. By this hand, I say 'tis very scurvy, and begin to find myself fopped in it.

Iago: Very well.

Roderigo: I tell you 'tis not very well. I will make myself known to Desdemona. If she will return me my jewels, I will give over my suit and repent my

195   unlawful solicitation; if not, assure yourself I will seek satisfaction of you.

Iago: You have said now.

Roderigo: Ay, and said nothing but what I protest intendment of doing.

Iago: Why, now I see there's mettle in thee; and even from this instant do build

200   on thee a better opinion than ever before. Give me thy hand, Roderigo. Thou has taken against me a most just exception; but yet I protest I have dealt most directly in thy affair.

Roderigo: It hath not appeared.

Iago: I grant indeed it hath not appeared, and your suspicion is not without wit

205   and judgment. But, Roderigo, if thou hast that in thee indeed which I have greater reason to believe now than ever, I mean purpose, courage, and valor, this night show it. If thou the next night following enjoy not Desdemona, take me from this world with treachery and devise engines for my life.

210   *Roderigo:*   Well, what is it? Is it within reason and compass?

Iago: Sir, there is especial commission come from Venice to depute Cassio in Othello's place.

Roderigo: Is that true? Why, then Othello and Desdemona return again to Venice.

Iago: O, no; he goes into Mauritania and takes away with him the fair Desdemona, unless his abode be lingered here by some accident; wherein none can
215 be so determinate as the removing of Cassio.

Roderigo: How do you mean removing of him?

220 *Iago:* Why, by making him uncapable of Othello's place—knocking out his brains.

Roderigo: And that you would have me to do?

Iago: Ay, if you dare do yourself a profit and a right. He sups to-night with a
harlotry, and thither will I go to him. He knows not yet of his honorable
fortune. If you will watch his going thence, which I will fashion to fall
225 out between twelve and one, you may take him at your pleasure. I will be
near to second your attempt, and he shall fall between us. Come, stand not
amazed at it, but go along with me. I will show you such a necessity in his
death that you shall think yourself bound to put it on him. It is now high
230 supper time, and the night grows to waste. About it!

Roderigo: I will hear further reason for this.

Iago: And you shall be satisfied. *Exeunt.*

Scene III: *Within the castle.*

Enter Othello, Lodovico, Desdemona, Emilia, and Attendants.

Lodovico: I do beseech you, sir, trouble yourself no further.

Othello: O, pardon me; 'twill do me good to walk.

Lodovico: Madam, good night. I humbly thank your ladyship.

Desdemona: Your honor is most welcome.

Othello: Will you walk, sir?

O, Desdemona—

5 *Desdemona:* My lord?

Othello: Get you to bed on th' instant; I will be returned forthwith.
Dismiss your attendant there. Look't be done.

Desdemona: I will, my lord.

Exit [Othello, with Lodovico and Attendants].

10 *Emilia:* How goes it now? He looks gentler than he did.

Desdemona: He says he will return incontinent.
He hath commanded me to go to bed,
And bade me to dismiss you.

Emilia: Dismiss me?

15 *Desdemona:* It was his bidding; therefore, good Emilia,
Give me my nightly wearing, and adieu.
We must not now displease him.

Emilia: I would you had never seen him!

Desdemona: So would not I. My love doth so approve him
That even his stubbornness, his checks, his frowns—
20 Prithee unpin me—have grace and favor in them.

Emilia: I have laid those sheets you bade me on the bed.

Desdemona: All's one. Good faith, how foolish are our minds!
If I do die before thee, prithee shroud me

In one of those same sheets.

Emilia: Come, come! You talk.

25   *Desdemona:*   My mother had a maid called Barbary.
    She was in love; and he she loved proved mad
    And did forsake her. She had a song of "Willow";
    An old thing 'twas; but it expressed her fortune,
    And she died singing it. That song to-night
30   Will not go from my mind; I have much to do
    But to go hang my head all at one side
    And sing it like poor Barbary. Prithee dispatch.

Emilia: Shall I go fetch your nightgown?

Desdemona: No, unpin me here.
    This Lodovico is a proper man.

35   *Emilia:*   A very handsome man.

Desdemona: He speaks well.

Emilia: I know a lady in Venice would have walked barefoot to Palestine for
    a touch of his nether lip.

Desdemona (sings):   "The poor soul sat sighing by a sycamore tree
40   Sing all a green willow;
    Her hand on her bosom, her head on her knee,
    Sing willow, willow, willow.
    The fresh streams ran by her and murmured her moans;
    Sing willow, willow, willow;
45   Her salt tears fell from her, and soft'ned the stones"—
    Lay by these.
    "Sing willow, willow, willow"—
    Prithee hie thee; he'll come anon.
    "Sing all a green willow must be my garland.
50   Let nobody blame him; his scorn I approve"—
    Nay, that's not next. Hark! who is't that knocks?

Emilia: It's the wind.

Desdemona (sings):   "I call my love false love; but what said he then? Sing willow,
    willow, willow:
55   If I court moe women, you'll couch with moe men."
    So get thee gone; good night. Mine eyes do itch.
    Doth that bode weeping?

Emilia: 'Tis neither here nor there.

Desdemona: I have heard it said so. O, these men, these men!
    Dost thou in conscience think—tell me, Emilia—
60   That there be women do abuse their husbands
    In such gross kind?

Emilia: There be some such, no question.

Desdemona: Wouldst thou do such a deed for all the world?

Emilia: Why, would not you?

Desdemona: No, by this heavenly light!

Emilia: Nor I neither by this heavenly light.

65   I might do't as well i' th' dark.
    Desdemona: Wouldst thou do such a deed for all the world?
    Emilia: The world's a huge thing; it is a great price for a small vice.
    Desdemona: In troth, I think thou wouldst not.
    Emilia: In troth, I think I should; and undo't when I had done it. Marry,
70   I would not do such a thing for a joint-ring, nor for measures of lawn, nor
for gowns, petticoats, nor caps, nor any petty exhibition; but, for all the
whole world—'Ud's pity! who would not make her husband a cuckold to
make him a monarch? I should venture purgatory for't.
    Desdemona: Beshrew me if I would do such a wrong
75   For the whole world.
    Emilia: Why, the wrong is but a wrong i' th' world; and having the world for
your labor, 'tis a wrong in your own world, and you might quickly make
it right.
80   *Desdemona:*   I do not think there is any such woman.
    Emilia: Yes, a dozen; and as many to th' vantage as would store the world they
played for.
But I do think it is their husbands' faults
If wives do fall. Say that they slack their duties
And pour our treasures into foreign laps;
85   Or else break out in peevish jealousies,
Throwing restraint upon us; or say they strike us,
Or scant our former having in despite—
Why, we have galls; and though we have some grace,
Yet have we some revenge. Let husbands know
90   Their wives have sense like them. They see, and smell,
And have their palates both for sweet and sour,
As husbands have. What is it that they do
When they change us for others? Is it sport?
I think it is. And doth affection breed it?
95   I think it doth. Is't frailty that thus errs?
It is so too. And have not we affections,
Desires for sport, and frailty, as men have?
Then let them use us well; else let them know,
The ills we do, their ills instruct us so.
100   *Desdemona:*   Good night, good night. God me such usage send,
Not to pick bad from bad, but by bad mend!   *Exeunt.*

ACT V

Scene I: *A street in Cyprus.*

    Enter Iago and Roderigo.
    Iago: Here, stand behind this bulk; straight will he come.
Wear thy good rapier bare, and put it home.
Quick, quick! Fear nothing; I'll be at thy elbow.

It makes us, or it mars us—think on that,

5   And fix most firm thy resolution.

Roderigo: Be near at hand; I may miscarry in't.

Iago: Here, at thy hand. Be bold, and take thy stand.

[Stands aside.]

Roderigo: I have no great devotion to the deed,

And yet he hath given me satisfying reasons.

10   'Tis but a man gone. Forth my sword! He dies!

Iago: I have rubbed this young quat almost to the sense,

And he grows angry. Now whether he kill Cassio,

Or Cassio him, or each do kill the other,

Every way makes my gain. Live Roderigo,

15   He calls me to a restitution large

Of gold and jewels that I bobbed from him

As gifts to Desdemona.

It must not be. If Cassio do remain,

He hath a daily beauty in his life

20   That makes me ugly; and besides, the Moor

May unfold me to him; there stand I in much peril.

No, he must die. Be't so! I hear him coming.

Enter Cassio.

Roderigo: I know his gait. 'Tis he. Villain, thou diest!

[Makes a pass at Cassio.]

Cassio: That thrust had been mine enemy indeed

25   But that my coat is better than thou know'st.

I will make proof of thine.

[Draws, and wounds Roderigo.]

Roderigo: O, I am slain!

[Iago darts from concealment behind Cassio, wounds him in the leg, and exit.]

Cassio: I am maimed for ever. Help, ho! Murder! murder!

[Falls.]

Enter Othello.

Othello: The voice of Cassio. Iago keeps his word.

Roderigo: O, villain that I am!

Othello: It is even so.

30   *Cassio:*   O, help, ho! light! a surgeon!

Othello: 'Tis he. O brave Iago, honest and just,

That hast such noble sense of thy friend's wrong!

Thou teachest me. Minion, your dear lies dead,

And your unblest fate hies. Strumpet, I come.

35   Forth of my heart those charms, thine eyes, are blotted.

Thy bed, lust-stained, shall with lust's blood be spotted.

Exit Othello.

Enter Lodovico and Gratiano.

Cassio: What, ho? No watch? No passage? Murder! murder!

Gratiano: 'Tis some mischance. The cry is very direful.

Cassio: O, help!

40 *Lodovico:* Hark!

Roderigo: O wretched villain!

Lodovico: Two or three groan. It is a heavy night.
     These may be counterfeits. Let's think't unsafe
     To come in to the cry without more help.

45 *Roderigo:* Nobody come? Then shall I bleed to death.

Lodovico: Hark!

     Enter Iago, with a light.

Gratiano: Here's one comes in his shirt, with light and weapons.

Iago: Who's there? Whose noise is this that cries on murder?

Lodovico: We do not know.

Iago: Did not you hear a cry?

Cassio: Here, here! For heaven's sake, help me!

50 *Iago:* What's the matter?

Gratiano: This is Othello's ancient, as I take it.

Lodovico: The same indeed, a very valiant fellow.

Iago: What are you here that cry so grievously?

Cassio: Iago? O, I am spoiled, undone by villains!

55   Give me some help.

Iago: O me, lieutenant! What villains have done this?

Cassio: I think that one of them is hereabout
     And cannot make away.

Iago: O treacherous villains!

     [To Lodovico and Gratiano.]

     What are you there? Come in, and give some help.

60 *Roderigo:* O, help me here!

Cassio: That's one of them.

Iago: O murd'rous slave! O villain!

     [Stabs Roderigo.]

Roderigo: O damned Iago! O inhuman dog!

Iago: Kill men i' th' dark?—Where be these bloody thieves?—How silent is this

65   town!—Ho! murder! murder!—What may you be? Are you of good or evil?

Lodovico: As you shall prove us, praise us.

Iago: Signior Lodovico?

Lodovico: He, sir.

Iago: I cry you mercy. Here's Cassio hurt by villains.

70 *Gratiano:* Cassio?

Iago: How is't, brother?

Cassio: My leg is cut in two.

Iago: Marry, heaven forbid!
     Light, gentlemen. I'll bind it with my shirt.

     Enter Bianca.

Bianca: What is the matter, ho? Who is't that cried?

75 *Iago:* Who is't that cried?

Bianca: O my dear Cassio! my sweet Cassio!

O Cassio, Cassio, Cassio!

Iago: O notable strumpet!—Cassio, may you suspect
Who they should be that have thus mangled you?

80   *Cassio:*   No.

Gratiano: I am sorry to find you thus. I have been to seek you.

Iago: Lend me a garter. So. O for a chair
To bear him easily hence!

Bianca: Alas, he faints! O Cassio, Cassio, Cassio!

85   *Iago:*   Gentlemen all, I do suspect this trash
To be a party in this injury.—
Patience a while, good Cassio.—Come, come!
Lend me a light. Know we this face or no?
Alas, my friend and my dear countryman

90   Roderigo? No—Yes, sure.—O heaven, Roderigo!

Gratiano: What, of Venice?

Iago: Even he, sir. Did you know him?

Gratiano: Know him? Ay.

Iago: Signior Gratiano? I cry your gentle pardon.
These bloody accidents must excuse my manners
That so neglected you.

95   *Gratiano:*   I am glad to see you.

Iago: How do you, Cassio?—O, a chair, a chair!

Gratiano: Roderigo?

Iago: He, he, 'tis he!
[A chair brought in.]
O, that's well said; the chair.

100   Some good man bear him carefully from hence.
I'll fetch the general's surgeon. *[To Bianca.]* For you, mistress,
Save you your labor.—He that lies slain here, Cassio,
Was my dear friend. What malice was between you?

Cassio: None in the world; nor do I know the man.

105   *Iago [to Bianca]:*   What, look you pale?—O, bear him out o' th' air.
[Cassio and Roderigo are borne off.]
Stay you, good gentlemen.—Look you pale, mistress?—
Do you perceive the gastness of her eye?—
Nay, if you stare, we shall hear more anon.
Behold her well; I pray you look upon her.

110   Do you see, gentlemen? Nay, guiltiness will speak.
Though tongues were out of use.
Enter Emilia.

Emilia: 'Las, what's the matter? What's the matter, husband?

Iago: Cassio hath here been set on in the dark
By Roderigo, and fellows that are scaped.

115   He's almost slain, and Roderigo dead.

Emilia: Alas, good gentlemen! alas, good Cassio!

Iago: This is the fruits of whoring. Prithee, Emilia,

Go know of Cassio where he supped to-night.
[To Bianca.]
What, do you shake at that?

120 *Bianca:*   He supped at my house; but I therefore shake not.

Iago: O, did he so? I charge you go with me.

Emilia: Fie, fie upon thee, strumpet!

Bianca: I am no strumpet, but of life as honest
As you that thus abuse me.

Emilia: As I? Foh! fie upon thee!

125 *Iago:*   Kind gentlemen, let's go see poor Cassio dressed.
[To Bianca.]
Come, mistress, you must tell 's another tale.
Emilia, run you to the citadel
And tell my lord and lady what hath happed.

                                                      [Exit Emilia.]

Will you go on afore?   *Exeunt [all but Iago].*
This is the night

130 That either makes me or fordoes me quite.   *[Exit.]*

SCENE II: *A bedchamber in the castle.*

Desdemona [asleep] in her bed. Enter Othello with a light.

Othello: It is the cause, it is the cause, my soul.
Let me not name it to you, you chaste stars!
It is the cause. Yet I'll not shed her blood,
Nor scar that whiter skin of hers than snow,
5 And smooth as monumental alabaster.
Yet she must die, else she'll betray more men.
Put out the light, and then put out the light.
If I quench thee, thou flaming minister,
I can again thy former light restore,
10 Should I repent me; but once put out thy light,
Thou cunning'st pattern of excelling nature,
I know not where is that Promethean heat
That can thy light relume. When I have plucked the rose,
I cannot give it vital growth again;
15 It needs must wither. I'll smell thee on the tree.
(He kisses her.)
O balmy breath, that dost almost persuade
Justice to break her sword! One more, one more!
Be thus when thou art dead, and I will kill thee,
And love thee after. One more, and that's the last!
20 So sweet was ne'er so fatal. I must weep,
But they are cruel tears. This sorrow's heavenly;
It strikes where it doth love. She wakes.

Desdemona: Who's there? Othello?

Othello: Ay, Desdemona.

Desdemona: Will you come to bed, my lord?

Othello: Have you prayed to-night, Desdemon?

25   *Desdemona:* Ay, my lord.

Othello: If you bethink yourself of any crime
      Unreconciled as yet to heaven and grace,
      Solicit for it straight.

Desdemona: Alack, my lord, what may you mean by that?

30   *Othello:* Well, do it, and be brief; I will walk by.
      I would not kill thy unpreparèd spirit.
      No, heaven forfend! I would not kill thy soul.

Desdemona: Talk you of killing?

Othello: Ay, I do.

Desdemona: Then heaven
      Have mercy on me!

Othello: Amen, with all my heart!

35   *Desdemona:* If you say so, I hope you will not kill me.

Othello: Hum!

Desdemona: And yet I fear you; for you're fatal then
      When your eyes roll so. Why I should fear I know not,
      Since guiltiness I know not; but yet I feel I fear.

Othello: Think on thy sins.

40   *Desdemona:* They are loves I bear to you.

Othello: Ay, and for that thou diest.

Desdemona: That death's unnatural that kills for loving.
      Alas, why gnaw you so your nether lip?
      Some bloody passion shakes your very frame.

45   These are portents, but yet I hope, I hope,
      They do not point on me.

Othello: Peace and be still!

Desdemona: I will so. What's the matter?

Othello: That handkerchief which I so loved and gave thee
      Thou gav'st to Cassio.

Desdemona: No, by my life and soul!
      Send for the man and ask him.

50   *Othello:* Sweet soul, take heed,
      Take heed of perjury; thou art on thy deathbed.

Desdemona: Ay, but not yet to die.

Othello: Yes, presently.
      Therefore confess thee freely of thy sin;
      For to deny each article with oath

55   Cannot remove nor choke the strong conception
      That I do groan withal. Thou art to die.

Desdemona: Then Lord have mercy on me!

Othello: I say amen.

Desdemona: And have you mercy too! I never did

Offend you in my life; never loved Cassio
60   But with such general warranty of heaven
As I might love. I never gave him token.
Othello: By heaven, I saw my handkerchief in's hand!
O perjured woman! thou dost stone my heart,
And mak'st me call what I intend to do
65   A murder, which I thought a sacrifice.
I saw the handkerchief.
Desdemona: He found it then.
I never gave it him. Send for him hither.
Let him confess a truth.
Othello: He hath confessed.
Desdemona: What, my lord?
Othello: That he hath used thee.
Desdemona: How? Unlawfully?
70   *Othello:*   Ay.
Desdemona: He will not say so.
Othello: No, his mouth is stopped.
Honest Iago hath ta'en order for't.
Desdemona: O, my fear interprets. What, is he dead?
Othello: Had all his hairs been lives, my great revenge
75   Had stomach for them all.
Desdemona: Alas, he is betrayed, and I undone!
Othello: Out, strumpet! Weep'st thou for him to my face?
Desdemona: O, banish me, my lord, but kill me not!
Othello: Down, strumpet!
80   *Desdemona:*   Kill me to-morrow; let me live to-night!
Othello: Nay, if you strive—
Desdemona: But half an hour!
Othello: Being done, there is no pause.
Desdemona: But while I say one prayer!
Othello: It is too late.
    (Smothers her.)
[*Desdemona:*   O Lord, Lord, Lord!]
    Emilia at the door.
85   *Emilia (calls within):*   My lord, my lord! What, ho! my lord, my lord!
Othello: What noise is this? Not dead? not yet quite dead?
I that am cruel am yet merciful;
I would not have thee linger in thy pain.
So, so.
Emilia (within):   What, ho! my lord, my lord!
90   *Othello:*   Who's there?
Emilia (within):   O, good my lord, I would speak a word with you!
Othello: Yes, 'tis Emilia.—By and by.—She's dead.—
'Tis like she comes to speak of Cassio's death.
The noise was here. Ha! no more moving?

95   Still as the grave.—Shall she come in? Were't good!—
        I think she stirs again. No.—What's best to do?
        If she come in, she'll sure speak to my wife.
        My wife! my wife! what wife? I have no wife.
        O, insupportable! O heavy hour!
100   Methinks it should be now a huge eclipse
        Of sun and moon, and that th' affrighted globe
        Should yawn at alteration.
Emilia (within):   I do beseech you
        That I may speak with you, O good my lord!
Othello: I had forgot thee. O, come in, Emilia.
105   Soft, by and by.—Let me the curtains draw.—
        [Closes the bed-curtains.]
        Where art thou?
        [Opens the door.]
        Enter Emilia.
        What's the matter with thee now?
Emilia: O my good lord, yonder's foul murder done!
Othello: What? Now?
Emilia: But now, my lord.
110   *Othello:*   It is the very error of the moon.
        She comes more nearer earth than she was wont
        And makes men mad.
Emilia: Cassio, my lord, hath killed a young Venetian
        Called Roderigo.
Othello: Roderigo killed?
        And Cassio killed?
115   *Emilia:*   No, Cassio is not killed.
Othello: Not Cassio killed? Then murder's out of tune,
        And sweet revenge grows harsh.
Desdemona: O, falsely, falsely murdered?
Emilia: O, Lord! what cry is that?
Othello: That? What?
120   *Emilia:*   Out and alas! that was my lady's voice.
        Help! help, ho! help! O lady, speak again!
        Sweet Desdemona! O sweet mistress, speak!
Desdemona: A guiltless death I die.
Emilia: O, who hath done this deed?
125   *Desdemona:*   Nobody—I myself. Farewell.
        Commend me to my kind lord. O, farewell!
        (She dies.)
Othello: Why, how should she be murd'red?
Emilia: Alas, who knows?
Othello: You heard her say herself, it was not I.
Emilia: She said so. I must needs report the truth.
130   *Othello:*   She's like a liar gone to burning hell!

'Twas I that killed her.

Emilia: O, the more angel she,
And you the blacker devil!

Othello: She turned to folly, and she was a whore.

Emilia: Thou dost belie her, and thou are a devil.

Othello: She was false as water.

135 *Emilia:* Thou art rash as fire to say
That she was false. O, she was heavenly true!

Othello: Cassio did top her. Ask thy husband else.
O, I were damned beneath all depth in hell
But that I did proceed upon just grounds

140 To this extremity. Thy husband knew it all.

Emilia: My husband?

Othello: Thy husband.

Emilia: That she was false to wedlock?

Othello: Ay, with Cassio. Nay, had she been true,

145 If heaven would make me such another world
Of one entire and perfect chrysolite,
I'ld not have sold her for it.

Emilia: My husband?

Othello: Ay 'twas he that told me first.
An honest man he is, and hates the slime
That sticks on filthy deeds.

150 *Emilia:* My husband?

Othello: What needs this iterance, woman? I say thy husband.

Emilia: O mistress, villainy hath made mocks with love!
My husband say that she was false?

Othello: He, woman.
I say, thy husband. Dost understand the word?

155 My friend, thy husband; honest, honest Iago.

Emilia: If he say so, may his pernicious soul
Rot half a grain a day! he lies to th' heart.
She was too fond of her most filthy bargain.

Othello: Ha!

160 *Emilia:* Do thy worst.
This deed of thine is no more worthy heaven
Than thou wast worthy her.

Othello: Peace, you were best.

Emilia: Thou hast not half the power to do me harm
As I have to be hurt. O gull! O dolt!

165 As ignorant as dirt! thou hast done a deed—
I care not for thy sword; I'll make thee known,
Though I lost twenty lives. Help! help! Ho! help!
The Moor hath killed my mistress! Murder! murder!

Enter Montano, Gratiano, Iago, and others.

Montano: What is the matter? How now, general?

170   *Emilia:*   O, are you come, Iago? You have done well,
        That men must lay their murders on your neck.
        Gratiano: What is the matter?
        Emilia: Disprove this villain, if thou be'st a man.
        He says thou told'st him that his wife was false.
175   I know thou didst not; thou'rt not such a villain.
        Speak, for my heart is full.
        Iago: I told him what I thought, and told no more
        Than what he found himself was apt and true.
        Emilia: But did you ever tell him she was false?
180   *Iago:*   I did.
        Emilia: You told a lie, an odious damnèd lie!
        Upon my soul, a lie! a wicked lie!
        She false with Cassio? Did you say with Cassio?
        Iago: With Cassio, mistress. Go to, charm your tongue.
185   *Emilia:*   I will not charm my tongue; I am bound to speak:
        My mistress here lies murdered in her bed—
        All: O heavens forfend!
        Emilia: And your reports have set the murder on.
        Othello: Nay, stare not, masters. It is true indeed.
190   *Gratiano:*   'Tis a strange truth.
        Montano: O monstrous act!
        Emilia: Villainy, villainy, villainy!
        I think upon't—I think I smell't!—O villainy!
        I thought so then.—I'll kill myself for grief.—
        O villainy, villainy!
195   *Iago:*   What, are you mad? I charge you get you home.
        Emilia: Good gentlemen, let me have leave to speak.
        'Tis proper I obey him, but not now.
        Perchance, Iago, I will ne'er go home.
        Othello: O! O! O!   *(Falls on the bed.)*
        Emilia: Nay, lay thee down and roar!
200   For thou hast killed the sweetest innocent
        That e'er did lift up eye.
        Othello: O, she was foul!
        [Rises.]
        I scarce did know you, uncle. There lies your niece,
        Whose breath, indeed, these hands have newly stopped.
        I know this act shows horrible and grim.
205   *Gratiano:*   Poor Desdemon! I am glad thy father's dead.
        Thy match was mortal to him, and pure grief
        Shore his old thread in twain. Did he live now,
        This sight would make him do a desperate turn;
        Yea, curse his better angel from his side,
210   And fall to reprobation.
        Othello: 'Tis pitiful; but yet Iago knows

That she with Cassio hath the act of shame
A thousand times committed. Cassio confessed it;
And she did gratify his amorous works
215   With that recognizance and pledge of love
Which I first gave her. I saw it in his hand.
It was a handkerchief, an antique token
My father gave my mother.
     Emilia: O God! O heavenly God!
     Iago: Zounds, hold your peace!
220   *Emilia:*   'Twill out, 'twill out! I peace?
No, I will speak as liberal as the north,
Let heaven and men and devils, let them all,
All, all, cry shame against me, yet I'll speak.
     Iago: Be wise, and get you home.
     Emilia: I will not.
     [Iago draws and threatens Emilia.]
     Gratiano: Fie!
225   Your sword upon a woman?
     Emilia: O thou dull Moor, that handkerchief thou speak'st of
I found by fortune, and did give my husband;
For often with a solemn earnestness—
More than indeed belonged to such a trifle—
He begged of me to steal't.
230   *Iago:*   Villainous whore!
     Emilia: She give it Cassio? No, alas, I found it,
And I did give't my husband.
     Iago: Filth, thou liest!
     Emilia: By heaven, I do not, I do not, gentlemen.
O murd'rous coxcomb! what should such a fool
Do with so good a wife?
235   *Othello:*   Are there no stones in heaven
But what serves for the thunder? Precious villain!
     The Moor runs at Iago [but is disarmed by Montano].
     Iago kills his wife.
     Gratiano: The woman falls. Sure he hath killed his wife.
     Emilia: Ay, ay. O, lay me by my mistress' side.   *Exit Iago.*
     Gratiano: He's gone, but his wife's killed.
240   *Montano:*   'Tis a notorious villain. Take you this weapon,
Which I have here recovered from the Moor.
Come, guard the door without. Let him not pass,
But kill him rather. I'll after that same villain,
For 'tis a damnèd slave.
     Exit [Montano, with all but Othello and Emilia].
245   *Othello:*   I am not valiant neither;
But every puny whipster gets my sword.
But why should honor outlive honesty?

Let it go all.
Emilia: What did thy song bode, lady?
Hark, canst thou hear me? I will play the swan,
And die in music. *[Sings.]* "Willow, willow, willow."
250   Moor, she was chaste. She loved thee, cruel Moor:
So come my soul to bliss as I speak true.
So speaking as I think, alas, I die.
(She dies.)
Othello: I have another weapon in this chamber;
It is a sword of Spain, the ice brook's temper.
255   O, here it is.—Uncle, I must come forth.
Gratiano (within):   If thou attempt it, it will cost thee dear.
Thou hast no weapon, and perforce must suffer.
Othello: Look in upon me then and speak with me,
Or, naked as I am, I will assault thee.
[Enter Gratiano.]
Gratiano: What is the matter?
260   *Othello:*   Behold, I have a weapon;
A better never did itself sustain
Upon a soldier's thigh. I have seen the day
That with this little arm and this good sword
I have made my way through more impediments
265   Than twenty times your stop. But O vain boast!
Who can control his fate? 'Tis not so now.
Be not afraid, though you do see me weaponed.
Here is my journey's end, here is my butt,
And very seamark of my utmost sail:
270   Do you go back dismayed? 'Tis a lost fear.
Man but a rush against Othello's breast,
And he retires. Where should Othello go?
Now, how dost thou look now? O ill-starred wench!
Pale as thy smock! When we shall meet at compt,
275   This look of thine will hurl my soul from heaven,
And fiends will snatch at it. Cold, cold, my girl?
Even like thy chastity.
O cursèd, cursèd slave! Whip me, ye devils,
From the possession of this heavenly sight!
280   Blow me about in winds! roast me in sulphur!
Wash me in steep-down gulfs of liquid fire!
Oh Desdemon! dead Desdemon! dead! Oh! Oh!
Enter Lodovico, Montano, Iago [as prisoner], and Officers; Cassio in a chair.
Lodovico: Where is this rash and most unfortunate man?
Othello: That's he that was Othello. Here I am.
285   *Lodovico:*   Where is that viper? Bring the villain forth.
Othello: I look down towards his feet—but that's a fable.
If that thou be'st a devil, I cannot kill thee.

[Wounds Iago.]
Lodovico: Wrench his sword from him.
   [Othello is disarmed.]
Iago: I bleed, sir, but not killed.
Othello: I am not sorry neither. I'ld have thee live;
290   For in my sense, 'tis happiness to die.
Lodovico: O thou Othello that wert once so good,
      Fall'n in the practice of a damnèd slave,
      What shall be said to thee?
Othello: Why, anything;
      An honorable murderer, if you will;
295   For naught did I in hate, but all in honor.
Lodovico: This wretch hath part confessed his villainy.
      Did you and he consent in Cassio's death?
Othello: Ay.
Cassio: Dear general, I never gave you cause.
300   *Othello:*   I do believe it, and I ask your pardon.
      Will you, I pray, demand that demi-devil
      Why he hath thus ensnared my soul and body?
Iago: Demand me nothing. What you know, you know.
      From this time forth I never will speak word.
Lodovico: What, not to pray?
305   *Gratiano:*   Torments will ope your lips.
Othello: Well, thou dost best.
Lodovico: Sir, you shall understand what hath befall'n,
      Which, as I think, you know not. Here is a letter
      Found in the pocket of the slain Roderigo;
310   And here another. The one of them imports
      The death of Cassio to be undertook
      By Roderigo.
Othello: O villain!
Cassio: Most heathenish and most gross!
Lodovico: Now here's another discontented paper
315   Found in the pocket too; and this, it seems,
      Roderigo mean t' have sent this damnèd villain;
      But that, belike, Iago in the nick
      Came in and satisfied him.
Othello: O thou pernicious caitiff!—
      How came you, Cassio, by that handkerchief
      That was my wife's?
320   *Cassio:*   I found it in my chamber;
      And he himself confessed but even now
      That there he dropped it for a special purpose
      Which wrought to his desire.
Othello: O fool! fool! fool!
Cassio: There is besides in Roderigo's letter,

325	How he upbraids Iago that he made him
	Brave me upon the watch; whereon it came
	That I was cast; and even but now he spake,
	After long seeming dead—Iago hurt him,
	Iago set him on.
330	*Lodovico:* You must forsake this room and go with us.
	Your power and your command is taken off,
	And Cassio rules in Cyprus. For this slave,
	If there be any cunning cruelty
	That can torment him much and hold him long,
335	It shall be his. You shall close prisoner rest
	Till that the nature of your fault be known
	To the Venetian state. Come, bring away.
	Othello: Soft you! a word or two before you go.
	I have done the state some service, and they know't.
340	No more of that. I pray you, in your letters,
	When you shall these unlucky deeds relate,
	Speak of me as I am. Nothing extenuate,
	Nor set down aught in malice. Then must you speak
	Of one that loved not wisely, but too well;
345	Of one not easily jealous, but, being wrought,
	Perplexed in the extreme; of one whose hand,
	Like the base Judean, threw a pearl away
	Richer than all his tribe; of one whose subdued eyes,
	Albeit unusèd to the melting mood,
350	Drop tears as fast as the Arabian trees
	Their med'cinable gum. Set you down this.
	And say besides that in Aleppo once,
	Where a malignant and a turbaned Turk
	Beat a Venetian and traduced the state,
355	I took by th' throat the circumcisèd dog
	And smote him—thus.
	(He stabs himself.)
	Lodovico: O bloody period!
	Gratiano: All that's spoke is marred.
	Othello: I kissed thee ere I killed thee. No way but this,
	Killing myself, to die upon a kiss.
	(He [falls upon the bed and] dies.)
360	*Cassio:* This did I fear, but thought he had no weapon;
	For he was great of heart.
	Lodovico [to Iago]: O Spartan dog,
	More fell than anguish, hunger, or the sea!
	Look on the tragic loading of this bed.
	This is thy work. The object poisons sight;
365	Let it be hid. Gratiano, keep the house,
	And seize upon the fortunes of the Moor,

For they succeed on you. To you, lord governor,
Remains the censure of this hellish villain,
The time, the place, the torture. O, enforce it!
370 Myself will straight aboard, and to the state
This heavy act with heavy heart relate.

Exeunt.

A Modest Proposal (1729)

Jonathan Swift
b. 1667 Ireland
d. 1745 Ireland

It is a melancholy object to those who walk through this great town or travel in the country, when they see the streets, the roads, and cabin doors, crowded with beggars of the female sex, followed by three, four, or six children, all in rags and importuning every passenger for an alms. These mothers, instead of being able to work for their honest livelihood, are forced to employ all their time in strolling to beg sustenance for their helpless infants: who as they grow up either turn thieves for want of work, or leave their dear native country to fight for the pretender in Spain, or sell themselves to the Barbadoes.

I think it is agreed by all parties that this prodigious number of children in the arms, or on the backs, or at the heels of their mothers, and frequently of their fathers, is in the present deplorable state of the kingdom a very great additional grievance; and, therefore, whoever could find out a fair, cheap, and easy method of making these children sound, useful members of the commonwealth, would deserve so well of the public as to have his statue set up for a preserver of the nation.

But my intention is very far from being confined to provide only for the children of professed beggars; it is of a much greater extent, and shall take in the whole number of infants at a certain age who are born of parents in effect as little able to support them as those who demand our charity in the streets.

As to my own part, having turned my thoughts for many years upon this important subject, and maturely weighed the several schemes of our projectors, I have always found them grossly mistaken in their computation. It is true, a child just dropped from its dam may be supported by her milk for a solar year, with little other nourishment; at most not above the value of two shillings, which the mother may certainly get, or the value in scraps, by her lawful occupation of begging; and it is exactly at one year old that I propose to provide for them in such a manner as instead of being a charge upon their parents or the parish, or wanting food and raiment for the rest of their lives, they shall on the contrary contribute to the feeding, and partly to the clothing, of many thousands.

There is likewise another great advantage in my scheme, that it will prevent those voluntary abortions, and that horrid practice of women murdering their bastard children, alas! too frequent among us! sacrificing the poor innocent babes I doubt more to avoid the expense than the shame, which would move tears and pity in the most savage and inhuman breast.

The number of souls in this kingdom being usually reckoned one million and half, of these I calculate there may be about two hundred thousand couple whose wives are breeders; from which number I subtract thirty thousand couple who are able to maintain their own children (although I apprehend there cannot be so many, under the present distress of the kingdom); but this being granted, there will remain an hundred and seventy thousand breeders. I again subtract fifty thousand for those women who miscarry, or whose children die by accident or disease within the year. There only remain an hundred and twenty thousand children of poor parents annually born. The question therefore is, how this number shall be reared and provided for? which, as I have already said, under the present situation of affairs, is utterly impossible by all the methods hitherto proposed. For we can neither employ them in handicraft or agriculture; we neither build houses (I mean in the country) nor cultivate land; they can very seldom pick up a livelihood by stealing, till they arrive at six years old, except where they are of towardly parts; although I confess they learn the rudiments much earlier; during which time they can, however, be properly looked upon only as probationers; as I have been informed by a principal gentleman in the country of Cavan, who protested to me that he never knew above one or two instances under the age of six, even in a part of the kingdom so renowned for the quickest proficiency in that art.

I am assured by our merchants, that a boy or a girl before twelve years old is no saleable commodity; and even when they come to this age they will not yield above three pounds, or three pounds and a half a crown at most on the Exchange; which cannot turn to account either to the parents or kingdom, the charge of nutriment and rags having been at least four times that value.

I shall now therefore humbly propose my own thoughts, which I hope will not be liable to the least objection.

I have been assured by a very knowing American of my acquaintance in London, that a young healthy child well nursed is at a year old the most delicious, nourishing, and wholesome food, whether stewed, roasted, baked, or broiled; and I make no doubt that it will equally serve in a fricassee or a ragout.

I do therefore humbly offer it to public consideration that of the hundred and twenty thousand children already computed, twenty thousand may be reserved for breed, whereof only one fourth part to be males; which is more than we allow to sheep, black cattle, or swine; and my reason is, that these children are seldom the fruits of marriage, a circumstance not much regarded by our savages; therefore, one male will be sufficient to serve four females. That the remaining hundred thousand may, at a year old, be offered in sale to the persons of quality and fortune through the kingdom; always advising the mother to let them suck plentifully in the last month, so as to render them plump and fat for a good table. A child will make two dishes at an entertainment for friends; and when the family dines alone, the fore or hind quarter will make a reasonable dish, and seasoned with a little pepper or salt will be very good boiled on the fourth day, especially in winter.

I have reckoned upon a medium that a child just born will weigh twelve pounds, and in a solar year, if tolerably nursed, will increase to twenty-eight pounds.

I grant this food will be somewhat dear, and therefore very proper for landlords, who, as they have already devoured most of the parents, seem to have the best title to the children.

Infant's flesh will be in season throughout the year, but more plentiful in March; and a little before and after: for we are told by a grave author, an eminent French physician, that fish being a prolific diet, there are more children born in Roman Catholic countries about nine months after Lent than at any other season; therefore, reckoning a year after Lent, the markets will be more glutted than usual, because the number of popish infants is at least three to one in this kingdom: and therefore it will have one other collateral advantage, by lessening the number of papists among us.

I have already computed the charge of nursing a beggar's child (in which list I reckon all cottagers, laborers, and four-fifths of the farmers) to be about two shillings per annum, rags included; and I believe no gentleman would repine to give ten shillings for the carcass of a good fat child, which, as I have said, will make four dishes of excellent nutritive meat, when he has only some particular friend or his own family to dine with him. Thus the squire will learn to be a good landlord, and grow popular among the tenants; the mother will have eight shillings net profit, and be fit for work till she produces another child.

Those who are more thrifty (as I must confess the times require) may flay the carcass; the skin of which artificially dressed will make admirable gloves for ladies, and summer boots for fine gentlemen.

As to our city of Dublin, shambles may be appointed for this purpose in the most convenient parts of it, and butchers we may be assured will not be wanting: although I rather recommend buying the children alive, and dressing them hot from the knife as we do roasting pigs.

A very worthy person, a true lover of his country, and whose virtues I highly esteem, was lately pleased in discoursing on this matter to offer a refinement upon my scheme. He said that many gentlemen of this kingdom, having of late destroyed their deer, he conceived that the want of venison might be well supplied by the bodies of young lads and maidens, not exceeding fourteen years of age nor under twelve; so great a number of both sexes in every country being now ready to starve for want of work and service; and these to be disposed of by their parents, if alive, or otherwise by their nearest relations. But with due deference to so excellent a friend and so deserving a patriot, I cannot be altogether in his sentiments; for as to the males, my American acquaintance assured me from frequent experience that their flesh was generally tough and lean, like that of our schoolboys by continual exercise, and their taste disagreeable; and to fatten them would not answer the charge. Then as to the females, it would, I think, with humble submission be a loss to the public, because they soon would become breeders themselves: and besides, it is not improbable that some scrupulous people might be apt to censure such a practice (although indeed very unjustly), as a little bordering upon cruelty; which, I confess, has always been with me the strongest objection against any project, how well soever intended.

But in order to justify my friend, he confessed that this expedient was put into his head by the famous Psalmanazar, a native of the island Formosa, who came from thence to London about twenty years ago: and in conversation told my friend, that in his country when any young person happened to be put to death, the executioner sold the carcass to persons of quality as a prime dainty; and that in his time the body of a plump girl of fifteen, who was crucified for an attempt to poison the emperor, was sold to his imperial majesty's prime minister of state, and other great mandarins of the court, in joints from the gibbet, at four hundred crowns. Neither indeed can I deny, that if the same use were made of several plump young girls in this town, who without one single groat to their fortunes cannot stir abroad without a chair, and appear at the playhouse and assemblies in foreign fineries which they never will pay for, the kingdom would not be the worse.

Some persons of a desponding spirit are in great concern about that vast number of poor people, who are aged, diseased, or maimed, and I have been desired to employ my thoughts what course may be taken to ease the nation of so grievous an encumbrance. But I am not in the least pain upon that matter, because it is very well known that they are every day dying and rotting by cold and famine, and filth and vermin, as fast as can be reasonably expected. And as to the young laborers, they are now in as hopeful a condition: they cannot get work, and consequently pine away for want of nourishment, to a degree that if at any time they are accidentally hired to common labor, they have not strength to perform it; and thus the country and themselves are happily delivered from the evils to come.

I have too long digressed, and therefore shall return to my subject. I think the advantages by the proposal which I have made are obvious and many, as well as of the highest importance.

For first, as I have already observed, it would greatly lessen the number of papists, with whom we are yearly overrun, being the principal breeders of the nation as well as our most dangerous enemies; and who stay at home on purpose to deliver the kingdom to the Pretender, hoping to take their advantage by the absence of so many good Protestants, who have chosen rather to leave their country than stay at home and pay tithes against their conscience to an Episcopal curate.

Secondly, The poor tenants will have something valuable of their own, which by law may be made liable to distress and help to pay their landlord's rent, their corn and cattle being already seized, and money a thing unknown.

Thirdly, Whereas the maintenance of a hundred thousand children from two years old and upward, cannot be computed at less than ten shillings a piece per annum, the nation's stock will be thereby increased fifty thousand pounds per annum, beside the profit of a new dish introduced to the tables of all gentlemen of fortune in the kingdom who have any refinement in taste. And the money will circulate among ourselves, the goods being entirely of our own growth and manufacture.

Fourthly, The constant breeders beside the gain of eight shillings sterling per annum by the sale of their children, will be rid of the charge of maintaining them after the first year.

Fifthly, This food would likewise bring great custom to taverns, where the vintners will certainly be so prudent as to procure the best receipts for dressing it to perfection, and consequently have their houses frequented by all the fine gentlemen, who justly value themselves upon their knowledge in good eating; and a skillful cook who understands how to oblige his guests, will contrive to make it as expensive as they please.

Sixthly, This would be a great inducement to marriage, which all wise nations have either encouraged by rewards or enforced by laws and penalties. It would increase the care and tenderness of mothers toward their children, when they were sure of a settlement for life to the poor babes, provided in some sort by the public, to their annual profit instead of expense. We should see an honest emulation among the married women, which of them would bring the fattest child to the market. Men would become as fond of their wives during the time of their pregnancy as they are now of their mares in foal, their cows in calf, their sows when they are ready to farrow, nor offer to beat or kick them (as is too frequent a practice) for fear of a miscarriage.

Many other advantages might be enumerated. For instance, the addition of some thousand carcasses in our exportation of barreled beef, the propagation of swine's flesh, and improvement in the art of making good bacon, so much wanted among us by the great destruction of pigs, too frequent at our table; which are no way comparable in taste or magnificence to a well-grown, fat, yearling child, which roasted whole will make a considerable figure at a lord mayor's feast or any other public entertainment. But this and many others I omit, being studious of brevity.

Supposing that one thousand families in this city would be constant customers for infants' flesh, besides others who might have it at merry-meetings, particularly at weddings and christenings, I compute that Dublin would take off annually about twenty thousand carcasses; and the rest of the kingdom (where probably they will be sold somewhat cheaper) the remaining eighty thousand.

I can think of no one objection that will possibly be raised against this proposal, unless it should be urged that the number of people will be thereby much lessened in the kingdom. This I freely own, and it was indeed one principal design in offering it to the world. I desire the reader will observe, that I calculate my remedy for this one individual kingdom of Ireland and for no other that ever was, is, or I think ever can be upon earth. Therefore let no man talk to me of other expedients; of taxing our absentees at five shillings a pound: of using neither clothes nor household furniture except what is of our own growth and manufacture: of utterly rejecting the materials and instruments that promote foreign luxury: of curing the expensiveness of pride, vanity, idleness, and gaming in our women: of introducing a vein of parsimony, prudence, and temperance: of learning to love our country, in the want of which we differ even from Laplanders and the inhabitants of Topinamboo: of quitting our animosities and factions, nor acting any longer like the Jews, who were murdering one another at the very moment their city was taken: of being a little cautious not to sell our country and conscience for nothing: of teaching landlords to have at least one degree of mercy toward their tenants; lastly, of putting a spirit of honesty, industry, and skill into our shopkeepers; who, if a resolution could now be taken to buy only our native goods, would immediately unite to cheat and exact upon us in the price, the measure, and the goodness, nor could ever yet be brought to make one fair proposal of just dealing, though often and earnestly invited to it.

Therefore I repeat, let no man talk to me of these and the like expedients, till he has at least some glimpse of hope that there will be ever some hearty and sincere attempts to put them in practice.

But as to myself, having been wearied out for many years with offering vain, idle, visionary thoughts, and at length utterly despairing of success, I fortunately fell upon this proposal; which, as it is wholly new, so it has something solid and real, of no expense and little trouble, full in our own power, and whereby we can incur no danger in disobliging England. For this kind of commodity will not bear exportation, the flesh being of too tender a consistence to admit a long continuance in salt, although perhaps I could name a country which would be glad to eat up our whole nation without it.

After all, I am not so violently bent upon my own opinion as to reject any offer proposed by wise men, which shall be found equally innocent, cheap, easy, and effectual. But before something of that kind shall be advanced in contradiction to my scheme, and offering a better, I desire the author or authors will be pleased maturely to consider two points. First, as things now stand, how they will be able to find food and raiment for a hundred thousand useless mouths and backs. And secondly, there being a round million of creatures in human figure throughout this kingdom, whose subsistence put into a common stock would leave them in debt two millions of pounds sterling, adding those who are beggars by profession to the bulk of farmers, cottagers, and laborers, with the wives and children who are beggars in effect; I desire those politicians who dislike my overture, and may perhaps be so bold as to attempt an answer, that they will first ask the parents of these mortals, whether they would not at this day think it a great happiness to have been sold for food at a year old in the manner I prescribe, and thereby have avoided such a perpetual scene of misfortunes as they have since gone through by the oppression of landlords, the impossibility of paying rent without money or trade, the want of common sustenance, with neither house nor clothes to cover them from the inclemencies of the weather, and the most inevitable prospect of entailing the like or greater miseries upon their breed for ever.

I profess, in the sincerity of my heart, that I have not the least personal interest in endeavoring to promote this necessary work, having no other motive than the public good of my country, by advancing our trade, providing for infants, relieving the poor, and giving some pleasure to the rich. I have no children by which I can propose to get a single penny; the youngest being nine years old, and my wife past child-bearing.